Solving Enigma's Secrets
The Official History of
Bletchley Park's Hut 6

Edited by
John Jackson

BookTower
PUBLISHING

First published by BookTowerPublishing 2014
Redditch, Worcestershire
www.booktowerpublishing.co.uk

Copyright John Jackson 2014

John Jackson asserts the moral right
to be identified as the editor of this work.

A catalogue record for this book is available from the
British Library

BookTower Publishing
ISBN 978-0-9557164-3-0

All rights reserved. No part of this publication may be reproduced, stored or otherwise be lent, re-sold, hired out or otherwise circulated without the publisher's prior consent in any form of binding or cover other than that in which it is published and without a similar condition including this condition being imposed on the subsequent purchaser.

CONTENTS

National Archives Note	9
Editor's Note	10
Original Editor's Preface	11
The Plan of the Book	13
Hut 6: An Adventure [Overview of Hut 6 by Stuart Milner-Barry]	17
Appreciation of Milner-Barry	51
The German Enigma machine	55

Period I: Pre-war and September 1939-January 1940: The Beginnings

CHAPTER 1: PRE-WAR THEORY   59

Introductory; Pre-war early theory; The first crib; Rods and wheel-breaking; The Indicating System and its vulnerability; Depth and turnover; New wheels and Indicating System: the goal-hunt; News from Poland; Polish methods of key-breaking.

CHAPTER 2: WAR: THE FIRST SUCCESSES   76

The outbreak of war; The Bombe and the Netz; The Jeffreys Sheets; Method of using the Netz; Early failures; Cillies and attempts at depth-reading; First breaks of wartime keys.

Period II: January-July 1940: Sitzkrieg, Norway, France – Start of Continuous Operational Breaking

CHAPTER 3: JANUARY-MARCH 1940   88

Red, Blue and Green; Successes and early organisation; Operational breaking: Rise of Yellow; The new Indicating System: first great crisis of Hut 6; Overwhelming importance of Red; Hand breaks.

CHAPTER 4: THE RULES OF KEYS   96

General considerations; The rules of Red; Results of the discoveries; Rules of other keys; Red keys: June 1940; Daily procedure in Machine Room; Liaison with France.

Period III: August 1940-May 1941: Britain Alone

CHAPTER 5: RISE OF BOMBES AND THE CRIB ROOM   104

General historical summary; Arrival of the Bombe: what it did; Establishment of the Crib Room; New discoveries on rules of keys: Brown; The origins of research: The function of Research; Early organisation and methods; Early triumphs; Summary.

Period IV: June 1941-December 1943: World War – the Great Period of Expansion and Consolidation

CHAPTER 6: GENERAL HISTORICAL SUMMARY 115
Features of the period; Increase of keys; Increase of personnel; Increase of machines; Growing complexity of organisation; Technical developments; General course of breaking; Liaison with Sixta; Liaison with Hut 3; Conclusion.

CHAPTER 7: DETAILED THEORY OF RULES OF KEYS 124
Sources of information; Air and Army; Divisions of the subject; Wheelorder rules: Army and Air; Clarkian wheelorder rule; Nigelian wheelorder rule; Monrovian wheelorder rule; Tricycle keys; Setting up of Committee on Rules of Keys; Ringstellung rules – Army and Air; Stecker Rules – Army and Air; Brown rules. GAF key repeats: Institution of key records; Limitation of the subject; Local keys; Keys constructed by the Cipher Office: repeats in 1941; 1942 – Quadrilateral repeats; Effects on breaking policy; Effects on intercept policy; Repeats in 1943 and 1944; Stecker/D repeats in 1945; Conclusion.

CHAPTER 8: GENERAL ORGANISATION OF MACHINE 146
AND CRIB ROOMS (LATER WATCH AND RESEARCH
The fourfold division; Location of rooms; Subordination of sub-sections; The differentiation of function; Dissatisfaction in the Machine Room; The problem solved; The formation of Research; The parentage system; Some special points; Summary.

CHAPTER 9: TRAINING SCHEMES IN HUT 6 155
Early training; The beginning of the schools; The RR school syllabus; Watch and Research training; The outline course and special talks; Other educational schemes.

Period V: January 1944-May 1945: the liberation of Europe: Hut 6 fights back against new German security devices

CHAPTER 10: GENERAL HISTORICAL SUMMARY 163
The determining factors; The techniques of cryptography; The organisation of cryptography; Importance of other sections to cryptography; Contribution of Hut 6 to intelligence.

CHAPTER 11: GERMAN SECURITY DEVICES – 1 166
REFLECTOR D (Part I)
General introduction; Reflector D in general; January-July 1944: The first menace; Illusory triumph; The BO mystery; The D-substitution; Greenshank and D; Red Ds: January-July; The overhanging menace; Preparations for August 1.

CHAPTER 12: GERMAN SECURITY DEVICES – 2   **176**
REFLECTOR D (Part 2)
August 1944-May 1945: Extension of D; Effects on breaking; D breaks; D captures; D rules; Summary of German use of D.

CHAPTER 13: GERMAN SECURITY DEVICES – 3   **185**
ENIGMA UHR, ZUSATZ STECKER AND NOT-SCHLÜSSEL
Enigma Uhr: The problem; Routine adopted; Extension of Enigma Uhr; Effect on breaking; Uhr notation; Summary; Zusatz Stecker: The May scare; A damp squib; Extent of change; The German idea. NOT-Schlüssel: Introduction; First system; First appearance of the NOTS; The saga of Guernsey or the Qwatch and the Forty NOTS; The plague of NOTS; NOT keys, new-style; Conclusions.

CHAPTER 14: GERMAN SECURITY DEVICES – 4   **204**
CY, RANDOM INDICATORS, WAHLWORTS, THE MOSSE CODE AND DOUBLE ENCODING
CY: Introduction; Extension of the practice; The German regulations; Effect on breaking; Conclusion. Random Indicators: The regulations; Extension of the system; Conclusion. Wahlworts: Introduction; Extension of wahlworts; German use of wahlworts; Effect on breaking; Value of wahlworts. The Mosse Code; Double encoding; Summary.

CHAPTER 15: CHANGE FROM WATCH/RESEARCH TO AIR/ARMY 220
Introduction; Stages of the change; Reasons for the change; Results of the change; Timing of the change; Unity of control; Organisation of the Watch: Introduction; The function of the Watch; Basic organisation; Division of keys between Watches; Watch A; Watch Q; Watch M; Watch R; BOVO; Administration.

CHAPTER 16: FINAL DEVELOPMENTS OF THE RULES OF KEYS 232
Introduction; The regular Air keys; Brown, Yak and Llama; Army keys; Rule of Ds; Summary.

CHAPTER 17: BOMBE CONTROL   **239**
Introduction; The problem; Intelligence value; Hut 6-Hut 8; Hut 6 Keys: Responsibility; Daily meeting; Priority list. Current Bombe Control: England; Washington (OP-20-G); Washington (Arlington); Conclusion.

CHAPTER 18: HISTORY OF THE MACHINE ROOM   **246**
(FORMERLY NETZ ROOM)
Historical outline; Expansion of the Room; The breaking of duds. Final set-up for Bombe control: Communications; Routine organisational jobs; Normal testing of stops; Special problems.

CHAPTER 19: RED. BLUE, PINK AND BROWN KEYS   **254**

General introduction; Red: A major German blunder; Breaking: 1940-1945; Supreme importance of Red; Blue and Pink; Brown: Introduction; Target for Tonight – Phase I: September 1940-May 1941; Target for Tonight – Phase II: December 1941- June 1942 (Brown II); The lull: Brown I; Attack and defence: Brown IV; Brown III; Conclusion.

CHAPTER 20: THE MEDITERRANEAN AIR KEYS   **275**

General; The triangle; The African campaign; The Italian Campaign; The Balkans; The last months.

CHAPTER 21: THE AFRICAN ARMY KEYS   **285**

General; The first breaks: 1941-1942; The re-entry into Chaffinch: April 1942; April-October: improvement in technique and increasing success; Phoenix: the difficulties of overseas interception; The wahlwort era – the Phoenix-Finch complex: December 1942-April 1943; Thrush (Sonder M/S Rom-Mallemes) and other keys.

CHAPTER 22: THE ITALIAN ARMY AND BALKAN ARMY KEYS   **296**

The Italian Army keys: General; Before the surrender of Italy: May-September 1943; Surrender of Italy and rise of Shrike and Bullfinch: September 1943-February 1944; Kingfisher: May-August 1944; Revival of Albatross: October 1944-April 1945; The Puffins; Sparrow; The Balkan Army keys: General; Before the Italian surrender: February 1942-September 1943; Surrender of Italy – appearance of Wryneck: September 1943-November 1944; Arrival of Russians and new Balkan set-up: November 1944.

CHAPTER 23: THE WESTERN AIR AND ARMY KEYS   **310**

Western Air keys: General; The breaking of Snowdrop; The pivotal importance of Red; The further growth of the re-encodement complex; D-Day; The period of regular breaking; Changes in emphasis; The decline of the West; Western Army keys: General; Before D-Day; D-Day and the first breaks; The first lull; The breakthrough; The second lull: October; The final battles: heavy traffic once again.

CHAPTER 24: GERMAN AIR AND EASTERN AIR KEYS   **329**

German Air keys: General; Research; The Watch; The first phase; The second phase; The third phase; The Eastern Air keys: General; The German advance; Key repeats; Hedgehog; The heyday of Research; The problem of the Luftflotten; The end.

CHAPTER 25: THE EASTERN ARMY KEYS, GREENSHANK   **346**
AND ALLIED KEYS
The Eastern Army keys: General; Initial advances: June-December 1941; Quiescence: 1942-1943; Spread of use of local keys: July 1943-December 1944; The final spurt; Greenshank and allied keys: The main feature of Greenshank; Breaks: 1939-1942; A blank wall; Inside information; The mystery solved; The last phase: statistics and summary; The associated keys: Falcon, Gannet II and Mallard; The breaking of Nuthatch; Grouse and the Wehrkreis CQ key; The role of WOYG (War Office Y Group).

CHAPTER 26: POLICE AND SS KEYS   **361**
General characteristics; History to the end of 1941; 1942: The Orange Age; 1943-1945: The Quince Age; Summary.

CHAPTER 27: MUSTARD   **378**
Introduction; Russian Mustard: Mustard I, IV; Mediterranean Mustard: Mustard II, III; Western Mustard and Cress; The end of the story.

CHAPTER 28: THE V-KEYS   **384**
General introduction; Corncrake; Ibis; Jerboa; Importance of the V-keys.

CHAPTER 29: SUMMARY AND CONCLUSIONS   **395**
General; How breaks are secured; How breaks can be prevented: the three desiderata; The two roads; The principle of over-protection; The German Enigma: theoretical and practical security; The failure of German efforts; Air and Army security; The special case of Greenshank; How to achieve security; The necessity of supervision.

APPENDICES

Note to Appendices on keys: English Key Names of Air and Army Keys	403
Note to Appendix I: First Break of Keys	409
Appendix I: First Break of Keys	411
Note to Appendices II-IV: General Use and Distribution of GAF Keys	417
Appendix II: List by German Categories of GAF Keys	425
Appendix III: Alphabetical List Under English Name of All GAF Keys	427
Appendix IV: List of County Keys	434
Notes to Appendices V & VI: General Use and Distribution of Army Keys	435
Appendix V: The Various Categories of German Army Keys Operative in March 1945	439
Appendix VI: List of All German Army Keys Identified During The War	442
GLOSSARY	**450**
INDEX	**471**

Note

[This Note was prepared by the National Archives and appears on the cover of each of the original volumes]

A photo-copy of the original book, written by the staff of Hut 6 in 1945/6. The original copy is to be found in the National Archives, HW43/72.

A note on this photocopy: The original 'History of Hut 6' was written by some of the staff of Hut 6, starting immediately after the end of the European war in May 1945, with reproduction and binding in 1946. Only a very limited number of copies were created at that time, being classified as 'Top Secret'. Similar end-of-war reports were prepared by all the other major units of the Bletchley Park war-time team. Most of these have been 'published' by being placed in the Public Record Office (now the National Archives) over the years from about 1979 onwards. This 'History of Hut 6' is one of the last to be released, first appearing in the National Archives only in June 2006. It is in three volumes, with Vol. III ending with a statistical appendix and a 24 page glossary. It appears that this general historical account was accompanied by a 'technical volume', which does not seem to have been published, and indeed does not now appear to be identified by GCHQ. (The titles are known of a number of end-of-war technical reports, each one dealing with the breaking of a particular cypher, whose publication is still withheld; maybe they constitute the 'technical volume').

The pages of the original have been reproduced by photocopying. The original is typed on the standard folio paper of the day, which is somewhat longer than today's A4. Because of the use of wide margins in the original, most of the text can be reproduced on A4 in the original size. But there are a few pages, such as the photocopy of the original book on the next page, where some size reduction has had to be made. In Volume I there are a few hand written notes on the text. (See p38, 44, & 51) [Editor's Note: these page numbers relate to the original document]. These seem to be original corrections made by Peter Twinn and Joan

Note

Clarke, who were never members of Hut 6 and so probably did not see this volume until they were asked to comment on some of the early history in it which had been challenged when the first volume of Harry Hinsley's great history [Editor's Note: This refers to the 5-volume British Intelligence in the Second World War] was proof-read in 1978. He had relied on some contentious material on the very early days to be found in this Hut 6 History; Peter worked with Dilly Knox in the summer of 1939 when information was obtained from the Poles, and Joan Clarke worked with Alan Turing in the summer of 1940 when the parallel board modifications to the first bombe were being tried out.

Editor's Note

The original Hut 6 Official History is in three volumes. Volume I dealt with cryptography involving the German Army and Air Force. This book reproduces Volume I, of which the final part is located at the beginning of Volume II in the original. The various appendices are to be found in the original Volume II and the glossary is in the original Volume III, so this book brings them all together into a single volume and includes an index, which is not available in the original History. The original three volumes are available at the National Archive, references HW 43/70, HW 43/71 and HW 43/72. The object in publishing this book in its original form is to bring it to the attention of a wider public. All royalties are going to the Bletchley Park Trust.

John Jackson
June 2014

Editor's Preface

[NOTE: The "Editor" in this case is the original editor]

The subject of the three volumes of the present work is the history of Enigma-breaking in Hut 6; and it is essential, above all, to stress the point that the history is necessarily incomplete and in a sense fragmentary. The whole process of breaking Enigma and using the results obtained is necessarily incomplete and in a sense fragmentary. The whole process of breaking Enigma and using the results obtained is a continuous chain of which Hut 6 was only one link. Other links in the chain were the intercepting stations, both at home and overseas, Sixta and, finally, Hut 3, who assessed and distributed the material presented to them by Hut 6.

It is impossible for any reader to comprehend fully the complete picture unless he reads not only this history but also those produced by what we have called the other links in the chain. Moreover, even in certain parts of the present work, a knowledge of certain matters which will be fully described in the History of Sixta – such as German callsign systems – is essential. However, every endeavour has been made not to trespass on the preserves of other sections and only to refer to them so far as is necessary to clarify the mutual relations existing between them and Hut 6.

In another sense, too, this book is incomplete. Much of what would otherwise have had to form a part of the history of Hut 6 has been placed in the separately compiled History of E/Breaking, Part II. The reasons for this step are given in the following section "The Plan of the Book".

Apart from the fact that the present work is, in its nature incomplete I feel it cannot but suffer to some extent from the inevitable drawbacks of a work by many authors. The expedient of composite authorship was, however, quite inevitable, as no single person was master of all the subjects that had to be treated. But the various Books are virtually independent entities: and it is hoped that in each case sufficient unity of plan has been attained by assigning the shorter Books to a single author and by planning the longer Books in considerable detail beforehand. It is believed that contradictions of fact have been removed; but it has not been thought necessary to be

Editor's Preface

nicely meticulous in suppressing any shade of differences of opinion,

and on certain points – such as, for example, the relative severity of the various crises, cryptographic and other, that shook Hut 6 – divergent standpoints will be apparent to the reader who, with the facts before him, can form his own judgment.

All the authors of his history were members of Hut 6; and the primary authority is simply the personal recollections of the authors. Naturally, however, all the documentary evidence available has been studied: this consists mainly of the regular reports of the Hut, published weekly since late 1941 or in some sections early 1942. Apart from this, special papers and sectional log books have also been consulted.

It will be noticed that for the first two years of the war the documentary evidence available is rather slight, and here in particular we have had to search the recesses of memory. Special difficulty was found to arise with the earliest history of all – that dealt with in Chapter One – as none of the authors arrived at Bletchley Park before January 1940; and though we have been careful to consult the few available documents and make enquiries of such personal sources as were available, it remains true that before January 1940 this history rests on secondhand evidence. This must excuse the comparative paucity of dates and occasional dubiety of minor facts in our prehistory; there is, fortunately, no uncertainty about the main course of events.

The purpose of this book is designed to fulfil is twofold. The first is to act simply as a historical record: in the preparation of this work I have noticed how difficult it has proved where no documentary evidence exists to attain absolute certainty on events that happened but five years ago, and, with the speedy dispersal of virtually all the staff of Hut 6, some permanent record clearly had to be compiled at once before the panorama began to dissolve in the mists of the past.

The other possible purpose is didactic. I have often felt that it would certainly have been interesting for us (if only for the sake of comparison) if we had been able to consult a history of the achievements of our predecessors in the First World War: and in the same way the present work might be of interest and possibly of use to our successors as, following in the footsteps of Oedipus whom we may claim as the first cryptographer they in their turn strive in their day and generation to read the riddle of the Sphinx.

29th September, 1945

The Plan of the Book

The plan of this history appears in detail in the following table of Contents, but a few general and preliminary remarks may be useful to the intending reader. The first section is a general introduction, a sketch of the whole history of Hut 6, from the pen of the Head of the Hut, P. S. Milner-Barry. This account should certainly be read before the rest of the book is tackled as it gives a delightfully vivid bird's-eye view of Hut 6 and its life. It is true that it contains some technical terms which may puzzle a reader who comes to this history with no previous knowledge of the subject, but the general lines of the story are clear, and any obscure details are best left to be clarifed by a second reading when the reader has delved further into the history.

After this introduction the history proper begins. Most of the main divisions or 'Books' correspond to the chief functional divisions of Hut 6, and indeed are such that as are almost inevitable in any cryptographic organisation. Traffic must be intercepted, then identified, registered, broken and then decoded. Each of these different operations was performed by a separate section of Hut 6, and to each a separate Book is devoted. The order given above (which is the normal chronological order) has been followed, except that for obvious reasons, breaking the traffic – the end of the whole process – has been placed first. It now remains to discuss the arrangement of the work within the various Books.

Book I: Cryptography deals with the actual breaking of keys and with the work of the cryptographic sections, i.e., Watch, Research and Machine Room. The treatment throughout is primarily historical. After an introductory description of the machine, five chapters follow on the main cryptographic periods of the war. Then two shorter chapters deal with the closely related subjects of Bombe control and the history of the machine room. Finally, we have a long chapter on the History of Special Groups of Keys and a short, final one of General Comments on Cipher security.

The Plan of the Book

Technical details and full descriptions of the processes involved have not been inserted in this history – these will be found in the separately published History of E/Breaking: Part II. There were three main reasons for taking this course:

- Even as matters stand, the Book on Cryptography is the largest division of this work, and if full technical details had been added, the Book would have reached too disproportionate a length.

- It was believed that there would be considerable gain to clarity of exposition if the technical and historical approaches to cryptography were firmly separated and dealt with in separate works. To deal with them in the same book would have meant that confusing changes of standpoint would have occurred rather frequently.

- Technically, the problems of Hut 6 were similar in many respects to those of Hut 8. It was possible to bring this out (as has been done) in a Joint Technical History, but the problems of Hut 8 could clearly find no place in the history of Hut 6.

The result of the course taken is that the treatment of cryptography in the present work is as little technical as possible (with a few exceptions to be later mentioned). This history is, in short, written for the layman, who should consult the Technical History for further details on any point that has aroused his curiosity. On the other hand, the professional cryptographer may well prefer to read the Technical History first, and consult the present work later for the purpose of filling out the historical background.

The exceptions previously referred to are found in Chapter 1.0 and Chapter 1.1 [Chapters 1 and 2 in this book]. These do contain a certain amount of technical detail, and in fact Chapter 1.0 [The German Enigma Machine] (which contains the unavoidable minimum of information about the machine) is taken directly from the Technical History. The only other comment worth making on Book 1 is that it deals with the early history of Hut 6 with which questions of technique are so closely bound up as to make impossible the rigid separation that is later enforced. In Book 1 the constantly increasing complexity of the general cryptographic situation is reflected in the increasing length of the historic chapters.

Book 2: Interception is much simpler in structure. The more technical side will be dealt with in other histories, and we have only striven to deal with the matter from the Hut 6 point of view. After a general introduction and a chapter on Stations and Communications, there follows a chapter on the routines and history of the Control Room, the Hut 6 section concerned with interception. This central chapter is followed by a shorter one on the rather special subject of Overseas Interception, a few General Comments and a brief Appendix on Hut 6 Liaison with WOYG [War Office Y Group – the intercept station at Beaumanor.]

Book 3: Traffic Identification is apart of Book 1, the longest. Its special peculiarity is that it deals almost wholly with the period from November 1943 onwards when Traffic Identification first became a problem and TIS – Traffic Identification Section – was set up. Again, the Book is arranged primarily by subject after a general introduction. The principle has been to describe, in the first instance, the normal routine of Initial Sorting and the work of the Duddery, then to discuss the more specialised work of Sector Investigation, first on the Air and then on the Army, with illustrations from specific sectors, and then to deal with the two great Traffic identification crises in some detail.

There is thus a steady progression from the simple to the complex. The final chapter 3.9 [not in this book] is in the nature of an Appendix containing a number of papers on special points, some of which are mainly intended for purposes of reference.

The remaining Books are very much shorter and, for that reason alone, have a clearer outline. In Registration and Decoding an attempt has been made to keep the basic routine quite separate from the refinements introduced to meet special problems and circumstances. The Statistical Appendix and Glossary are naturally mainly designed for reference.

It should perhaps be emphasised that the Books are to a great extent independent, and though the order adopted seemed to us the best, there is no very cogent reason why the reader should not pick and choose among the Books to suit his taste. But it is certainly advisable to read through in order whichever Book is chosen.

Hut 6: An Adventure

[Editor's Note: This overview of the Hut 6 story was written by (Sir) Stuart Milner-Barry, former Head of Hut 6.]

General Retrospect

So much has happened in the past five years, and at such a pace, that much of what happened, especially in the early days, is hidden in the mists. It is difficult even to recall the atmosphere in which we worked, let alone actual events or incidents in any sort of order. The story, both on the technical and historical side, is set out by various hands, all of them much more capable than I should be at describing the work and the fortunes of their own sections. All that I can try to do is to sketch very briefly and in the broadest outline the picture as a whole, to trace the development of the organisation, selecting what seem to be the most important points and pointing out the mistakes that we made. Even this will be a very partial and one-sided affair, for I shall only deal incidentally with the other members of the Enigma combine – the stations, Sixta, the bombe huts, Hut 3.

The whole process formed one whole and Hut 6 had to have the closest and most intimate relations with all of them. The longer the war went on and the more difficulties the Germans put in our way, the more our affairs became mixed up together and the closer the collaboration had to become. That held good just as much for our external relations as for those between the different departments of Hut 6; but this story does not pretend to be more than the story of Hut 6. The work of the intercept stations and of Sixta in particular seems to me to have become steadily more difficult and more important in the relation to the whole, particularly in the final stages, and this ought as far as possible to be borne in mind in reading the following pages.

There is a further caution which I would like to give. I was intimately concerned with the beginnings of the Crib Room and, as it later on developed, with the Watch; and only became Head of the section in the autumn of 1943. What I have to say about the first four years, then, is inevitably written from a rather narrow standpoint. In particular, I had little or nothing to do with the development of interception or with that of what was known as 'WTI' and subsequently grew into Sixta. That was Welchman-Colman, Welchman-Blair Conyngham and subsequently Welchman-Lewis. The struggles to obtain adequate interception facilities went on unremittingly for the first few years of the war and they were, of course, vital to the ultimate success of the firm. But the main part of that battle had been won by the time I took over.

Again, it was [Gordon] Welchman, with his strange and uncanny knack of grasping the ultimate significance of things who fought throughout for the recognition of the importance of WTI. Many of us, myself certainly included, thought that this was just a fad, and it is in fact true that the cash value as an aid to breaking of the whole log reading and Fusion Room organisation in the first few years of this war was extremely meagre. In fact, in my view, we could have done perfectly well without it. But Welchman's prescience was to be brilliantly justified after his departure, when the knocking down of the various props which had made identification almost a rule of thumb matter – first discriminants, then changing frequencies and finally encoding of call-signs – made the cryptographer largely dependent on the complete and accurate knowledge of the German W/T organisation which Sixta had steadily been building up.

Then what had been from the cryptographers' standpoint a luxury became a basic necessity of life and, if Welchman had not fought for its development in the early years, we should have had no hope of weathering the storms which nearly overwhelmed us in the last eighteen months. However, if one was not at the centre of things and therefore could not have a proper overall view, the Crib Room was the next best place to be. Just because we had no identification difficulties to speak of, breaking really was a matter almost entirely for cryptographers. At first it was cillies, but with a tightening of German security regulations on this side, cillies were largely superseded by cribs, which became and remained to the end the standard method of breaking Enigma keys. So the Crib Room, as it then was, was in the key operative position, and to concentrate in the early years on the cryptographic side of things should not produce too distorted a view. Moreover, it was a logical function of the Crib Room, as the chief breaking agency, to take charge, under Welchman, of bombe policy generally and of our relations with Hut 3 and with the naval sections. These were and remained the most important matters of general policy to be decided.

They were, perhaps, more crucial, though simpler, in those days. There were far fewer bombes in proportion to the work to be done and, therefore, though there were far fewer keys, there was a much more serious tug-of-war between them. Later on there were so many bombes that even with a much greater number of keys and a much heavier programme of work there was much greater play, and the chance of a really serious clash between vital operational keys (e.g., a Russian convoy and a decisive battle in Egypt) were greatly reduced. 1942 and 1943 saw the development in embryo of the liaison between cryptography and intelligence, which was developed to a high degree of sensitivity under Manisty as head of the Watch.

I shall say next to nothing, too, of the technique of bombe design nor of the battles which were successfully fought to provide us with enough tools to do the job at the breaking as well as at the intercepting end. That again, under the Director, was almost entirely Welchman's achievement, not only when he was Head of Hut 6, but when he was translated to a higher sphere. It will be clear, I hope, that alike in interception, in WTI, and in the production of high-speed machinery I took over in October 1943, a concern in which all I personally had to do was to see that proper use was made of the tools which the foresight of others and especially my predecessor had provided. Many dramatic and spectacular events occurred in the final eighteen months, which make them one of the most exciting experiences it is possible to imagine. But the spadework which enabled us to emerge from them in good shape had all been done long ago.

1940

To go back to the beginning, which from my point of view is February 1940, some time after the first break had been made (on the old indicating system, by means of females). It is not at all easy now to recapture the atmosphere of those days. The main sensation of the bewildered newcomer was that he was participating in a miracle which he was entirely incapable of comprehending. I may say that this sensation has never entirely left me and that no amount of success staled the thrill of a break, be it on the most cast-iron crib or the most obvious of cillies. That is no doubt the advantage of a non-mathematical mind, which is incapable of grasping how man or machinery or both combined can possibly find the right solution out of 150 million million (is it?) possible answers. However, breaks were certainly occurring, though hardly on an operational basis. The traffic was mostly days or weeks old and very dull at that (quite trivial on Red or Blue). But even to the least imaginative it was obvious that the enemy was not perfecting his wireless technique or exercising his cipher operators for fun. This was the considered opinion of Hut 3 (total strength: Saunders, Edgar, Lucas).

Nevertheless, it was an act of faith to put the Hut on a 24-hour basis. This was done chiefly to avoid the Registration Room having an accumulation of some 15 hours' traffic – 6pm to 9am – to deal with in the morning. But I can still remember Welchman talking about "dealing with the traffic on an operational basis" at a time when the 'phoney war' was still in progress, and when the terms carried no significant meaning to me. Nor did they to the higher authorities (I do not, of course, refer to the present Director). The innovation was not only thought to be a strange fad, but dangerous to the morals of a mixed community. Indeed a total of three girls (which was all that we required) was thought to be insufficient to ensure the observance of the proprieties; and presumably on the principle that the men would be overworked by such large numbers, a minimum of six was insisted upon. It was therefore necessary to bring in three members of the Netz Room to act as dummies, a precaution that was dropped by tacit consent after a short interval. The experiment was duly launched and was a great success. Several of the original members of that shift – David Gaunt, Michael Banister, Sheila Dunlop and June Canney – remained with us to the end, or almost. And very good fun it was, cooking eggs and bacon in the kitchen ourselves in the middle of the night with copious draughts of tea and unlimited jam.

And it was also very fortunate or very providential because no sooner was the night shift in full swing than the Germans invaded Norway. Traffic jumped up on a new key, Yellow, and we found ourselves breaking currently. However, our triumph was short-lived because, although we lasted out the Norwegian campaign, and the intelligence content immediately verified the predictions of Hut 3, the Germans then changed their indicating system and Hut 6 met with its first and last check in the continuity of breaking, at any rate on the main Air Force keys.

I can remember most vividly the roars of excitement, the standing on chairs and the waving of order papers, which greeted the first breaking of Red by hand in the middle of the Battle of France. It was never surpassed, and equalled only I think by the first breaking of Brown later on in the year. In later times the nearest approach was the first break of

Light Blue in (I think) March 1941. This occurred when the first party of American visitors was being shown round Hut 6 and must greatly have astonished any of them who had the idea that the British were a phlegmatic race. Highlights of this kind were naturally rarer in the modern age, but, though sentiment was more restrained, a good deal of the same underlying tension communicated itself when Oliver Lawn broke Uncle D in the small hours of January 2, 1944 – a short-lived triumph, but an extremely dramatic one. (Welchman and Rees achieved the same feat with the mysterious Uncle Charlie, also on the night shift in bygone days).

However, naturally this first break of Red was the greatest event of all, because it was not only, in effect, a new key, which is always exciting, but because we did not then know whether our number was up altogether or not. The first bombe was not then in action, nor had cribs as yet been thought of (except probably in the fertile imagination of Welchman, ranging as usual a long way ahead of the event). So the break had to be by hand on new technical methods invented by the experts of the Machine Room. As was to happen again and again, we were assisted at precisely the right time by the enemy, because this was the heyday of cillies and of the ringstellung tip (the 'first message' cluster) without which hand-breaking would have been impossible. The Machine Room experts proceeded to sixes all round the wicket for the rest of the Battle of France and part of the Battle of Britain.

The volume of traffic on the one key was enormous – over 1,000 messages one day, which was broken at 5am. I cannot now imagine how, with our primitive methods of collecting and registering traffic, and our tiny staff for decoding it, we managed to cope at all. Anyway, the job got done somehow, the Battle of France was lost, the miracle of Dunkirk occurred, the Battle of Britain was won, and Hut 6 settled down for the winter. Not, however, before the threat of invasion had caused plans for a mobile Hut 6 to be far advanced, and even the team selected. The selection of a very small team of girls from 100% volunteers caused almost the most serious crisis in our personal relations that I can remember. Fortunately the emergency never came to pass, for I really think that those excluded (in nearly every case on the grounds of physical condition alone) would have stowed away in the lorries rather than be left behind.

The dying down of the battle was followed almost immediately by a marked improvement in German security, and the autumn of 1940 witnessed the birth of the Crib Room. I had been entirely sceptical of the possibility of ever finding or recognising standard routine messages of the requisite length, and only the persistence and optimism of Welchman, independent it seemed to me of any evidence, induced me to make the attempt. We then set up the Crib Room by removing the young men from the Registration Room, leaving the young men in the Machine Room to carry on the more technical machine side of breaking, including testing, finding ringstellung, etc., as well as cillies and hand attempts. The arrangement most unfortunately became crystallised, and a disastrous and, as it ultimately proved, quite unnecessary split was created for which I must take the chief blame. I will say something more about it and its consequences later on.

The remaining major cryptic event of 1940 was the breaking of Brown and its exploitation as an operational key. Nobody knew what its contents would be and the most extravagant hypotheses were entertained. It proved a delightful and most entertaining key cryptographically, because although the traffic was small, the density of cribs and of cillies was phenomenal. Never before or since have so many, and such gross breaches of the most elementary rules of cipher or procedural security been committed, as by the specialists of beam bombing. They never learnt and the German signals officers apparently were powerless to intervene. It was also extremely exciting, because of course the object of the exercise was to discover the target before it was too late to be of use to the Air Ministry. The handling of Brown, moreover, gave us our first insight into the necessity of close liaison between intelligence and cryptography, because we had to decide whether we would pull all the (two or three) available bombes on the full range of wheel orders, starting early in the morning on the overnight cribs; or wait until two or three messages were gathered together, after which it was any odds that cillies would effect a substantial reduction in wheel order. The first course was obviously extravagant, but gave a much better chance of getting the result in time. It meant leaving Red and later on Light Blue (GAF in Africa) to take care of themselves till later in the day, urgent though they might be. Thus was born the idea of Hut 6/Hut 3 liaison, though 1942 was far advanced before it was placed on an official basis.

1941

1940, of course, was a time unique in history. Never again did we have quite the same sense of fighting for our lives, because however bad things were later, I doubt if the man in the street ever seriously contemplated losing the war. So the 'life or death' feeling never quite repeated. Cryptographically, too, 1941 was a comparatively uneventful year. We settled down to a routine of breaking Red on cribs and in March Red was joined by Light Blue, the initial breakthrough and exploitation of which was very exciting. All the same, all through this year there persisted, at any rate in my own mind, the sensation that it was all much too good to be true, that any day now the enemy would discover and that we should wake up one morning to find that it was all over. In retrospect one sees these fears to have been much exaggerated, but the technique of cribs was in its early stages and nobody appreciated what a powerful weapon was being forged. Moreover, our fears were justified to the extent that for a short period in the autumn it really did look as though we were in imminent danger of losing both Red and Light Blue. For some time we hung on to both by the slenderest of threads.

In those days the effects of getting into a jam were much more noticeable than they were later, because with only two or three keys work simply came to a standstill if nothing broke for a few days, and the whole Hut descended rapidly into the darkest abyss of despair. It was almost worth descending into the abyss, though, for the pleasure and thrill of emerging from it. It would always happen that everything would come right all at once, a whole series of back days would tumble out one after another and everyone trod on air. One of my most vivid recollections of those early days is of listening anxiously as one neared the old Hut 6 for the sound of the decoding machines. After some days of silence, a cheerful clatter from within caused one to enter the Hut at the double. Later on it was never quite the same. Jams and bad times were just as frequent, but even if all the important keys went wrong together, there was usually a good deal going on that prevented a complete impasse.

1941 was not without its highlights. There was the message about the attack on Crete and then there was the sinking of the Bismarck. It saw, too, the beginnings of the long fluctuating campaign in Africa and of the Hut 6 struggle with the Chaffinches, a story complete in itself and one of the most fascinating jobs we ever did. Those days were not well documented, for the writing of regular sectional reports did not begin till the spring of 1942. I think we made an initial break in April (the key was called AF5); that we did not do much good till the autumn; and that after getting much valuable intelligence for the autumn campaign we lost grip after the Rommel retreat and did not get in again until the spring of

1942. On the whole, though, 1941 was a dullish year, made particularly depressing for the Machine Room by the dearth of cillies and the advance of mechanisation; so that each new addition to the highly powered cryptographic staff was regarded with apprehension or dismay by the original inhabitants. In other directions we had the utmost difficulty in recruiting staff, and another recollection of that year is of incredulity at hearing my own voice say "10 Downing Street" to a taxi driver at Blackfriars and arriving unopposed – the first and no doubt the last time that I shall find myself inside those doors. It seems a long time ago now.

1942

1942 was the annus mirabilis. At the beginning of that year the Germans suddenly realised that there was no objection, and obviously great advantage in security, in making a large number of different keys for the different major units of the GAF. However, with characteristic blindness, the enemy undid much of the good that this step might have done him, for instead of making up entirely separate keys, he rehashed old ones on a delightfully simple plan which the ingenuity of Mr Parker soon uncovered. The effect of this was that, every other month, the majority of Air Force keys were in our hands for the decoding, and a tremendous boom ensued which taxed our resources to the utmost. In June, the Decoding Room was decoding 1,170 messages a day (about half the figure for the closing months of 1944). In August over 500 breaks were made, double the previous best, and 50 keys in all were recognised. This result was achieved on the ridiculous total (by subsequent standards) of 29 bombes. By October the worst of many major crises had arisen in the Decoding Room and the Registration Room, but we were eventually saved by the autumn influx of university candidates and the setting up of schools to train them.

Not only was there all this commotion on the Air side, but 1942 was the great year of the African campaign, culminating in the Battle of Alamein and the long retreat of Rommel towards the final catastrophe in Tunisia. It saw the development of an entirely new technique, that of re-encoding; for the Army keys in Africa split into several components, and all of them were closely interconnected. Here again for a long time I remained very sceptical about the practicability of ever making use of re-encodements, on the grounds of variations in spelling and abbreviations etc., change of address and other alterations. Dudley Smith, who at that time constituted the Crib Room Research section – a new and important innovation – worked away a long time at re-encodements between, I think, Gadfly and Chaffinch. Eventually the renewed breakthrough in April was made by Bannister guessing a straight beginner, but Smith, who had been confident always that the re-encodement method could be made to work, was certainly most unlucky.

He was baulked on one occasion by the ill-luck of a corruption in the original Gadfly text from GANZER to PANZER, in a context where PANZER made equally good sense and was passed without comment by Hut 3. If the corruption had been to any other letter than a P, the correct emendation would no doubt have been made. Moreover, the German encoders' mistake effectually prevented any possibility of obtaining the correct solution on the Chaffinch, because in the right position the bogus P crashed with P in the Enigma text. I mention this in some detail because it seems to me a classic instance of the part played by luck in our affairs, and because it might so easily – though in fact it did not – have delayed by weeks our re-entry into the African Army keys at a most critical period. One could, of course, easily name equally extraordinary instances in which the luck ran in our direction, and with equally providential consequences.

Be that as it may, the re-encodement technique had clearly come to stay, and in fact there proved to be no more interesting and enjoyable side to cribbery. In passing, it is worth remarking that of all the egregious errors committed by the Germans, the folly of sticking the same time of origin in the preamble of two encodings of the same passage was the worst. It enabled us quite gratuitously to pick up the vast majority of re-encodements on 'kisses' – the comparison of GTOs between messages on different keys. They thereby reduced what should have been principally a WTI job – the comparison of routeings – into a largely mechanical routine operation; though, of course, knowledge of callsigns, units involved etc., was still highly desirable.

The Chaffinch pot boiled away merrily all the summer and autumn and there were several vitally important operational GAF keys as well, such as Red, Primrose, Locust and Scorpion. (The last one named was front-line tactical matter of the highest degree of urgency, but it providentially repeated the Primrose key of the preceding month. This enabled us to send the keys out to Africa, and to have the traffic decoded on the spot from messages intercepted locally). The Crib Room became a hive of activity and it was necessary to expand it very quickly. It was about this time that the experiment was tried of promoting from other rooms,

Hut 6: An Adventure

such as the Registration Room, the best available girls. This experiment, frowned upon by the more conservative, proved an immediate success; but it still further increased the discontents of the Machine Room cryptographers, who in the absence of cillies or hand attempts or other suitable material for their virtuosity, found themselves more and more in the position of hewers of wood and drawers of water for the Crib Room, who were having all the fun. However, the business of the key repeats, which by our then artificial separation was a Netz Room function, served to disguise the fact that an untenable situation was developing.

It was during this summer that the liaison with Hut 3 was put upon an organised basis by the setting up of 3L. It was the first time, I think, that a definite attempt was made to guide the Hut 6 effort by the light of known forthcoming Allied intentions. This was the effort to get a grip on Locust well in advance of the August convoy to Malta. As I remember, we were not on this occasion told the nature of the forthcoming operation, but later on – I think first on the occasion of the African landings, in which Locust was also in the forefront of the battle – the broad character of the operation was revealed to senior officers in Hut 6. This was an essential step for the intelligent direction of cryptographic policy. The liaison thus established worked almost without friction or serious disagreement, with both parties on an equal footing, until the end of the war. It would be impossible to over-rate its importance in the combined Enigma effort, but it worked so well that it has virtually no history.

At the same time more systematic consultations were arranged with Hut 8 and Block A (Naval Section). There was danger of really serious conflict of claims here, because there was no overriding intelligence authority that could balance the claims of the Admiralty against the War Office, and we had to work out our own solution. It was a question of the best use of the bombes at a time of the greatest stress, with the U-boat warfare at its peak and the decisive battle being fought in Egypt. The decisions, which had to take account of highly technical considerations, could only be taken by the man on the spot in the light of the best intelligence advice he could get. We solved the problem by setting up a rota of bombe directors or dictators from Hut 6 and Hut 8, who had plenary powers during their turn of duty for deciding on the distribution of the bombes. We were very lucky that the really crucial occasions were so rare, but the decisive factor in avoiding serious conflict of opinion was the broad-mindedness and clear-headedness of Alexander, the Head of Hut 8. The directors seemed to vary considerably in the calibre of their judgment, but they all did their best, and decisions were rarely if ever taken on what might be called party political lines.

The problem became less acute as the output of bombes increased. The naval keys did not proliferate like the Army and Air Force and therefore the total requirements of the Navy loomed less large. Nor did they grow more difficult as did those of the Army. In the end it was almost always possible to find bombes without more than temporary inconvenience for urgent naval demands, and it became possible to disband the directors and put the problem on the basis of long-term discussions of policy. This was done by holding weekly meetings at which intelligence and cryptography from both camps were represented, and broad lines of priority were agreed upon. These meetings, too, were a success, and occasions of serious disagreement hardly ever occurred. This again was due to the fair-mindedness and impartiality of the intelligence representatives. I usually felt that they leant over backwards in their determination to give full weight to the intelligence needs of the other services.

1942 ended with the tide of battle definitely turned in favour of the Allies. The landings in Africa had been successfully carried through, and the stage was set for the final battle of Tunisia. The last month of the year, however, was marred cryptographically by the arrival of wahlworts or nonsense words on the Finches, not apparently a general security measure but the invention of some local security officer in the Italian theatre. They were clearly destined to prove a major obstacle to breaking, because though they set no intrinsically new problem they enormously multiplied the job to be done. They meant running a crib perhaps in several different positions, or perhaps several versions in several positions, instead of one version in one position. This could be overcome, in theory, by a sufficiency of bombes, but until the supply of bombes, particularly of Washington bombes which could run shorter cribs, caught up with the demand, we were bound to be seriously handicapped.

1943

As 1941 to 1940, so 1943 to 1942 was something of an anti-climax. It was very much of a transitional period in many respects. Key repeats in the Parkerian sense ceased, and the breathless pace slackened. Old Hut 6 finally burst its bounds and in the spring we moved into our palatial new quarters in Block D. At first we appeared to rattle about like peas in a pod, and it seems fantastic to suppose that within a year or so we were again clamouring for more room and knocking down walls to provide it.

Hut 6: An Adventure

We were still digesting the autumnal influx of the new staff. The African campaign lasted till May and the Finches ended up in March with a blaze of glory. In April they became virtually unbreakable, and the decision was taken in consultation with Hut 3 to abandon the impossible task of trying to break Bullfinch and to concentrate on breaking new ground in preparation for the next round. By that time the battle was clearly won, and it did not matter whether we broke it or not. Hut 6 for prestige and Hut 3 for news interest would no doubt have liked to pursue the Finch to the bitter end, but it could not be justified on grounds of strategy.

The most important event of the spring was the setting up of the Watch by the amalgamation of the Machine Room and the Crib Room and the setting up of a separate Research Section on a completely larger scale. (Both Machine Room and Crib Room had had their own Research Sections for some time previously, for the investigation of unbroken keys or the exploitation of non-operational ones. But this was a new unified organisation under Major Babbage.) There is now little doubt in my mind that it was a mistake not to have done this earlier, but the reasons were not purely historical or conservative. It had been argued by the supporters of the status quo, on the one hand, that the Crib Room were not mathematically-minded and would therefore be ill-fitted to cope with the more technical aspects of the machine; and on the other that the Machine Room were mathematically-minded and were therefore not likely to be proficient at cribs and re-encodements, which were thought to require a linguistic or humanitarian background. There was an element of truth in this reasoning, but also a good deal of prejudice on both sides. The Machine Room undoubtedly felt that with the gradual lessening in importance of their side of things they had been elbowed out, and were now being deliberately kept out of the more entertaining aspects of Hut 6 cryptography. The Crib Room reacted against what they took to be an unjust aspersion and partially justified it by standing somewhat jealously on their privileges.

The decisive argument in favour of the change was that it was absurd and uneconomical to have one man finding a crib on a key and solemnly passing it to another expert to find the cillies. Great saving of labour and efficiency would be achieved by having the complete handling of a key done by one man; and even had the logical case not been so strong the psychological case for removing the Machine Room grievance was overwhelming. It is quite arguable, I think, that we were so busy during 1942 that a large-scale change of this kind could not have been effected without considerable sacrifice of exploitation; and that we did all that could then be done, by having visitors from the Machine Room for courses in the Crib Room as opportunity offered. However, the setting up of the Watch, which was Welchman's last major reform, produced an immediate and permanent improvement in the atmosphere which ever afterwards became, I think, quite as happy as that of any Room in the Hut. The main damage was that it came too late to restore the morale of one or two very able members of the Machine Room, who went off to do outstandingly valuable work in other sections. It was soon found that the mathematical education was as good as any other for cribbery and re-encodement work; and that those unversed in the mysteries of mathematics could nevertheless make a surprisingly good showing at the more technical aspects of machine cipher, though naturally they could not rival the experts in this sphere. Now up to this time – say the spring of 1943 – Research had been something of a poor relation. Certainly it was not so in the eyes of Welchman, who always saw the long-term importance of things more clearly than anybody else. But the main weight of Hut 3's interests lay naturally in the operational keys on which immediate action could be taken, and my own bias was certainly in favour of the immediate and urgent objective as against the more remote. Therefore, with a limited amount of bombe time available, the difficulty had always been to see that Research keys, whether being handled by Machine Room Research or Crib Room Research, did not get squeezed out altogether. I do not think, in fact, that we made any unfair distribution, or that we could have devoted substantially more time to Research than we did, without adversely affecting operational work. But I am very conscious that the inhabitants of the Research Sections must have felt that they were ploughing a lonely and unappreciated furrow. From time to time we made the experiment, regarded as a pretty daring innovation, of allocating two or three bombes as a definite minimum for Research work, and in this way we usually managed, even at times of the acutest stringency, to keep the flag of Research flying. But for long periods we barely achieved even that.

In the early spring and summer of 1943 all this was changed. With the collapse of resistance in Tunisia our main theatre of operations closed down and did not reopen till the invasion of Sicily and the mainland. There were not wanting those who said, not for the first time, that the great days of Enigma were over: that with the Germans forced back into Fortress Europe, and eventually into their own territories, they would

Hut 6: An Adventure

have less and less need to rely on wireless as their main channel of communication: that Fish would supplant Enigma as the vehicle of all high-level strategical material, and so on. All of these predictions were to be gloriously falsified in the great days of the invasion of Italy, of the second Battle of France, and of the final Battle of Germany. But in 1943, while we were waiting for the move into Sicily, there was certainly a lull; and this was clearly the time for switching our main attack on to Research keys, especially Army keys, with the idea of finding out anything and everything that we possibly could about the strength and disposition of the enemy in Europe. There were, at this time, very few operational keys left – only three or four – and therefore the newly-founded Watch had a very lean and depressing time, which tried everybody's morale as highly as 1941. What we did, therefore, was to transfer a considerable number of cryptographers to the Research Section. It had for a while all the bombe time it needed and made very good use of it. Taunt and Roseveare were the leading men on the GAF side, Gaunt and Nicoll on the Army, with Babbage and Aitken as the senior partners.

By this time we had developed a sound and flexible organisation for transferring keys from one category to another. The general principle was that a key was handled by the Watch, i.e., on a 24-hour basis, if:

- it had operational urgency; and
- it was currently breakable

If it was currently breakable, but not but not important enough to break every day or extravagantly, it was handled by 'Research' – in this sense an obvious misnomer; and similarly, however urgent and important a key was, there would be no sense in handling it in the Watch if it was not currently breakable. Keys of this type, therefore, were handled by Research, more patiently, and in a calmer atmosphere. The division of work between the two Registration Rooms corresponded with the allocation of keys as between Watch and Research at any given time. Incidentally, the qualities required for dealing with keys in the Watch are largely different from those needed for Research, and this imposed a limit on the freedom of movement of cryptographers from one section to another.

One disadvantage of this constitution was that, except at rare intervals such as the summer of 1943, the transfer of keys was largely one way. This, of course, was inevitable. As soon as a key developed operational urgency, and became breakable through the efforts of Research, a claim would be put in by the Watch to have the key transferred. It thus appeared that Research did all the dirty work, and as soon as their spade-work had been crowned with success, the baby was snatched from them. I, as Head of the Crib Room or the Watch, appeared to be greedily grabbing keys from Research just as soon as they began to look really interesting and to become good fun cryptographically. Claims of this kind, however logical and inevitable and even if admitted to be so, could hardly be put forward or strongly pressed without a good deal of heart-burning, particularly when the claimant was the man who was going to have all the fun. Among many instances of this, one of the clearest was the transfer of the Finches to the Crib Room in May 1942, just before the Rommel offensive, a short while after they had been resuscitated from the grave by Dudley Smith and Banister. I think if one were making a blueprint of a constitution, and not dealing with a living organisation and a process of evolution, one would avoid difficulties of this kind, which could easily have led to time-wasting delays, by putting the whole cryptographic effort under one head: so that a decision would be taken in one man's mind rather than on arbitration between conflicting claims. That no serious delays or damage was caused, even though the arbitration nearly always had to be one way, was due to the essential reasonableness and broadmindedness of the Research party and the loyalty with which they suppressed their own feelings. In the end, after a further process of evolution and in very difficult circumstances, we did achieve what appeared to be a more logical and satisfactory structure; but of that more hereafter.

However that may be, it was a good thing that the lend-lease worked in reverse in the summer of 1943. Indeed, the heyday of Research really lasted until the spring of 1944, though naturally the invasion of Sicily and subsequently of Italy in the autumn of 1943 brought the Watch to life again with a jerk. There was plenty to do then, because Army keys, such as Albatross, Cormorant, Shrike, and subsequently Bullfinch, were mostly extremely difficult. Their expensiveness, combined with that of Army Research, was such that for a time at least in September, Air Research had a lean time, and a system of rationing had again to be adopted. This again was an inevitable consequence of the fact that the emphasis of intelligence leant more and more heavily in the direction of the Army. It was the Army that we had to meet and beat in the field before we could finish the war and GAF keys were prized more and more for the light they could throw on the Army than for an intelligence they could give about the outclassed GAF. This situation was accepted and understood by the

Roseveare/Taunt combination. They pursued an essentially secondary role with the utmost vigour.

Fortunately I was able to assure them honestly that we should all be fully operational in the final stages. (In any case, the strength of the GAF, or at any rate the value of intelligence about it, was seriously undervalued at headquarters. I noticed no lack of anxiety about the strength, dispositions and intentions even of a depleted GAF around D-Day, nor even as late as the eve of the Ardennes offensive.) It was a great advantage at this stage and right up to the end to have daily contact with 3L. They sat in on the daily meetings which we held every afternoon `to consider and arrange in order of priority the material produced by both branches of the Research Section, and to relate it to the probable demands of the Watch keys. In this way we had the benefit not only of day-to-day tactical advice on the varying merits and urgency of keys, but of long-term views and assessments by which cryptographic policy and effort could be guided.

In October Welchman became AD (Mch) [Assistant Director, Mechanisation] and I took over as Head of Hut 6, leaving the Watch in Manisty's hands. All I need say about this is that I need never have given another thought to the Watch either in organisation or on the side of 3L policy; and this though the last 18 months, for the Watch as for all other sections, brought a host of new problems. Its efficiency and happiness were equally assured. This was just as well, for my attention was violently distracted by a storm which blew up in a quite unexpected quarter.

It was in September that the Germans, almost without warning, dropped discriminants from Army traffic, thereby destroying our main means of identifying the keys. Now discriminants and the whole business of unidentified and dubiously identified traffic had been the province of a few highly skilled specialists with – as was properly their job – very much of a 'research' outlook. This was appropriate to a small percentage of unidentified traffic, but quite different methods and aptitudes were required when it was a case of dealing in bulk with a large mass of traffic. What was wanted now was not the patient investigation of each piece of traffic by the skilled worker, but a largish organisation which could formulate rules for identifying the great majority of the traffic correctly. The essential thing, if we were not to be swamped, was to boil the problem down again to the routine identification of traffic by rule of thumb methods; to be prepared to sort a lot of traffic wrongly, provided that it was sorted somehow. It is no disparagement to the experts who had so far been charged with the investigation of unidentified traffic to say that they were not fitted by temperament to deal with the new situation, any more than one could have transferred the whole Research Section into the Watch, or vice versa.

Now, for some reason, and most blamably, we failed properly to appreciate that what the Germans had done on the Army they would almost certainly do later on the GAF, a vastly bigger problem because of the far greater volume of traffic. Nor did we take at all adequate steps to see that the Army were managing all right with their problem. Apart from any other considerations, the existing staff was ludicrously small even to form a nucleus for training purposes. The experts did their best and worked all hours, but they were overwhelmed. This was the situation when we had about a week's warning at the end of October that discriminants would be dropped from the GAF at the beginning of November. We had had two months in which to prepare and had wasted them. We never made the same mistake again.

In my opinion, this was easily the most dangerous period we ever went through. It would take far too long to describe even in outline the measures which were put into force, nor how they were just in time to be effective, before the flood of unidentified traffic at the beginning of November swamped us. There was only one man with the quickness and clearness of brain and the originality of mind needed to construct a new framework, and that was Davies; and only one man who could get all the tools together, dot the 'i's and cross the t's and actually put the thing into operation, and that was Gaunt. These two saved the side and no other pair could have done it, nor I think either of them alone. But it was a nightmare to live through. I should certainly not forget that Winton, whom I had asked to sand down in favour of Davies, could not have responded more loyally both then and later. But naturally his own staff felt that he had been hardly done by and a great deal of unavoidable heartburning was caused. It was much the most disagreeable decision I was ever forced to take, but not the most difficult, because I had no doubt whatever at the time, and have had none since, that it was the only possible one.

Anyway, a new section called the 'TIS' was set up – with an auxiliary called he 'Duddery' run by David Gaunt – which in effect steered the identification of the Watch keys. The principle and methods of identifying by frequency and callsign were not, I think, difficult, but there was an enormous lot to be done in the way of training the staff and codifying the routine. All this will no doubt be dealt with by the proper authorities in their own sections. An incidental effect was that the whole of the new staff collected in the autumn in preparation for the second front was swallowed up in the increased complexities both of identification and, subsequently, of decoding. But by the end of the year the crisis was definitely over, only to be succeeded by a new and still more formidable menace, that of Uncle D.

1944
By comparison with 1944, everything that had happened since 1940 seemed almost tame. It included January 1st, the cheap, unlooked for, and illusory triumph over the Uncle: April 1st, the change to the F book which, in spite of months of preparation, almost knocked us out in the first 48 hours; May 1st, the famous 'damp squib' stecker change so much dreaded in advance; Enigma Uhr, D-Day itself with all that it meant in the months of preparation before and the enormous explosion of traffic afterwards; the Battle of France with the Western Army keys coming into their own at long last; August 1st, the culmination of months of sinister distribution of Uncle D; the invention of Duenna to cope with Uncle D, and other D-breaking machinery; the autumn slump when we realised the war was not over; November 1st, the encoding of callsigns by the Army so brilliantly handled by Beaumanor. A year with which nobody with imagination could ever forget, but one which is such a crowded canvas, that within the limits of this survey it is quite impossible to deal with it except in outline.

Let me first dispose of Uncle D. The most elaborate preparations were made for a massed hand attempt on the assumption of a total introduction of the new reflector on January 1st. As is well known, the Germans handed the wiring to us on a plate by using B and D indiscriminately with the same key – an egregious mistake in which they persisted to the end, though, as the supply of reflectors increased, it happened from time to time that a key was wholly, or almost wholly, using Uncle D. In nothing were we more fortunate than the misuse which the enemy made of this decisive weapon. Anyway, we scored our dramatic triumph and breathed again, but not for long. For, to our horror, a new reflector appeared after ten days, another ten days afterwards, and so on, until eventually we became convinced that the reflector was pluggable. Up till August, its use was extremely restricted – only on a part of Red – but from April onwards sinister references appeared to a projected extension of the range, and we waited in monthly anticipation of snuffing out. However, not passively.

Many heads had worked on the problem of devising mechanical means of combating the monster, and eventually various possibilities were thrown up, three of which – Giant, Duenna, and the Arlington Autoscritcher – did noble work. Throughout this period we owed much to Alexander, the Head of Hut 8: the whole Uncle D campaign on all fronts, including new and improved versions of the hand attempt, was guided by him as chairman of the Uncle D Committee. It was one of his greatest services to Hut 6. For months it seemed we must lose the race, that devastating extensions by the Germans must take place long before the counter-machinery was ready. To the anxious spectator, our progress (though probably spectacular) was maddeningly slow, but the enemy was also (though he too may have been distributing as fast as he knew how) extremely dilatory. And what was more important, when the dreaded extension took place in August, it was on the same stupid lines as the original introduction. All the same, mishandled as he was, Uncle D remained a major and increasingly serious menace, though not till April 1945, when it was too late to matter, did he actually threaten to unfasten our grip on the major operational keys. In the meantime, Duenna and her allies did all and more than could have been expected of them, though as it turned out, their services were not required until the end in the most vital regions. But in April 1944, all this was hidden in the future, and dread of Uncle D was one of the major preoccupations of the year.

Next, the F book. It was known that the Germans were preparing to substitute the F book of callsigns for the Bird book, and after the hideous experience of the dropping of discriminants, we were determined not gain to be taken by surprise. The effect of the change was, of course, that until we had got the hang of the new F book allocation, we could make no use of predicted callsigns, on which our whole sorting system was now based. On the other hand, we could expect that within a matter of weeks, provided we could go on breaking, we should accumulate enough data to work out the new system and be back where we were before. It was therefore essentially a temporary crisis, though liable to be very fierce while it lasted.

Very elaborate – too elaborate – plans had been drawn up, but even so we were knocked off our balance by the sheer flood of unidentifiable traffic which poured in upon us. The plans therefore broke down, and a state of chaos threatened, and for some, most unpleasant hours actually reigned. Even now I am not very clear what were the precise measures which we took to restore the situation, beyond ruthlessly scrapping a lot of our carefully prepared machinery, which proved to be too cumbersome. But somehow or other the crisis passed of itself, and matters improved very rapidly. This experience taught all of us some invaluable lessons, which enabled us to deal with the intrinsically much worse crisis of February 1, 1945 (GAF encoding of callsigns) in every way more calmly and competently. It taught us to make our plans as simple as possible, or if they could not be simple, at least to scrap too soon rather than too late; and above all, to make sure that as many people as possible of those who would actually have to operate the plans should have a hand in the drafting of them, and should clearly explain them to their colleagues. These precautions we had not taken thoroughly enough and we paid dearly for lack of them.

The other distinguishing feature of this episode was that we were brought for the first time into the closest contact with Sixta on an operational basis. As I said in the introduction, in my view the contribution made by Sixta increased enormously in the last 18 months, and became a vital factor in a sense in which it had not been previously. As soon as discriminants were dropped, TIS as an organisation for the sorting and identification of traffic was relying upon – was turning to operational use – the background of knowledge of the German Order of Battle and W/T system which Sixta had built up, and it could not have functioned without Sixta. Now, in the F book crisis, Sixta came along and showed us how to identify units and subscribers with the callsign prop knocked away; a tour de force which they did not have to perform for many days, but which they were destined to have to adopt as part of their normal routine when the encoding of callsigns brought us to our final test.

And finally, the F book crisis demonstrated once more that the Watch could rise superior to any difficulties of breaking, as they were to demonstrate after D-Day, and the much more long drawn-out crisis of February 1, 1945. It is said, indeed that the Watches in Hut 3 noticed nothing abnormal in their supply of intelligence, at a time when the scene of excitement and confusion in Registration Room 1 defied description, and would certainly have shaken even the imperturbable Group Captain, had he had the misfortune to witness it.

To come back now to the second front, which in all the alarms and excursions of Uncle D, F book, thrice-daily stecker, and Enigma Uhr, dominated all our thoughts and plans during the early months of 1944. I have said already that the difficulties of identification swallowed up all our D-Day reserves some eight months beforehand; so the last and greatest expansion was asked for and authorised with the influx of 130 Wrens into the Registration Room and Decoding Room during the spring and early summer. But mere weight of bodies was by no means the greatest of our difficulties in these rooms, to whose problems I will return later.

The first essential was to set the stage cryptographically. It was clear that the Second Front would confront us with far more operational keys than we had ever had before, and it was essential to practice the Watch in dealing with them. Moreover, we knew well from experience that enormous advantages accrue from taking over keys on to an operational basis well in advance of the actual operations, so as to accustom the cryptographers who would have to deal with them to their characteristics. This argument is in no way vitiated by the fact that, under the impact of a shock such as the Normandy landings, these keys themselves would certainly lose their characteristics and develop new ones. The point was that, if only we could get a grip of some of the main keys beforehand, our knowledge of them might help us to tide over the critical transitional stages and to go on breaking until they developed well-defined new traits. With this double object in view then, we transferred as early as March some of the main French keys, such as Snowdrop and Jaguar, back to the Watch. At the same time we began to transfer back our key men from Research, while Manisty continued to recruit and train fresh cryptographic staff from every likely source. As we hoped, our knowledge of the invasion GAF keys proved valuable on D-Day and the weeks following.

With the Army keys we could not do this in advance. There was practically no traffic on the Western Army, so they had to wait perforce till after D-Day. But we had a very strong party working under Douglas Nicoll on those Western keys in Research, and a very good party in Registration Room 2. We also arranged to make a room available so that the minute the time was ripe, we could transfer the whole party on to a fully operational basis as a part of the cryptographic Watch, with the corresponding Registration Room 2 outfit transferred to Registration Room 1. With that we had to rest content.

The main task of May was to go round the Registration Room and the Decoding Room and try to bring everything up to concert pitch. What we had to fear there was an explosion of traffic so devastating that it would swamp our existing routines, and we had to decide beforehand what we could afford to scrap (in many cases in the most literal sense, by using the waste paper baskets). The worst bottleneck that suggested itself was in the initial sorting, that is, the sorting to identified keys, by means of a frequency guide, as the traffic came off the conveyor belt. It was obvious that if, as we must expect, we had a flood of traffic and a much higher number of urgent operational keys, intolerable delays would be caused at the initial stage. At the last moment, only just in time for the new routine to be adopted, R. C. Baker of the Control Room hit on the match-winning device of sorting in a different way, by serial instead of by frequency. This was much more economical and efficient and time-saving, and just made all the difference between coping and not coping at the crisis. Numerous other improvements and simplifications were made, all with the basic object of getting as much as possible of the operational traffic through as quickly as possible; but none was as important or far-reaching as this.

The Decoding Room was the final port of call. Once more the speedy passage of the operational traffic was our main concern. In this connection I made one reform which shocked the best instincts of the stalwarts of that room, and which also, I think, was accepted with no enthusiasm by Hut 3. This was the so-called 'spotty messages' routine, whereby poor texts were left on one side in hopes of a better one coming, and if none did were ultimately scrapped. Now the skill of the expert decoder lies in this very matter of extracting the last ounce from the filthiest text, and it was entirely against the best traditions that the fullest effort should not be put forth against them: it appeared to put a premium on the slapdash or slovenly workers. Nevertheless, it appeared to me that the overriding necessity of getting as much of the important traffic through as quickly as possible demanded this innovation, and I believe that in the most critical period it fully justified itself. However, it was never popular anywhere, and everybody was very thankful when relaxation of the pressure enabled us to return to our former and better standards.

I do not think it is boasting to say that all these preparations fully justified themselves, and that D-Day for Hut 6 could hardly have gone better than it did. The Watch broke practically all there was to be broken of the enormous volume of operational Air traffic. They lived on the old cribs for a day or two, then they lived on re-encodements until the cribs settled down again, which they did when the Germans had redisposed themselves and recovered from the original disorganisation. The Registration Room, Decoding Room and Duddery just and only managed to cope, the Decoding Room output rising from 1,600 before D-Day to a peak of 3,000 a fortnight later. Traffic began to appear on the Western Army keys, and the transfer to the Watch and Registration Room 1 was made within a few days. Both the cryptographic and registration Army parties had to be expanded very rapidly, but they too kept their heads above water. By the time the Battle of France was in full swing, they were producing intelligence worthy of our greatest days. In sum, we had swung more fully than ever before, on to an operational basis, and all the sections concerned stood the strain and did their jobs. Actually, the level of traffic fell away as quickly as it rose, which was just as well, because I do not think we could have maintained the peak level for any length of time.

Now for the rest of 1944. First of all, the GAF. In August came the long-dreaded expansion in the use of Uncle D. It meant a lot more work for the cryptographers and we broke a prodigious number of reflectors from then onwards, but it did us little harm otherwise: and output showed a negligible decline. In September, however, a serious slump in the intake of traffic occurred on both Air and Army, a serious anticlimax which was trying for everybody. In October we took a further important step in organisation, affecting both the cryptographic and identification sides. It had long been obvious that with the ever-narrowing circles around fortress Germany, it would become increasingly difficult to maintain clear-cut distinctions between the various geographical fronts. The areas would get mixed up with each other both for cryptography and identification. This was particularly obvious on the Air side, because of the universal Air key, Red, which was liable to be connected with any other key, and therefore we tackled the Air side first.

Since it was becoming impossible without loss of efficiency to segregate GAF keys into groups, the logical course was to abandon the time-honoured distinction between Watch and Research, to pool the total Air cryptographic resources and to put the whole under one management. There was no need and no intention to treat all the keys as of equal urgency, because we had already, in the Q Watch, an admirable instrument for taking care of the less urgent or less tractable keys. A similar course was adopted in TIS, where the distinction between operational and non-operational keys had long lost any relevance. It was clear that there was no logic in having one body – the Duddery – dealing with the Watch keys and another dealing with non-Watch. The problem of the GAF could only be dealt with satisfactorily as one whole. These measures met with marked success, particularly in the greater concentration of effort which it was possible to bring upon the Eastern Front group of keys. The Taunt/Roseveare combination was now reunited and the months of October and November gave us the completest picture we have ever obtained of the GAF in all sectors.

Now for the Army side. The Western Army party had had its crowded hour during the battle of the Falaise gap and the pursuit across France, which must have made up for any amount of dreary and discouraging waiting. However, the glory departed as suddenly as it came, and with the Germans behind the Siegfried Line, they were once more reduced to sitting about and waiting. I spoke optimistically of 'jam tomorrow' and said that the final battle would be theirs, and prophesied better than I knew; but it is not easy to take long views when you are disconsolately reading a book or knitting, and their morale slumped badly. It was not improved, nor was that of the section as a whole, when the initial success of Rundstedt's offensive in the Ardennes showed that we had been taken off our guard, and suggested either that Ultra was losing its potency or that someone had blundered. Neither was true without qualification or extenuation, but it was difficult to explain without appearing to explain away; and coming as it did on top of the general disillusionment created by over-optimistic pronouncements, the shock was considerable.

Nor, in the meantime, was the enemy by any means done with on the security side. Nothing in the fight which he put up in the closing stages was more remarkable than the activity and energy of his security officers, nor the discipline which enabled his operators to carry out new and exceedingly complicated security devices. In November he embarked on the Army side on the long-dreaded system of random or encoded callsigns, which meant that our last prop for identification was knocked away. It was at this point that Beaumanor achieved its crowning triumph, and so for the matter of that did the overseas Army intercept stations as well. They fought and won this battle almost off their own bat, so that the very elaborate preparations made by ourselves and Sixta proved to be largely unnecessary. They were lucky in that the Germans committed their habitual mistake of taking two bites at a cherry, and introduced the three-daily frequency changing before the callsign encoding; so they had been given time to accustom themselves to the pattern of frequency changes. Even so, that detracts little from an outstanding achievement. It will be seen that as the Germans got better and better at camouflaging everything to do with their wireless system, so the problem was pushed further and further back from Hut 6, first to Sixta and then to the stations themselves, because it was in the last resort the individual operators who now had to make suggestions based on similarities of procedure and so forth, for the continuity of their own groups. We were more and more in the position, not of doing the sorting and identification job for ourselves, but of so organising ourselves that we could make the most effective and immediate use of the help which we were receiving from outside. That is why I said at the beginning that the rôle of the earlier members in the chain, the stations and Sixta, became steadily more important.

Not, however, that our own task became any easier. On the contrary, the organisational problems became steadily more complicated. Now it had been clear for some time that in the end we should have to do for the Army what we had done for the Air in October, and for precisely the same reason. One could only do the identification job properly by treating the Army traffic as a whole, with the same group of experts working upon it; and this had already been done in the division of TIS into TIS (Air) and TIS (Army), under a common head. Cryptographically, the high-level general keys tended less and less to confine themselves to one particular Army group or area, while re-encodements from any area or key might provide an entry into any other. Again, therefore, the distinction between operational and non-operational traffic, while still partially valid for intelligence, could no longer be maintained for cryptography. To get the best results for cryptography, it was necessary to bring all the Army cryptographers together; and to get the best results from the cryptographic effort as a whole, it was necessary that the Army and Air sections should be jointly administered, for the policy that dealt with the bombes and with the priorities of keys, not only of Air against Air and Army against Army, but of Air against Army, could only be efficiently directed by one man. Nor, on the basis of divided responsibility, could one have made the best use of the available cryptographic resources, which involved frequent and rapid redisposition of forces between the two sections, in accordance with the changes in the difficulty or importance of various Air and Army keys.

The final act of 1944, then, was to say goodbye with regret to the conception of Research as a separate entity, to put the Army all in one room – the old Research – and to put all the Army registration in the old Registration Room 2, leaving Registration Room 1 for the Air. Major Manisty took administrative charge of the Air and Army Watches and Q Watches, and Miss Hollington of the two Registration Rooms – again for better use of the available personnel, and because so many problems of administration were common to both, and could not be settled in one room without reference to affairs in the other. For sentimental reasons the change s were not popular, but I think the critics would even then have admitted that the logical case was conclusive, and that the practical difficulties – space, distance from the operational centre, etc., – could be overcome. And we could feel by the end of 1944 that we had in the long course of the years, not arbitrarily or violently, but by evolution and persuasion, evolved a simple, compact and logical organisation with which to face the final battle.

1945: Finale

The story of 1945 is simple and clear-cut. On the Air side it comprised the final battle of February, the longest and hardest of any of our crises, but victoriously surmounted in the end. On the Army side, there was a crescendo of success from February onwards right up to the end, so that though the Air had a record of almost uninterrupted success for five years, the Army, with on the whole the much more difficult task, had the satisfaction of doing their best and most complete job in the closing months of the war. The Air were going down hill in April, but bad though Uncle D was, their difficulties were caused principally by the enemy going down hill still faster.

I was always glad that February 1st happened. It showed that the Germans could do the worst they could think of and still fail to shake off our grip. Once again Davies was the moving spirit behind all the plans which were made, the man who could see the problem as a whole, and who could produce and formulate the constructive ideas to deal with every part of it. But much more than before, it was an operation in which everybody played his part, not only once the battle was joined but in all the preparations beforehand. No doubt for that reason and because we had learnt by experience, it was a much better conducted operation than that of April 1st in the year previously. The first few days were extremely tense, but there was never any feeling that matters were getting out of hand. The worst difficulties were those of the cryptographers, and they had some extremely bad days in which they were obviously under great strain and fearing in their own minds the possibility of defeat.

I never had any real doubt that they would find the cribs without anything to find them by, and so in the end it proved. The course of events is shown by the drop in our output from 1,800 or so in January to 1,000 or less, around which level it hovered for the first three weeks of February. Then there was a distinct turn for the better, and the level became stabilised at 1,200-1,300. At the end of the month it began to climb steeply again, and by the second week in March we were back again in our full stride. Of course, for the rest of the war a lot more traffic got lost in the wash and never correctly identified than ever before, but by and large we could claim to have achieved a pretty complete victory. The new regime meant very much harder work all round, particularly, I think, for the stations and for the Control Room. But at the same time it made life very much more interesting, and I think that on balance those departments at least were happier after the change than before. The Germans continued, as usual, to spoil to a considerable extent the effects of their own ingenuity, for first of all the system of encoding was so complicated that they gave up changing every day and made the same callsign do for three consecutive days – an inestimable saving for us. And secondly, they managed things in such a way that they quite unnecessarily started repeating the same cycle of callsigns over again for various groups, leaving us with no work at all to do except find the repeat. But by the time we were able to take advantage of these mistakes, we had already broken the back of the problem in its most sinister form.

Finally, the end of the Army story. The Western Army party sadly rejoined their colleagues in the old Research quarters, and the Registration party moved back to Registration Room 2 now known as Registration Room Army. Now, because on balance the Army keys had always been the most difficult, and therefore remained in the category of Research (I exclude, of course, the African and Italian Army keys), and because they were remote from the bustle and activity of the Air Watch and the Machine Room and Decoding Room, those rooms had never developed the same 'feel' of operational urgency as the ones nearer the scene of action; the sense of doing things in a chain, so that if a piece of paper or a menu or a decode gets held up at one link in the chain, it will cause corresponding delays all the way down. Partly to combat this psychological difficulty, but chief because it was essential if we were really going to handle Army traffic in bulk on an operational basis, we ordered, in November, when these changes were made, a conveyor belt from Registration Room Air to Registration Room Army and a reverse one to carry decoding traffic back. This came into operation in February, and in the nick of time. For, from then onwards, the traffic increased steeply, and so did the success of the cryptographers and the value of their success. Instead of dissipating their traffic over a wider and wider range of keys, as on the Air Force; the Army, in the closing stages, concentrated more and more of their high-grade traffic on just a few general keys, such as Falcon, Avocet or Puffin. So the contribution of the Army section at the end surpassed that of the Air in quality, and rivalled it in bulk. And the Army sections had the satisfaction of becoming every bit as operational as the Air, with the conveyor belt sometimes needing as many as three or four girls to stoke it with decodes on their way over to Hut 3.

So, in the first three weeks of March, the last preparatory phase before the crossing of the Rhine and the final battle, we were going as well as we had ever done. April, by contrast, was rather an anticlimax. The Army went on as strongly as ever and the Air cryptographers were busy enough, but the advance of the allied armies overran and destroyed a number of old favourites among our keys. Others simply disintegrated in the general mêlée. Traffic fell off very sharply, and in the lovely April weather there was nothing to do but sit about and pray that the end would not be long delayed. In the last week or two operations were conducted in an unreal atmosphere against a background of ever more lurid and fantastic melodrama. And so to the first week of May, when the Control Room were taking down messages in clear from the stations and enjoying a bigger thrill from them than they had ever had before.

The final message of surrender signed by Jodl for Dönitz and Keitel, sent in the small hours of May 7th, came both to the Control and Registration Rooms, and was known all over the Hut on the night shift. It is worth recording, I think, that my appeal to all rooms that it should not be passed on to the day shift was honoured in full, and that the first news they had was in the public announcement, after lunch, on the German wireless. That seems to me, of its kind, one of the most remarkable episodes in our history. I don't suppose that a leakage at that stage would have done any great harm, but it seemed a pity to spoil the Prime Minister's fun – though in the end the Germans spoilt it for him.

Postscript

I am very conscious, on finishing this hasty narrative of Hut 6, of how incomplete the record is; that some big subjects are barely glanced at, and others not at all. Some names crop up in the course of the story, others not at all. This is not to say that the names which do appear are more important to the story than those which do not. There is no reference, for instance, to Fran Braithwaite of the Control Room; to Mary Wilson, the perpetual head of the Netz Room (later Machine Room, taking on the old and honoured title of Machine Room, most of whose original functions it performed to admiration); to Harold Fletcher, to whom more than to any one man the happiness of the staff was due; to Mrs Queening MBE, who succeeded Gaunt as head of the Duddery, and rivalled any man in her technical ability and stamina; to Major Dennis Babbage OBE, the Chief Cryptographer to Anne McLaren, the invaluable ADC; to Sheila Dunlop, who graced three of the most important posts in the Hut and was invariably to be found in the tightest places at the worst time; to Major Bundy and his American contingent, who ought to have a chapter to themselves; to the principal heads of shift in the Air Watch, John Monroe and Howard Smith; and to many others far too numerous to mention by name. All of them played an indispensable part in the story of Hut 6; but Hut 6 was bigger than any of its members and they should, perhaps, remain anonymous.

Hut 6 was fortunate in its birth and more fortunate in the job it had to do; most fortunate of all in that by a series of coincidences and lucky chances, mistakes galore by the enemy mixed with his superb efficiency, it was enabled to do its job to the end. I would like to say something on the personal aspect of this organisation, which was far the most important and which was the main reason why it was to many of its members a unique experience.

First, a small body coming together in a time of desperate urgency is bound together by ties much closer and more intimate than can be found in a larger and more impersonal organisation. It was the common determination of all to strive to preserve something of this atmosphere, however vast and complex the organisation became. It is perhaps too difficult to analyse anything so intangible, but so far as we laid down for ourselves any guiding rules of policy to achieve this aim, they went along these lines. We tried to keep the human and personal element in the forefront the whole time. The biggest mistake we made, the neglect of the Machine Room cryptographers in 1941 and 1942, was due to neglect of this factor. We had to remember that, among the girls especially, we had a staff which was doing a job that, in itself and apart from the objects of the exercise, was desperately dull routine work, and much more monotonous than girls with an academic background, rightly or wrongly, felt they could expect. Whether we could have done better with a different type of labour is a very big question, on which I shall not enter. At any rate it would have meant an organisation run on quite different lines. The point is that the monotony of the work (I am thinking principally of Registration work) was itself deadening to the mind, and that made it much more difficult to maintain the vivid imagination of the importance and urgency of the enterprise, which was essential if staleness and lassitude were not to mar our efficiency. Because the work could *not* be done efficiently as a matter of meaningless routine with the surface, or barely even the surface of the mind, and anybody who did it like that was no good.

An added and very serious difficulty was the violence in the fluctuations of the work. Because of the steadily increasing complexity, the long-term curve was always upward, and the policy of continuous expansion was absolutely right. But time and again we had longish periods when there was far too little to do, and nothing is more demoralising than to have a boring job and not enough of it. In that respect, the Decoding Room were lucky, because nearly always they had too much to do. The physical wear and tear were greater, but the psychological problems were less.

How did we try to combat these deadly enemies of staleness and boredom? First, by sparing no trouble to arrange leave when people wanted it, allowing people to choose heir own days off, to change shifts and so on. I am sure that nobody who had to plan an organisation of the size to which we eventually grew would ever have thought of anything but fixed shifts and fixed days off, rotating according to a predictable plan: simply because of the immense simplification and saving of labour which such a course would have ensured. Nevertheless, I am convinced that the opposite course, to which we stuck throughout, repaid us manifold, not only on human considerations but in the actual efficiency with which the work was conducted.

Secondly, by information. I would myself have liked to go further in the direction of disseminating 'inside information' than was possible if the guiding principle of security was accepted, that nobody should know more of the content of the material than was essential for the proper conduct of the job. I would have liked to interpret this dictum rather more elastically. However, it is not of information of this kind that I am chiefly thinking, but of information about the activities of Hut 6 itself, of the state of the game generally on all fronts, of the whys and wherefores of particular changes of routine, and of the broad objects at which particular changes of organisation were aimed. I think it is impossible to explain too much, or to publish one's explanations too widely; and essential, except for overriding personal reasons, to be frank and to put all the cards on the table; also to put them on the table as simply as possible, so that anybody can understand. The results of this are often disappointing, because only the lively and alert will read what is written, and the amount of personal talk and explanation that one can give is strictly limited. But something percolates, and it is there for anybody who is interested. The more everybody can be encouraged to try to comprehend the overall picture, the better. The Hut 6 organism never became so complicated but that anybody who was so minded could understand in broad outline – which is all that was required – what it was all about.

Thirdly, go round and talk, or perhaps rather to encourage other people to do the talking and to listen, so as to get the 'feel' about what the man in the street is thinking, whether about the work or the war or billet or anything else. One can learn more in this way than by any number of formal interviews. The night shift is the best time for this, for there are fewer people about. It has a more friendly atmosphere than any other and people are more companionable and more talkative. Again, I think one is far more likely to do too little rather than too much in the way of aimless wandering. It is also a good excuse for postponing the duller jobs.

Fourthly, discipline. In the sense of issuing formal orders, this hardly ever existed: orders were nearly always given in the form of requests, and accompanied by explanations. Here again the reasons were partly historical, though I think in any case the system, where it is appropriate at all, is likely to give the best results. When we began, there was in any one room no hierarchy; the people doing the job were all on the same level. As things became more complicated, it was obviously impossible to maintain this agreeable anarchy; somebody had to be responsible, if administration was to be carried on at all. So the system of heads of shift grew up, an innovation looked at askance in the early days – chiefly because those appointed, chiefly in the girls' Rooms, were extremely reluctant to appear to push themselves forward or to assume any kind of authority over their colleagues and friends (on rare occasions they went to the other extreme). So any kind of authority there was, was dependent on leadership and authority and not any kind of sanctions. In nothing was Hut 6 better served than in the calibre of its heads of shift in all sections. It was they who really ran the Hut and they were the anonymous heroes and heroines of the story. The great thing about them was they were all so keen on the job. They had a genuine sense of responsibility, not in a heavy or pompous fashion, but because they realised how important their job and that of the Hut was, and they retained the same sense of excitement and high adventure which was the essential background of our work. Without that stimulus, I don't know whether it would have been possible to run a section which involved so many comparatively high-powered people doing work that involved so much drudgery, on anything like the lines which we adopted.

I should like now to try and appreciate how far these methods succeeded and where they failed. It was, as I have tried to describe, a very loose and informal organisation with only an indispensable minimum of formal routine meetings. I left heads of departments with a very free hand in their own department and in nine cases out of ten accepted their advice without question; confining myself to making sure that I understood pretty clearly what was going on and to encouragement. They did the same by their head of sub-sections, and heads of sub-sections by heads of shift. Each department would have its own meetings of heads of shifts whenever it felt like it. When major changes threatened, we would all get together at all levels, but avoiding as far as possible the monster general gatherings at which it is almost impossible to get anything done. As far as possible, therefore, each Room took care of itself. But the more complicated matters became, the more closely did the affairs of each department become entangled with the affairs of every other, and our own with other sections such as Sixta, Hut 3 and the stations. In the end we found it necessary to set up special liaison committees between the different departments. I think this was a good idea, but the war came to an end before the committees had got fully into their stride. The guiding principle all along was not to lay things down from on high, but to bring everybody into consultation, to get general agreement and to make everybody feel participants and not cogs in an unintelligible machine.

It is easy to enunciate high-sounding abstract ideals of this kind, not easy to carry them out in an organisation of 550 people divided up into at least nine largish groups (Watch Air/Army, Registration Room Air/Army/ TIS Air/Army, Machine Room, Decoding Room, Control); and it would be absurd to maintain that we fully carried our intentions into effect. But it is true to say that the only Rooms which caused me real anxiety over a long period were the two Registration Rooms. That was emphatically not due to any shortcomings in those who were charged directly or indirectly with the responsibility of running them, but simply to the fact that they were much the most difficult Rooms to run. To the psychological problems which loomed more largely in that section than any other I have already referred; but there were plenty of other worries. First, the Rooms were used as a reservoir from which the expansion of other sections doing more highly technical work was fed. Sooner or later nearly all the most promising recruits were transferred in this way, so that the turnover was much higher there than elsewhere. Moreover, those who by reason of ability and personality were best fitted to lead, were naturally those most sought after elsewhere. The difficulty was to find enough girls of the high calibre required for the very harassing and responsible job of head of shift, who could stand the racket indefinitely and would waive the possibility of promotion to much more interesting work.

Secondly, it was a vast Room – over 30 a shift – far too big for adequate supervision and with far too many different kinds of routine. The complaint was common and had a real foundation, that the routine had to be changed so often and the same girl only came back to the same job at such rare intervals, that she never properly mastered it. The obvious answer to that is specialisation and sub-division, so that one team does certain jobs, e.g., sorting, and others, e.g., registration But the objection to that was, that all the jobs were intrinsically so dull, that the only way of keeping even reasonably fresh was to have plenty of change and variety.

Thirdly, the rooms suffered much more from dilution than any other, except the Decoding Room, which was a much easier problem. There was a much longer tail, and however cunningly the head of shift might dispose of her resources, the weaknesses were liable to let her down. Everything therefore in that section militated against everybody's being on their toes and on top of the job all the time, and this was most noticeable not only in a great deal of needless inaccuracy, but in the speed with which urgent traffic was handled. It was always possible in a short campaign to bring the speed up to the highest possible level. There was no reason why it should not have stayed there, but it never did; as soon as one's foot was removed from the accelerator, the speed began to slip back. I am sure it was lack of imagination, the deadening effect of monotonous routine over a long period. It is one thing to be told that speed means lives, another to realise it. In a smaller room one might have overcome this deadweight of inertia; with the governing conditions what they were, I am convinced that nothing but Prussian methods would have succeeded; and equally clear that we had immeasurably more to lose than to gain by adopting them.

It is easy to criticise the Registration Room, because standing on the centre of things and serving all other departments, it stood to be shot at, and had nobody to shoot back at. Its mistakes were bound to be observed, and neither its merits nor its difficulties were always fully appreciated. In all the circumstances, I think it did at least as good a job, and perhaps a better, than could reasonably be expected, even though that job never came anything like as near to 100% efficiency as did those of other rooms. If I were to run Hut 6 again, I would organise the Registration Room differently; but I have no idea how. The great thing about the Registration Rooms was that you could always rely on them to rise to an occasion. In Registration Room Army, if there was more work to do than they could get through, they worked overtime till it was done; not once in a while, but for weeks on end, not as a special spurt, but as a matter of tradition. In Registration Room Air, which bore the brunt of nearly all our worst crises, the more hectic things were the better they liked it. Their heads of shift worked two shifts; they were full of good ideas of how to improve the routines; the best girls, including neish ones with no old Hut 6 tradition, worked as though they were 1940 volunteers; and the Room as a whole accepted without complaint the inevitable stoppage of leave. In all things they were not peculiar to Hut 6, but it did them, perhaps, more honour. That they responded in this way, was due, I think, partly to the fact that we tried to treat a staff of 500 in the same way as a staff of 50 – as individuals and not as units.

Philip Stuart MILNER-BARRY

To round off the sketch of Hut 6 history just given it seems imperative that another pen should estimate the individual nature and the extent of the personal contribution of P S Milner-Barry, the second Head of the Hut, to the success and happiness of the whole organisation.

Before October 1943 Milner-Barry, as head of the Crib Room and then of the Watch, had already set his mark on Enigma cryptography. In these years he accomplished his most vital technical achievement, his pioneer work in cribbery; he set the Crib Room on its feet and none ever surpassed him in his flair for picking out the essential message from a miscellaneous mass of traffic or in his skill in manipulating difficult re-encodements. Yet, as time passed, increasing responsibilities of internal organisation and liaison with Hut 3 inevitably debarred him more and more from the technical field; and by his success in these new tasks he stood forth as Welchman's natural successor in October 1943.

In nothing, perhaps was Hut 6 more fortunate in that the differing talents and capabilities of its successive heads were so admirably adapted to the circumstances of the times in which they assumed their responsibilities. Milner-Barry himself has already well depicted Welchman's peculiar genius; but if his originality of mind, strong mechanical bias and imaginative vision were invaluable assets for one presiding at the birth of an infant organisation and planning its future growth, no less were his successor's administrative and diplomatic talents ideal for controlling and directing the life of an institution grown to adult stature.

By October 1943, indeed, Welchman's main work for Hut 6, the provision of the tools to do the job in the shape of sets, bombes and cryptographers, was virtually done; but in the sphere of organisation many improvements were possible. Hut 6 had expanded from small beginnings in a natural but at times unplanned and haphazard manner (to take one example only, the Quiet Room, which performed a logically separate function, was administratively, as it was historically, a sub-section of Control). And a great part of Milner-Barry's work was dotting I's and crossing t's, tying up loose ends and removing anomalies generally. For a Hut of several hundred members the loose organisation of 1940 was no longer sufficient. At the time of Milner-Barry's assumption of office, the higher authorities were requesting each section to prepare a description of its organisation, and the paper on the organisation of Hut 6 drawn up by Milner-Barry shows clearly his keen interest in this aspect of his new responsibilities. The paper in question was by far the fullest account of the subject yet produced.

But, of course, much had to be done apart from this work of codification. Many changes in organisation proved necessary (whether through German security measures or war developments) and some of these were fundamental. Throughout all these changes Milner-Barry's synoptic vision as a whole – his ability to see the Hut 6 picture as a whole – and his foresight – found the right path. He was able to see the Hut not only as it was at any given moment but as a dynamic and developing organisation. And by an intelligent appreciation of the probable effect of German moves – and our moves – on the problems presented to Hut 6 he was able to play the Hut 6 game so that plans were ready for all probable contingencies and yet not so rigidly based as to be incapable of opportunist alteration if the unexpected happened. It was largely owing to this planning for which Milner-Barry was ultimately responsible that Hut 6 was never overtaken by events.

In his execution of changes (as distinct from their conception) Milner-Barry showed a rare combination of firm resolve and diplomatic finesse. Except in urgent emergencies, all proposed changes were thoroughly discussed with all parties affected, and the protests of outraged conservatives were patiently heard. While Milner-Barry was rarely, if ever, deflected from a course he had decided on, he was thus able to secure his way in such a manner that even opponents of the solution adopted felt their case had been fully considered. This ensured at least a moderately cheerful acquiescence, the more readily forthcoming as experience continually vindicated the soundness of Milner-Barry's judgment.

Still another important element in Milner-Barry's success was that while constantly endeavouring to systematise the organisation of the Hut, he never fell a victim to an unbridled craving for schematic perfection. He never, as his own final remarks show clearly, ignored the human element. So, to the end, there were some anomalies in the Hut 6 'constitution' which to the last was alive and flexible, never rigid and fixed. It is easy to conceive that others – the Germans, for instance, might have planned a Hut 6 (quite possibly very efficient in its Prussian way) run on very different lines, an organisation more logically administered where the chain of subordination would be more precisely defined. But in such an organisation the true flame of Hut 6, the spirit of free enquiry and camaraderie, would have flickered and died. Milner-Barry gave the Hut the more definite shape it needed without sacrificing its soul. His successful preservation in a Hut of some 500 persons the spirit that animated the original nucleus of some 50 was not the least of his achievements.

The German Enigma Machine

Purpose
The German Enigma machine is a mechanical device for performing a varying simple substitution on the successive letters of clear text.

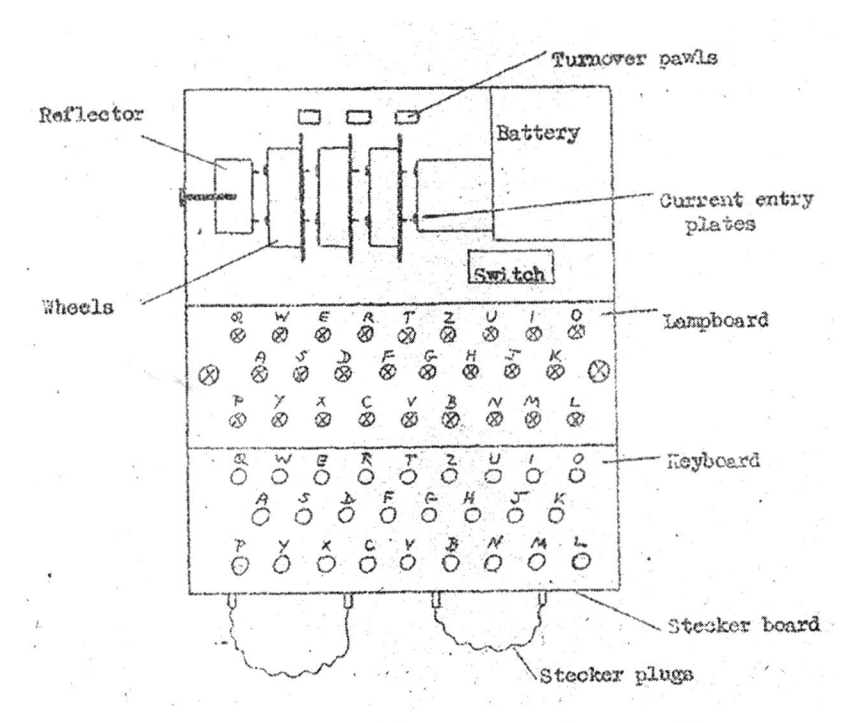

Diagram 1: Layout of the German Enigma Machine

The machine is contained in a wooden box about a foot square and six inches deep. It consists of three WHEELS (Walzen) mounted between the CURRENT ENTRY DISK (Eintrittswalze) and the REFLECTOR (Umkehrwalze), together with a KEYBOARD (Tastenbrett), LAMPBOARD (Lampenbrett), STECKER BOARD (Steckerbrett), BATTERY and SWITCH. The lid of the box contains spare lamps, plugs, etc., and the whole is fitted with a handle for carrying. See Diagram 1.

The German Enigma Machine

The current entry disc is a ring of 26 terminals (the CURRENT ENTRY PLATES), and these are connected in alphabetical order – via the stecker board – to the key and lamp contacts. See Diagram 2.

Each wheel has on one side 26 pin terminals, and on the other 26 plate terminals. The 26 pins are connected to the 26 plates in a hatted [random] order. On the right hand side of the wheel (as it stands in the machine) is a toothed cogwheel. On the left hand side is a metal TYRE (ring), marked with the numbers 1-26 in order, settable in any position by means of a clip, and provided with a TURNOVER NOTCH on its extreme left hand edge. The notches are in different tyre positions on each wheel. (The Naval Enigma Machine has three further wheels – VI, VII and VIII. Each of these has two turnover notches – at points diagonally opposite each other on the tyre – and the notch positions are the same on each of the three wheels.) Any three wheels, in any order, may be in the machine at a given time.

The reflector is a ring of 26 pin terminals which are connected together in pairs. (Normally the B reflector was used. Latterly, however, a pluggable one – D – was introduced on GAF keys and a few Army keys.) When wheels are in the machine the 26 current entry plates are connected together in pairs by electrical paths through the wheels, the reflector and back again through the wheels. The actual connections depend on the wheels involved and their positions. (Wheel positions are read off from windows on the cover of the machine.) The pressing of a key sends current through the stecker connections into the machine. The current emerges at the contact of another key, and the corresponding lamp lights up.

The stecker board has two sockets corresponding to each letter. These are made to take 2-pin double-ended STECKER PLUGS (the pins are of different sizes to prevent accidental inversion). When the stecker board is not plugged the connections between the current entry plates and the key and lamp contacts are straight – viz., A to A, B to B, C to C etc. The insertion of a stecker plug between, say, L and V is equivalent to interchanging these letters on both keyboard and lampboard. (See Diagram 2).

Every time a key is pressed one or more of the wheels turns over – thus altering the substitution. This motion is controlled by three TURNOVER PAWLS at the back of the machine which engage with the cogwheels and turnover notches.

The effect is as follows - the right hand wheel turns over once each position, irrespective of the motions of the other wheels. The middle wheel turns over whenever the right hand wheel is in a 'turnover position'. The left hand wheel and the middle wheel turn over whenever the middle wheel is in a 'turnover position'. This last type of turnover is called a 'double turnover' or (quite illogically) a 'middle wheel turnover'. (A wheel is said to be in a 'turnover position' when a notch on its tyre is ready to engage its appropriate pawl. The window readings in such positions – called TURNOVER LETTERS – are as follows:

- Wheel I: Q
- Wheel II: E
- Wheel III: V
- Wheel IV: J
- Wheel V: Z
- Wheels VI, VII, VIII: M and Z

Method of use

The 'machine setting' consists of:

- Wheel Order: three wheels in a definite order, read from left to right.
- Ringstellung: tyre settings on the three wheels, also read from left to right.
- Stecker: the cross-plugging on the stecker board, usually ten pairs, involving 20 letters. (The remaining six letters are unaltered.
- Reflector plugging: when the pluggable D reflector is used.

To encode a message, the three wheels are set at certain positions – called the 'message setting' – and the keys corresponding to the letters of clear text are pressed successively. The lamps which light up give the letters of the encode. The turnover(s) actually occur before current enters the machine, so that the pairing 'clear text-encode' refers to the position immediately following the position actually set up. Also, from Diagram 2, it is clear that the relation between clear text and encode is reciprocal – a fact which makes encoding and decoding exactly similar processes.

The machine gives a substitution only of the letters of the alphabet to each other. Alphabetical conventions must therefore be adopted for figures, punctuation marks, brackets, etc. Also, because of the way the machine is constructed, no letter can encode itself.

Four-wheel machine

The Naval 4-wheel machine is exactly similar to the above except that the reflector is replaced by a 'reflector plus wheel' combination. The wheel is on the right of the combination. It may be set at any combination, but does not move during encoding. The reflector is thinner than the normal one, but mounted in the same way. The wheel may be either Beta or Gamma, the reflector either Bruno or Caesar.

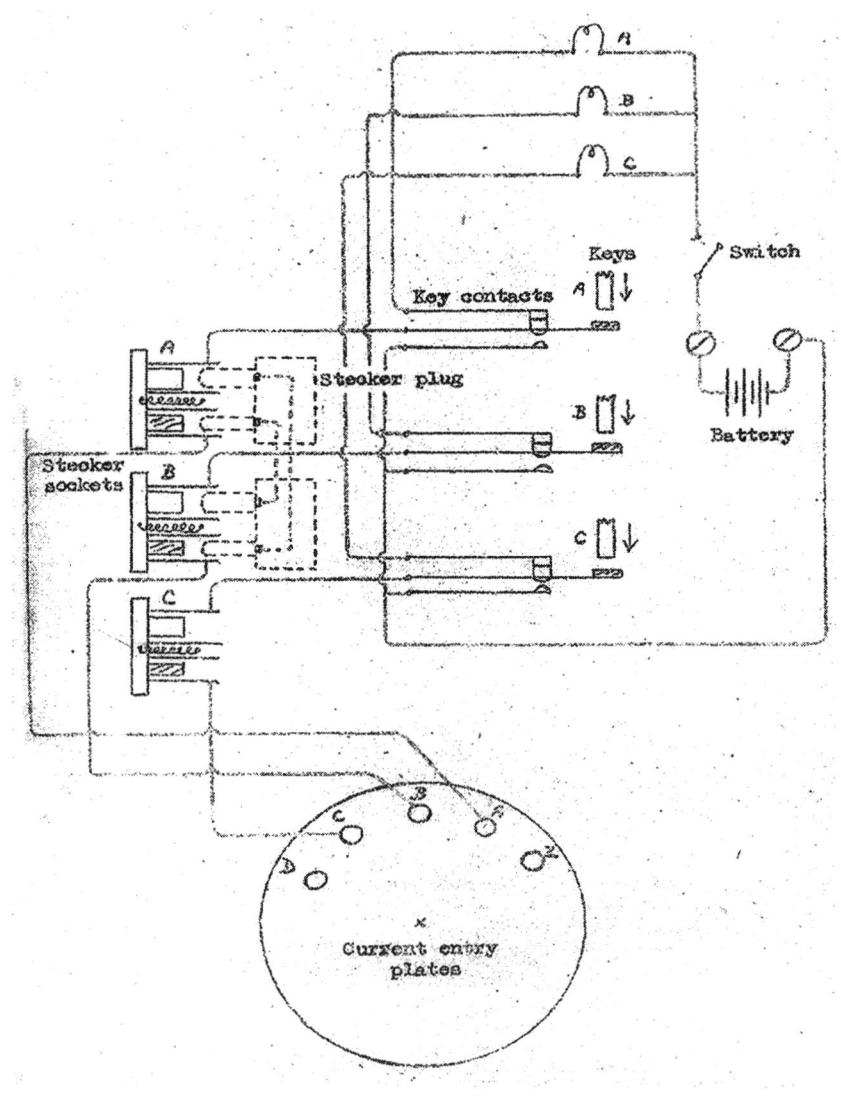

Diagram 2: The Wiring of the German Enigma Machine

Period I
Pre-War & September 1939 - January 1940: The Beginnings

Chapter 1
PRE-WAR THEORY

"I don't believe there's an atom of meaning in it", said Alice.
"If there's no meaning in it", said the King, "that saves a world of trouble, you know, as we needn't try to find any. And yet I don't know", he went on, spreading out the verses on his knee, and looking at them with one eye; "I seem to see some meaning in them, after all."

Lewis Carroll, Alice in Wonderland

Introductory

Although Hut 6 did not exist as a building and can hardly be said to have existed as an organisation before January 1940, the nucleus of its original members was assembled at the beginning of the war. As early as October 1939 there was a fairly full knowledge of the cryptographic problem as it then was, and work was already in hand on the devising of methods and apparatus for its solution. All this knowledge was based on pre-war information. We could not be certain that the enemy had not modified the Enigma machine in readiness for the outbreak of war, and we did have information that he had done so. It was not until January 1940 that this particular fear was set at rest by the breaking of a war-time key.

In the late summer of 1939 we received vital information about the Enigma from Polish cryptographers, culminating in the reconstructed machine which they presented to us in October 1939. Without this the work of Hut 6 would have been postponed for many months, for although advances might have been made in the theory, we could have taken no practical steps before capturing a machine, which we did not do before the Norway campaign. Certainly we did not collect anything like sufficient data for breaking the machine before then.

Pre - War Theory

As it was this first capture that came rather as an embarrassment than otherwise, lest the enemy should, as a result, introduce new wheels or other security devices. It was shortly followed by a great improvement in the indicating system, but it is doubtful whether this was a case of cause and effect, rather than a step that was bound to be taken as soon as the enemy realised the weakness inherent in the old system. Although routine breaking did not begin before 1940, the real dividing line between groping theory and operational practice coincides with the arrival of the information from Poland. This event would make a suitable starting point for our history, but a brief summary of our earlier work in this country and in Poland will add to the completeness of the picture which we will try to present.

Pre-War: Early Theory

The first crib
Machines of the Enigma type had been familiar to us for several years. An unsteckered version, the commercial Enigma, was on the open market, and a similar machine, with three wheels and no stecker, had been used by the Germans during their intervention in the Spanish Civil War and solved by (Dilly) Knox. Some time before the war – the provenance and date are unknown to the writer, but the latter was certainly prior to February 1939 – there had come into our possession a clear text, its Enigma equivalent, and the key with which the encipherment had been performed. This key contained stecker and provided our first information of this additional complication. The crib was attacked without success by various people at different times throughout the first six months of 1939. The stecker had merely the effect of imposing a substitution on the clear text letters entering the machine and the inverse substitution on the enciphered letters emerging. With the stecker known in this case, the effect of this substitution could be stripped off, so that we had effectively a crib on the unsteckered machine.

Rods and wheel-breaking
The method of recovering the wiring of an unsteckered machine from a crib was sufficiently well-known, though it was later to be given greater precision; it had been used with success by Knox in his solution of the earlier machine. The theory is too complicated for explanation here (a full account is given in the first part of the technical volume), but some of the basic notions involved may be briefly indicated. Most important of them is the idea of a "rod". Suppose we have an Enigma wheel with known wiring. We denote the positions of the 26 left-hand terminals of the wheel by a, b

... z. Left and right here apply to the wheel as it would be looked at when in position in the machine, though here we are considering the wheel in itself with no reference to the rest of the machine. Note that a, b ... z and A, B ... Z are attached to the positions of the terminals, that is actual fixed points in space, and not to the terminals themselves.

Suppose the wheel is in a position which we may call, arbitrarily, position 1. At this position the point a is joined by an internal wire of the wheel to, say, the point T. Now let the wheel rotate (in the direction z, y, x ...) into position 2. A different wire now joins 'a' to, say, Z. Proceeding thus, we obtain a sequence of 26 letters, say:

T Z E Y L X M W I V K U J A L S I R F Q C Q V N Q N

which we will call the a "rod". Similarly, we obtain the rods of b, c ... z, the wheel starting position being the same in every case. Note that the 26 letters of the a rod in this example are not all different. Like letters arise from parallel wires; of the 26 cross-wires of a wheel at least two must be parallel, so that a rod necessarily contains at least two letters the same. (This is true of an Enigma-type wheel with an even number of terminals. It is not necessarily the case of the number of terminals is odd.) Each rod clearly contains in itself full particulars of the wiring and the rods are not, therefore, independent. The connection between them is easily seen. Suppose at a certain wheel position a particular wire joins, say, q to S. When the wheel moves one step (in the direction of z, y, x ...) this same wire will now join p to R. Thus, if a letter occurs at a certain position on a given rod, the next letter in the alphabet occurs at the preceding position on the rod next in the sequence a, b, ... z. This "diagonal property" enables us to write down all the other rods given the a rod, and we thus obtain the "rod square":

```
     1  2  3  4  5  6  7  8  9 10 11 12 13 14 15 16 17 18 19 20 21 22 23 24 25 26
  a  T  Z  E  Y  L  X  M  W  I  V  K  U  J  A  L  S  I  R  F  Q  C  Q  V  N  Q  N
  b  A  F  Z  M  Y  N  X  J  W  L  V  K  B  M  T  J  S  G  R  D  R  W  O  R  O  U
  c  G  A  N  Z  O  Y  K  X  M  W  L  C  N  U  K  T  H  S  E  S  X  P  S  P  V  B
                        N                                              Q
                     O                                              R
                  P                                              S
  z  M  S  Y  D  X  K  W  L  V  H  U  J  T  I  Z  K  R  H  Q  E  P  B  P  U  M  P
```

Pre - War Theory

The column 1(the particular choice of column is, of course, arbitrary) is known as the "wheel upright".

Consider now the wheel in position in the machine at the right-hand side. We can identify the points A, B, ... Z with the terminals of the entry plate (Eintrittswalze). Suppose now we have a plain text and its cipher equivalent. Each constatation of this implies a pairing of two of the points A, B, ... Z by electrical connections through the three wheels and reflector and back again. If the starting position of the right-hand wheel is known or assumed, this pairing implies a pairing of two of the points a, b, ... z, say a and b by electrical connections through the two left-hand wheels and reflector and back again. So long as the two left-hand wheels do not move, that is in general for a stretch of 26 consecutive positions of the right-hand wheel, this pairing of the points a, b or ab rod pairing, will persist. There will be for the stretch 13 such fixed pairings, which may be regarded as the pairings of the composite reflector formed by the reflector proper and the two "fixed" left-hand wheels. Thus among the 26 rod pairings determined by the successive constatations in the stretch of crib there will be several which will occur more than once. It is from these considerations that we can, given a crib, attempt to recover the wheel upright (and therefore the wiring) of an unknown wheel.

It is necessary to assume the positions (at intervals of 26) when the middle wheel turns over. With a long crib it may not be necessary to make all 26 assumptions in turn. We can assume that the turnovers come in certain stretches, say of five or six positions, at intervals of 26 and confine our attention to the remaining stretches. We can, in this way, cover all possibilities with five or six different assumptions of turnover areas. Since the wheel wiring is unknown we can, with no less of generality, assume that the right-hand wheel is in position 1 for the first constatation of the crib.

Consider now two consecutive constatations within a non-turnover stretch, say at right-hand wheel positions 8 and 9. Provided – and this is a most important point – that we know the wiring of the machine from keyboard and lampboard to the (double) terminals of the Eintrittswalze, these constatations can be translated into pairings of the points A, B, ... Z – let us say W/X and I/M. Now it may be the case that the wire of the right-hand wheel which is opposite W in the eighth position and that opposite I in the ninth, both lead to the same fixed point on the left-hand side, or, in other words, that W and I are the eighth and ninth letters of a particular rod. If this is so, then X and M are necessarily the eighth and ninth letters of another rod, the two rods being paired through the "fixed" left-hand position of the machine. Because of the diagonal property of the rod square this hypothesis and its consequence can be translated into properties of the wheel upright and we may say that if D is immediately above Q on the upright, then E is immediately above U.

We may alternatively assume that W and M, and therefore also X and I, are consecutive on a rod. In this case we can say that, if D is next above U on the upright, E is next above Q. Every pair of consecutive constatations within a non-turnover stretch gives us similar pairs of hypotheses and consequences about consecutive letters of the upright. By taking constatations 2, 3, 4 ... apart we get similar hypotheses and consequences about letters at these distances apart on the upright. It is clear that all these hypotheses and consequences interlock. The technique, therefore, is to take a promising hypotheses (one which gives the same consequence several times) and to follow out the chain of consequences until either a contradiction is reached or the upright is filled in. It may, of course, be necessary to make subsidiary hypotheses from time to time. In case of failure we must proceed to a new hypothesis for the positions where the middle wheel turns over. Once the right-hand wheel is determined we can take all the crib pairings through it and translate them, thus, into pairings through the two wheel Enigma constituted by the reflector and the two left-hand wheels. A similar process is then employed to recover the wiring of the middle wheel and finally those of the left-hand wheel and the reflector itself.

In the preceding account we have associated the letters A, B ... Z with consecutive terminals of the Eintrittswalze. It was customary, however, when this was known, to name the terminals by the keyboard and lampboard letters to which they were connected. For the machines with which we were familiar, the terminals were connected to the keys (and lamps) in the order in which these appeared on the machine, the 'typewriter' order:

QWERTZUIOASDFGHJKPYXCVBNML

The fixed points opposite these terminals on the left-hand side of the right-hand wheel were named by the corresponding small letters. When the rods q, w, e, r ... were written out under each other, they would thus form a rod square with diagonal QWER ... This convention had the

Pre - War Theory

convenience that a clear-cipher equivalence through the unsteckered machine could be translated at once from the rod square into a rod pairing. The rod square diagonal was known as "the diagonal of the machine".

The process of the wheel-breaking which we have sketched presupposes the knowledge of the diagonal. Without this knowledge the problem is much more difficult and it requires a very long crib – about 2,000 letters – or a very specialised one, as for example a knowledge of all the 13 pairings through the machine at each of nine consecutive positions together with two pairings at a tenth position. Information was not at our disposal, and it was therefore necessary to guess the diagonal. The obvious guess was QWERTZU ... L. When this failed, this order was tried in reverse with equal lack of success. The correct diagonal, which is in fact ABCD ... was either not tried or, if it was, and the evidence is conflicting on this point, the attack was not pressed home. When, months later, we had definite knowledge of the diagonal, the crib was again attacked and the wheel wiring successfully determined [Editor's Note: A handwritten comment states *It fell out very quickly then (Twinn)*], but by then the problem was an academic one.

It is difficult not to feel that the alphabetical diagonal should have been considered earlier, but it must be remembered that, from a constructional point of view, it is a most improbable one. In the various Enigma-type machines in which the security depended on multiplicity of turnovers, the diagonal adopted was always the constructionally obvious QWERTZU... It is difficult to see why the Germans should have adopted a different practice in this case, especially since heir notion of stecker gave what was, in effect, a device for the arbitrary hatting of the diagonal. The only argument in favour of the alphabetical diagonal would seem to be that it is a rather more convenient one for a theoretical study, but this was a very small point. The unfortunate fact remains that the diagonal was not guessed and the breaking of Enigma was thereby probably postponed for six months.

In addition to the attack on this crib, there was being examined in the spring and early summer of 1939, traffic bearing all the characteristics of encipherment with the Enigma. The most obvious characteristic, common to all machine encipherments, was the flat distribution of letters. But what made the use of the Enigma particularly certain was the indicating system employed. The system that was being employed in early 1939 continued right through to the end of April 1940. This system will be described later. Most of the research work that was being done in the spring of 1939 was on traffic of earlier years which, while in clear continuity with current traffic, employed a primitive and most revealing system of indicating.

The Indicating System and its vulnerability

Traffic on one key could be identified by its Kenngruppen or discriminants. A discriminant consisted of a group of three letters and each key had four discriminants. The first five-letter group of an Enigma message consisted of two dummy letters followed by a discriminant group, whose three letters could be in any order. On a few occasions the dummy letters occurred at the end of the first group. The linking together of the four discriminants used by a key could usually be done from an examination of the first groups of a message with several parts. (At a considerably later stage the use of different discriminants for the different teile of a multi-teile message was forbidden). When several messages on the same key were written out under each other, a certain set of six consecutive letters at the same position in each message was seen to have significant characteristics. This was the indicator group. Its position varied from time to time but was fixed for a particular key: it was always near the beginning of the message and started at the beginning of a five-letter group. A number of such indicator groups, written under each other, might present the following appearance:

A	M	V	B	L	S
C	T	U	K	Z	C
A	R	K	B	R	Z
C	T	K	K	Z	Z
D	O	C	E	Q	V
D	T	V	E	Z	S

It will be seen that each occurrence of A in the first column is followed by B in the fourth, similarly D in the first is followed by E in the fourth, T in the second by Z in the fifth and V, K in the third by S, Z respectively in the sixth.

Generally, the occurrence of a letter in column n (n = 1, 2, 3) implied the occurrence of a definite associated letter in n + 3. This phenomenon makes the indicating system fairly obvious. Part of the key consists of

Pre - War Theory

a Grundstellung, or basic setting of the three wheels. Each message is enciphered at a message setting (or inside indicator) at the choice of the operator. In order to disguise this setting, which must be conveyed to the recipient in order that he may decipher the message, it is enciphered twice at the Grundstellung, and the resulting six letters sent as indicator group. The recipient sets up his wheels at the Grundstellung and deciphers the indicator group, obtaining the result, say, X Y Z X Y Z. The message setting is thus X Y Z. This double encipherment of the message setting is a good check against faulty encipherment or transmission, but it has a fatal weakness, as the sequel will show.

Given a sufficient number of indicator groups of the preceding type, it is possible, with a certain amount of inspired guesswork, to read them all, and this with no prior knowledge of the wheel wiring or stecker (if any). This feat was frequently performed. A detailed account of the technique occurs elsewhere, but the method can be lightly sketched here.

The explanation is simpler if we start the wrong way round, assuming the solution known. At any position the machine imposes a reciprocal transformation on the letters of the alphabet. This transformation, consisting of 13 letter pairings, was known loosely as the "alphabet" at the particular position. Let us call the six machine positions immediately following the Grundstellung positions 1, 2, 3, 4, 5, 6. Suppose the alphabet at position 1 is:

(AM) (BZ) (CQ) (DX) (EL) (FG) (HK) (IJ) (NY) (OP) (RU) (ST) (VW)

and the alphabet at position 4 is:

(AL) (BY) (CE) (DR) (FX) (GH) (IN) (JS) (KT) (MV) (OZ) (PW) (QU)

Suppose now that A is the first letter of an indicator group. A is the result of enciphering M. Therefore, the message setting begins with M. When it is enciphered at position 4 we get V, therefore V is the fourth letter of the indicator group. Similarly, B in the first place, implies O in the fourth. We give the complete list of consequences:

<u>Column 1</u>: A B C D E F G H I J K L M N O P Q R S T U V W X Y Z
<u>Column 4</u>: V O U F A H X T S N G C L B W Z E Q K J D P M R I Y

A more compendious notation can be used for this table of consequences. We have A in column 1 implies V in column 4. V in column 1 implies P in column 4. P in column 1 implies Z in column 4 and so on. This can be expressed in the form:

(AVPZYISKGXRQE) (BOWMLCUDFHTJN)

These are two distinct cycles of 13 letters, both EA and NB being regarded as consecutive. It two letters are connecting in either cycle, then the occurrence of the first in position 1 of the indicator group implies the occurrence of the second in position 4. We call the above expression the "box" of indicator columns 1 and 4. We now "box together" the alphabets at positions 1 and 4, that is we take any letter, say A, and we write after it its pair in alphabet 1, in this case M. After M we write its pair in alphabet 4, which is V, after V, its pair – W – in alphabet 1 and so on. The final result is: (AMVWPOZBYNIJSTKHGFXDRUQCEL) – a cycle of all 26 letters. If we take alternate letters of this cycle starting with A, we get: AVPZYISKGXRQE and starting with M we get: MWOBNJTHFDUCL.

The first of these is one of the 13-cycles of the indicator column box, the second is the other 13-cycle written backwards. Consider now the problem as it would be presented. Given enough indicator groups, we should have the data to form the box of two 13-cycles of indicator columns 1 and 4. There are 13 different ways in which the letters of the second cycle, written backwards, can be inserted between alternate letters of the first. We thus obtain 13 possible 26-cycles for the box of alphabets of 1 and 4. Each is a possible solution, the alphabet being read off direct from the box.

In this example the indicator column box consists of two 13-cycles and the alphabet box of one 26-cycle, but this will not happen in every case – there may be a larger number of smaller cycles. What we can say, however, as a little consideration will show, is that for every cycle of length 'm' seen in the indicator column box, there must be another cycle of the same length, the two combining to form a 2m cycle of the alphabet box. Given the complete box of two indicator columns, we can always find a finite number (12 or more) of pairs of alphabets at the corresponding positions. Hence, boxing similarly columns 2 and 5 and columns 3 and 6 we deduce 12^3 or more possible sets of alphabets at the six positions. Any such solution will decipher each indicator group in the form XYZXYZ.

In theory, any one of these solutions is as good as another, but in practice this is not so. This is because the message settings, being at the operators' free choice, tended not to be perfectly random. In particular, it was unlikely for a message setting to contain a repeated letter, and any solution giving a lot of such settings could be rejected. The most powerful criterion at that time was "the middle vowel". It was assumed that pronounceable trigrams would be popular as settings, and therefore any of the 13 or so possible solutions of the 2, 5 alphabet box which gave a large count of vowels for the second letter of the setting, would have a good chance of being correct. If such a solution stood out convincingly it reduced the possibilities by a factor of 13. It was usually found that among the sets of settings produced by the different solutions of the other alphabet boxes, one was clearly better than the rest, as containing such likely pronounceables as GUT, WAL, FRO etc., and keyboards like ASD, PYX, RFV, OKL etc. Such choices were very much commoner in the early days, and there was rarely any doubt about the correctness of the solution found.

Depth and turnover

Once the message settings had been determined for a day's traffic it became possible to locate, at least approximately, the positions of the turnover notches on the middle and right-hand wheels. This was done by "setting messages in depth". If two plain language texts are written out one under the other and the "clicks" (occurrence of the same letters at the same place in each) are counted, there will in general, because of the irregular distribution of letters in language, be more than one click for every 26 letters, which is the random expectation of two texts consisting of arbitrary jumbles of letters. There is also the chance of a repeat of several consecutive letters arising from a common word or syllable. This high "repeat rate", which varies with the nature of the plain text but which was in the neighbourhood of one in 17 in the kind of German plain texts that we met with, will clearly persist if the two texts concerned are both enciphered at the same position of the machine. Texts enciphered at different positions have a random repeat rate when counted level.

Suppose now we have two messages whose settings have been determined as GUN and GUT. If the right-hand wheel has a single turnover at one of the positions N to S inclusive, the second message will be enciphered with a starting position 20 preceding that of the first. If the turnover is at one of the positions T to M inclusive, then the starting point of the second message will be after that of the first. If the hypothesis of a single turnover is right, the correct alternative can be determined by staggering the messages appropriately and counting the repeats. In one case the count will be flat and in the other that of plain language. Similarly, we may be able to limit the possible turnover positions of the middle wheel. Thus two messages with settings DER, EFR may have a convincing level count, perhaps with a long initial repeat. This suggests that the middle wheel has turnover position E, so that EFS is the wheel-reading immediately following each of the above settings.

By methods of this sort the existence had been established of three wheels with turnover positions Q, E and V, the wheelorder varying from day to day. These turnover positions were actual window readings of the wheels, so that the turnover notches were necessarily on the tyre and not on the main body of each wheel, as had been the case with some types of machine we had seen.

The knowledge of any particular day of the alphabets at the six positions following the Grundstellung was not in itself sufficient for the discovery of the wheel wiring. To obtain further evidence attempts were made to get cribs by "reading messages in depth". With the wheelorder and message settings known for a day's traffic, all messages could be set at their correct relative positions and numbers of depths or overlaps obtained of parts of messages enciphered at the same position. The theory of reading such depths is simple enough, but the practice is difficult in the extreme. Suppose we have four Enigma messages in depth:

....	T	P	N	E	V	K	Z	...
....	X	P	N	E	V	L	T	...
....	Y	P	I	S	Q	Z	C	...
....	R	P	M	N	D	O	A	...

The letter P occurring at the same position in each text is likely to be the encipherment of a common letter such as E. If this is so, it suggests the possibility that the clear text of PNEV, common to the first two messages, is the common tetragram EINS. On this hypothesis we can, because of the reciprocal property of the machine, read additional letters of the last two messages. We have clear text:

....	E	I	N	S	...
....	E	I	N	S	...
	E	N	.	.	...
	E		E	.	...

This looks promising and can be made the basis of further hypotheses. With no prior knowledge of message contents, however, reading in depth is an unrewarding pastime. Even with a reciprocal machine like the Enigma it is doubtful whether anything but a few isolated fragments can be read in general on a depth of less than 20, and such depths were unobtainable with the small volume of traffic at our disposal, and no effective progress was made on these lines. (In the years to come, many ingenious feats of depth-

Pre - War Theory

reading were performed, but always with strong presumptive evidence for the probable clear text of one or more of the messages.)

New wheels and Indicating System: the goal-hunt

The use of three wheels, giving six possible wheelorders appears to have continued on German Army and Air Force keys until the end of 1938, when two extra wheels, giving a choice of 60 wheelorders, were introduced. Roughly contemporaneous was the change in indicating system. The first group, as before, contained the discriminant, but the characteristic effects of a fixed Grundstellung disappeared, and instead each message had a three-letter group in the preamble. It was an obvious guess that each message now had its own individual Grundstellung, represented by this trigram, for the encipherment of its (repeated) setting.

This hypothesis was soon verified and the position of the indicator group determined by writing under each other the texts of messages with the same trigram preamble (or "outside indicator") and looking for repeats three apart. The indicator group was found to be consistently in positions 6 to 11, immediately following the five-letter dummy and discriminant group. Thus we might have the following pairs:

	Outside Indicator			Letters 6 - 11				
(i)	A	M	V	S	**T**	Z	U	**K**	N
	A	M	V	L	**T**	A	M	**K**	Q

Here the repeat of T is followed by a repeat of K three places on. Evidence was also obtainable from pairs of messages whose outside indicators were one or two apart. Thus:

	Outside Indicator			Letters 6 - 11				
(ii)	A	X	T	L	**A**	C	M	**Z**	R
	A	X	U		**A**	D	V	**Z**	E	K

| (iii) | A | E | C | M | **V** | U | X | **L** | Q |
| | B | F | D | | **V** | L | S | **L** | U | A |

| (iv) | A | L | Q | N | S | **T** | Z | U | **B** |
| | A | M | S | | | **T** | V | Q | **B** | X | C |

| (v) | A | D | Q | P | Z | **Y** | X | L | **V** |
| | B | F | S | | | **Y** | C | Q | **V** | A | D |

(ii) is a straight verification of the hypothesis. (iii) is a verification only on the further hypothesis that the middle wheel has E/F turnover, so that the second letter of the first inside indicator and the first letter of the second are both enciphered at the same position BFE (and there again three places on). Similarly (iv) suggests (but does not prove) that the right-hand wheel has Q/R turnover, and (v) that the middle and right-hand wheels have respective turnovers E/F, Q/R.

Evidence of this kind established, first, the position of the indicator group and then the existence of two wheels with turnovers J/K and Z/A in addition to the three with the turnovers Q/R, E/F, V/W which were already known. The examination for "clicks three apart" of the appropriately staggered indicator groups of messages with adjacent outside indicators was known as the goal-hunt. More important than the clicks or goals that were scored, were those that were not. Thus (iv) above only suggests that the right-hand wheel is that with Q/R turnover, but if the pair had been:

(ii)   A   L   Q   N   S   T   Z   U   B
       A   M   S   T   V   Q   D   X   C

The fact that T is <u>not</u> followed by a click three places on proves that the right-hand wheel cannot have Q/R turnover.

The new indicating system, lamentably bad thought it proved to be when we knew the wiring, came as a serious setback to the attack on the uncompromised machine. Since it was no longer possible to break the indicators, the chance of a depth crib became still more remote – few depths were discovered, let alone read.

News from Poland

The preceding pages roughly indicate the lines of attack in the first six months of 1939. Within another month the whole position had been radically changed. At the end of July Knox went to Poland and met the cryptographers there. He returned with the startling the news that the Poles had, with varying success, been reading Enigma for several years.

It is historically uncertain how the Poles obtained the wiring of the wheels and machine, and it was not a subject on which they were very communicative. Certainly they made extensive use of secret agents and it is most probable that they obtained photographs of keys and messages

Pre - War Theory

with clear text. The essential fact that the machine diagonal was alphabetical they admitted to have discovered through one agent, though they claimed, no doubt with justice, that "nous aurions pultrouver par mathematique".

[Editor's note: The original document in the National Archives has a handwritten note to say that:

The statement that the Poles learnt <u>through an agent</u> [original emphasis] 'the essential fact that the machine diagonal was alphabetical' was a misunderstanding. The only agent information used in breaking wheels 1, 2, 3 was provided by the French (Bertrand from German traitor Asché), and consisted of key sheets.

[General Gustave Bertrand was the head of the French cipher organisation and Asché was the code name of Hans Thilo Schmidt, who worked in the German Army cipher office.]

However much the Poles had depended on agents for their basic information there is no question that they were highly talented men, and that, with limited resources, they had performed brilliant work. In the course of the next three months additional information was given about their methods of breaking and finally, at the beginning of October, we received a reconstruction of the Enigma itself. Owing to some unexplained error, the wiring of the two wheels with turnovers J/K and Z/A was interchanged, a confusion which was later to cause us a certain amount of worry, fortunately short-lived.

Polish methods of key-breaking

The methods of key-breaking adopted by the Poles are such as readily suggest themselves. There were essentially two methods, corresponding to the two different indicating systems. We consider, first, the original system, with settings doubly enciphered at a fixed Grundstellung. In the first place, the message settings and the alphabets at the six positions following the Grundstellung were found in the way we have already described. The boxes of alphabets 1 and 4, 2 and 5, 3 and 6 were formed and their "shapes", i.e., the lengths of their apparent cycles, noted. These boxes are of alphabets through the steckered machine, but it is clear that stecker have no effect on the shape of the boxes of the alphabets at two given positions, and that the actual boxes themselves can be obtained from those formed for the unsteckered machine by imposing on the latter the transformation represented by the stecker. The Poles therefore had catalogues of the box-shapes of unsteckered alphabets three apart for all positions and each of the six wheelorders (there were only three different wheels when this indicating system was in use.) From these catalogues they could determine possible values for the wheelorder and basic setting of the Grundstellung (i.e., the setting relative to some standard ringstellung), namely, machine positions for which the boxes of alphabets 1 and 4, 2 and 5, 3 and 6 following had the required shapes.

Such a solution, having been found, the steckered alphabet boxes would be matched against the corresponding ones for the unsteckered machine. In this matching, cycles of the same length would be "slid" against each other and the correct position would have to yield a reciprocal correspondence, the stecker transformation, between the letters of the boxes under comparison. This requirement was a severe one, so that from the possible solutions given by the catalogue, the correct one could quickly be picked out. The solution thus found gave the wheelorder and stecker. To complete the key it was necessary to find the ringstellung. To do this it was sufficient to determine the basic setting (referred to the standard ringstellung) of any one message, the key ringstellung being the difference between the (known) tyre-reading and this basic setting. This was performed by rodding a short crib, such as the common beginner ANX. With the stecker known, such a crib could be translated into a crib through the unsteckered machine. For each assumed absolute starting position of the right-hand wheel the constatation of this crib could be transformed, as previously described, into rod pairings through the two left-hand wheels and reflector (since the tyre-readings are known, so are the positions at which the middle wheel turns over, so that these can be avoided or taken account of).

Of the 26 sets of rod pairings thus obtained, further examination would first be made of those with confirmations (the same rod pairings arising from two or more constatations). The absolute positions, if any, of the two left-hand wheels which gave rise to such a set of rod pairings could be obtained by reference to a catalogue of pairings through two wheels and reflector (it is not clear if the Poles had such a catalogue) or, with only 26^2 positions to try, simply by trial and error. Any such possible absolute setting thus determined for the three wheels could be tested by further decoding, and a correct one would immediately determine the key ringstellung.

When the new indicating system was introduced (with the message setting doubly-enciphered at an arbitrarily chosen setting, the outside

Pre - War Theory

indicator of the preamble) a method of attack was worked out which was based entirely on the weaknesses inherent in the system. It made use of a mechanical device known to us as the cyclometer. This consisted essentially of two unsteckered Enigmas (whose wheels were turned by hand) wired together so that the output of each went straight to the input of the other. The circuit, which contained a lampboard, was completed by pulling an appropriate switch on a board containing a switch for each letter of the alphabet. We have seen how the boxes of the alphabets at two machine positions break up into even cycles. Thus if the alphabet at one position contains the pairs AX, CY, DF, GH and that at the other contains the pairs AH, CD, FG, XY, the box will contain the eight-cycle (AXYCDFGH), successive pairs of letters in this cycle being pairs of the two alphabets alternatively. If the two Enigmas of the cyclometer were set at the two positions concerned, then the depression of the switch corresponding to any one of the letters of this cycle would light up the lamps attached to each of its letters, and only those lamps. In particular, if the alphabets at the two positions had a common pair, say LM – then (LM) constituted a two-cycle and only the lamps L and M would light up when either of the switches L or M were pulled. The chance of two alphabets having at least one common pair is about two-fifths. When it happened, the two machine positions were said to be "female" with respect to each other.

Suppose now we have a message whose outside indicator and indicator groups are:

    A M K   X C P X O R

At each of the positions AML, AMO (referred to the unknown ringstellung) the letter X has the same encipherment, namely the first letter of the unknown message setting. These positions are "female three apart". The distance of three was commonly tacitly understood and we should say "there is a female on X at AML". In this the machine is steckered. If we are considering the alphabets through the unsteckered machine at AML, AMO we can say that these alphabets have a common pair, namely the letter steckered to X and that steckered to the first letter of the message setting.

The procedure was to pick out a number of these females, preferably on the same letter, from the indicator groups. The absolute settings were, of course, unknown, because the ringstellung was unknown, but the relative positions were determined by the outside indicators. Wheelorders were attacked in turn, the total number to be tried having been reduced by the goal-hunt previously described. A ringstellung was first presumed and cyclometers set up for each of the female pairs of positions. If these all proved to be genuinely female, this ringstellung gave a possible solution for further examination. Otherwise a new ringstellung was tried, and so on, through all 26^3 possibilities. The effect of a change of ringstellung could, of course, be obtained by the appropriate rotation of the Enigma wheels in all the cyclometers, the relative positions of any two Enigmas remaining unchanged.

One person could operate each cyclometer, testing for female positions by the switchboard. A ringstellung hypothesis for which all the cyclometers simultaneously registered females was a possible solution. Among the letters shown up as female by a particular cyclometer there must occur in the correct position that steckered to the repeated letter of the associated indicator group. With several females on the same letter, therefore, the rejection of wrong positions was usually fairly rapid. In any case, a possible solution gives, in addition to the ringstellung, sets of possible stecker for the various female letters. And since, from a hypothesis of the stecker of any particular letter we can, by virtue of the indicating system, deduce the stecker of a letter three apart from this in any indicator group, the rejection of wrong hypotheses for the female letters and the building up of the complete stecker in the right case was a simple if laborious process.

This method of solution, through essentially simple, required a high measure of concentration, and in the absence of a powerful reduction in the number of wheelorders to be tried, it was intolerably expensive in man-hours. The Poles, therefore, were casting about for some more economical exploitation of the female letters of indicator groups. The solution they arrived at, the method of the Netzverfahren, was adopted by us. It will be described later.

Chapter 2
War: the first successes

The outbreak of war

Within a month of the declaration of war we had received full particulars of the machine from the Poles, together with a reconstruction of the machine itself. At the same time they told us, however, that the Germans had changed everything at the outbreak of war. Although they advanced no evidence for this statement and gave no details, it was so intrinsically probable that we were prepared to believe it. It was obviously right to proceed with the assembly of apparatus for breaking, even though this might yield us only the decodes of pre-war traffic. While this was being done an intensive examination was made of current traffic for external evidence of the method of encypherment. At first, probably because of the lack of adequate wireless cover, it did seem that there had been a change of indicating system, but as the evidence provided by the goal-hunt accumulated it became fairly clear that this was not the case. It also became reasonably certain, from the same evidence, that the Germans were still using wheels with turnovers at the old places. This did not mean that there might not have been a change in the wiring of wheels or reflector or both, but our confidence was somewhat restored.

Meanwhile, a certain amount of practice was obtained in the breaking of traffic of the previous year which employed the old indicating system with fixed Grundstellung, and for which there were only six wheel orders to try, the possible permutations of the three original wheels. There was also at lest one notable achievement in breaking on the rods from a small crib deduced by depth reading. Rodding, as we have so far described it, is a method for discovering the wheels and their starting positions from a crib on the unsteckered machine. With more finesse and considerable more work, it can, in certain favourable cases, be adopted when the machine is steckered. However, in addition to the assumptions of right-hand wheel, rod position and middle wheel turnover position, it is necessary to make hypotheses for the stecker of one or more letters.

Solving Enigma's Secrets - The Official History of Bletchley Park's Hut 6

The technique is thus, from all these hypotheses, to deduce rod pairings and the stecker of other letters. Full details will be found in the articles in the technical volume on Rodding and SKO – Stecker Knock-Out – but a simple example will sufficiently illustrate the basic ideas involved.

Suppose we have on the steckered machine the crib:

. . .	P	C	B	P	L	A	Q	R	. .
	N	U	L	L					

and that we are investigating simultaneously the stecker hypotheses P/A, B/N. Suppose, further, that the right-hand wheel is known, that the middle wheel does not turn over in the stretch under examination and that for the P-N constatation the right-hand wheel is at a different position – say position 3 – relative to the standard ringstellung. We have then to choose the rods which have A (the stecker of P) and B (the stecker of N) in the third positions. Suppose there are the rods 'm' and 'x'. These rods – they were written out on strips of cardboard or wood – are laid out in groups under the crib thus:

		P	C	B	P	L	A	Q	R	. . .
		N	U	L	L	.	.	.	.	
Rod 'm'	-Q	Z	A	X	N	R	E	S	L	M . . .
Rod 'x'	-U	L	B	V	E	S	P	C	Y	U

Under the B-L constatation, the rod letters are N-E. By hypothesis B is steckered to N. If, therefore, we are correct in all our assumptions it follows that L is steckered to E. Having now the stecker P/A, L/E we can lay the rods for the P-L constatation, namely the rods with A and E in the sixth place. Also, under the fifth letter of Enigma text, L, the letters of rods 'm' and 'x' are E-P. Since L/E is a stecker pair it follows that the corresponding letter of clear-text is steckered to P, and is, therefore, A. This suggests that the crib can be extended to NULLA (QT).

This example illustrates the possibility of making further deductions about stecker and rod pairings and also how one can read or guess at clear-text beyond the crib. The process is clearly cumulative. If enough rod pairings are established for a given stretch, it may then become possible to discover by reference to a catalogue or otherwise, for what left-hand and middle wheels and for what positions of these wheels these rod pairings are valid. A solution of this last problem immediately gives us all 13 rod pairings, with consequent possibilities for further stecker and clear-text deductions.

The great number of different initial hypotheses to be tried makes a hand break on the above lines normally impracticable without a very long crib. The Germans, however, introduced the device of stecker, like other devices in the years to come, in piecemeal fashion. It was not until 1940 that the practice of having ten stecker pairs to a key became general. In 1938 there were usually only four or five, with a probable increase to seven or eight in the latter half of 1939. With only a few steckered letters, therefore, there was a strong chance that any particular letter was unsteckered, or 'self-steckered', as it was often called. Thus, the probability of the correctness of hypotheses could be judged by the number of self-stecker deductions to which they gave rise.

The Bombe and the Netz

Two instruments for solving were soon under consideration and development – the bombe and the Netz. The former, a piece of high-speed electrical machine, was far wider in its scope than the latter. It was designed to break a day's traffic either on the indicators or by means of a crib, while solution by the Netz depended entirely on the continuance of the indicating system then in force. Bombe theory, however, was only in its infancy, and it was obvious in any case that a long time must elapse before theory, however sound, could be translated into an efficient machine. The Netz, on the other hand, presented few technical problems in the preparation of apparatus and appeared a theoretically sound method of solution which should be ready for regular operation within a reasonably short time. Preparation of the Netz was therefore a most urgently important work, and this was early put in hand. Nevertheless, since the bombe, in its finally perfected form, was far and away the most important piece of apparatus used by Hut 6, it would be as well to describe simply at this early stage of its history, when it existed only as an idea, what exactly it was designed to do and how it was proposed to do it. Suppose we have a crib for the beginning of a message:

    P Z U K L O A R E Y Z M L D C E E X V B R K U .
    A N X L F L X K D O X E I N S S I E B E N . . .

There are normally 60 wheelorders to be tried. Let us suppose we are testing a particular one. The absolute wheel position is unknown for any constatation, for we know neither the ringstellung nor the individual message setting, both of which are necessary to determine absolute position. We do, however, know the relative machine positions for any two constatations. This statement is not perfectly true because of the turnover uncertainty. Thus normally the two consecutive constatations P-A, Z-N occur at machine positions 1 apart. If, however, there is a turnover of the middle wheel between the two, it is proper to say that the two machine positions are 27 apart, and similarly allowance must be made for the possibility of a simultaneous rotation of all three wheels. It is clear, however, that a sufficient number of hypotheses about the position or approximate position of the turnover will account for all possibilities. For the examination of any particular hypothesis, therefore, it is legitimate to assume that the statement above is correct. For simplicity we assume that there is no turnover of the middle wheel in the crib stretch of the example. We first assume that the absolute wheel positions (referred to standard ringstellung) of the successive constatations are ZZA, ZZB, ZZC etc:

```
ZZ    A B C D E F G H I J K L M N O P Q R S T U V W X Y Z
      P Z U K L O A R E Y Z M L D C E E X V B R K U . . .
      A N X L F L X K D O X E I N S S I E B E N . . . . .
```

The different constatations can be formed into a linkage of which we show part, with the assumed wheel positions written on the links:

```
          ZZA         ZZG         ZZK         ZZB
    P ─────── A ─────── X ─────── Z ─────── N
                                │
                                │ ZZC
                                │
                                U
```

If, say, R is enciphered by S at position ZZA of the unsteckered Enigma, then the stecker hypothesis P/R implies the stecker A/S. If now S and V are paired through the unsteckered Enigma at ZZG, we deduce from A/S the further stecker X/V and so on. An initial stecker assumption for any letter of the linkage implies the stecker of all the other letters of

War: The First Successes

the linkage. Suppose now the links to be replaced by Enigmas set at the appropriate positions, and that the output of the Enigma at ZZA is wired straight into the input of that at ZZG, the output of this into both the Enigma at ZZK and that at ZZC, and so on. Then, given suitable recording devices, we can see, without attempting to go into technical details, that by putting in electric current at a given point of the first Enigma, or in other words, by making a definite stecker assumption for P, we can read off the stecker of all other letters of the linkage. Should we thus get a consistent stecker "story" we shall, if it is the right one, be able to check our results and obtain further stecker either from crib constatations not used in the linkage or by further tentative deciphering of the message: from the complete stecker to the complete key is a short step which need not detain us here. If the story is inconsistent we must make a different stecker assumption for P, and when all 26 have been examined, proceed to a new set of wheel positions, the relative positions of any two Enigmas remaining unchanged. For each particular wheelorder and linkage there are thus 26×26^3 or 26^4 hypotheses to be tested.

This, then, very roughly, is the Bombe – a set of Enigmas which could be plugged into each other according to a predetermined linkage. The Enigmas were to be electrically driven, moving on to a new set of positions automatically when all stecker hypotheses had been examined (also automatically) at a given set of positions.

So far we have considered a linkage obtained from a crib, but it is readily seen that the message indicators themselves provide material for such a linkage. Thus a message with outside indicator and indicator groups gives the links

```
            A   M   K           S   U   T   L   O   Y
            AML     ?           AMO
        S   ___                         ___         L
            AMM     ?           AMP
        U   ___                         ___     Q
            AMN     ?           AMQ
        T   ___                         ___             Y
```

The letters here indicated by queries are the unknown letters of the message setting. There is no objection to joining such links as the above together to form a linkage for investigation by the bombe. Twice as many Enigmas are needed to form an equally powerful linkage (the power of a linkage being measured inversely by the number of solutions that it admits). On the other hand we do not have to make different hypotheses about the turnover positions of the two right-hand wheels since, for any particular wheelorder, these are determined by the outside indicators. Further, the correct bombe story immediately determines the key ringstellung.

For the bombe as originally designed it was necessary that the linkage should consist of several closed circuits with a common letter. For the crib of our example such a closed circuit is the following:

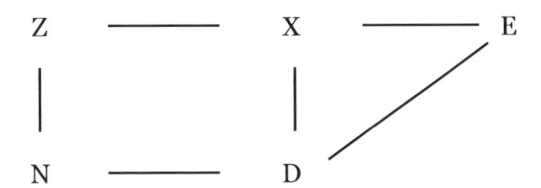

```
Z ——— X ——— E
|       |      /
|       |     /
N ——— D
```

At a given set of Enigma positions an initial stecker hypothesis for E, when taken round the circuit in a given direction will yield in turn stecker deductions for D, N, Z, X and finally E again. For the correct hypothesis the two values for the stecker E must be the same – a chance of one in 26. With four such closed circuits through E we expect on average one set of Enigma positions and one stecker for E which will satisfy the requirements for any particular wheelorder.

For a bombe on these lines it was that hoped that it would be unnecessary to make 26 different stecker assumptions for E each time. A certain assumption – say E/N – would be made. If this happened to be correct, well and good. If not, it would lead, after one passage round the circuit to different stecker for E, which again would travel round the circuit and yield further stecker. In this way all letters other than N would also be deduced as possible stecker for E except possibly one particular letter – say R – which could not be reached from the initial (wrong) assumption: E/R would then be a potential solution.

The notion just described gets over the need for making 26 stecker assumptions at each stage. In other respects, however, it is extravagant in that it requires a particular kind of linkage which it might not always be possible to construct, and also in that the possible correctness of a story is based on the examination of the stecker of one particular letter.

War: The First Successes

It takes no account of that a stecker hypothesis for one letter implies stecker deductions for all other letters of the linkage. The requirement that all these deductions should be logically consistent with themselves and with the original hypothesis is a much more stringent one than that considered above. What then was really needed was a device which, without sacrificing the advantage of making all 26 stecker assumptions for a particular letter effectively in one, would make use of <u>all</u> the information that could be deduced from the linkage. It was the solution of this problem that characterised the great advance in bombe theory which was to be made in the spring of 1940.

[An apparently 'officially sanctioned' (according to the National Archives) handwritten note is appended here in the original Volume 1 by Joan Murray (née Clarke), who joined Bletchley Park on 17 June 1940. The note ('Comment by JELM') is dated 23 February 1978, and is as follows:

'As I understand it, from memory and Prof's Book (written in 1940), this description does not apply to any stage of bombe design. The original plan for simultaneous scanning (i.e. testing all 26 stecker assumptions at once) did <u>not</u> rely on one passage round the circuit leading to a different stecker for the input letter and thus to another passage round the closure(s). "Pye simultaneous scanning", being engineers' planned implentation of the problem as put to them, used 26-phase power supply for the 26 assumptions.

The other, i.e., the logic for simultaneous sanning using the diagional board, was only discovered (by Alan Turing) after Gordon Welchman's idea of the diagonal board for the purpose of getting 'the complete set of consequences of a hypothesis... to reject any position in which a certain <u>fixed-for-the-time stecker hypothesis</u> led to any direct contradiction including on a secondary chain.'

Before leaving this subject for the time we may perhaps give the origin – possibly apocryphal – of the actual word "bombe". The Poles are said to have had in mind a rather Heath Robinson device for dealing with the problem, in which the signal of a potential solution would be the dropping of a heavy weight to the floor. This weight was the bomb, or, in French – which they used for communication with us – "bombe".

The bombe, however, was still very much in the air and the Netz held the centre of the field. We have described how the Poles, armed with cyclometers, attacked the weak points of the indicating system. It was clear, however, that the method was clumsy and extravagant in that every attack involved a fresh search for female positions three apart.

Solving Enigma's Secrets - The Official History of Bletchley Park's Hut 6

What was wanted was some method of recording wheel order positions for all wheel orders in a form which could be readily applied to the solution of a particular problem. After a good deal of consideration it was found that the Netz, now to be described, represented a reasonably simple and manageable solution of the problem. The Netz were square sheets of paper (other materials were experimented with but not used in practice) in which the required information was recorded by punched holes. For each wheelorder there were 26 sheets, one corresponding to each position of the right-hand wheel. Every sheet was divided into four squares, each of which in turn was divided into 26 x 26 smaller squares identified by row and column letter. Suppose for the wheelorder considered, the position DXL (referred to standard ringstellung ZZZ) was female with the position DXO, three further on. This fact would be recorded by a hole punched in sheet L in the square with row D and column X. This hole would actually occur at four places in the sheet, the four big squares of the sheet being duplicates of each other. All the holes were punched by hand by a team of girls, the female positions (we use "female position" here and later to mean a position female with that three further on) having previously been marked in on the sheets. These positions were detected by a machine known as the "Mouse" in the form of strokes printed on master sheets. The accuracy of the top line of produced by the Mouse was tested by "Waterwheel", a device operated by the turning of a handle, one person turning and another checking the female positions which were indicated by the flashing of an electric bulb. The tediousness of the latter work was enlivened by the discovery that the operation could be performed to waltz time.

The preparation of the Netz occupied a considerable time. The writer arrived at Bletchley Park in the middle of December 1939, just in time to assist at the ceremonial (and somewhat eccentric) punching of the two-millionth hole by the then Director (<u>editor's note</u>: *this was Alistair Denniston*). (The pedant will discover for himself that a complete set of Netz contains less than two million holes. The discrepancy can be attributed either to pardonable exaggeration or to the fact that a second copy was being produced for the use of the French cryptographers, now strengthened by a contingent of Poles, who had made good their escape).

The Jeffreys Sheets
Before going on to describe the method of using the Netz, we may briefly mention here the Jeffreys sheets (these were named after John Jeffreys, one of the pioneers of Enigma-breaking), which were also produced in

the first months of the war. These recorded, also in the form of punched holes, the pairings through two wheels and the reflector. There was one sheet for each pairing containing 26 x 26 rectangles. Each rectangle had a row and column lettering corresponding to the position of the two wheels, and the rectangle itself was divided into 5 x 4 squares corresponding to the 20 possible wheelorders. A hole punched in one of these squares thus indicated a wheelorder and wheel position for which the pairing written on the sheet was valid. The information to be transferred to the Jeffreys sheets was first recorded in catalogue form, one to each wheelorder. (The five wheels I-V were known as Red, Purple, Green, Yellow and Brown respectively. The wheel orders 1-3-5, 2-3-4 etc., were called ROGOB, POGOY etc., and the catalogues of pairings through two wheels and reflector BOGOX, POROX, YOPOX and so on). The use for which the Jeffreys sheets were intended will readily be guessed. If an attack based on rodding on the right-hand wheel alone yielded a possible solution requiring, say, the rod pairings al, e.g., hx ..., the sheets AL, EG, HX ... would be superimposed. Any hole right through would indicate a possible combination and positions of the first two wheels for which all these pairings were valid. In practice the vulnerability of the indicators made the rodding attack unnecessary even if it should ever be possible, and for long the bulky cupboard-full of Jeffreys sheets languished unused. Later on in the war, when the Netz had become historic relics, the Jeffreys sheets came into their own for a few halcyon months, when an unintentional gift of stecker by the enemy made rodding once again a practicable technique.

Method of using the Netz
The cyclometer attack, as we have seen, was a method of finding a wheelorder and ringstellung for which a certain number of positions (strictly, pairs of positions three apart) were female. The Netz provided a much simpler solution of this problem.

Suppose the indicators from a day's traffic on a given key yielded eight or more female positions (eight was generally considered the necessary minimum, otherwise, unless the number of wheelorders could be drastically cut down, either by the goal-hunt or by the "cillies" later to be described, there would be too many possible solutions for convenient testing. For each assumed ringstellung of the right-hand wheel we took the eight sheets (of the wheelorder set that we wished to try) for the corresponding absolute positions and superimposed them, staggered horizontally and vertically with respect to each other.

The relative stagger between any two sheets was, horizontally, the distance between the left-hand wheels, and vertically, the distance between the middle wheels for the two females concerned. The sheets were by means of a simple grid of squared paper fixed at one corner of the table. Any hole through the eight sheets gave us eight female positions for that wheelorder which had the required displacements relative to each other. This was a possible solution for further testing. It gave us the ringstellung at once, and the determination of the stecker and the correctness or otherwise of the position was soon performed by hand on cyclometers.

Early failures
We have already described how a limitation of the possible wheel orders could be obtained from a comparison of the indicator groups of messages with adjacent outside indicators. All the outside indicators of a day's traffic on one key were recorded on a Foss sheet, divided into 26 x 26 rectangular compartments each identifiable by a row and column letter. Thus AEC would be recorded by the letter C and a message reference number entered in square AE. A routine examination was made of this Foss sheet for pairs of outside indicators capable of leading to goals, that is such that the machine positions for the encipherment of the six-letter inside indicator would overlap by 4, 5 or 6 given a suitable wheelorder.

Several days' traffic after the beginning of the war had good wheel order reductions and a sufficiency of females, so these were attacked first. It so happened, unfortunately, that these all involved wheels IV or V and, owing to the mistake about the turnover positions of these wheels, both the wheelorder deductions and the setting of some of the wheels were at fault. Some half dozen days were tried altogether, though all 60 wheelorders when the goal evidence did not positively reject any wheel order. One after the other they went down and a general gloom descended. Within a few weeks it was lifted again when an emissary took a duplicate set of Netz to Paris and there discovered the confusion between the two wheels. These few weeks were not, however, wasted, for it was in this time that the existence and importance of 'cillies' were first recognised, a discovery of far-reaching consequences.

Cillies and attempts at depth-reading
These repeated failures made us fairly certain that the Germans had, after all, introduced some innovations at the beginning of the war, the most popular guess being that they had brought in a new reflector. In

order to break this we needed a long crib, and the only way to get a crib was to read a depth. It was as a means to this unlikely end that we first expected cillies to be most useful. From the decoding of pre-war traffic it was noticed that the German operator often took as his outside indicator the final position of the three wheels at the end of the preceding message. By so doing he saved himself the trouble of altering the wheels for the encipherment of the message setting. Since the message setting was often obviously selected, either as a 'keyboard' setting like PYX, RFV, CGU etc or a 'pronounceable' like HAN, WAL, MAR, CIL etc., it was possible, by 'subtracting' from the outside indicator of a message the number of letters in that preceding (excluding the 11 letters of the discriminant and indicator groups) to find what the setting of the previous message was, on the assumption that 'cillying' had taken place. (The pronounceables were often the first three letters of proper names, e.g., MARtha, WALter, CILli – and it was this last which gave the name of the process, since CIL was the setting of one of the first messages in which the practice was observed). The result of the subtraction depended, of course, on which wheels were assumed in the middle and on the right, and therefore a correctly guessed cilli generally implied a reduction in the number of wheelorders.

Looking for cillies became a popular pastime and, though at first we over-estimated the amount of cillying and believed cillies that we should later have been extremely sceptical about, we did nevertheless get impressive-looking wheelorder reductions on some days. We did actually, in our enthusiasm, suspect that new wheels were in operation because on some days we could find no cillies on the old turnover assumptions. On one such day, one of us deduced the existence of a new wheel with two turnover notches. If such a wheel were assumed, a noble array of cillies was obtained. It must be said that this hypothetical wheel did not command general belief. The actual subtraction was first done by the sliding of measuring strips (the number of units of length being the number of letters of the message) against a long strip consisting of the alphabet written out several times. These "snakes" were clumsy, and later we used a simple subtractor involving a transparent numbered grid 26 units wide and about 10 deep (to allow for a message length of 260), which could be slid over a 26 x 26 card in which each square had its appropriate row and column letter entered. Finally, when it became almost second nature to work quickly in the scale of 26, all such aids to subtraction were gradually dropped.

The attempt at depth-reading in order to find a crib on which to break the hypothetical new reflector was short-lived, but it was interesting practice. We chose a day with several good cillies and had all the messages on the key punched out on "Banbury sheets", so-called because they were prepared by a printer at Banbury (Oxfordshire). These were strips of paper on which were printed some 300 columns of letters, each column consisting of the alphabet written vertically. If, say, the 197th letter of the message were P, then a hole would be punched in row P, column 197. The process of counting the repeats between two messages at a given staggered distance could be easily performed by superimposing the sheets and counting the holes through both. The sheets for each message were labelled with reference number and cilli value, if any. All messages with good cilli values like WER were counted level with the rest, any which gave a count considerably better than random could be tested further by counting them, at the appropriate stagger, with the several WFNs, which were the basis of the story. Messages with cilli values near WER were counted against this both level and at a stagger of, say, 1 to 50 either side to see whether anything remarkable showed up. However, in the end, we did not succeed in getting anything better than a rather dubious depth of about seven, which was quite impossible to read.

First breaks of war-time keys
The attempt at depth-reading was abruptly terminated at the end of the year when our emissary returned from Paris to tell us of the muddle between wheels IV and V and with the great news that a key had been broken (October 28 Green) on the Netz sheets he had taken with him. Immediately we got to work on a key (October 25 Green) for which, by cillies and goal-scoring, the wheel orders had been convincingly reduced to three only. This, the first war-time Enigma key to come out in this country, was broken at the beginning of January 1940.

We eagerly awaited the opportunity to find the answer to the next great question: had the Germans made a change in the machine at the New Year? While we awaited a suitable day, that is one with enough females for our purpose, several other 1939 keys were broken and we began to get evidence of the extent and nature of cillying. At last the favourable day arrived and it had, besides the requisite number of females, several good cillies to cut down the wheelorder. The sheets were laid, the stories tested, and Red of 6 January 1940 was out. Other keys soon followed and Hut 6 (at the beginning of January we had moved from Elmer's School into a new wooden building) was beginning to get into its stride.

Period II
January-July 1940: Sitzkrieg, Norway, France –
Start of Continuous Operational Breaking

Chapter 3
January-March 1940

Red, Blue and Green

As we have seen, it was not until January 1940 that there was any approach to current breaking in Hut 6, and not until three months later that we reached the stage of continuous current breaking on any key. The position in January 1940 was as follows. Our resources in sets were not sufficient to enable us to intercept large quantities of traffic, and indeed it is certain that in comparison with later periods no great volume of traffic was being passed just now.

Nevertheless three different keys (or colours) - keys were originally distinguished by colour names – hence arose the use of 'colour' as a synonym for key were thus early recognised — Red, Blue and Green. These are the three 'primaries' among the mass of nearly two hundred keys that Hut 6 was to recognise, name and break. Of these keys *Red*, the general GAF key, was recognised a few months later as the most urgent and important of all Enigma keys and retained this place for four years, during which it was broken daily with very few exceptions. Even in the last year of the war, though Red was dethroned from its intelligence primacy, it was still at the cryptographic centre of Enigma-breaking. There can be no question that Red was in general the most important and famous key of the war.

Blue was the closest analogy to Red among GAF keys by virtue of its universal nature, but from any other standpoint far inferior. With rare exceptions its content was always practice messages – it was the

Luftwaffenmaschinenübungsschlüssel. Compared with Red it was broken seldom, largely because its intelligence value was almost nil: its dignity as one of the three 'primaries' was very honorary indeed.

Green (known also as Wehrkreis and later as Greenshank) presents a very different picture. In its own way it almost paralleled the renown of Red and it had the honour of confronting Hut 6 with some of its most difficult cryptographic problems. No colour that was so much worked on was broken more seldom and none had a higher standard of cipher security. Throughout the war Green was the key of the Wehrkreis or Army Commands into which the Greater Reich was divided. It would be false to claim that its position was on the same as that of Red. There never was any general Army key as Red was the general Air key, but there are respects in which it was the closest Army equivalent to Red. There never was any other Army key which last for so long a period as Green, and during all its life it was valid over an immense area.

Success and early organisation

The Netz method proved in practice very effective and when breaks had once started they came rapidly. From January to March 1940 we broke some 50 keys of Red, Blue and Green, and this is not accounting an appreciable number of 1939 keys that were also broken in this period. Every 1940 day broken had ten stecker pairings; the 1939 days all seven or eight. While we did not break a day between 28 October 1939 and 6 January 1940, it is reasonable to suppose, in view of what was later discovered about the systematic habits of the Germans, that the change to ten stecker took place on 1 January 1940.

The organisation of Hut 6 was at this time of the simplest. There was no necessity for a night shift or sufficient staff to man it, so a two-shift system was, in general operation. The sections of Hut 6 were:

NR (Netz Room):	engaged in "shoving the sheets"
MR (Machine Room):	arranging the data in suitable form, for the NR, checking stories and completing the key.
RR (Registration Room)	
DR (Decoding Room)	

Looking for wheel order tips by cillies was still regarded as an esoteric mystery. It was for a time presided over at 'the cottage' by Dilly Knox, assisted by occasional visitors from Hut 6. Knox had been the pioneer worker on Enigma in this country and his energy and enthusiasm had been an inspiration to all in the early months. When the Enigma had disclosed its secrets and Hut 6, under Gordon Welchman, was firmly on its feet, Knox and his cottage party turned their attention to new problems.

Operational Breaking

Rise of Yellow

The first indication of the new era of operational breaking came with the Norwegian campaign. The invasion of Norway by the Germans resulted in the immediate rise of a new key passing considerable quantities of traffic. This phenomenon of a rise of a new key coinciding with the opening of a new campaign was often to be repeated and arose naturally from the German system of key distribution. When a new land campaign was planned the armies involved were allotted one or more keys (according to the size of the operation) and these keys came up in strength as soon as the campaign started. It also followed that on the successful conclusion of a campaign, or on the establishment of land-lines in sufficient quantity, the key might dwindle or even vanish as quickly as it had arisen.

These points are illustrated in the brief history of Yellow (as the Norway key was called), which lasted in quantity from 10 April to 14 May and was broken from 15 April to 14 May inclusive. Yellow continued to use the single indicator system even after other keys had changed to the new system, soon to be described, and the amount of traffic was large enough to make continuous and regular breaking in the sheets possible. Yellow decodes in content referred to the GAF, yet the key was technically an Army key, i.e., one issued by the Army cipher authorities. This became *clear* later from several points, as, for instance, its key rules. At the time, however, the distinction between Army and Air keys could not be fully realised, and it was not until 1942 that it was quite clear they formed fundamentally different sets. It is odd – in view of the fact that during the war, Army keys were in general harder to break than Air keys – that the first key to be broken continually for a month was an Army key. But this was only possible because of its use of an indicating system already obsolescent.

The new Indicating System: first great crisis of Hut 6

On 29 and 30 April 1940 a new indicating system appeared on some of our traffic. This was called the double indicator system, and was characterised by two – not one – three-letter groups in the preamble. In the message itself the discriminant group remained as before. Thus, to all appearance, the message proper began in the sixth place, as proved to be the case. It might be mentioned here that at a later date, the Germans put the discriminant – if used at all – as a third trigram in the preamble and started the message in the first place.

The change did not come as a surprise: we had in decodes clear warning hat some change was envisaged. Here it should be noted that in cryptography, it is impossible to over-estimate the value of regular daily breaking, particularly in giving timely warning of any new complications the enemy is planning. Throughout the whole history of Hut 6 there were extraordinarily few examples of any innovation in German technique of which we did not have adequate forewarning. It will be realised that in examining traffic we had always to be on the lookout for messages that gave information of this nature and as a safeguard, it was arranged at an early date that Hut 3 should send back to Hut 6 for investigation, any relevant 'key messages', as they were called.

As soon as the first hints of a new system had been observed, speculation on its nature became widespread throughout Hut 6: and the correct answer was soon guessed. It was thought that the first three-letter group was still the outside indicator and the second three-letter group must be the encode of the message setting, starting from the position of the outside indicator. Fortunately, it was easily possible to prove that this theory was correct because, with crass stupidity, the Germans on 29 and 30 April employed both systems simultaneously on Blue – so we broke on the old system and checked up on the new. In May, all colours adopted the new system except Yellow, which continued to use the old system till its demise, and was still broken by the Netz method.

At one blow a catastrophe had fallen. In the course of its history, Hut 6 had to face many a crisis, but from some points of view, this was the most serious. In later crises we had at least a tremendous background of knowledge and experience of the whole German cipher system, a staff sufficiently large to undertake if necessary the most laborious hand operations, and a large reserve of complicated cryptography machinery.

But in May 1940 our whole system of breaking had been rendered useless at a moment when we had none of the above advantages. True, the bombe, which still provided a solution to our problems (given a crib) was in production, but the first machine was not expected to arrive for several months yet it arrived in August – and how were we to fill in the interval? Besides, if we did not make any breaks till then, how could we expect to write out cribs when the bombe came?

It was a godsend for the whole future of Hut 6 that, in May and the following months, German cipher security was so hopelessly bad that the enemy failed to reap the advantages they should have attained by the great improvement in their indicator system which they had carried out on the eve of their great Western offensive. Not for the last time, the carelessness of German cipher clerks wrecked the well-laid plans of their cryptographers. Yet the severity of the crisis can be measured by the fact that – apart from Yellow, which was on the old system – no key was broken in Hut 6 for about three weeks, the longest gap in breaking from January 1940 to the end of the war. Had the German cipher security been anything like adequate, we would have been fortunate indeed to get the first break on the new system within three months.

Overwhelming importance of Red
On 10 May the German attack in the West altered the whole interception situation. After a two-day's wireless silence, traffic suddenly rose to hitherto unheard of dimensions, and quick decisions had to be taken in view of our limited resources in sets. It was obvious from mere volume that one key – Red, the general GAF key – was of paramount importance, and the decision was made to concentrate on this key and drop everything else that in the view of our cryptographic resources and the possibility of breaking. There can be no doubt that in view of our cryptographic resources and the possibility of breaking this decision was absolutely correct. It is almost certain in view of our later experiences that there was in existence at this time a large quantity of Army traffic of high intelligence value and readily breakable on the mechanical resources we began to get in a few months. But very little of it could have been broken in summer 1940, as these resources were not yet available, and we were right to concentrate on what we <u>could</u> break. In what follows, we shall sketch as briefly as possible the general theory of the hand breaks on which we kept going. A later section will outline the daily routine adopted, but for the details of technique the reader must consult the technical volume.

Hand breaks

It is, in general, impossible to break any Enigma key with an adequate indicating system unless one has a crib – using that word in its widest sense as the clear language equivalent of a section of cipher text. The hand breaks of 1940 depended on the use of a specialised type of crib – the cilli – combined with a severe limitation of the number of machine positions to be tried. A machine position means a wheel order/ringstellung combination. There are 60×26^3, i.e., about one million such positions.

Cillies have already been referred to, so it is only necessary to summarise the essential points, which are:

1. A cilli occurs when a cipher clerk, after encoding a message, proceeds <u>without moving his wheels</u> to encode the next message, i.e., when the ending position of one message is the outside indicator of the next message. The setting of the message is the cilli.

2. If a cipher clerk has cillied, it is possible by subtracting the length of the message from the next outside indicator to arrive at the cilli – or, more accurately, to arrive at several alternative possibilities (according to the wheelorder assumed) for the message setting.

3. As message settings were selected by the free choice of the German operators, they were often non-random and fell into a number of popular categories – e.g., keyboards, pronounceables, nearnesses and a few other groups. In 1940 such non-random settings were particularly common – in mobile warfare cipher security is the first casualty.

4. So, after subtraction, we may be able to select the true message setting from the alternative possibilities (normally four) by recognising it as one of a favourite group. This gives us a three-letter crib and normally a wheelorder reduction. Of course, this recognition of the setting is the point of cillying, i.e., subtracting messages in a search for cillies, and, <u>as normally used</u>, cilli means a recognisable cilli, one spotted by subtraction as at least possibly correct.

5. Finally, a number of cillies on the same key make up a cilli

story. They can be used together as the relative machine positions are known and their self-consistency in wheelorder reduction and possibly in type provides an internal check on their correctness.

But before a handbreak can be considered there must also be a ringstellung reduction. Here we come to the "ringstellung tip", also named Herivelismus after its discoverer J.W.J. Herivel. It appears that it is in accordance with human nature when setting up a key in a machine:

1. To put the right wheelorder in the machine and then

2. To set the clips in the right position.

These steps *can* be taken in the reverse order, but the order given above was in point of fact normally adopted by Hut 6 and obviously also by German cipher clerks.

Now it is quickly seen by experiment that if the ringstellung is set up after the wheels are in the machine, then the reading showing in the window is near the ringstellung. If, in addition, the cipher clerk encodes his first message without moving his wheels, then the outside indicator of his first message is somewhere near the ringstellung – in practice it tended to be either "dead", i.e., exactly right or completely "in step", i.e., with each letter of the same distance on or back. Thus it was sometimes possible to deduce the ringstellung exactly or within narrow limits from an examination of the first messages of various operators. One, for instance, on a Kestrel day, the exact ringstellung was sent no fewer than five times and on 24 March 1943 Quince the first six messages on the blist had, as outside indicators XNF, XNF, XMF, WMD, APH, XNF – the ringstellung being, naturally, XNF. It is clear that this is a kind of laziness strongly akin to cillying – both depend on the German operator not moving his wheels, when on grounds of cipher security he should. It is thus not surprising (though it was very fortunate, especially in 1940) that cillies and ringstellung tips tended to arise on the same keys and often from the same men.

Now it is essential in attempting a hand break to have the number of positions considered worth trying severely limited, probably by cillies and ringstellung tips combined. How big a range can be covered depends to some extent on the material available, but even with ample material, i.e., a good cilli story, one would hardly undertake more than 180 positions <u>at the outside</u>, and one might well think twice before tackling more than 60. During this period most hand breaks were on a much smaller scale: the normal minimum was three positions, i.e., three wheel orders and a dead ringstellung. Assume for the sake of argument that we are making a hand attempt and that we have been fortunate enough to try in the first instance the correct wheelorder and ringstellung, i.e., the correct position. It is clear that our problem is solved and that we have broken the day if we can find the stecker. So what we want is a method of working out the correct stecker when we know the correct positions and have a series of cillies, i.e., steckered constatations at known positions of the machine.

In practice it is very easy to do this by setting up a German machine to any of the positions in question and then using the principle of "stecker implication" – i.e., that if it is known that at a given position of the machine, W decodes as E, then any assumed stecker of W gives rise to one, and one only, stecker of E. If, for instance, AG is a pairing through the unsteckered machine, then W/A implies E/G and W/G implies E/A. This is perhaps <u>the</u> fundamental principle of all Enigma breaking.

Thus, by assuming any stecker for one letter, we get the stecker of another letter and so proceed to a third and so on until we either get a contradiction (proving our first stecker assumption was wrong) or begin to get confirmation when we suspect the day is out. The correct story is always recognised by confirmations and self-stecker, and it was thus in these early days a great thrill when this happened. In due course, the miracle became almost a routine, and yet the magic of a hand break of Enigma never wholly faded into the light of common day.

It is obvious that for hand breaks, any further limitation of wheelorder, ringstellung and stecker (beyond what can be deduced from cillies and ringstellung tips) is invaluable. Hence arises the practical importance of the rules of keys that were now discovered. But this subject deserves a section to itself.

Chapter 4
Rules of Keys

General considerations

The subject of Rules of Keys is a large theme that runs throughout the whole history of Hut 6 from the summer of 1940 to the end. Sections on it will therefore be found in each of the subsequent periods and a reader who wishes to trace the historical development of the whole subject is advised to peruse these in succession. The present section is a general introduction, including the initial discoveries of summer 1940.

Even as early as spring 1940, before continuous breaking had started, several people in Hut 6 had already started looking for rules of keys, i.e., had begun to examine meticulously the various keys broken and try to find any sort of pattern construction. The main difficulty in such research is that one does not know precisely what one is looking for – to know this one would have to have guessed the rule already. All one can do is to arrange the available material in any way one can think of that might be helpful, and then examine the results. The psychological nature of the investigation is pronounced. What one is looking for is an insight into the mind of the German keymaker to discover the rules or principles by which he works. There are numerous pitfalls in this search, of which three may be mentioned.

Firstly, the sceptic might doubt whether there are any rules at all. There is no absolute necessity why keys should be made up on any system. Why should they not be absolutely random? The answer to this difficulty lies not in logic but in psychology. It seems to be an inherent trait of human nature – and not least perhaps of the German people – to seek to introduce system even where there is no need or desirability for system to exist. This explains both why rules of key exist and why – despite all sceptical arguments – people persist in looking for them. In short, the ideal of randomness is as difficult for the layman to achieve as it is for the mathematician to define.

The second difficulty is that it is not necessarily easy even when an apparent rule is discovered to look at it from the same angle as the enemy and to express it in his way, and unless this can be done, we may not appreciate the full significance of our discoveries. A good example of this is the Nigelian wheel order rule discussed later. It was discovered that most GAF keys took their wheel orders from what appeared an arbitrary list of 30. The question at once arose whether this was the whole story or whether there was behind this rule an elaborate system of picking the order of the wheel orders, where this apparent rule was merely a consequence – possibly an undersigned consequence – of some system which we never understood.

The third difficulty is more obvious: that of distinguishing a rule in the strict sense – i.e., a regulation observed by the keymaker – and a mere tendency. This can only be done on the basis of much evidence of broken keys considered in accordance with the laws of probability. A strong tendency, even if of short duration, may be almost as useful as a rule.

It has been mentioned above that the first investigation into the actual keys we had broken began in spring 1940. No progress was made then and none could be expected as there was not sufficient material on which to work. In general, nothing much can be done in this sort of investigation until there is about a month's keys – as complete as possible – ready for analysis. It also happened that the original tentative investigations considered the whole key as a unity, and we were soon to see that this was the wrong method.

The rules of Red

From 20 May onwards Red was broken daily for months, and indeed years, on end. It was not long before rules were discovered for each of the three constituent elements of the key – wheel order, ringstellung and stecker. All the rules described below were discovered in June 1940 and confirmed on the evidence of May and the following months.

<u>Wheel Order</u>: Red was found to obey both the non-clashing rule and the non-repeating rule. The first rule was that on any two consecutive days in the same month the same wheel could not be used in the same place. By this alone, if any one day was out, the wheel order for the next day was automatically reduced to 32 instead of the usual 60. The non-repeating rule, which was never quite so absolute, simply laid down that within a month the same wheel order was not used twice.

<u>Ringstellung</u>: If for the first 26 days of any month the ringstellung were written down in three columns, each column contained all the

letters of the alphabet once, and once only. Days past the 26th chose their ringstellung arbitrarily.

Stecker: Consecutive stecker, i.e., A/B, C/D etc., were never used. A/Z was allowable, showing that the keymaker looked at the alphabet from a linear and not a cyclical viewpoint. Also, the keymaker strove to avoid repeated stecker pairings in the same month. It was not possible to avoid such pairings altogether, for there were only 300 legal stecker pairings and it was proved by later events that all keys must have been made up as if for 31-day months. The evidence supported the theory that repeats were allowed rather more freely with the first five days of the month.

Results of the discoveries
These discoveries had two consequences: they were of immediate practical assistance in breaking Red, especially on the hand methods then in vogue, and they definitely fixed the future lines of research into rules of keys. On the first point, the influence of the wheel order and ringstellung rules in reducing the number of positions to be tried is obvious, and about the 26th one had an excellent chance of fixing the ringstellung dead, while the stecker rules greatly facilitated the picking out of the correct story by inspection from several plausible alternatives. Stories could be rejected out of hand on a consecutive stecker and it was a bad mark against them if they threw up stecker clashes. In fact, the immediate effect of these discoveries was to lead to the quick breaking of several obstinate missing keys.

On the second point, the concept of a key block became clear. It was obvious from the rules that the keys of a calendar month formed a unity to the Germans. We were to discover that each month's keys were issued as a whole on a key sheet and given a key number. Thus the future theory split into two sections – discovery of rules within a key block and comparison of different key blocks. This last section led, in 1942, to the discovery of key repeats.

Rules of other keys
One further point should be stressed. The rules already discovered were valid – as far as we knew for Red alone. They had later to be tested for each new key broken. By July 1940 we had, apart from Red, broken some Blue, some Green, a lot of Yellow and a single day of a key called Purple. How far did these keys obey the new Red rules? Often there was

Solving Enigma's Secrets - The Official History of Bletchley Park's Hut 6

simply insufficient evidence. It looked, however, as if Blue obeyed the rule against consecutive stecker, while clearly Green and Yellow did not. Yellow also did not observe the non-clashing wheel order rule or the Red ringstellung rule. It had, however, been previously discovered that Yellow was using another ringstellung rule by which all the letters of the alphabet were used in blocks of approximately nine days, as under.

May 1	ALO	May 8	OBZ
May 2	ENF	May 9	VMG
May 3	IBJ	May 10	EWQ
May 4	GKD	May 11	IYC
May 5	CHM	May 12	LDR
May 6	NXA	May 13	SFJ
May 7	HPU	May 14	A)(KT

After the discovery of the Red ringstellung rule this was put aside as an oddity, but it was to reappear later and be known as the Army ringstellung rule.

Rules of Keys

Red keys: June 1940

To illustrate the above points, the Red keys for June 1940 are now appended:

DATE	WHEEL ORDER	RINGSTELLUNG
1	514	GMP
2	321	RYK
3	215	VDG
4	531	NTZ
5	124	ZHB
6	312	EXO
7	423	TPJ
8	154	KBF
9	352	CRX
10	541	SIT
11	123	JUH
12	214	WAY
13	345	FWN
14	512	QLA
15	135	BGS
16	451	HOW
17	143	MSE
18	235	WCL
19	543	DJQ
20	341	OZC
21	152	INU
22	245	XEI
23	534	AVR
24	315	UKD
25	432	PFM
26	154	**LOV**
27	543	HDS
28	132	SXK
29	354	XGN
30	521	HPC

Daily Procedure in Machine Room

It may be helpful in filling out the picture of Hut 6 in summer 1940 if a brief account is given of the daily routine in the Machine Room (MR), which at this date was certainly the nerve centre of the Hut. The MR worked three shifts: 0000-0800, 0800-1600 and 1600-2400. This three-shift system continued to the end, but for practical reasons the night shift later ended at 0900, and there were sufficient personnel for three or four members for each shift. The main object each day was to break the current Red, and this was frequently accomplished during the day shift, and occasionally even before 0800 — the day when Red was broken on a hand attempt at 0500 was long remembered as a record at the time. The traffic was examined in the first instance on the registers, which were a continuous list of messages by each station, giving the essential details of the preamble, including the first two groups of the message. The Red discriminants were quickly identified and it was the custom of the registrar — the member of the shift whose primary responsibility it was to examine the register — to underline Red discriminants in a red pencil. This enabled one to see at a glance what messages were on the Red key and the practice was later extended to underlining other keys in appropriate or conventional colours.

The registrar also subtracted all messages, paying particular attention to known cilli frequencies, and noted any possible cillies he discovered. The listing of first messages and search for ringstellung tips was another important part of the work. A third was the AN-sheet — the 'fossing' [Editor's note: *recording outside indicators of messages*] of the first two letters of all messages and the counting of any with an additional bigram. The idea was to pick up depths, i.e., two or more messages encoded at the same message setting, which would of course show this by a plain language count instead of a random count. Figures were worked out later for the chances of various counts being genuine. Roughly speaking, a depth should have a count of at least 1/18 instead of the average 1/26. The justification for the initial bigram test was that, in general, the commonest single beginner to German messages was the word AN.

At a later date the AN-sheet was given up as being insufficiently productive of results, but in 1940 it paid good dividends. It is possible (as

Rules of Keys

is shown in the technical book) to use a fit or Banbury as it was called in a hand attempt, and also if one of the message cillies we know the setting of the other one. In a period where cillying was plentiful and keyboard settings were frequently used, it was quite likely that 'fits' would arise with keyboard cillies, and in fact on one day no fewer than ten NMLs were discovered.

If, as a result of the above investigations enough material was discovered for a hand attempt, this was organised forthwith, and if desirable the work was split up among the whole shift. (The methods deployed are discussed in detail in the technical book). It should be understood that at this period, the organisation was extremely informal, and there was none of the fairly rigid differentiation of functions between the various members of a shift that later proved necessary. In general, everything was a matter of ad hoc arrangement. Unbroken back days were considered by the same people who were attempting to break the current day.

As can be guessed, with only one major key to break (and in fact only one key was being taken in quantity) it happened that if Red came our early, the evening shift was unemployed so far as operational work was concerned. On these occasions the members of the shift occupied themselves in a more or less systematic way with any general problem that attracted them – in particular the discovery of the original rules of keys and the first investigations into what was to become known as 'the dottery' – were made in these quiet hours. It is never very easy in an expanding organisation like Hut 6 to get a perfect correlation between the work to be done and the staff available at any moment. One constantly has either too large or more often too small a staff for immediate needs. But the experience of 1940 suggests that, while in general once the organisation has got going on a large scale and the main lines of advance seem clear, it is preferable to have too small rather than too large a staff, there is a good deal to be said in the early experimental stages when the main technical problems are still to be solved, for having a small excess of staff over strict operational requirements. At this stage, if the right staff is available, leisure time spent in free experiments is unlikely to be altogether wasted.

Liaison with France

The subject of this section is rather by itself and not clearly connected with any of the preceding sections, but it obviously deserves brief notice. The liaison to be described was not confined to the period under discussion, but extends from the beginning of the war to the fall of France. During this time there was a constant interchange of cryptographic information between Hut 6 and the corresponding French organisation, and our allies were fully informed of the technical processes we were using and of our future plans — i.e., the bombe. In particular, all keys broken by either side were interchanged and in fact one of the important days that established the new indicating system was broken by the French. The keys broken in France were, however, much fewer in number than those broken here. This was probably due to the fact that their mechanical resources were even more rudimentary than ours were.

When the fall of France was clearly imminent, this regular intercourse was broken off and henceforward, until liaison with America became an important factor in 1943, Hut 6 fought its war alone. Had the war taken the course anticipated by the Allies in 1939, France would have played a significant part. The fall of France caused much anxiety in Hut 6, not only for general reasons, but for fear lest the Germans should find out that we had been breaking their traffic, and the methods we were using. Such knowledge on their part would have been disastrous for our future success — for apart from more far-reaching changes of the machine they might have brought into force — they would certainly have done something to eliminate cillies if they had realised their practical importance. It is due to our allies to state that it is now clear from the lack of German security devices at this time that they secured no information of cryptographic value from the French. So, fortunately for Hut 6, this dangerous moment (when the Germans had their best chance of securing an insight into our breaking methods) passed over without any appreciable damage being done.

Period III
August 1940-May 1941: Britain Alone

Chapter 5
Rise of Bombes and the Crib Room

General historical summary

This vital period, corresponding to one of the major crises of the war, is the time when the foundations of Hut 6's success were at last firmly laid. It is the immediate prelude to the great central period of consolidation from June 1941 to December 1943, when an adequate solution was found for all technical problems that had presented themselves to that time. But, from this time, the complexity of the German key system and the complexity of Hut 6 for breaking, increase together. It consequently becomes more and more difficult to treat the subsequent periods in strict historical sequence. Hence this general historical summary, and then to add special chapters on those sides of the period under review which demand detailed treatment.

The principal event of this period was the coming of the first bombe, Agnus, in August 1940 followed quickly by two others. On 17 March 1941 Jumbo, the eponymous bombe of a new type, arrived after exhaustive trials at Letchworth and quickly proved its value. With the bombe, cribbery became more important, though cillies were for long a valuable line of attack, especially on new keys. However, the Crib Room was set up as a separate entity on 1 October 1940, and rapidly developed and expanded.

While Red remained the largest colour, its size had dropped since the Battle of France and our growing resources enabled us to intercept more varied types of traffic. Thus more colours were broken and towards the end of this period two new keys – Brown and Light Blue – had joined Red in the category of regularly broken colours. At the same time a number of other colours had been broken on several occasions: Blue, Green, Orange,

Violet, AF5 (later to be called Chaffinch) and Onion. Most of these were broken at least in the first instance by the Research section which, in a very tentative way, had its beginnings in autumn 1940. At this stage it had no permanent membership, and was simply composed of two or three people seconded from the routine shifts for a week or two at a time to work on the 'odd colours'. It naturally happened that breaks of these new colours developed the theory of Rules of Keys, in particular the case of Brown. Another development was the recognition of re-encodements between one key and another as an important subject of investigation and the first breaks on re-encodements. The immediate operational use of Hut 6 breaking in this period hinged on Brown – which surpassed Red in urgency and importance. But no fewer than three of the new keys – Brown, Light Blue and Chaffinch – were closely connected with the current development of the war, as is made clear in the separate key histories later.

To conclude this summary, reference must be made to what was, at the time, an exciting, though somewhat mysterious development – the breaking of Reflector C on cillies. Disquiet had been aroused by some reference to a new reflector, and its quick conquest was regarded as a triumph of major importance. Of two multi-teile messages on a Norwegian frequency 1180, one came out on the normal Red key, while the other was dud. But the dud message provided some cillies to pronounceables, not exceptionally strong in themselves but very convincing in their agreement with the Red wheel order. Moreover, cillies had occurred in the decoded message. So it was assumed that this obliging operator had encoded the first message with Reflector B and the later message on the new Reflector C, and it did not take long before C was broken on this assumption. The method adopted was that of rodding through each wheel in turn. As is pointed out in the technical volume, the later invention of the half-Enigma gave a quicker mechanical method of solving the problem.

Reflector-breaking became commonplace in 1944, but the breaking of C has its unique place as the only time when it was possible to perform the operation on cillies. The practical results of the triumph were disappointingly meagre, as the Germans used Reflector C to such a small extent that the reason for its introduction remains obscure. On Hut 6 traffic it was used for a few weeks only on its original frequency and then disappeared. Its later use on some Naval keys does not fall within the confines of this history.

August 1940 - May 1941: Britain Alone

Arrival of the Bombe: What it did

The arrival of the bombe or spider — Britain's secret weapon — (strictly speaking there is a technical distinction of some importance between these two terms. The later term 'spider', after being frequently used in autumn 1940, was superseded in common use by the earlier term 'bombe', which will be generally employed in this work), is the most complicated piece of cryptographic machinery invented by Hut 6, with the possible exception of the reflector-breaking machines of 1944, all of which were, to a greater or lesser extent, modelled on it. In an earlier chapter of this book a sketch was given of the original conception of the bombe. What follows is thus to some extent recapitulatory, but it must be mentioned that the bombe, as finally constructed, differed in an important respect from the original conception. It was no longer necessary to construct a closed linkage and it was possible to use the principle of stecker implication to its full extent.

How this was done is explained in the technical volume. In the present non-technical treatment of the subject, it is desirable to attempt no more than to describe, as briefly as possible, *what* the bombe does without tackling the far more difficult subject of *how* it does it.

The material presented to the bombe is a 'menu', i.e., an equation consisting of a number of steckered constatations at known relative settings. These constatations can arise either from a series of cillies with which may be combined a beginner or signature on a cillied message, or a crib, i.e., the plain text equivalent of part of an Enigma message. (It is not possible to use *two* crib messages except in special cases, e.g., depth).

If the cilli or crib story is correct then there is at least one machine position (out of the $26^3 \times 60$ possible positions) where a consistent set of stecker can be found to satisfy the equation represented by the menu <u>and</u> to satisfy in addition all the constatations <u>not</u> used on the actual menu.

Now, if we suppose that the correct position is known or at least reduced to such narrow limits that all possible positions can be tried by hand – as happens on a cilli story where there is a good ringstellung – then we can break the day by the stecker knock-out principle, i.e., by making up a menu and then trying all possible stecker pairings for one of the letters on the menu and following up the implications. As was said earlier, an initial wrong assumption is rejected on stecker contradictions – an initial correct assumption is verified by confirmation and self-stecker.

Now what the bombe does is do just this on (if necessary) the full range of approximately one million positions. In every single position the bombe assumes all possible stecker pairings for one letter on the menu – known as the input – and works out the consequences of this initial assumption. Broadly speaking, the bombe stops at and records all positions that give possible answers, and the "stops" are tested by hand as described above. And the machine works so fast that it is able to run through an entire wheelorder in about a quarter of an hour.

Thus the bombe does over a vast range what any single person can do over a small range on an ordinary Enigma machine. It is, of course, only able to act in this way because of its greater scale and complexity. Thus, in a hand attempt, it is customary to use only <u>one</u> Enigma which is set in turn at each of the positions required. But in the bombe we have a series of Enigmas which are set before the run starts at relative positions corresponding to the constatation on the menu and which travel in perfectly synchronised motion from one position to another.

The arrival of the bombes in August 1940 meant great changes in the organisation of Hut 6 which will be described later. In the first place, it underlined the necessity of a study of the art of cribbery and a careful recording of all messages that might turn out to be cribs – hence the rise of the Crib Room (CR). In the second place, there was a constant – and as time went on, increasing – demand for two types of work: making up menus for the bombes and testing stops sent over from the bombes. The repairs and maintenance of the bombes were too technical to be trusted to Hut 6 and were from the beginning in the hands of a capable staff of mechanics in a separate establishment. The actual running of the machines was done by trained Wrens.

The making up of menus – a more complicated affair in some ways at first than it was later – was the business of the Machine Room and so at this period was the testing of stops. As time went on this last task became so heavy that a separate section of the Hut was set up as a Testing Room to do this work. Historically this room was a descendant of the old Netz Room and carried on the name – although it was now meaningless – until 1943 when, on the formation of Watch and Research, as the main cryptographic sections, the Netz Room became known as the Machine Room. This was a far more appropriate title as by then practically all the normal testing work was done by girls of the MR, and consequently they possessed most of the Enigma machines used in Hut 6.

August 1940 - May 1941: Britain Alone

Establishment of the Crib Room

The breaking of Enigma on cribs had been considered as an academic question from the earliest days, but with the arrival of the bombe the problem assumed the most vital importance, for any key could now be broken if 20 to 40 letters of the text of any message could be correctly guessed.

On 1 October 1940, the Crib Room was formed, consisting of four men who had previously been engaged in registration, under the leadership of Stuart Milner-Barry, who had been studying the cribbery problem. At this time cillying was still common and there were only two bombes. Constantly, therefore, problems of priority on the bombe arose. Should a 60% crib on Brown start running on 60 wheel orders early in the day when there was also ready a 90% shot on Red and cillies would probably later reduce the Brown wheel order? In general, the answer was that cribs were run where possible on cillie wheel orders, and were only run on all wheel orders if they were thought certainly correct. So then the circumstances demanded, a very high percentage of accurate guesswork from a section totally without experience in the work, and the successes achieved right from the beginning were a remarkable tribute to the energy and ingenuity of its members.

Methods improved as time went on, but the beginnings of most of the elaborate Watch technique of later years can be seen in the early days of the Crib Room. Routine messages were spotted from the typed books and, if good enough, details of their form and identification marks were entered in folders. To quote from a note on the work of the Crib Room, written in May 1941:

Likely looking messages are usually identifiable by a combination of length, frequency, time of origin, time of intercept, call sign, whether KR [immediate] etc. The actual analysis is performed by trying all known variants, and if possible, thinking of forms which might have occurred but have not done so. Finally the crib is graded A, B or C according to whether it permits e.g.:

Only one favourite form;

Two or more favourite forms, etc., etc.

Thus crib records were highly organised from the first, but the most satisfactory method of keeping them up-to-date was not brought in until long afterwards. In the early days the traffic was sent through after decoding to Hut 3, and later returned for the entry of cribs. This frequently resulted in delay in the observation of new cribs and new forms of old ones. Hence the system of 'EP-ing' (entering *en passant*) was introduced, whereby each message was inspected by a member of the Crib Room before being sent through to Hut 3. But this was not till much later. In the early days the Crib Room Log, which was from the beginning used to pass on information from one shift to another, contains many references to the non-entry of cribs, and the difficulty of recovering the messages once the intelligence people had begun to work on them.

Exploitation of re-encodements was, until 1942, in a rather primitive stage. The 1941 account quoted above says:

> *Occasionally profitable are <u>exact or almost exact</u> re-encodements from one colour to another, e.g., Red to Light Blue or Brown.*

Methods of using re-encodements when the texts were not letter-for-letter the same, had yet to be discovered by sheer necessity in the Chaffinch era. Meanwhile, the art of cribbery was steadily developed, the members of the section becoming gradually surer in their touch as they gained experience which was to be the foundation stone of the latter successes of the Hut.

New Discoveries on Rules of Keys: Brown

During the period under review the most important discoveries in the sphere of Rules of Keys were concerned with Brown. This unique key is in many respects unquestionably the most interesting of all keys broken by Hut 6. Its initial break was one of the greatest sensations of Hut 6 history. Brown is treated from a more general standpoint later, but here we confine ourselves to its key peculiarities.

Brown was first broken on cillies on 2 September 1940, and the key had six pairs of stecker and 14 self-steckered letters. This was the first known occurrence of a 1940 key with fewer than 10 stecker, but that this was no isolated fluke was proved by the subsequent Brown breaks which all revealed six or seven stecker pairs. This peculiarity put Brown in a class by itself, at least so far as the then known keys were concerned: it will be remembered, however, that all the 1939 keys broken had fewer than 10 stecker, and it is natural to consider Brown in this respect as the last

August 1940 - May 1941: Britain Alone

survivor of an old order. It was clear from later discoveries that the Brown keys were not made up in the central GAF Cipher Office, and we tended to picture the Brown keymaker as the doyen and diehard Tory of his class.

As soon as a sufficient number of Brown keys were available for examination, we looked to see whether the Red key rules were observed. It was at once clear that Brown obeyed none of these rules – not even that against repeats of stecker pairings within a month – though with the limited number of stecker, this rule would have been easy to keep.

But in December 1940 an important discovery was made. It was noticed that since 15 October 1940 Brown had been pairing its stecker – i.e., in every pair of days, one day had six stecker pairs, another seven, and between them the steckered letters accounted for every letter of the alphabet. This meant that if one of the pair days were out, 12 or 14 self-steckered letters were known on the next day, e.g.:

Brown Stecker

| 15 October | A/F | I/V | J/U | M/T | O/S | T/X | R/Y |
| 16 October | B/K | C/E | D/G | H/Z | L/W | N/Q | |

Unlike some key discoveries, this was of immediate and vital importance for breaking, for not only were the chances of hand breaks – not inconsiderable in any case due to frequency of cillies, ringstellung tips and the half chance that any particular letter was self-steckered – immeasurably increased, but apart from cillies altogether one might, with half the stecker known, break 'on the rods'. [*A rod was one of a series of pasteboard strips, 26 for each wheel, giving the contacts through the wheel at the 26 wheel positions of each letter of the alphabet.*] (See the chapter on rodding in the technical book). This latter possibility was exploited at once, and within a few hours of the discovery of the rule, 12 December Brown was out on the rods – the first break of any key in this way. A rush of rod breaks followed in the next few days and, in general, in future it was only necessary to run Brown on the bombe one day in two at the most.

It was discovered from the way the rule worked that the Brown key month was not the calendar month but ran from the 15th of one month to the 14th of the next. Hence, whenever the month consisted of 31 days, the 14th was an odd day. It also follows from this that the Brown keys must have been made up <u>for the particular month in which they were used</u>, otherwise the pairing would not have fitted in for such a month as 15 February- 14

March 1941. This is opposed to the general practice of the GAF Cipher Office, where it is clear that keys were made up for a 'standard month' of 31 days so that they could be readily transferred from month to month if this were desirable.

The pairing rule did not hold before 15 October, though there is a rough approximation to it on 11-12, 13-14 October. It did hold consistently from 15 October 1940 to 14 May 1941, during which time Brown was broken almost daily. There were very few exceptions to the strict rule in this period – once or twice there were slight slips which may have been due to a typist's error in copying out the keymaker's script. They all consist of one letter being steckered in both keys and consequently one being unsteckered on both pair days. Apart from this, the only oddity is that on 15 and 16 March 1941 there were only six stecker pairs, F and Z being unsteckered on both days. After 14 May Brown repeated back keys for ten days and this was followed by a period when little Brown was broken. It appears, however, that the stecker pairing rule came to an end with the March-April key – at any rate it did not hold in the June breaks.

To conclude this chapter something should be said about how other keys were behaving. Red continued to observe the rules of June 1940, except that after December, the ringstellung was abandoned. Light Blue (which began to be broken fairly regularly in March) behaved precisely like Red: non-clashing and non-repeating wheel order, no consecutive stecker and avoidance of repeated stecker. Of the other keys broken – Blue, Green, Orange, Violet, Chaffinch and Onion – none was in a sufficient quantity to warrant any far-reaching deductions.

The breaking of 28 February Light Blue was an important milestone for Hut 6 history in that, after this time, everyone <u>expected</u> a key to have 10 stecker pairings. The discovery of the peculiarities of Brown was necessarily unique, and the fact that in the log of the period it is explicitly noticed that the Light Blue key had 'ten stecker just like Red' betrays that no *a priori* assumption was made that this would be so. But when Light Blue had been broken, the general opinion of the Hut seemed to regard the question as settled – we had then direct knowledge of seven keys, and six of these had used 10 stecker from 1940 on. Henceforward, Brown was put on one side as an exception. We would have been surprised to find another key like it, and we never did. However, for a month or two in 1944, Llama, a home-made Sonderschlüssel [*a special key*] used in Albania, had a large number of self-stecker.

Origins of Research

Function of Research

Machine Room Research – or MR2 – began in a very informal manner in autumn 1940 and gradually obtained a more permanent and stable position. It was obviously desirable as soon as we become aware of the large number of keys that existed and felt ourselves in a position to devote some of our resources to intercepting hitherto unbroken keys that a separate body should be entrusted with the specific task of trying to break the 'odd colours' — as they were called to distinguish them from the current colours, Red and Brown, broken daily by the routine shifts in Machine Room and Crib Room.

Early organisation and methods

At this stage no permanent organisation was set up. The section had a variable membership, consisting at most of two to three persons at a time. In the great majority of cases they were seconded from the Machine Room routine shifts for a week or a fortnight. Normally the researchers worked 'permanent days'. Their initial numbers were not sufficient for three shifts, but the type of work did not demand working a 24-hour day.

The methods adopted in tackling their problems were in essence the same as those used on routine shifts and previously described – the search for cillies, ringstellung tips and depths – except that the work was not done currently but several days late and that subtractions and the rest of the routine were not performed on the register but on the 'blist' [originally the 'Banister List'], a list of all messages on a key arranged not as the traffic came in but in German Time of Origin, which in most cases corresponded to the order of encoding. In these early days there were few blists to look at, and there was considerable competition for those which, on past evidence, were considered most hopeful. There was more work than might have been imagined for the principal odd colour, Green, was well covered at this period and passed considerable quantities of traffic.

It was the duty of the researchers to use every means they could devise for breaking the traffic and for that reason to acquaint themselves with whatever was known about the W/T background of the colours with which they were concerned. At this period such information related mainly to Green. In fact, however, the finding of a cilli story was by far the most likely means of securing an initial break – too little was as yet known of the art of cribbery to expect correct guesses at what messages in an unknown key might say. With only two colours being broken regularly the day of re-encodements was not yet. It was natural that the researchers should be drawn from the Machine Room and not, as yet, from the Crib Room. In any case, the Crib Room's limited membership did not permit the establishment of a research section now, but if a break was secured the traffic was examined by the Crib Room from the crib point of view.

Early triumphs

The history of the more important groups of colours broken by Hut 6 is recounted in a later chapter which will contain many of the triumphs of Research, as for most of the war new keys were dealt with by Research in their initial stages. But the earliest successes should be mentioned here to give a picture of the variety of the early work.

If the researchers were fortunate enough to make considerable progress with a colour, and its contents were sufficiently important to make current breaking desirable, the key would quickly be transferred to the routine shifts. This happened with Light Blue, key of the GAF in Africa, which was, after several near misses, broken on cillies in March 1941 and almost at once taken over as a current colour. Cillies, re-encodements from Red and cribs all combined to give Light Blue a flying start, and is perhaps the classic case of the Research ideal – to break a new important key soon after its appearance and hand it over to the routine shifts as soon as possible. Shortly after, a similar initial entry was made into AF5 (Chaffinch) on cillies, but in this case full success had to wait for a later cillie break in September 1941.

But apart from Light Blue and Chaffinch the researchers had two major triumphs in this period. The first was the breaking of 19 November Green on a hand attempt. By the rarest of lapses on this most secure of keys there was a keyboard cilli story and a good ringstellung. The second important break was an entry into Orange 10 December on a nearness story – a break secured on the memorable 12 December, the same key on which the Brown stecker pairing rule was discovered.

This Orange day was the first war-time break of a new class of keys – the SS keys. In this case it proved possible to exploit the initial break and four days were broken in January 1941 on a crib called Fehlanzeige – the first crib to secure any regular success on a Research key. But the early disappearance of this key left us nothing to work on but cilli stories – which were available at not too long intervals – but had the annoying habit of being rather sketchy and insufficient. For a considerable period Orange was a tantalising colour, raising one's hopes only to cast them down. It was possible to try quite a number of days – sometimes on laborious hand attempts – but to break very few. For example, in the four months from February to May 1941, only one break was achieved – 22 March by hand.

Green (later called Greenshank) proved much less easy to exploit. Two methods were tried at the time and also much later. One was running the address AN STELLV GEN KDO RCEM in some form or other on suitable messages, but this, though with some support from the day broken, was failed *ad nauseum*. The second line of attack was the famous 'Banburismus' [*a mechanical method of counting messages together with the object of discovering fits (two or more messages on the same key and at the same machine setting)*] method. This is the only way of breaking an Enigma key that does not presuppose the ability of writing out the clear equivalent of cipher text. However, its utility is severely restricted by the unfortunate fact that it postulates a great quantity of traffic – probably at least 400 messages. So Green, apart from, of course, Red which could be and was broken on more normal means, was the only Hut 6 key that could be attacked by Banburismus, but the most pernicious attacks failed.

Banburismus was often used successfully in Hut 8 (*the naval section*) and a full description of the method as applied to Naval problems will be found in the technical volume. It was not till march 1942 that Greenshank was broken again, and 19 November 1940 had at least the distinction of being pored over years after as the latest available evidence!

Summary

This brief account of the early work of MR Research may serve to show the general place that Research – which came to include the crib side also – played in Hut 6. Research was the pioneer cryptographic section, breaking new ground and extending the frontiers of what was known. It was not <u>always</u> true that new keys were treated by Research in their first days. Later, keys closely connected with Watch keys would be treated currently from their first appearance. Still, by and large, new keys were the province of Research. It inevitably happened that, the more successful Research was, the more was its own share of work limited – the area of the unknown grew less and less. In the end, as we shall see later, Research died as a separate organisation largely in virtue of its own success, but this self-immolation is a measure of its triumph. Broadly speaking, at the end, so much was known, that there were no more cryptographic worlds to conquer.

Period IV
June 1941-December 1943: World War – the Great Period of Expansion and Consolidation

Chapter 6
General Historical Summary

Features of the period

This long period of over two and a half years is not the time when Hut 6 reached the peak of its success, if success is to be measured by the quantity and quality of the intelligence sent to Hut 3. On those standards, the peak is in the last period of the war, probably especially in the months following D-Day. Yet the period now under consideration is the greatest central epoch in Hut 6 history, the time when, thanks to increase of resources all round – sets, personnel and bombes – we got so completely on top of the enemy's cipher system (especially on the Air side) that all the ingenuity of his subsequent innovations failed to shake off our grip.

At the end of this period Hut 6 could claim that practically every key which was passing a large amount of traffic (Greenshank was the most notable exception) was being broken with at least fair frequency and that a satisfactory solution had been found to every technical problem with which the enemy had so far confronted us. The salient features of the period are the great increase in the number of keys recognised, named and broken, corresponding increases in our personnel and machine strength combined with a growing complexity in our administrative arrangements, great developments in the regular technique of breaking, the frequent use of several new methods made possible by GAF key repeats, a much greater concentration of attack than before on the not immediately operational keys so far as this could be done without detriment to those of operational value, and improved liaison with Sixta

General Historical Summary

and Hut 3. It will be convenient now to devote a paragraph to the above tendencies which will serve as an introduction to more detailed treatment later where this is desirable.

Increase of keys

A certain proportion of this may be fictitious and represent merely the discovery by our greater interception resources of keys that were in use already. But when full allowance is made for this factor, there can be no doubt that there was a vast increase in the number of keys issued and used by the enemy. For this there were two main reasons:

a. the initiation of new campaigns by the Germans or their preparations to meet expected attacks by the allies, and

b. the splitting up of keys by the Germans themselves because of the alterations in their systems of key distribution and allocation.

Examples of (a) were the appearance of Mustard, Vulture and Kestrel in June and July 1941 immediately after the attack on Russia, and the appearance of Albatross and Cormorant in May 1943 in anticipation of Allied attacks on Sicily and Italy. Examples of (b) were, on a small scale, the breaking up of Kestrel into several geographically distinct keys in August 1941 and the similar disintegration of Raven in December 1943; and, on a larger scale, the complete reorganisation of German key allocation in January 1942 when Fliegerkorps keys were carved out of Red. It should also be noted in passing that matters sometimes worked the other way round: German changes in key distribution might occasionally lead to the disappearance of a key (as Light Blue died in January 1942), while the same effect might be obtained on the conclusion of a campaign. The most conspicuous instance of this was the unlamented death of Phoenix and the Finches in the Cape Bon peninsula. But for this period such cases were exceptional. For German keys, the forces of new creation and fission were still stronger than those of death and amalgamation.

Increase of personnel

The new fields opened up demanded staff increases in every section of the Hut. The main cryptographic sections (Watch and Research in the latest terminology) were considerably expanded not only by new arrivals from outside, but also by recruitment from other sections of the Hut –

especially the former Netz Room, now renamed the Machine Room. This section, too, was considerably strengthened to deal with the increased number of bombes and took over all the normal testing of bombe stops. In 1943 the constant influx of newcomers made it necessary for us to prepare a short course in cryptography and make other general educational arrangements. In this year also began the American 'invasion', destined to add welcome fresh blood to the Watch, Research and many other sections of the Hut.

Increase of machines
Along with the increase in personnel there was a considerable increase in our bombe resources. This was, indeed, a first priority in the eyes of those responsible for the administration of the Hut, and without their persistent clamour for more and more bombes, Hut 6 simply could not have achieved anything like its actual success. The priority problems in this field were by no means straightforward as there were always the rival policies of concentrating on standard machines, i.e., aiming at mere quantity, and the more adventurous course of experimentation. Further, the requirements of Hut 6 and Hut 8, competitive users of the bombes, tended to differ. Experience taught us that you can scarcely have too many bombes – the more you have the more you use them up by embarking on long drives which you could never contemplate if you had not a superabundance of resources.

And thus, despite the large number of bombes produced here, Hut 6 would have suffered severely from insufficient mechanical resources – particularly in 1944 – had not the mass production of America come to our aid. Machine construction on a vast scale was in fact the peculiar contribution of America to Hut 6's success. In its full development the story belongs rather to the final period of the war, but even in the latter half of 1943 we were already getting substantial aid both from the military bombe at Arlington (Virginia) and the naval bombes at Washington – witness especially the break of Bullfinch on a date stagger in December 1943, a form of attack which would have been inconceivable without American bombe resources.

Growing complexity of organisation
A natural consequence of the growth of work and of numbers was an increasing degree of specialisation in most sections and a growing com-

General Historical Summary

plexity in the general organisation of the Hut. As far as the cryptographic side was concerned this resulted:

a. In Machine Room Research (or MR2) being put on a more stable and continuous basis with a couple of permanent members assisted by a staff of visitors from the routine shifts, and,

b. In a corresponding Research section of the Crib Room being set up under the name of CR2. We now had two pairs of sections – MR1 and CR1, MR2 and CR2 – each pair dealing with the same material from a somewhat different standpoint.

It was realised that however naturally this division had arisen, it was wrong in principle and persistent attempts were made to correct the error and arrive at a closer integration of cryptographic effort. Eventually, when the ground had been carefully prepared, MR1 and CR1 were formally united as the Watch, while MR2 and CR2 were also amalgamated as the Research section and at the same time their membership was set on a permanent basis. These important developments, which coincided with the abandonment of the old Hut and our move to the newly-constructed Block D, are fully discussed later.

Technical developments
These fall under three main heads:

a. (a) cribbery
b. (b) re-encodements
c. (c) new methods of breaking

The theory of cribbery reached its final development by the end of 1943. Afterwards it was mainly a matter of employing known principles. Our experience in 1941-1943 made us familiar with all the different types of messages, and through this experience we became able on occasion to guess cribs on the slenderest of evidence. The important Army distinction between ordinary and Staff keys was first apparent from our observation of Chaffinch decodes in 1941 and 1942.

While re-encodements were first used successfully in March 1941 it was not until the present period — and particularly not until the great extension of keys in January 1942 — that they really came into their own. In anticipation of this multiplication of keys a mechanical means of discovering potential re-encodements (soon to be known as 'kissing') was instituted on Air keys in December 1941 and at a later date the method was applied to Army keys also. The technique of working re-encodements underwent a great development, and on the African Army keys in particular, a chain of re-encodements became the recognised method of exploiting an initial break. Experience was also gained in what is often a most difficult task — working a re-encodement to Enigma from some other cipher (e.g., Fish). The peculiar trouble in such cases is to make adequate allowance for changes in punctuation.

The new methods of breaking came into their own in 1942 through the remarkable series of GAF key repeats to be described in a later section. These made it possible on occasion to break a key by (1) rodding, (2) by running a 'hoppity' menu. The last two of these were new methods: (2) had not been used in Hut 6 practice until 1942 (though it had been employed by Hut 8, and hence the mechanical device was ready for use), and (3), though developed in theory in autumn 1941 and once used in Hut 6 practice, did not come into its own till 1942. Apart from these strictly technical developments, fresh discoveries in the Rules of Keys – particularly as regards GAF wheel orders – increased the number of breaks by saving bombe time. And the curious story of the HOR-HUG stecker on Orange (see the section on SS keys) led to a new kind of rodding – rodding with half the stecker known. This, it is true, was not in principal different from rodding Brown on known self-steckered letters, but in practice was somewhat harder.

General course of breaking
Throughout this period supreme emphasis was placed on the Mediterranean keys – on the Air side Red, Primrose, Locust, Scorpion II and later Puma. On the Army side, Phoenix and the Finches up to May 1943 and later Albatross, Cormorant and Shrike, but as far as possible without detriment to this priority we attempted to break anything in sight. On the Air side we succeeded in breaking many Luftgau and Fliegerkorps keys, including some on the Eastern Front, also large quantities of Mustard, the GAF Y key, and of the Weather keys more than enough to satisfy all intelligence claims. On the Army side we made increasingly successful inroads into the Balkans and tried to break Vulture on every opportunity, though we could seldom get any long sequence of breaks. We also scored sporadic successes on Kite, Osprey, Robin, Gannet and a few other keys.

General Historical Summary

Of the SS keys, Orange and Quince were both broken frequently, and in the case of Orange, cheaply, so long as the HOR-HUG stecker lasted.

It should be noted that (especially in 1942), the key repeat system made it more than ever absurd to organise our Air breaking on a basis of intelligence priorities alone, for no-one could tell whether a key of negligible intelligence value in one month might not prove to be of the highest cryptographic value in helping to break an important operational key the next month. In the GAF key world, everything was so interwoven and interlocked that the only safe rule was *to try to be in a position to break any key on demand even if one did not have the resources to do so regularly*. If this ideal was achieved, then we could take full advantage of any key repeats that were discovered and also be reasonably certain of not missing any discoveries. As a step in the latter direction, it was a definite point of policy to have an exceptionally vigorous drive on the 1st of every month and to attempt to break on that day every identifiable key, no matter how trivial might be its content.

Liaison with Sixta

During this period liaison with Sixta – the organisation responsible for log reading and 'fusing' together all information of W/T interest – became closer than formerly, though not yet so intimate as in the last period of the war. But even at this stage liaison with Sixta was invaluable for securing to Hut 6 up-to-date information on all W/T matters that might affect cryptography. Sixta's special responsibilities were:

   a. working out new W/T systems by evidence of logs, call signs, direction-finding etc;

   b. discovering re-encodements by charting, log reading and other methods;

   c. answering specific enquiries about routeing of messages, indicators, etc., and;

   d. bringing to the notice of the cryptographers any significant log chat.

No official liaison body was ever set up between Hut 6 and Sixta. Contact was maintained by day-to-day intercourse between the parties concerned, who were in most cases the Fusion Room officers on behalf of Sixta and members of the Crib Room or Machine Room (later Watch and Research) on behalf of Hut 6.

Liaison with Hut 3

The importance of liaison with Hut 3 was that only in this way could Hut 6 receive adequate guidance as to the intelligence priority of various colours, i.e., which colours were most important and most urgent to break. The two categories did not necessarily coincide — final decisions could not be made on intelligence values *alone*. Hut 6 had to weigh these in the light of cryptographic probabilities, otherwise we might have gone on failing poor shots on important colours, while good shots on less important colours waited. But it was at least essential that Hut 6 should know as accurately as possible what the intelligence priorities were – and this information could only be supplied from Hut 3. So from the earliest days an informal liaison grew up, and in 1942 this had progressed so far that in some instance advance information of war moves was passed on to senior members of Hut 6 so that they could, if necessary, reconsider their breaking policy. But at this stage the need was felt for a more regular link and a separate section (known as 3L) was set up in Hut 3, one of whose functions was liaison with Hut 6. Henceforward (except in emergencies) all advice on intelligence priorities (for breaking and decoding alike) came to Hut 6 from Hut 3 through 3L and it was one of the functions of the Head of Hut 6 to keep in constant touch via 3L with the general intelligence background.

After the formation of Watch and Research the liaison with 3L became still more formal and official. In July 1943 a daily meeting (taking place normally at 5pm) had been arranged between officers of the Watch with the Head of the Research Section and the Head of the Hut to discuss the bombe programme for the next 24 hours. This meeting was required because the very length of the Research programme to be run on the bombes made a clear system of grading necessary. In September 1943, this meeting, known as the Lage Conference, was extended to include a representative of 3L. At this conference the general cryptographic situation – including the bombe resources available – was set forth by representatives of Watch and Research, the general intelligence situation was explained by 3L, and finally, after any questions from either side, the Lage, i.e., the list of jobs to be run, was arranged in an order of priority that struck a fair balance between the claims of Intelligence and Cryptography. The Lage Conference remained as a useful piece of machinery till the end of the war. Its final form is discussed in the section on the Organisation of the Watch.

Conclusion

It may be useful to add here a brief list of the important dates of this period, including the first breaking dates of the more famous new colours:

1941

June	First breaks of Vulture and Mustard
August	First break on the dottery
September	Beginning of regular breaks of Chaffinch
December	Beginning of regular breaks of Vulture

1942

April	Discovery of HOR-HUG stecker
	Discovery of GAF key repeats
May	Greenshank of 5 March broken
June	First break of Phoenix
August	New record of 508 breaks in one month
October	New record of 555 breaks in one month
December	First use of regular wahlworts, i.e., nonsense words affixed to the beginning and end of messages

1943

June	First break of Albatross
October	First break of Wryneck
December	First break of Bullfinch

It should also be mentioned here that during this period the Germans adopted various security measures. The most widespread change of this nature was the permutation of wheel order, finally adopted universally in some form or other. This was clearly an anti-depth device, and from this angle is in the same category as later German security measures (e.g., Zusatz stecker and Enigma Uhr). The German cryptographers were obsessed to an excessive extent by the fear of depth which, in fact, was very rarely used as a means of breaking. But, their anti-depth device did, at any rate, rule out the Banburismus method as a practical one for Hut 6, and certainly ensured the failure of the Banbury attempts on Greenshank in 1942, as on this key the alteration of wheel order was particularly thorough.

The first step in wheel order change — as far as we knew — was taken by the GAF in October 1941 when Red and all other Air keys (except Brown which, as usual, came into line later) adopted the system of AM and PM wheel orders — i.e., at 12 noon the wheels in the machine were taken out and simply reversed, this also reversing the ringstellung. The German Time of Origin of any message determined whether the AM or PM wheel order would be used.

In July 1942 a more radical change was made on all pure Army keys. Three wheel orders were used daily from 0000-0759, 0800-1559, 1600-2359 respectively, the permutation being cyclic: ABC, CAB, BCA. Later, when the key began at 0300, all the times were put three hours on. In September 1942 the GAF came into line (Brown, as usual, lagging), as also did Orange, then the principal SS key. By December 1942 Quince had also adopted the system of X, Y, Z wheel orders as they were called. The system was by now virtually universal: it should be stated that the wheel order first used on any day — i.e., the AM or X wheel order — was the basic one printed on the key-sheets and, as such, the relevant wheel order for key rules.

Two Army keys (Greenshank and Nuthatch) were found to use a different system. Both employed all six permutations of a basic wheel order, the order of the changes being variable and decided by a daily changing table. The times of alteration were irregular — on Nuthatch, when the key started at midnight, they were 0000-1115, 1115-1330, 1330-1500, 1500-1700, 1700-1800, 1800-2400. The basic wheel order – which was presumably written on the key-sheet — was that with the wheels in ascending numerical order and not necessarily the first wheel order of the day. Further details of the wheelorder peculiarities of these keys will be found in the section "Greenshank and Allied Keys".

More isolated security measures such as the ringstellung peculiarities of Orange and Mustard are dealt with in the special key histories, while the W/T camouflage measures at the end of 1943 — viz., the dropping of discriminants on Army keys in September and on Air keys in November — are discussed in the book on Traffic Identification.

Chapter 7
Detailed Theory of Rules of Keys

Sources of information

With the large number of breaks in this period our general knowledge of the workings of the German cipher system greatly increased and it became possible to treat rules of keys in a more systematic manner. The principal source of our deductions and conclusions remained the actual keys broken in Hut 6, but a subsidiary source of value was the examination of captured keys and documents. It was not until summer 1944 that these began to arrive in Hut 6 in large quantities, but at least one important point was confirmed by captured documents as early as 1941.

Air and Army

The fundamental distinction of Air and Army keys first became clear in 1942. These two types of keys were found in general to obey so divergent rules that it was obvious that the GAF cipher office was distinct from the Army cipher office or offices. This was most clearly shown by the remarkable key repeat system on the GAF which reached its climax in 1942: this system to which the relatively few Army repeats provided no real analogy is dealt with fully in the next section. The divergence is also suggested by the fact that the GAF and Army used different discriminant books for, to the Germans, the discriminants – which appeared on the key-sheets – were an integral part of the key. Thus, in considering key rules, it is necessary to make a sharp distinction between Air and Army keys. In our conventional key nomenclature, Army keys were given bird names, while Air keys were called after colours, insects, flowers or various types of animals.

The SS keys (fruit names) are in the wide sense Army keys, but had to some extent peculiar key rules, and were possibly made by a separate SS cipher office. Indeed, it was never quite clear whether all the 'pure Army keys' – i.e., Army keys excluding SS keys – were constructed in one office or not. In the case of Air keys it is clear they were all constructed in a central office except for Brown (which was always in a category of its own) and a few locally issued special keys.

Divisions of the subject

The theory divides naturally into four parts, which will be dealt with in the following sub-sections:

1. Wheel order rules
2. Ringstellung rules
3. Stecker rules
4. Brown rules

Wheelorder rules: Army and Air
On Army keys wheel order rules were conspicuous by their absence. Even the fundamental Air rules of non-clashing and non-repeating wheel orders were frequently broken by the Army and the SS. In fact, the incidence of clashing wheel orders in this period was, as a rule, not less than random, and sometimes one could almost have given a preference for the clash.

On Air keys on the other hand (excluding Brown — this is to be understood from now on) these rules were observed with very few exceptions, and in themselves gave helpful wheel order reductions. At various times however, other more precise rules were discovered, and these now fall to be described.

Clarkian wheelorder rule
This rule held on Red and Light Blue from August to November 1941 and was named after its discoverer, L.E. Clarke. To follow the subsequent discussions, the reader should refer to the Table of Wheelorders which is inserted here. The rule states that, in the same column, no wheel is followed by a consecutive wheel: 5 and 1 are not, however, regarded as consecutive. It will be noticed that there are only some half-dozen breaches of this rule in the four months. Its effect is, supplementary to the normal non-clashing and non-repeating rules and the conjunction has a powerful effect in reducing wheelorders — in general (apart from the non-repeating rule — four to ten legal wheelorders are left. It is also usually possible to reduce a Clarkian sandwich to a single wheelorder — see examples of this in the table.

Before August 1941 the rule is not very noticeable, though there are no actual contradictions in Light Blue of July. But in view of the numerous gaps in that month and the bad record of Red, it is very doubtful if the rule really held then. In December it broke down definitely on Red, though on Light Blue a preference for Clarkian wheelorders was even yet worthwhile, but the demise of Light Blue at the end of December meant the end of the rule. Before leaving this subject it ought to be mentioned that with the Clarkian rule there was a tendency for wheel orders to run in cycles – at least two well-marked cycles of eight appeared. These are marked A and B on the Table. This phenomenon naturally made prediction of the day's wheel order a popular parlour game in the Machine Room and attempts were made to discover a deeper system in the sequence of wheel orders within a month. However, as in the later case of the Nigelian wheel orders, all such attempts proved abortive.

Detailed Theory of Rules of Keys

Table of Clarkian wheel orders – August to November 1941

Day	RED					LIGHT BLUE			
1	154	235	425		421	123	(231	253
2	431	451			153	451	(453	521
3	253	124	531		325	134	B(125	145
4	425	351	124		541	512	(341	312
5	142	135	352			154	(513	154
6	325	452	524			431	(235	432
7	153	214	241	412	125	254	(542	215
8	524	531	513	135		512		543
9	342	243	135			435	351	321
10	514	415	452	524	241	153	523	153
11	231	231	(215)			321	241	435
12	315	513	541	415		543		251
13	152	345	214	(231	412	125	132	524
14	324	521	345	(453	254	341	354	342
15	541	254	(512)	(125	531	513	521	514
16	213	532	13	B(341		135	(254)	(231
17	435	315	351	(513		352	421	(453
18		143	523	(235	524	514	253	(125
19		421	245	(452		241	435	B(341
20	542	253	321	(124		423	152	(513
21	314	435	154	541	521	251	315	(235
22	531	152	412	213		534	543	(452
23	215	(321	543	435		152	(321	(124
24	452	(145	315	153		325	(145	351
25	124	(423	132	(321	215	143	(423	135
26	341	A(251	514	(145		415	A(251	
27	513	(534	342	A(423	514	231	(534	
28	235	(312	(125)	(251		413	(312	
29	451	(154	453	(534		145	(154	
30	134	(431	231	(312	341	421	(431	
31	352	---	415	---	513	---	215	---

NOTE: In the above table A and B represent the two long cycles of wheelorder referred to. Wheelorders closed in brackets are not <u>known</u> from breaks, but are the only legal Clarkian ones. Breaches of the Clarkian rule are indicated by underlining the offending wheels. It may be worth mentioning the Clarkian sequences, which are:

    1: 3, 4 or 5 – not 4
    2: 4 or 5; 1, 2 or 3 – not 2
    3: 1 or 5
    4: 1 or 2; 3, 4 or 5 – not 4
    5: 1, 2 or 3 – not 2

Nigelian wheelorder rule

This second and far more important rule lasted on the majority of Air keys for just two years, i.e. May 1943 to the end of the war. Like the Clarkian rule, it was a supplement to the ordinary non-clashing and non-repeating conditions. It stated that all Air keys selected their wheelorders *not* from the complete list of 60, but from a list of 30, known as Nigelian after the discoverer, Nigel Forward. This discovery had naturally a tremendous effect in reducing the number of bombe hours per menu, especially towards the end of a month. The obvious difficulty that all keys had to be made out for a 31-day month (to allow for transferences in the event of compromises) was got over by a relaxation of the rule for the first five days on any month. On these days a repeated or non-Nigelian wheelorder was permissible. (Actually the 1st and 2nd were the dangerous days — the 3rd, 4th and 5th days have records only a little worse than days after the 5th). In practice, therefore, up to the 5th we ran on the normal legal wheelorders with a reference only for Nigelians. After the 5th we gave preference for Nigelians and excluded wheelorders used since the 5th, and as soon as it was considered safe to declare the key Nigelian we ran on Nigelian non-clashing non-repeating (since the 5th) only. How soon the final declaration was made depended on the importance of the key and the strength of the cribs normally available. At the beginning of each month general principles were laid down for the more important keys. And, as even the best established wheelorder rules were sometimes broken, it was always open to the Air Head of Shift, on sufficient reason, to run any particular crib on illegal wheelorders.

Detailed Theory of Rules of Keys

TABLE OF NIGELIAN WHEELORDERS

132	235	312	342	421	514
142	241	314	345	425	523
145	243	321	354	432	524
152	245	325	413	512	531
153	251	341	415	513	534

The discovery of the Nigelian wheelorders gave rise to an interesting problem. Was the selection purely random or dictated by some system? The very peculiarity of the rule and in particular the fact that there are only 30 and not the convenient 31 Nigelian wheelorders, suggested the probability of a system, but the list of wheelorders (given above in the order usually adopted for writing out) seemed at first sight quite arbitrary. However, closer examination reveals that each wheel occurs precisely 18 times. This suggests that one object of the rule was to level out the incidence of occurrence of the several wheels and thus avoid any unintentional favouritism of a particular wheel.

A still more detailed analysis discloses that the wheelorders fall into ten triads, each triad consisting of three out of the six permutations of any selection of wheels. This certainly looks like intention, and explains how the figure of 30 is arrived at. But it is unfortunately impossible to reduce each triad to the same pattern. If, to secure standardisation, we arrange each triad so that a wheelorder reads down and across in the first, second or third row and column, and that we also have a "diagonal" from top left to bottom right, we have six triads of the pattern:

Six triads of the pattern: A B C
                            B A C
                            C B A

Three of the pattern: A B C
                            B A C
                            B C A

And one of the pattern: A B C
                            C A B
                            C B A

128

The basic Nigelian wheelorder – i.e., ABC in the above patterns – are 132, 152, 153, 241, 325, 342, 413, 415, 425 and 534 with each wheel occurring twice in the second position. It does not seem possible to carry any further the analysis of the Nigelian list and no system was ever discovered by which the permutations into monthly key blocks were arranged.

Monrovian wheelorder rule
It should be mentioned that apart from Brown and the local keys such as Yak, Llama, Raccoon etc., which were never Nigelian, there was in some months a non-Nigelian minority of Air keys. Some of these keys – but by no means all – were found to obey the Monrovian law, named after its discoverer, Major Monroe. By this rule the five wheels were all used on any two consecutive days in the month. It will be seen that a Monrovian wheelorder, like a Clarkian, is a purely relative conception. This rule was never so absolute as the Nigelian and it is usual to find one or two exceptions even on keys where it is generally held – nor was it ever very widespread. Till the end of 1943, Monrovian keys were October Primrose, November Primrose, Squirrel and Cockroach and December Leek, Puma, Hornet and probably Beetle.

Tricycle keys
To conclude this subject of wheelorder we should mention one interesting, if completely unimportant, survival. In 1941 and 1942 we broke several days of 'Tricycle', as it was called, a type of traffic that used the old outmoded indicating system of encoding the message setting twice at a fixed Grundstellung. All the days broken used a permutation of the wheel order 1, 2, 3, and it was suggested that Tricycle only used these three wheels, hence the name. While this hypothesis was hardly decisively proved (as owing to lack of traffic and its low intelligence priority we were able to secure very few breaks), it is not so fantastic as appears at first sight, for it is known that wheels 4 and 5 were later additions to the Enigma machine, and it is not unreasonable to suppose that a key which was still in 1942 using the obsolete indicating system described above, might still keep to the original six wheelorders. The traffic was Abwehr in content and not directly connected with the German armed forces, and even in 1942 there was no wheel order permutation in the course of the day.

Detailed Theory of Rules of Keys

Setting up of Committee on Rules of Keys

The discovery of the Nigelian wheel order rule in August 1943 had an important consequence. It may have been noticed that rules were often not discovered till several weeks or months after they had come into force. This is to some extent inevitable, as a new rule cannot be discovered till there is a sufficient body of evidence to make the necessary deductions. However, it was clear that the problem of discovering key rules at the earliest possible moment had to be taken up more thoroughly than before. Consequently, a small committee was set up to issue reports on such questions at suitable intervals and strenuous and successful attempts were made to induce parents of keys to write out each month's keys on a key-sheet. The key-sheet system – which corresponded to the German layout – had been first introduced in 1942 – but had somewhat lapsed till it was generally revived in September 1943) in a form which was more suitable for analysis of rules than the daily entries in keybooks. It is these records and reports that are the main authorities for the history of key rules since September 1943. (The question of key parentage is discussed later.)

Ringstellung Rules – Army and Air

Army ringstellung rules

It is again convenient to treat the Army first because of the relative lack of variety in its key rules. In the autumn of 1941, during the British offensive in Libya, a number of army keys — Chaffinch I and II, Phoenix and corresponding Reserve keys for November 1941 and Phoenix and Phoenix Reserve for December – were captured and sent back to us. They were closely examined (all the more so as they were the first captured key-sheets seen in Hut 6), and a ringstellung rule was quickly noticed. Every letter of the alphabet was used in blocks of eight or nine days — the exact divisions are to be seen in the table below — namely, the first five days form an odd set using up 15 letters of the alphabet, days 6 to 13 plus two letters from the 14th form a complete alphabet, the remaining letter of the 14th, one letter from the 23rd and all the intervening letters form a second alphabet and the rest of the month gives us a third. Occasionally there are slight errors in the system, and it should be noted that there are some variations in the method of splitting up the ringstellung letters on the 14th and 23rd (see the following example for the orthodox method).

Immediately after the rule had been discovered it was confirmed by a captured document giving instructions for the use of the Enigma.

In the course of hints for constructing emergency keys this document recommended that the letters of the alphabet be written out on small discs and that 24 of these be chosen to form the ringstellung of eight consecutive days, a rudimentary version of the ringstellung rule.

The rule had previously been used on Yellow in 1940, and soon after its discovery in November 1941, it was found to hold on Vulture and also sometimes on Orange – though never on any other SS key. However, until January 1944, when it disappeared, the rule was observed by most Army keys – the list included Yellow, Chaffinch, Phoenix, Vulture, Orange, Sparrow, Shrike, Bullfinch, Raven and Wryneck I – occasionally, though its observance could never be assumed in advance. In general, the rule was no a great deal of help in breaking, except towards the end of a period. The colours on which it proved most useful were Phoenix and Orange, where the occurrence of cillies and (in the case of Orange) the known HOR-HUG stecker made hand attempts possible if the ringstellung could be guessed.

EXAMPLE OF THE ARMY RINGSTELLUNG RULE
(Phoenix, January 1943)

Day	Ringstellung	Day	Ringstellung
1	AZS	17	YFQ
2	UIM	18	HKV
3	DRW	19	OTC
4	NTH	20	
5	LBP	21	JXE
6	SFJ	22	MGP
7	HMD	23	WC(U
8	OBY	24	AQL
9	KVG	25	ZIS
10	ZIQ	26	OKG
11	ETX	27	VEX
12	RLC	28	HTK
13	WAN	29	RBP
14	D)PU	30	NJD
15	LIS	31	YFU
16	NWB		

Air ringstellung rules

The Air keys at times observed ringstellung rules, but again these could not be counted on in advance. Many key-sheets show no rule at all in this respect, and each case had to be examined on its merits. It must also be remembered that for the period with which we are now dealing – despite the high break figures – there were still comparatively few complete months broken and Air ringstellung rules do not show up clearly unless a very large percentage of the month is out. The most regular colours were Red for the whole period, and at intervals, Locust and Primrose. To the end of 1943 two main rules can be distinguished:

1. The old ringstellung rule used in 1940 and covering the first 16 days of the month, and:
2. The 31-day rule, an extension of the above by which all the letters of the alphabet were used in each ringstellung column, but the five repeats were irregularly distributed and not lumped together at the end.

The first rule was the better from our point of view as the position of the repeat letters was fixed. But on the whole neither rule was of much assistance to breaking after 1940. It must be remembered that in 1942 all key rules were completely overshadowed by the key repeats which were fundamental to our whole breaking practice. The 26-day rule ended on Red in December 1940, but revived in 1943, and was used on January and June Red, January, February and March Locust and April Primrose. The 31-day rule was, so far as we can tell, used principally by Red, but we have much more evidence for Red than for any other colour. It first appeared on Red in May 1942 and was used till August when it vanished till fleeting reappearance in February and July 1943. Once or twice a curious intermediate rule occurred by which all the letters of the alphabet with one repeat were used in the first 27 days – examples are Red of February and March 1943, and Hedgehog of June. The above selection of facts may serve to show how variable and confusing is the whole subject. The numerous key-months not mentioned either show no rule at all or give insufficient evidence.

Stuttering ringstellung

To conclude the ringstellung rules it should be mentioned that there was a marked prejudice against "stutterers" – i.e., ringstellung with a repeated letter. By chance these should be 11% of the whole, but we can only collect 91 examples. Three of these are on Brown, one on Yak, 15 on SS keys (mainly Orange) and the rest on Army keys with Falcon I and II principal offenders. It is noteworthy that all the examples except appear in 1944 and 1945 and that there is no regular Air key on the list. One double stutterer occurred – GGG on Falcon I of 8 December 1944.

Stecker Rules – Army and Air

Air rules and tendencies
Here, for once, the Air rules are simpler and may be taken first. The rule against the use of consecutive stecker is one of the most absolute ever discovered. Brown, a few locally issued special keys and the NOT-keys of 1944-1945 are exceptions. But, of the of the many thousands of Air keys regularly broken or captured, <u>only one</u> (Mayfly, 16 March 1944) had a consecutive stecker, and the chance of any given ten-stecker key having a consecutive stecker is approximately ½. This rule was one of the most consistently useful of all, as in running Air keys on the bombe, CSKO [*Consecutive Stecker Knock-Out – a device by which a bombe could be made to reject solutions involving consecutive stecker*] could be and was regularly used. The non-repeating stecker rule was also generally observed, though it was never again of such practical use in breaking as in the early days of hand attempts in 1940. More interesting was that on most keys there was a constant tendency – it can hardly be called a rule – to diagonalisation (how natural the tendency to diagonalisation is may be inferred from the fine example provided by the nomenclature of the Bletchley Park buses), i.e., the use of stecker pairings which form a diagonal on a Foss sheet. An excellent example is the stecker of Primrose, 22 July:

A/Y, B/X, C/W, D/V, E/U, F/T, G/S, H/R, I/Q, M/Z

where only the last pair is out of step. But there are many examples on other days of a smaller number of pairs on the same diagonal. If a particular key is noticed to be behaving like this frequently in a month, it is possible to try a still unchosen diagonal for the stecker of unbroken days, and on Primrose at least one triumph was achieved in this way. Again, it happened once that the right story was picked out on a dottery attempt by choosing diagonal stecker pairings, but obviously it is very seldom that one can bring off such a *tour de force*. From time to time persistent attempts were made to discover a complete system in the arranging of GAF monthly sets of stecker. It was not impossible or unreasonable that the Cipher Office should have devised some means for reading off sets of stecker from a square or some similar figure so that, as far as possible, there would be no repeats of the month. But we were unable by analysis of keys to arrive at such a system, and we must perforce come to the conclusion that the German key-maker made up his sets of stecker on no other system except that – possibly by setting out his stecker pairings on a Foss sheet as we did – he endeavoured by eye to avoid repeats.

Army rules in general and particular
Army keys never obeyed the Air law against consecutive stecker, though many keys had periods when consecutive stecker were very rare. Still, it was never possible, without undue risk, to use CSKO. The SS keys, on the other hand, generally used consecutive stecker pairings to a more than random extent. The captured Army key sheets of 1941 did not reveal any helpful stecker rules. The pairings were not even written in alphabetical order except that the first letter in each pairing was the earlier in the alphabet. Otherwise the order seemed quite arbitrary, except that in some keys there was a very rough and not very useful pattern in the first column – a pattern (if we can call it so) which merely consisted in a progression in the alphabet of alternate initial letters or the like.

But, though there were no useful rules, particular Army keys were always liable to throw up odd and ephemeral rules which were so confined in their applications, as to throw some doubt on the natural hypothesis that all Army keys were made up in a single central office like the Air keys. To the end of 1943 these Army stecker rules fell into two classes: (1) special stecker patterns, and (2) stecker repeats within a month. Under the first head must be cited the rule on Chaffinch II by which A and B were self-steckered on alternate days. The best example is July 1942 when out of 15 days broken, A or B was self-steckered on 13, and in general the sequence was alternate. In September A or B or both were unsteckered on all 20 days broken, but the alteration was not well observed, and in October the rule (with exceptions and an increasing disregard of the alternate aspect) appeared on all the Chaffinches. There were also occasional signs of its appearance on Orange, but here the certainty of the HOR-HUG stecker made us prefer to ignore entirely this rather uncertain rule.

A more interesting and much more useful stecker pattern occurred on Albatross in July 1943. Most of the keys in this month showed the phenomenon known as "stepping stecker", i.e., stecker pairings all the same distance apart in the alphabet. Thus on 1 July the stecker ran:

A/D, E/H, F/I, G/K, J/M, L/O, N/Q, P/S, T/W, U/X

with a difference of three (G/K is an error), while on the 4th we had:

A/G, B/H, C/I, E/K, J/P, L/R, O/U, Q/W, S/Y, T/Z

with a difference of six. It should be mentioned that addition does not carry over at the end of the alphabet, hence it sometimes happens that the last stecker pairing is outside the system, as on 12 July we had:

B/I, C/J, F/M, H/O, K/R, L/S, N/U, P/W, Q/X, T/V

Fortunately, in July the differences also were in sequence – we were able to break sufficient days to make it apparent that the full sequence must be 34567XX, 34567XXX, 34567XXX, 34567XXX, where X denotes a day without stepping stecker. Once this pattern was realised we knew that on 20 days out of 31, every letter either self-steckered or steckered to, at most, two definite other letters and it was possible to use this considerable stecker limitation on both hand attempts and bombe menus. It was particularly useful in making weakfish cilli shots runnable – with cribs it was, generally speaking, unnecessary to run even with the slight risk involved. In September 1943 stepping stecker again appeared on Albatross, but on this occasion the sequence of differences was too irregular for successful prediction.

On Wryneck I, the other principal Balkan key, similar repeats were found to exist in October and December. In October the repeats occurred at slightly irregular intervals of 15 or 16 days. In December the 16 days interval was universal, days 17-31 repeating the stecker of days 1-15. The Wryneck repeats were not exact – but this disadvantage was offset by the greater strength of the Wryneck cribs and by repeats of the other key components. It was discovered that November Wryneck was the basic month – this was apparent from its observance of the Army ringstellung rule. The wheelorder and ringstellung of November Wryneck were used in different shuffled blocks in October and December, the ringstellung

Detailed Theory of Rules of Keys

being sometimes permuted. The combination of all these factors meant that towards the end of December 1943 it was possible to predict the Wryneck wheelorder, the ringstellung letters and the approximate stecker. The result was that for a brief period Wryneck enjoyed the distinction of being broken currently in the Watch until the end of the repeats in January 1944 sent it back to the normal Research status of Balkan Army keys.

Brown Rules

Brown is best considered separately. Its special peculiarity is that, at times, the rules regarding wheel order, ringstellung and stecker were so rigid that it was possible to attain the ideal of the investigator of key rules – i.e., to generate a key from its predecessor and simply write the answer down. In June, after a long period of successful breaking, Brown was virtually lost by one of the many temporary eclipses, mainly due to paucity of traffic, to which this colour was liable. When, in December 1941, regular successes were again achieved, Brown was found to have split into two keys – German and French, later known as Brown I and II. It is advisable to follow the career of these two keys separately, always remembering that the Brown key-month ran from the 15th of one month to the 14th of the next.

Brown I early developed the habit of choosing its self-steckered letters in a continuous or nearly continuous block, e.g., 31 December 1941 had O/P, Q/R, S/T, U/V, W/X, Y/Z, A/B with C to N inclusive self-steckered, and 15 January 1942 had A/N, B/L, C/K, D/J, E/I, F/M, G/H with O to Z inclusive self-steckered. This block rule was sometimes conjoined with the old stecker pairing rule as, e.g., 18 and 19 February which had, respectively, B to O and P to A self-steckered and sometimes, with a variety of the rule by which, on both pair days, we have a different set of self-stecker, but the whole alphabet is not used up, e.g., on 15 and 16 January the runs of self-steckered letters were from O to Z and then from C to N.

The tendency to blocks of self-stecker lasted till April, but the pairing rule continued much later and was observed in most months up to June 1943 (15 November-14 December 1942 was an exception). Apart from the strict pairing rule, namely, that all letters steckered one day are unsteckered the next, and that the steckered letters on the two days account for all the letters of the alphabet, a modified rule was often employed by which the second regulation is waived. This relaxation suited the tendency to the frequent use of only <u>five</u> stecker pairs, which arose in October 1942, and must be considered as a throwback to the sparing use of stecker in the pre-war days. More interesting was the tendency to "universal stepping" which appeared occasionally on Brown I. However, the duration of this rule was always uncertain and it came up at irregular and unpredictable intervals. The first occasion it arose was on 25 January 1942 when there was a strong tendency to step on wheelorder, ringstellung and stecker with occasional deviations, particularly in the case of wheelorder – otherwise the wheelorders would repeat themselves after a cycle of five days. A few examples will indicate how the rule worked and it will be seen that it was sometimes possible to write the key down:

Jan

25	452	MAI	A/B	O/Z	P/W	Q/X	R/V	S/T	U/Y
26	513	AOE	A/U	C/W	E/Y	G/H	J/O	K/Q	M/S
27	123	HPF	B/V	D/X	F/Z	I/K	J/P	L/R	N/T
28	135	CQG	A/G	C/W	E/X	K/Q	M/S	O/U	
29	241	DRH	B/H	D/X	F/Z	J/M	L/R	N/T	P/V
30	352	ESI	A/G	C/J	E/Y	M/S	O/U	Q/W	

The sequence continued more or less in this style till 14 February. Later (20 March 1942) stepping on the ringstellung came into force again along with the old stecker pairing. Thus from 20-26 March we got the following series of ringstellung, stepping two on each wheel: AOD, CQF, (ESH), GUJ, IWL, KYN, MBP. (Note that the bracketed ringstellung is an inference and that there is a slight deviation in the last of the series).

Brown II has a less colourful career. When it was first broken in quantity in January 1942, it obeyed the stecker pairing rule and apparently continued to do so till 14 April. Four later April days (26-29) show no stecker rule at all, but late in June the stecker pairing was again observed. Brown II never observed the self-stecker block rule, nor the stepping rules, nor did it ever use only five stecker pairs. It confined itself to the normal Brown practice of six or seven stecker, until the fateful day – 12 October 1944 – when Brown II was broken – and proved to have ten stecker, like any common or garden key.

This discovery was a great shock, as it suggested that Brown was at last abandoning its peculiarities, now endeared by long association, and coming into line with other keys. Apart from sentiment, the use of ten stecker would inevitably make Brown harder to break by ruling out the stecker pairing rule and eliminating the traditional resource of the "clonk" – see the history of Brown in a later chapter. Although Brown II quickly disappeared, these forebodings were not unwarranted, for on 15 July 1943, Brown I adopted ten stecker and Brown III, a new key that appeared in autumn 1943, had ten stecker from the beginning. Yet, despite the loss of its main hallmark, the Brown keys always maintained a place of their own – to the end they used consecutive stecker freely and refused to adopt any of the normal Air key rules.

GAF Key Repeats

Institution of key records
In the summer of 1941 records were started of the component parts of the keys recovered, i.e., wheel order, ringstellung and stecker. The records were instituted on the assumption that, as discriminants were known to repeat, it was possible that the other parts of keys w4ere also likely to be used again. From the account of the discriminant system it can be seen that this was completely wrong, but the time spent in compiling the records and in their upkeep, declared considerable dividends.

Limitation of the subject
For the purpose of this report one class of key repeat is ignored. This is the one where a back key is used again, either as a day-for-day repeat or in some form of shuffle, because of the non-arrival of the current key. The detection of these was a routine matter and presented little or no inconvenience. This was particularly true as in the majority of cases we were we were forewarned by reading the message giving the German units concerned the necessary instructions. The repeats under discussion are those made deliberately in the construction of keys. It is interesting and ironic that, from the evidence, it seems that repeats occurred in greater numbers whenever, as a security measure, additional keys were introduced. Presumably the extra labour required so infuriated the key compiler that he resorted to repeating portions of old keys.

Local keys
Before covering the larger field of keys constructed by the Cipher Office it may be interesting to look at locally-made keys. Where the status of a unit did not officially entitle it to a key of its own, but circumstances arose which made one necessary, then the unit applied to its Luftgau [*areas into which Greater Germany was divided for military administration*] for one. Such a key was made up by the Luftgau without reference to the Cipher Office. Whether this was regarded by some of the Luftgau as an imposition is not known but it was quite common for such 'Sonder' [*special*] keys to be constructed from others. Noteworthy were the following examples:

    a. <u>Scorpion II and III</u>: Fliegerführer Afrika, during the 1942-1943 winter campaign employed, apart from his official key, two others. Scorpion II was a shuffled version of Primrose of the month before. Scorpion III was a shuffled Blue of the month before.

    b. <u>Crab (Fliegerführer Luftflotte 1)</u> in August 1942 employed a hatted version of Wasp of June 1942.

    c. <u>Yak (Fliegerführer Kroatien)</u> was a consistent repeater, but showed originality in that it used to employ back versions of itself as a basis for keys.

Keys constructed by the Cipher Office: repeats in 1941
Although repeats appeared in these keys throughout the war, 'fashions' were continually changing. However, a historical account is the easiest way of discussing the various types of repeats. [Note: The following account covers the entire war and so exceeds the time limits normally observed in this chapter. Most of the repeats, however, arise in 1941-1943. Some additional remarks on the later repeats will be found later.]

    <u>May 1941</u>: Red of the 18th and Violet of the 1st had the same stecker. There was no 'diagonal' or other pattern to the stecker, so the repeat can only have been deliberate. However, no other Violet days were broken and the repeat was not discovered until two or three months afterwards when the records were being compiled so that no capital could be made of this.

    <u>September 1941</u>: Red stecker repeated Red stecker of February 1941 on a straightforward day-for-day basis, with the exception that as the basic month only had 28 days, some days were used twice. This meant that once the pattern of the repeat was established (about the 4th of the month) the rest of the month was broken by hand. This was providential

as it coincided with the start of General Auchinleck's offensive [*in North Africa*] and enabled us to concentrate all our bombes on other important keys, such as Light Blue and Chaffinch.

1942 – Quadrilateral repeats

This year was the zenith of the repeats. The effects upon the various sections of Hut 6 organisation were far-reaching. 1st January marked the introduction by the Germans of separate Fliegerkorps keys and an increased number of Luftgau keys. This extra labour apparently caused the Cipher Office to adopt the expedient of repeats on a wholesale basis. The *January* repeats gave little indication of what was coming. They were:

a. Hornet stecker repeating Light Blue (July 1941)

b. Leek stecker repeating Blue (July 1941) and

c. Primrose and Gadfly sharing the same monthly set of stecker

The three repeats were not on a day-for-day basis but were on patterns which were discovered and this enabled us to determine beforehand which back day's stecker had been used.

February brought the first of the 'Quadrilateral Repeats'. The key compiler made a set of keys for one month in the normal manner and then cut them in half: wheel order and ringstellung in one half and stecker and discriminants in the other. These halves were then united differently and issued as keys for the next month. This practice was symbolised by us as:

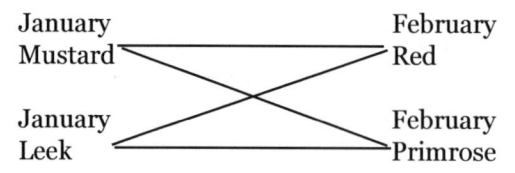

```
January               February
Mustard               Red

January               February
Leek                  Primrose
```

where the diagonal lines represent wheel order and ringstellung, and the horizontal lines stecker and discriminants. From the diagram it is obvious why these repeats came to be called Quadrilaterals.

The habit grew steadily from one quadrilateral in February to ten in October and December. When it is realised that ten quadrilaterals meant repeats of 20 keys from November into 20 keys of December, it can be seen that the possibilities for breaking are many. Further assistance was given us after the first quadrilateral in February when the 'Reverse Quadrilaterals' appeared. This system meant that when we found that Mosquito and Leek of July had been used to compile Primrose and

Snowdrop of August, we could be certain that Primrose and Snowdrop of July were the basis for Mosquito and Leek of August. The beauty of the system was that part of the repeat could be established from the external characteristics of the traffic, i.e., a discriminant repeat meant a stecker repeat.

Effects on breaking policy
Our breaking policy had to be completely revolutionised. Previous to the quadrilateral repeats, pressure of time had forced us to abandon a key if it was unbroken in a few days. It now became extremely important that as many keys of the first day of the first month of the pair should be broken. This was so that any repeats in the second month of the pair should be established as soon as possible, and even as late as 28 September we broke Cockroach of 1 September. Having assembled an assortment of keys for day one of the first month, the messages of day one of the second were examined for discriminant repeats from the month before. Any such repeat meant that the stecker also repeated, and by combining this stecker with the available wheel orders and ringstellung in turn, the resultant keys were tried until a German text was obtained. In this way the repeats were established in a very short time, for example, Blue of 1 October 1842 was broken before midnight on 30 September owing to the different between German time and Greenwich Mean Time (GMT).

Effects on intercept policy
Before 1942, the lack of sets and intercept operators had forced us to discourage vigorously the taking of any traffic on a key which could not be broken or which was not operationally important. With the introduction of the quadrilateral system, however, this policy had to be revised. No one could tell whether a very minor but breakable key might not be partially repeated by an operational and vital key in the following month. To meet this contingency the so-called 'insurance policy' was introduced. By this system daily cover was arranged so that known cribs on all keys were intercepted and then the group dropped. In this way, even if the keys were never attempted during the current month, at least the cribs were available in the following month if needed.

The following are extracts from *An Appreciation of the Enigma Situation: June to December 1942*, written by Welchman and Colman:

> *(1) ... ... the key repeats which were expected in August could only be exploited by maintaining cover on the minor GAF groups during*

Detailed Theory of Rules of Keys

July and there was no means of knowing which would prove to be useful ... A good deal of bombe time was used in August on the minor GAF keys but some of this was applied to the breaking of July keys which helped to break August keys with a resulting decrease in bombe time spent on Red and the principal Mediterranean Air keys in August. In all 396 GAF keys were broken in August for 5,719 bombe hours, an average of 14 bombe hours per key, against 138 keys in July for 7,549 bombe hours, an average of 55 hours per key. Thus the key repeats not only increased the number of breaks but also reduced the total bombe time and enabled more bombe time to be spent on the Mediterranean Army keys.

(2) The history of Locust deserves special mention. One day was broken in January and one in March. As a result of the scanty knowledge of the traffic obtained from these two breaks it was possible to break Locust again in June, at the time of a Malta convoy, with the help of a cilli and a partial key repeat from May Foxglove. Nineteen days of June Locust were then broken, but breaking could not be continued in July. In August a key repeat led to the breaking of nearly all the July days as well as nearly all the August days. In September breaking again stopped, although crib cover was fully maintained, and in October a key repeat again made it possible to mop up most of the previous month's keys as well as most of the October ones. In November, when the key became of first-rate importance operationally (the North African landings), the knowledge gained enabled us to go on breaking without the assistance of key repeats, although a heavy expenditure of bombe time was needed.

(3) ... ... it was possible to discover cribs in some of the minor air keys and to arrange special crib cover during September. One result of the October repeats, which has since proved to be important, was that Celery was broken for the first time and was found to possess a good crib.

(4) ... ... it appears that the man who prepares the GAF keys is changing his habits and that the repeats may not be quite so helpful in the future as in the past.

Repeats in 1943 and 1944

The repeats continued in 1943, but on a very much reduced scale and in a more complicated and less helpful manner. Four keys of one month were separated into their *four* component parts, shuffled and remade into four keys for the next month. This meant that discriminants no longer gave any assistance, and repeats could only be established after an initial break had been made and then only if the corresponding day of the basic keys had been broken in the previous month. This lengthened the odds against our discovering the repeats. Between April and July 1943 there was prevalent a habit of issuing exactly the same key on four key sheets, but with different discriminants. This was completely unexpected and was only discovered when two of the four keys involved were broken and compared. After the practice was discovered, then every time a key was broken, a mammoth all-against-all decoding had to take place until it was established which other sets of discriminants decoded on the key. This had to be done every month as the sets of four keys differed monthly.

In the last three months of 1943 the only repeats found were confined to the ringstellung. The monthly set of ringstellung for a key of one month was divided arbitrarily into three or four blocks of days, the blocks shuffled and used for another key for the next month. The number of blocks made from a monthly set and the days comprising the blocks varied from key to key. This coupled with the fact that from our point of view the ringstellung was the least difficult part of the key to find made repeats of little value to us. During 1944, repeats were almost non-existent so far as we could establish. However, towards the end of the year one or two isolated cases of stecker repeats did occur.

Stecker/D repeats in 1945

The introduction of Reflector D pairings as an integral part of a key led to repeats being found of a completely new character. In the past, repeats always occurred between parts of a key serving the same function, but in 1945 cases were found where stecker pairings had been used to construct reflector pairings. The original records for finding repeats were known as 'Parkerismus' and were kept up by hand and the necessary comparisons made by eye. D pairings employed 24 letters (excluding J and Y) and stecker only 20, and the manual system of recording, instituted in 1941, did not permit of comparisons between the two. On the principle that with the GAF Cipher Office 'you never knew' it was obviously worth making the comparisons and a new and mechanical method was devised

Detailed Theory of Rules of Keys

of recording and comparing stecker and D pairings. These comparisons showed three cases of five common pairings and one of four, but the outstanding results were the following:

A

Snowdrop 22 Jan 45	A D E F G H I J K W U Q S Z M N O V X Y		B C L P R T		

Red D 1st Period Jan 45	A D E F G H I U Q S Z M N O	K X	B W	P V	C L R T

B

Snowdrop 18 Jan 45	C D H I L O P Q R U J Z M S N V T Y W X		A B E F G K

Hyena D 1st Period Jan 45	D H I L O P Z M S N V T	R U C W X Q		A B E F G K

The partial repeats can be dismissed as happening by chance, but the two given in detail are obviously the result of deliberate intention. This is further proved by the pattern of the changing process. When considering this process two points should be borne in mind:

1. when constructing a D-plugging, J and Y, by the construction of the machine, must be omitted.

2. for some unaccountable reason the GAF Cipher Office had a deep-rooted objection to pairing consecutive letters together, either in a stecker or in a D.

The process seemed to be this:

a. Lift all pairs not involving J and Y directly into the D

b. The letters to which J and Y are paired in the stecker are paired together in the D. If these letters are consecutive (as in example A) the process is altered — see (d) below.

c. Take the unsteckered letters in alphabetical order and pair them 1 and 4; 2 and 5; 3 and 6. These obviously cannot give consecutive letters.

d. Where operation (b) gives a consecutive pairing, take the offending letters and pair them with the 1st and 4th unsteckered letters. The remaining unsteckered letters are paired 2 and 5; 3 and 6 as in (c) above.

The pattern of the dates of the stecker used can also be explained. The monthly key list of the GAF Cipher Office is dealt with fully in the section on GAF discriminants and in January the first read: Red, Indigo, Gorilla, Beetle, Hyena, Jaguar, Gadfly etc. From this it can be seen that 22 January fitted to Red gives 18 January up against Hyena. It is therefore obvious that D pairings have been allotted to the keys in their Cipher Office order and that stecker pairings have been used in consecutive day order to provide those D pairings.

This has all been gone into in great detail because it was never able to be proved further owing to the fact that although every key issued had D pairings printed on it, they were not all used. Thus we did not obtain the necessary evidence to corroborate the theory, but the theory is sound, and had it been more widely used it is extremely probable that we should have been able to reconstruct the pairings, at least for January 1945, without having to break them.

Conclusion

It must be emphasised that, theoretically, if the enemy is not breaking your keys then you can use repeats, partial or otherwise, as much as you like, although there is a chance that a capture may give you away. If, however, you feel you must use repeats, then use them in a completely patternless manner so that even if the enemy does establish that one key is constructed from another, he can only ascertain which day is used for which day by breaking both without the aid of the repeat. From all this it seems that one of the most desirable attributes of a key compiler is full confidence in the ability of the opposing cryptographers.

Chapter 8
General Organisation of Machine and Crib Rooms (Later Watch and Research)

The fourfold division
During this period there were four separate sub-sections directly concerned with breaking:

>Machine Room 1
>Machine Room Research (or Machine Room 2)
>Crib Room 1
>Crib Room Research (or Crib Room 2)

MR1 and CR1, as the operational sections of MR and CR were frequently referred to without the numeral. But here, for the sake of clarity, MR will be used to refer to MR1 and MR2 together and so with CR. MR1 and CR1 were also sometimes referred to as the routine shifts.

They dealt with operational colours on a current, three-shift basis. MR2 and CR2 dealt with all other colours on a non-current basis, i.e., examining the traffic on an average two days late, with the ultimate objective of handing over to the routine shifts any colour that could be worked up to a point where it was currently breakable, provided that its intelligence importance justified the transfer. MR2 and CR2 worked, in general, on day shift.

This fourfold division grew up by degrees. MR1 was the lineal descendent of the Machine Room of the early days of Hut 6. CR1 was formally started in October 1940 (though cribs were first used in August), MR2 first began in autumn 1940, but it was not for the best part of a year that it had any permanent or assured status in the shape of a fixed nucleus of members. The early routine of all these sections has already been described. CR2 came much later. It began on a small scale in April 1942, but cannot be said to have got going as a permanent organisation till September 1942, when D M Gaunt took over its organisation.

Location of rooms
MR1 and CR1 were necessarily always located in neighbouring rooms at the nerve centre of Hut 6, centrally placed for communication with

Registration Room, Decoding Room and the bombe huts. One of the party, normally a member of CR1, was in direct control of the bombe situation. MR2 and CR2 were by no means so fortunate and lived a very nomadic existence. Hut 6 was simply not large enough for its inhabitants and so sections not strictly necessary for operational breaking had to seek accommodation outside. After several migrations, MR2, CR2 and the corresponding Registration Room (RR2), found rooms in the Main Building which were satisfactory in themselves, but inconveniently remote from the rest of the Hut, a matter particularly awkward in 1942 when the vagaries of key repeats caused frequent tie-ups between research and current colours. Finally, the space problem was solved by the completion of Block D and the transfer of all sections of Hut 6 to premises which seemed at the time palatial, an illusion speedily dispelled.

Sub-ordination of sub-sections
Administratively, both MR sections were under one head (Major D W Babbage) as were both sections of the CR (Mr P S Milner-Barry). This administrative division cut clean across the division of keys with which the various parties dealt. MR1 and CR1 dealt with operational keys, MR2 and CR2 with non-operational. But there were graver objections than purely technical administrative anomalies to the illogical system that had grown up. As was eventually realised by all the leading figures in the Hut, the MR/CR division was wrong in practice.

Differentiation of function
In terms of work, the distinction was as under:
　　MR responsibilities included keeping an eye on Rules of Keys, cillying and keeping cilli records, organising hand attempts, making up bombe menus, dealing with the bombe stations on technical matters, testing (or supervising the testing of) bombe stops and, finally, seeing the prompt completion of the correct story.
　　CR responsibilities included keeping crib records up-to-date, discovering cribs and handing them to the MR to be made up, finding and working on re-encodements, controlling what was being run on the bombes and keeping in close touch with the W/T background as was necessary for the efficient discharge of the above duties. Certain functions, such as working on depths or rodding, fell within the uncertain borderline between the two Rooms.
　　There was something very artificial and arbitrary in this division of

General Organisation of Machine and Crib Rooms

responsibility between the two sides of breaking. Indeed, Hut 6 could never have got on without the closest liaison between MR1 and CR1. Every day, questions would arise which neither party could settle on its own. Was a crib produced by the CR strong enough to run on wheel orders contradicted by a rule or a cilli? Again, the MR might discover one or two cillies, but not enough to run, i.e., to make up into a bombe menu. Then they had to approach the CR, cillies in hand, and ask if cribbery could supply a beginner or signature for the message concerned. Similar questions would arise between MR2 and CR2. At one time a system was adopted by which the MR, after examining blists, noted any cillies and wheel order preferences in a special notebook which was later consulted by the CR. But all such makeshifts emphasised the illogical nature of the barrier that had grown up, and moreover, there was always the danger of some important scrap of information not being passed on.

Dissatisfaction in Machine Room

The MR/CR divorce had another consequence of the evils that may arise from an organisational error. During summer 1940 the MR had been the nerve centre of the Hut, but as cribs became the main standby this altered, and by autumn 1941 the boot was very much on the other foot. CR1 was in the ascendant and its members alone were in close touch with the intelligence authorities in Hut 3, and were alone in being able to make vitally important decisions of bombe policy. Meanwhile, MR1 members (with only occasional hand breaks to console them), felt themselves degraded from their former proud position, to be little more than menu-makers and testers of stories. Not that these occupations are in themselves useless or dishonourable – but they were too routine and mechanical to occupy the full powers of the persons concerned. Hence there was considerable dissatisfaction in MR1. (MR2, for reasons to be mentioned later, had not so much of a grievance. But at this time, most members of MR2 were temporary visitors from MR1, so MR2 could not fail to be to some extent influenced by the general MR discontent.) This feeling came to a head in autumn 1941 when several meetings were held to try to find a solution. In 1942, while the grievance remained, the situation was not so acute as new MR methods of breaking – in particular the dottery – provided a temporary palliative. While not wishing to exaggerate the discontent and while anything like an actual explosion was avoided, this was a serious personnel management crisis, but fortunately the problem was successfully resolved. Once the faulty system was corrected, the staff difficulties vanished, proving they were not caused by personal incompatibilities but by organic maladjustments.

Problem solved

So, in 1941-1942 we were faced with two evils:

1. There was an artificial distinction between two aspects of breaking, and;
2. The machine experts were being relegated to a position that did not give sufficient scope to their abilities.

Clearly, the proper solution to *both* difficulties was to unify the two sides of breaking, and all parties agreed on this as a desirable reform. But reforms, however desirable, cannot always be carried through at once, and to attempt an immediate amalgamation would have led to chaos as neither party was ready to take over the other's work. Technical knowledge had first to be interchanged, so a series of visits was arranged by which members of MR1 spent a week or two in CR1 and learned the routine, and vice versa. Finally, when it was considered that this preparatory fusion had gone far enough, the formal amalgamation was arranged. For practical convenience its execution was deferred until shortly after the move from the old and cramped Hut 6 to the spaciousness of Block D. In February 1943, MR1 and CR1 married as the Watch, set forth on a new and auspicious career. At the same time, the Netz Room (now a valued auxiliary to the other cryptographic sections) assumed the time-honoured title of the Machine Room.

Formation of Research

At the same time a similar amalgamation took place between MR2 and CR2, who united to form the Research Section. The Watch was placed under the control of Mr Milner-Barry, formerly Head of the CR, and Research under Major D W Babbage, formerly Head of the MR. This removed the administrative anomaly mentioned earlier. This amalgamation had also been prepared beforehand by tuition in MR methods given to members of CR2, and by cribbery carried out on certain keys by MR2. However, in the Research Sections, the division between MR and CR had never been so rigid, and so the fusion presented a simpler problem. The reasons for this difference are interesting.

Because (at least in 1940) the natural means of entry into new keys was by cillies — the MR speciality — MR2 was, as we have seen, inaugurated

General Organisation of Machine and Crib Rooms

much earlier than CR2. However, in the early days, breaks secured by MR2 were examined by CR1 from the crib standpoint. But it soon happened that CR1, whose numbers were for some time far too small for their growing responsibilities, became so occupied with cribbery and re-encodement work on important operational colours, that little time was left for sustained effort on the less urgent research cribbery. At the same time, some members of MR2, realising the artificiality of the distinction between MR and CR methods, began on their favourite and adopted keys (the keys of which they were the parents - see later) to make independent investigations into the field of cribbery.

So, when the staff situation at last permitted us to establish CR2 as a separate sub-section, there were already certain keys which, by long-standing agreement, were treated for cillies and cribs alike by MR2. This arrangement — which suited both parties as CR2 had its hands full with other work — was allowed to continue until the formation of the unified Research Section. The keys that were thus wholly taken over by MR2 were Brown (when it was not a routine commitment), Orange I and II, Mustard and Quince. In addition, when the eventual amalgamation was definitely planned, a number of other colours, such as Cockroach and Snowdrop, were taken over for varying periods by MR2 members. So, long before the fusion, MR2 and CR2 had done much to break down the wall of partition, and hade already secured unity of control on certain keys.

Parentage system

This seems a suitable moment to discuss the parentage system was an essential part of the organisation of Watch and Research. This was a system of specialisation virtually forced on us by the rapid proliferation of keys. In Hut 6 history, about 200 distinct Enigma keys were identified, named and broken, and sometimes nearly half of that number existed simultaneously. No one person could have but a general knowledge of this vast key complex. In 1940 — and even 1941 – one man might still cover the whole field in some detail, but later this was impossible. What could still be attained was a thorough knowledge of machine technique, a mastery of the theory of cribs and re-encodements, a general knowledge of a large group of keys — usually Air or Army, which, it became clear, were separate key systems – and a detailed and intimate acquaintance with several keys within this group. Hence there grew up — more or less simultaneously in the CR and MR2, although the word, I think, is a CR invention — the parentage system, by which one (or sometimes more than one) person 'adopted' — i.e., made himself responsible for the welfare of — a certain key or group of keys. This was done with the approval of the head of the section concerned, and did not affect his ultimate responsibility for breaking. The parentage system, although already existing in embryo, did not come fully into force until the Watch/Research set-up was achieved, as only from then on did parentage imply full responsibility for both cribs and cillies.

The dangers inherent in an excess of specialisation were seen and guarded against. Changes in the allocation of keys to parents were made at intervals — sometimes at short intervals — and hence many members of Hut 6 had parental experience of a number of different keys. These changes were supervised by the head of the section or sub-section concerned. His general objects were to dispose of his cryptographic resources to the best advantage, i.e., to make full use of the special talents of each individual, to ensure that each key got its fair share of attention (in the light both of intelligence value and cryptographic possibilities), to combat the enemies of boredom and staleness by shifting round the duller and more hopeless tasks and, finally, to see that everyone had enough to do, but not more than he could reasonably be expected to cope with. (This last was sometimes difficult when the work of the section was either very busy or very slack but, if necessary, transfers of staff to and from other sections were arranged). Apart from this general post at intervals, it was expected that every member, while specialising in his own colour, should take an intelligent interest in the remaining work of the section. Parenthood had a somewhat different meaning to Watch and Research — a difference that arose inevitably from their varied methods of work. Research parenthood (on keys that were broken with any frequency) was a full-time occupation. Normally the parent did *all* the work on his key, examining blists, preparing menus to be run on the bombe and entering the traffic when the day was broken. (Normally Research keys were decoded in bulk, then sent to the parent for examination before being passed on to Hut 3). This ensured the individual supervision of records that is especially invaluable on difficult colours — in general, Research keys were more difficult than Watch ones. In most cases there was also no urgency in breaking, hence on a parent's day off his work could simply be left over, although, naturally, a foster-parent had to take over during long leave.

General Organisation of Machine and Crib Rooms

By contrast, Watch parenthood was part-time, although the parent is spoken of in the singular, all major Watch keys had more than one parent. The parent's main duty was to look after the general interests of his child, and in particular to keep crib records in a systematic form. In the Watch, the breaking of keys of operational value (as most were) had to be a continuous process, therefore every member might have to take a hand in breaking *any* Watch colour, and so had to know something of *all* Watch colours. Any member might discover and prepare cribs to be run (although the decision as to what should be run was reserved to the head of shift), and in general the entering of Watch traffic was performed by a person on each shift set aside for this sole purpose — not necessarily the parent of the key being entered. Thus it was never the case that on Watch keys that the parent did *all* the work — the burden was one that varied very much with the state of the key and the enthusiasm of the parent. It was also generally true that the busiest time for a Watch parent was when his child was sick, for then he had to nurse it back to health. The busiest time for a Research parent was when his child was in vigorous health, for then he had a lot of entering to do.

From 1942 on there was an intermediate category of colours looked after by the Q-Watch or 'Qwatch' [Quiet Watch – the part of the Watch intended to deal with rarely broken or non-operational keys], a body of cryptographers who worked (mostly on Air keys) in the closest collaboration with the Watch proper. Indeed, in its early days the Qwatch was often called the 'fourth Watch' to distinguish it from the three routine shifts. The Qwatch looked after keys which for some reason, e.g., difficulty or inferior intelligence value, were not suitable for full Watch treatment, but were yet so closely connected with Watch colours that it was judged inexpedient to banish them to the outer darkness of Research, and also on occasion nursed back to health full Watch keys that had 'gone bad'. There was normally a lively interchange of both keys and personnel between Watch and Qwatch. Qwatch methods were essentially a compromise between those of Watch and Research. Its members worked on more current material than the researchers, but specialised rather more than did the Watch proper, and did most of their entering by bulk. In the last period of the war, the Qwatch idea gained ground markedly and eventually ousted the older Research conception.

Some special points
The reader may feel inclined to ask two questions:

1. Why is it that Hut 6, in 1940, made what was later recognised to be a radically unsound distinction between MR and CR?

2. How was it that this unsound division and the tension it caused made so little difference to the practical success of Hut 6?

The fundamental answer to (1) is probably that the art of Enigma cryptography found its main development in a different direction from seemed likely in the summer of 1940. Then it looked as if cillies (helped by Rules of Keys) were to be the trump card, and the majority of cryptographers were so fully occupied with pursuing this line of attack that they neglected the alternative of cribs – not then usable in the absence of the bombe. It is possible that, had the bombe been with us a few months earlier, the cilli method would not have got such a start over the crib method, and so not have attracted such an excessive preponderance of attention and effort. Ultimately, the error was a natural enough failure to forecast correctly future developments. One moral is that we should never neglect to develop a new breaking technique even if, at the time, it seems unlikely that it will be required. (Compare the technique of the dottery, worked out in 1941 at a time when it seemed unlikely that we would have many occasions for using the method, which came into its own in 1942 as a consequence of an unpredictable series of key repeats.)

The answer to (2) is partly that the evils were counteracted by close liaison between the parties concerned. But the fundamental answer is that the practical success of a section such as Hut 6 (so far, at least, as the directly <u>cryptographical</u> work is concerned) does not depend <u>primarily</u> on a faultless internal organisation – desirable as this may be to secure smooth working in all departments. Granted that the nature of the cipher is known and that a practical method of breaking has been devised, success will be measured by, first, the provision of staff adequate in numbers and quality and, second, the provision of sufficient mechanical aids, i.e., in our case sufficient bombes. Perfect organisation is, at best, in the third place, and the success of Hut 6 is due to the fact that, on the whole, throughout the war the above two conditions were well met.

Summary

The final moral of the MR/CR story is that, while in a complex cryptographic organisation like Hut 6 a considerable degree of specialisation is unavoidable as between interception, traffic analysis and cryptography, it is undesirable that there should be any watertight

General Organisation of Machine and Crib Rooms

divisions *in the initial process of breaking*. Any specialisation that is necessary here should arise from divisions of the material to be broken, e.g., Watch/Research and later Air/Army – not from different lines of approach to the same material.

After the fusion, all members of Watch and Research looked at the problem of breaking as a whole and used MR or CR methods as best fitted the occasion. The routine of the Rooms in such matters as a separate log for each key, approached more nearly to that of the crib sections, but there was a general unification of records. Research was comparatively soon again divided into Air and Army Research, and this was a forerunner of the final reorganisation to be described later.

Successful as the fusion undoubtedly was, it would be untrue to say that the old MR/CR division left no traces. It had gone too deep for that to be possible, and as has been said earlier in the Introductions, the two aspects of cryptography do tend to appeal to different types of mind. Although many became versed in both techniques, in other cases the original bias and native forte was always discernible, but such a degree of specialisation is desirable. Granted the general knowledge of the whole breaking process that was secured by the success of the fusion, there was everything to be gained by permitting individuals to pursue the higher levels of theory in accordance with their particular bent. Fortunately, it also happened that throughout this history of Hut 6 there was work to be done suited to all varieties of cryptographic taste and talent. So, in the final period – January 1944 to the end – when cillies were least important, the use by the Germans of Reflector D and Enigma Uhr presented new technical problems and allowed us to gather a belated autumnal harvest from the gnarled tree of machine theory.

On the general questions of the rival merits of the cilli or crib methods of breaking, honours must be adjudged even. If, for the greater period of Hut 6, most breaks were secured on cribs, the initial entry into many important keys was made on cillies, and without cilli breaks we would not have obtained our invaluable crib evidence. The value of cilli breaks is thus immeasurably greater than any mere calculation of their number can show. If we wish to sum the merits of the two lines of approach in a sentence, it is that MR methods first broke the Enigma and CR methods kept open the breach. But, to say which was more important is to ask whether it is the upper or lower blade of the scissors that cuts the paper.

Chapter 9
Training Schemes in Hut 6

Early Training

The need for special courses of training for new members of Hut 6 was first felt in autumn 1942. Before then, training had been essentially individual. New members of the Hut would be given an introductory talk on the machine and a series of subsequent talks varying from section to section, but no effort was made to build up training schools or to draw up programmes of work in progressive courses. Training came from doing the work itself, in the company of others who had been doing the work for long enough to gain experience of the routine and knowledge of the techniques.

A member of the Machine Room, for instance, would not only have to learn about the machine in general, but also about the exploitation of cillies, the making of menus, the working of the bombe and a mass of other technicalities, for which members were considered good learners in view of their particular interests and previous education. [This section covers a period during which the term "Machine Room" was used in two senses. To avoid ambiguity in the present section, Machine Room is used in its original sense, referring to the machine cryptographers, and the older term – Netz Room – is used for Machine Room in its second sense.]

In the Crib Room, the entering of typed books provided the quickest means of learning to recognise and discover cribs. The visiting system in the CR and MR gave a chance for this individual system of cryptographic training to be put to good use. It was considered useful psychologically to introduce members of the Registration Room and Netz Room to the broader aspects of work of the Hut. They came as visitors, and saw something of the final process in the handling of Enigma traffic.

Promising pupils who showed a special aptitude for key-breaking might be retained in the Watch or Research. Other pupils, it was believed, would go back to their routines refreshed and invigorated, and see the final purpose of their often tedious work. Throughout, the general maxim was applied that experience is the best teacher.

Beginning of the schools

It was with boom conditions of work and with a steady increase of staff from the end of the University year 1941-1942 that the need for more formal and planned instruction arose. The members of the Decoding Room required a good deal of practice and some instruction, and this section led the way. In August 1942 it was decided to set up a DR school, and after difficulties of space had been overcome, it was duly inaugurated on 14 September. The Registration Room School followed later that month. Here, new staff were taught the background of blisting, a little about W/T, the system of key distribution and naming, and the various registration routines – and given supplementary talks by other members of the Hut on such topics as discriminants, methods of breaking and Control. Visits to the bombe Hut and to Sixta were also arranged to catch a glimpse of the wider picture and see the wheels go round. The course was useful enough to be extended in scope. In October it was used as a refresher course for members of the RR, who had not previously had the opportunity for any systematic tuition.

In the pioneer organisation of the RR School were laid the foundations of the systematic training of all new members of the Hut and of the specialised cryptographic training for members of Watch and Research. If 1942 saw a great increase in the totals of DR, NR and RR staff, 1943 saw the largest single increase from outside to the cryptographic staff that had ever taken place. No new member from outside the Hut entered the cryptographic sections between January 1942 and April 1943. Then the flood-gates were opened. First, three members arrived from Bedford, then a batch of four undergraduates from Cambridge in the early summer, then a bunch of Americans. There was also a further intake of cryptographers from the NR, RR and DR.

But it was not merely a question of increasing numbers. The scope of the work was becoming more difficult at this time. The fusion of the MR and CR meant that the knowledge of the average member had to be more varied than ever before, and in the case of the new member, a great deal more had to be learned at once. Most of the new arrivals were not mathematicians, and the machine side of the work demanded systematic and detailed instruction.

However, it was not until the arrival of the university intake that a Watch Course was drawn up. The earlier arrivals in 1943 did the RR

School course and followed this up with a week in the Qwatch, entering typed books and having an occasional talk on bombes and cillies. Three weeks' probationary work was then done in the Watch. This consisted of one turn on each of the shifts, while the prospective member learned the routines by helping to carry them out. Sometimes one or two weeks followed in Research, particularly for individuals whose success was not quite certain.

In June 1943 a committee was set up to see how this system, which had been applied in the case of visitors, could be improved and extended to cater for the university intake, and a detailed plan was drawn up. It was agreed that all new members of the Hut destined for the Watch should go first to the RR School, where they would learn something not only of other people's problems, but also of the cryptographic background as a whole.

The RR School syllabus
At this point the RR School, with a course which lasted for a fortnight on a two-shift basis, became a much more formal institute of instruction than before. Below is the syllabus, first drawn up in October 1942:

(I) W/T
1. Wireless Sending, Morse etc.
2. Organisation of a wireless station; Signals office, operators etc.
3. The message itself; Preamble (frequency, length, callsigns, and how to look them up, discriminants, practice in colouring the register etc; Text (five-figure groups, dupes etc)
4. Wireless Working; Use of callsigns; Control and CQ; Stars, Kreis, Netz etc.

(II) The Machine
1. Details of turnover mechanism; ringstellung clips, tyres, stecker etc;
2. Keys: Setting up of a key.
3. Encoding and decoding messages; The Indicator system.
4. Cillies and ringstellung tips: how they arise.

(III) Hut 6 routines

1. Blisting: Practice.

2. Naming of keys: Traffic summaries.

3. Routine jobs in RR1 and RR2: Control jobs.

4. Key repeats.

5. Fag systems.

(IV) Elements of breaking: bombes, menus etc.

This ambitious syllabus was taught by varied methods. The course as a whole was in the hands of an experienced member of the RR – in one case of the NR – who was competent to deal with certain aspects of the course very well. The bulk of the course, however, was taught indirectly by means of papers, which had been drawn up by experts in their respective fields. Much was also put across in lectures by "outside" speakers, including members of the Watch and Research. Visits were arranged wherever possible, and the whole of the syllabus was designed to be as practical as possible, and to give unity and direction to the work of the Hut as a whole.

Watch and Research training

For those members going on to Watch or Research, a further course was now drawn up, systemising a good deal that had never been systemised before. The syllabus was drawn up in two parts:

I   The Machine
II   Cribs and re-encodements

The first part of the course was expressly designed to give a much wider machine background to members of the Watch than was general at the time.

Part I

1. Cillies: their nature and types: Practice in subtraction of cillies and deducing wheelorders: Breaking on cillies.

2. Ringstellung tips: how to find them.

3. Hand attempts: Difference between English and German ringstellung. Females: The cyclometer etc.

4. Breaking on the bombe: Cribs and menus: What the bombe does: Its construction: Different types of bombes: Jumbos: Different types of menus: Cilli menus: Hoppities.

5. Rodding: Theory and practice.

Part II

1. General talk on cribs: Statement of the problem: Routine messages: Spotting the crib message: Guessing what it says: Aids in spotting the message – length, GTO, callsigns etc.
2. The crib folder and conventions of entering.
3. Types of cribs and different forms of cribs: Cycles: Security methods against cribs – location of address, wahlworts etc.
4. The preparation of a crib – unduped and contradicted letters, checking of unduped teleprint etc.
5. Talk on re-encodements: How they arise: How they are spotted: Fitting the German: Stagger stretches: Teil-breaking: Linked stagger stretches: Routine REs: Comparison cards and folders: Partial REs: REs from non-Enigma.
6. Talk on the organisation of Watch and Research.
7. Stray points to be cleared up:
    (i) Boils and form sheets
    (ii) Depth
    (iii) Construction of keys
    (iv) Rules of keys
    (v) Sources of information
    (vi) Crib cover

The main method of driving these points home was by means of 12 practical exercises, based where possible on "real life" examples and graded in terms of their difficulty:

1. Hand attempt: cillies plus ringstellung (keyboards) (Rating: Easy)
2. Hand attempt: Cillies plus ringstellung (nearnesses) (Rating: Easy)
3. Depth reading: Robinson fun and games (Rating: moderately easy)
4. Re-encodement exercise (Rating: difficult)
5. Depth reading (Rating: Easy)
6. Hand attempt: cillies plus ringstellung (various) (Rating: Difficult)
7. Dottery (Rating: Easy)
8. Dottery (Rating: Moderately Easy)
9. Dottery (Rating: Moderate)
10. Dottery (Rating: Difficult)
11. Re-encodement (Panzer RE) (Rating: Moderate)
12. Hand attempt (Rating: Moderate)

In the second part of the Course, and in the supervision of the exercises, various members of the Watch acted as instructors and guides. Parents were detailed to talk about their own keys and the Qwatch became a school, attached to the main establishment. Various improvements were suggested in the arrangement of the course. With a large number of keys, the week or more of entering in the Qwatch had become somewhat dull and monotonous, and the last groups of people to do the course had this week extended and interspersed with days of routine shift, working on the keys on which they had been instructed. After this experience of current working, they went back to the Qwatch for a spell of two or three days' revision. In the case of the American contingent, a special room was set aside and the course was given in a classroom atmosphere with competitive impetus, at least in the solution of the exercises.

By these means, new members of Watch and Research were given a wide background before setting out as fully-fledged operational staff. In the Watch itself, there was still something to learn of the division of labour and the allocation of jobs, and it became customary to send all new members to work for at least a week in the NR, where they would not only test stops and find ringstellung, but learn something of the liaison with the bombe Hut and its outstations. The NR itself had a vast amount of educational training to carry out, for its numbers increased more rapidly than those of the Watch, and it was losing experienced members regularly to Watch and Research. Special papers were written outlining the work of the Room and members were gradually initiated into the more specialised tasks.

The outline course and special talks

The value of the Watch course as a general introduction to Enigma and its breaking was plain, and it was felt that an outline course on the same lines would be of value to others besides the members and potential members of the Watch. So a short course was drawn up to last two or three days, which could be attempted by visitors from other departments. It was divided into three lessons, each of which lasted preferably for a day, and each of these lessons had its appropriate exercises:

Lesson 1:   The Machine and hand-breaking;
Lesson 2:   Bombe-breaking by cribs and the finding of ringstellung;
Lesson 3:   Cribs and re-encodements and how to find them.

Each of these lessons had its appropriate exercises. For members of the RR in training, talks on the work of the Watch were regularly given by members, who would discuss not so much the different methods of breaking as the part played by Watch and Research in the total effort of Hut 6 as a whole. The ideal method of tackling a key would be considered as a problem – and the value of complete traffic, tidy blists, comfortable hours and expert attention being balanced against urgency and speed in the breaking of operational keys. The Watch would become a demonstration centre for interested and curious novices, who would have the functions of the different shift members explained to them on the spot.

Other educational schemes

Three other detailed educational schemes need some attention in this discussion in Hut 6 methods of training. The first was the special menu-making course inaugurated in December 1943 and developed in 1944, when members of the RR were drawn into the cryptographic organisation to relieve pressure, particularly on the Army Watch. They were taught in two main lessons:

Lesson 1: Machine turnover: Cribs: Why written out in banks of 26:
The turnover assumptions implicit in menus and the meaning of the "relative positions of constatations": Types of stretches chosen for menus: Strength of menus: Practical menu-making: Methods of menu-making – ringing "females" and noting triangles, checking, phantoms and bracketed letters, bombe copies etc.

Lesson 2: Top and tail menus: Cilli menus: Hoppities: Delayed hoppities.

These two lessons were supplemented by much practice work, and of course it was merely necessary to be taught the essentials of this subject in order to set off on the job. Practice was the best teacher.

The second educational scheme was organised in collaboration with Sixta, and was designed for training TIS members. After the abolition of the regular use of discriminants in September 1943, it was felt that TIS members should be taught something of log reading, D/F and other branches of W/T. A course was arranged and held at the end of 1943, but because of the pressure of work, it was never possible to give everyone the opportunity of taking the Course.

The third educational scheme was connected with the Hand Duenna

Training Schemes in Hut 6

attack projected in July 1944 to meet the dreaded extension of Reflector D. When it was found that there was no immediate need to put into effect the complicated organisation prepared beforehand, the enterprise was transformed into a trial run. It was unique in so far as it demanded a detailed educational training for Wrens at Stanmore as well as members of the Hut itself. Four bays of bombes at Stanmore were to be put out of action, releasing 60 Wrens per shift. These Wrens were to be taught and supervised by one shift leader from the Hut.

The understanding of the Hand Duenna technique required a Netz Room background, and those with this knowledge and experience were well supplied, under the leadership of the technical adviser (O H Lawn, a member of the Watch), to do the teaching of the shift members. Many members regretted that the scheme had not been undertaken operationally, but the teams at Stanmore did a trial run, which would have been of considerable value in facing new contingencies.

This was the last general experiment in training. From this time until the end of the war, new technical problems and new situations were faced by existing staff and techniques evolved by a progressive adaption of existing knowledge.

Period V

January 1944 – May 1945: The Liberation of Europe – Hut 6 Fights Back Against New German Security Devices

Chapter 10
General Historical Summary

The determining factors
Complicated in the extreme as is the detailed history of Hut 6 in the final phase of the war, the main determining factors are twofold:

1. The decisive assault on Fortress Europe launched on D-Day;

2. The bringing into force of new German security measures.

It will be convenient to discuss the effect of these factors under four main heads: the technique of cryptography; the organisation of the cryptographic sections; the importance of other sections to cryptography; the contribution of Hut 6 to Intelligence.

The technique of cryptography
The new devices introduced by the Germans (in particular D and Enigma Uhr) brought about a remarkable renaissance of machine theory. Old problems that in the past seemed merely academic – and also new problems – had to be tackled and mastered, in particular the invention and improvement of D-breaking machines was (so far as Hut 6 was concerned) the climax of cryptographic mechanisation.

The organisation of cryptography
This was scarcely affected by the new German devices, but underwent many changes both in anticipation of D-Day and as a result of it. The main developments were the transference of the principal Western Air

General Historical Summary

keys to the Watch in May 1944, the setting up of the Army Watch just after D-Day, and — as a consequence of the general contraction of the fronts and the increased interlinking of previously separate keys — the gradual alteration of our whole breaking set-up from a Watch/Research to an Air/Army basis. This important development — the last major administrative change in Hut 6 — was finally completed at the beginning of December 1944 as is fully discussed later.

Importance of other sections to cryptography

A marked feature of the whole period is the increased dependence of the cryptographer (wandering in the confused labyrinth of W/T camouflage — culminating in call sign encoding — and the key compromises inevitable in fluid warfare) upon the helpful thread of the traffic analyst. Inevitably, liaison with TIS [Traffic Identification Section] and Sixta becoming ever closer, TIS, in particular, took over two important cryptographic functions:

a. responsibility for the identification and naming of 'unknown' keys – in particular the Barnyards;

b. responsibility for dealing with captured keys i.e., identifying the keys and seeing that any available traffic was decoded. In the last year of the war, Hut 6 was constantly under fire from an increasing barrage of captured documents and machines. The documents, after examination by TIS, were filed and catalogued by the chief cryptographer, Major Babbage.

Contribution of Hut 6 to Intelligence

The new German security measures of all kinds might, properly handled, have virtually stopped the flow of operational intelligence from Hut 6 to Hut 3. Very largely through German mistakes, this result was never achieved. However, our success was not unaffected. Several keys (in particular Puma), were finally ruined by D, and the encoding by calls signs on the GAF caused a serious drop in Air decodes from which we never made a complete recovery. But on the whole the luck of Hut 6 held good, and to the end we decoded currently most of the vital operational traffic.

From the standpoint of the quantity and quality of the intelligence sent to Hut 3, our peak year was 1944. The peak period – for quantity at least – is about a fortnight after D-Day when, for about a week in the key book, over 30 keys appear as broken on each day. The statistics of the total number of breaks put 1944 easily above other years. In 1942, through the incidence of key repeats, it would sometimes happen that more keys would be broken at one time, but there are many months in 1944 that top the 1942 record of 550 breaks.

On the Army side, in particular, 1944 witnessed an immense advance. Although we should not forget the valuable intelligence provided by the African Army keys in 1942-1943, still Hut 3 had never previously seen Army traffic of such high quality as on the best keys of 1944 – the Bantams, Ducks and Puffins. The importance of Army keys relative to Air constantly increased, and towards the end, when the Air difficulties were most acute, the Army decodes sometimes surpassed the Air in number and quality. This was a reversal of the situation that prevailed for most of the war, but the Army experts, who had had in general the hardest cryptographic task, cannot be grudged this final hour of triumph. In 1944-1955, first Italy, then the West – finally even the East – was held in fee, and on the Army side, as on the Air, the cryptographic encirclement of Germany was complete.

On the standards of quantity of breaks, quality of intelligence and general all-round cryptographic success, 1944 saw Hut 6 at its best. At the height of its resources in personnel and machine power, the Hut worked flat out, particularly in the weeks immediately following D-Day. By the unanimous testimony of the generals in the field, the contribution to the victory now made through the ULTRA intelligence which flowed to the Continent as regularly as PLUTO's oil, can scarcely be over-rated. However, the success of 1944 could never have been achieved without the patient spade work of the preceding years, but it is none the less true that on the final analysis, 1944 was Hut 6's finest hour.

Chapter 11
German Security Devices -1
Reflector D (Part 1)

General Introduction

Between January 1944 and may 1945 the Germans introduced a large number of security measures. Some were of a W/T camouflage nature and had their effect on cryptology in that they made proper traffic identification more difficult. Other enemy measures were essentially cryptographic, i.e., they affected the actual process of encoding and thus influenced our methods of breaking. It will be convenient to classify the various devices adopted into three groups:

    a. mechanical gadgets which involved the provision of an addition (or Zusatzgerät) to the standard Enigma machine;

    b. alteration of the key;

    c. encoding rules

The separate devices adopted are as follows:
- (a)   1. Reflector D
        2. Enigma Uhr
- (b)   3. Zusatz stecker
        4. Notschschlüssel
- (c)   5. CY
        6. Random indicators
        7. Wahlworts
        8. Mosse Code
        9. Double encoding

Before proceeding to discuss these devices in turn and the countermeasures we adopted, one or two general points should be noticed. Firstly, these new German tricks were of very unequal value and importance. As might have been expected, technically D and Uhr were far more important than the rest, and indeed D as a potential menace to our cryptographic success was much more serious than the rest of the bag of tricks put together. Class (b) was a minor nuisance to the cryptographers, but not much more, while class (c) did not, on the scale, fundamentally affect our breaking methods though they did make breaking more expensive and difficult.

Secondly, it should be stated that while the German security drive of 1944 was on a more thorough scale than previously, some of the devices had been used earlier or were on the lines of measures previously adopted. Such pre-1944 anticipations of the 1944 devices will be referred to later under individual cases.

Reflector D in general
Uncle D, as he was affectionately known, was a household word in Hut 6 from January 1944 to the end. For the first half of the year he was also shrouded in a black cloak of mystery and the secret of his true identity and nature gave rise to much ingenious speculation. In what follows it is proposed to discuss Uncle D and all his works in historical sequence, making clear at each point the extent of our knowledge: in the technical volume the reader will find a full discussion of the methods used for breaking reflectors. D, as it affected Hut 6, was primarily a GAF security device, and this at once leads to a division of the history into two sections:

1. January to July 1944

2. August 1944 to May 1945

Up to and July 1944 D was confined to Red among GAF keys. From August on its range was extended and consequently the number of Ds recovered rose rapidly. From January to July we recovered 21 Ds; from August to the end of the war 379. This later figure includes just over 100 by capture.

January to July 1944

The first menace
On 23 December 1943, Hut 6 received an unwelcome jolt. A Red message was intercepted on a Norwegian frequency which gave instructions that a new reflector – called Umkehrwalze Dora – was to come into force on 1 January 1944. It was not clear from the message whether the new reflector was to be used on part of the Red system, or on all of it – or even whether it was to be confined to Red at all. We felt that there was a reasonable chance that the Germans would make the error of using the new reflector only on a part of Red. But preparations had to be made for

German Safety Devices - 1

the less favourable possibility that Red as a whole might go over to the new reflector and thus, at a stroke, become unbreakable by our normal method – the bombe.

Hut 6 was then suddenly faced with the possibility of a first-class cryptographic crisis which was liable to result in the loss for an indefinite time of the principal GAF key – Red – the cornerstone of all Air cryptography and still at the top of the intelligence ladder. Recurrent crises were not unusual in Hut 6 at this time – only recently, in November 1943, the Germans had dropped the regular use of discriminants on the Air and a radical change of W/T set-up was now expected every month. But this was a crisis of a new order. A new reflector, if it came into universal use, would – until broken – make all our hundreds of bombes so much waste metal. Until we had solved the D mystery our whole breaking technique was jeopardised.

Yet, while no-one minimised the gravity of the impending crisis and the seriousness of the ordeal through which Hut 6 might have to pass, it would be wrong to imply that the cryptographers viewed the prospect as an unalloyed tragedy. It had been so long since they had been forced to direct their minds to the higher reaches of theory that many felt a distinct exhilaration at the thrill of a difficult problem. The very completeness of our conquest of the Enigma, the very perfection of our technique, seemed at times to make it all too easy and monotonous. Certainly 1944 was destined to dispel quickly any such feeling. D was only the first – although the most serious – of a host of new problems. Yet probably most of those closely involved in the solution of these new difficulties would agree that the increasing interest of the work was, on balance, a more than adequate compensation for the additional labours involved.

Meanwhile, preparations were made in the last week of 1943 for the worst, i.e., that Red would go over wholly to D. At the time there was only one way to tackle the problem, i.e., to break by the hand SKO method (D-breaking machines were not yet in existence, nor thought of) on a long crib – which could probably only be attained by an RE [re-encodement] from some other key. It was realised that if D was universally introduced our only chance was an RE from some other cipher. But there was nothing we could do about this but wait until 1 January and see what happened. We held a number of meetings at which the SKO technique was explained and discussed. In all this activity, Mr Alexander, Head of Hut 8, was prominent and his experience — for Hut 8 had had to use SKO on several occasions, was invaluable. (While the technique was known in outline, few members of Hut 6 had any practical experience in SKO.

The method had never been successfully employed in Hut 6, no doubt because the need for it had never arisen). These meetings were attended by the cryptographers of Watch and Research plus selected personnel from the Machine Room. From this band it was proposed to draft a team for the SKO operation if necessary, while those not selected would have to go on breaking in the normal way any keys unaffected by D.

It must be remembered that, at this stage, no-one had or could have any conception of the true nature of D. It was thought of as a fixed reflector like B or C. We were prepared for a hard struggle to break it, but it was imagined that once broken our troubles were over. Herein ignorance was bliss – the stoutest hearts might have quailed in those last days of 1943 had it been possible for us to realise the hydra-headed nature of our veiled antagonist.

Illusory triumph
Perhaps no single day in Hut 6 history was more memorable than in prospect than our D-Day, New Year's Day 1944. Breaks that on other days had become matters of course recaptured their old thrill and any who had forgotten in daily routine the meaning of our achievement, had a fresh realisation of the truth of the statement: 'The breaking of Enigma is a daily miracle'.

The first break was that of Leek at 1100, hailed as never was a Leek break before or since, as it proved that D was not a universal presence. This was followed by the vital break of Red at 1150. All the traffic already in came out on the key we had discovered, and for some time we wondered whether Uncle D was but a false scare. But after dinner it became clear that messages on the Norwegian Auto and some on the GHQ Auto were not coming out. A reasonable beginner — SEQSXFREDX — was then rodded on one of the Norwegian messages, assuming the Red stecker, wheel order and ringstellung (which gave the turnover on the rods). What was obviously the correct story was discovered, but there was no hole through the Jeffreys sheets, therefore the presence of a new reflector was proved. The rodding was then continued through the middle wheel and the wiring of the reflector established by Oliver Lawn at 0130 on the morning of the 2nd. (For the process employed see the technical volume.) The method soon became routine, and was eventually speeded up by new apparatus, but this was the first occasion we had required to use it — except for the break of Reflector C on cillies in 1940). D was unmasked and the crisis was over – or so we fondly thought. Alas for the vanity of human wishes! How soon was the cup to be dashed from our lips!

The BO mystery

For the moment the skies were clear. Arrangements were made to have bombes, hand machines and Decoding Room machines fitted with the new reflector. This could easily be done by plugging, and within the first week of January at least one Red key was broken on a crib run on D. Meanwhile, a set of D rod catalogues was ordered to be a companion to the existing B set and the hypothesis that Greenshank was on D and hence (as we supposed) now breakable was canvassed. But, on 11 January, Uncle D struck again.

The D traffic did not come out on the wiring already known. In the same manner as before, a new wiring was recovered which had one pairing only – BO – common with the first D. This showed that D was a many-sided device and a much more formidable threat than we had imagined. To anticipate events, we found that about every 10 days a new D came into force on Red and every D had the common pairing BO. Up to the end of July, 20 Red Ds were broken and given serial numbers.

A great controversy followed as to the nature of the device. Argument turned principally on the significance to be attached to the fixed pairing BO, but it was by no means clear what theory this peculiarity supported. Two main theories were propounded:

  a. that D was pluggable and hence each of the countless possible variants would have to be broken individually when used, or:

  b. that D was a device with a limited number of positions and hence capable eventually of a complete once-for-all solution.

Various ingenious theories on the nature of this device were suggested by the imaginative members of the Hut. The simplest idea was that D consisted of a basic fixed reflector with another thin wheel next to it, rotating through 26 positions. This was in accordance with naval practice, and if it had been true we could have broken the basic D on three positions (assuming D1, D2 and D3 were consecutive), or on some seven or eight if the succession of Ds was random. The main weakness of this theory is that it is at least unlikely that a common pairing would have appeared in such a D-family.

It is however, needless to pursue our speculation in detail. Largely from the difficulty of forming any other watertight hypothesis, the pluggable theory gradually gained ground, and was finally proved correct by the capture of the Red key-sheet for June 1944 with the D pairings on it. To remove all doubt, the column containing these pairings was headed:

STECKERVERBINDUNGEN AN DEN UMKEHRWALZE

The D pairings were written vertically in three columns of four pairings each. For the month there were three Ds, each covering approximately ten days.

D Substitution

We have spoken of 12 pairings only, but our Ds had 13 pairings – 12 variable and the fixed pairing BO. It was therefore clear from this discrepancy alone that the German system of notation for D pairings was different from ours, but as we had previously broken some of the Ds now captured, it was easy to work out the relationship between the two systems. The transformation is shown in the following table:

ENGLISH	GERMAN	ENGLISH	GERMAN
A	A	A	A
C	Z	B	Z
D	X	C	Y
E	W	D	X
F	V	E	W
G	U	F	V
H	T	G	U
I	S	H	T
J	R	I	S
K	Q	K	R
L	P	L	Q
M	O	M	P
N	N	N	N
P	M	O	M
Q	L	P	L
R	K	Q	K
S	I	R	J
T	H	S	I
U	G	T	H
V	F	U	G
W	E	V	F
X	D	W	E
Y	C	X	D
Z	B	Z	C

German Safety Devices - 1

It will be noticed that (starting from A = A) one alphabet runs backwards and the other forward, omitting the letters BO in the English alphabet and JY in the German, which correspond to the permanently fixed pairing. The discovery was important in two ways:

1. for its reference to Rules of Keys, and:

2. because in future we could translate captured Ds into our own notation.

For all general purposes, we continued to use the English notation.

Greenshank and D

So far we have spoken of Red Ds only, and as for the GAF, D was so far confined to Red. But even before the end of 1943, there was a strong suspicion – based on the failure of several good Falcon REs – that Greenshank, the prize of prizes for Army Research, was using a new reflector or a new wheel. The gradual growth of this suspicion is clearly seen in the reports of the period, as confidence of success is replaced by baffled dismay. So strong had the suspicions grown, that the best RE – on 7 October 1943 – was run through all <u>Naval</u> wheel orders and reflector combinations at Washington.

It is therefore not surprising that Army Research quickly decided that D was the answer to the Greenshank riddle and strong psychological stories that appeared early in 1944 were run unsuccessfully on the then known varieties of D. But success depended on the truth of the 'limited variety' theory of D, and as the pluggable theory gained ground, the running of Greenshank on known Ds was more and more discouraged.

The possibility remained of a break by SKO, and in any case, there was a strong feeling that whether we broke a Greenshank day or not, a SKO experiment was well worth undertaking for the sake of practice – we might yet have to do the job in dire earnest. Accordingly, towards the end of February 1944, a team of four people with occasional visitors conducted an experimental attack on Greenshank of 7 October 1943. This failed to break the day (probably because it was not possible to press the attack home – only two out of five right-hand wheels were tried) but (as the report properly emphasises) gave useful information on the best technique to adopt. The time that would have been required to do the complete job was estimated at about a fortnight for relays of five people working continuous shifts.

It is emphasised in the report on this experiment that the best method to tackle any particular SKO problem can only be determined in the light of the peculiarities of the available crib. In a favourable case the time required may be much reduced. This point was quickly driven home by one of the great personal triumphs of Hut 6 — the break of Greenshank of 27 April 1944 — on a re-encodement of some 200 letters. This feat was effected in about a week by taking full advantage of an equidistance in the crib and gambling on our chances, by trying only the most favourable hypotheses to reduce the labour involved to proportions that a lone worker could contemplate. It was universally recognised as a fitting reward that fortune should have at length smiled on Lionel Clarke, who had chased Greenshank with relentless determination for four long years.

This break made it highly probable that Greenshank was using D as the BO pairing appeared (The D was named DG1. Much later it was given a D number in the regular series as D194), and this supposition was fully confirmed by the later Greenshank breaks in 1945. We were soon able to establish that the common key (For, as is elsewhere explained, Greenshank used two keys on the same day) used the same D — but we could break no days near at hand by running on the D we had recovered. But though the truth was early suspected it was not until much later that we were able to demonstrate that Greenshank changed its D daily.

Red Ds: January to July
Meanwhile, the Red Ds were being broken regularly and with no great difficulty. It was soon discovered that there was some uncertainty about the date when the second and third Ds of the month would come into force, but this caused little serious trouble in practice. During these relatively quiet months, Air Watch got constant practice in breaking Ds, and a general speed-up of the process was soon achieved by the construction of suitable tables and the convenient invention of the 'half Enigma' [a type of hand machine in which the terminals of the reflector may be connected direct to the lampboard]. The only breaks in the steady progressions of three Red Ds a month was caused by two Red compromises. In the first case (March) the reserve key came into force on the 10th but no D was used – hence in March there is only one D. But in June the reserve key (which came into force in the middle of the month) had its own D, and so we got four Ds in that month. The

conclusion is obviously that in March the reserve Red key had no Ds printed on it, while in June it had.

The overhanging menace
During this time we could never forget the Sword of Damocles. We were more or less all right if things went on as they were, but we could not always rely on the Germans making the egregious mistake of using B and D on the same key — sooner or later there would be a great extension of the use of D. The references in decodes to the continuous distribution of Ds to units were decisive on this point. Sooner or later it was clear, D would extend to more keys, and some fine day we might discover that Red or possibly some other even more important key would be unbreakable as being 'wholly D' or 'nearly wholly D'.

So, through this period, while the TIS experts classified all references to D, noted its distribution and endeavoured to discover the principles underlying its use, the Uncle D committee, chaired by Mr Alexander, held regular meetings to discover, if possible, a real defence to the menace of a 'wholly D key'. Most attention was paid to mechanical D-breaking devices, for it was realised that though we might *have* in an emergency to use hand methods, they were too slow and too expensive in the labour required to be really feasible as a means of operational breaking. Machine experiments were set on foot, both here and in America, and as a result the various D-breaking machines described in the technical volume were evolved. Of them all, Duenna — a machine invented by American experts as a result of discussions with Mr Alexander, who visited the US in connection with this problem — proved in practice most successful (it is fair to remember that it had a start over most of its rivals) and a hand method — Hand Duenna — was elaborated as a standby in case the full crisis came on us before the machines were ready.

Had the Germans known how easily they could have checkmated us! Yet to imagine this presupposes that they had some idea of our successes against Enigma, and it is clear that they had no conception of the extent of our victory. Also, slow as their proceedings seemed to us, it may be that they were distributing Ds as fast as they could. However, the first day of every month – despite several alarms – passed with no change in the situation, but at last it became apparent from references in July, that something was really going to happen on 1 August.

Preparations for 1 August

Elaborate preparations were made for 1 August — our second D-Day. Careful co-ordination of records was clearly necessary and and this was organised by the Qwatch, while through the parents of various keys, a list of Air cribs was drawn up with special attention to any that offered possibilities for Duenna or hand SKO. Except for a few special frequencies which had declared their position in advance, it was impossible to predict what messages would be on B or on D, and careful assessment of probabilities would clearly be required before we could give up a key as 'wholly D'. On the Research keys, the class of those that could be broken or failed on B within a few days, but were hopeless on D, was distressingly large. This was due to the great demands of D-breaking machines compared with the bombe (see the figures in the technical volume), and boded ill for our prospects if there was a serious extension of D. But with the perennial optimism engenered by so many narrow escapes in the past, we still hoped that the Germans would continue to mix up B and D, and so, in the popular phrase, hand us their reflector on a plate.

Chapter 12
German Security Devices - 2
Reflector D (Part 2)

Extension of D

To a considerable extent our optimism was justified. By 2 August three distinct Ds had been broken — disproving the pleasing illusion that all keys might share a common D — Red, Cricket and Gadfly, and others rapidly followed. There was no significant extension in the use of D on Red, and at least five keys — Ocelet, Puma, Yak, Snowdrop and Daffodil — were free from D. There was also no appearance of D on Army keys.

However, it was not long before we realised that the nightmare of a wholly D key was no fantasy. Wasp, the key of Fliegerkorps IX, went over wholly to D on 5 August (this was at the time a deduction from its failure to come out, but was proved later), the first — and not the least serious of our defeats by our shadowy antagonist. Later, the Wasp Ds for the second and third periods of August were recovered by running shots on the only non-D frequency — the Nosegay fag — but it was obvious that Wasp, as a nearly 100% D key, was hanging by a hair.

From later evidence and our general knowledge of the GAF Cipher Office it is possible to state that what really happened in August was this: prior to August 1944 only the Red key sheet had Ds printed on it. Now, it is believed that in the GAF cipher office a number of keys were made up and then the key number and discriminants added in a fixed order which determined the nature of each key. On this theory, not until the discriminants were added was the nature of the key known. Thus, before August 1944 the Red D must have been made up when the discriminants were added, and not when the key was composed. But from August on it is simplest to suppose that every key, when made up, had its quota of Ds added before the keys were identified by number and discriminants. This theory is not contradicted by all the available evidence.

On this theory it follows that from August 1944 every GAF key had a set of Ds attached, i.e., every key was liable to use D. But it does not follow that every key *did* use D. First, certain units might not have D distributed to them. Second, even if an operator had D, there is a lot of evidence to show that D was so unpopular with German cipher clerks that they would not use it without explicit and repeated orders. It is possible from our actual breaks to draw up the following table of the first use of D on various keys:

1944:	August	Gadfly, Cricket, Jaguar, Cockroach, Snowdrop, Hyena, Wasp, Pink, Lion, Mosquito.
	September	Beetle, Gorilla.
	October	Mustard
	November	Puma, Narcissus, Yak, Daffodil, Leopard.
	December	Ocelot
1945	January	Aster, Lily.
	February	Skunk, Wallflower, Indigo.
	March	Marmoset, Moth.
	April	Gentian.

This table gives a general picture of the gradual increase in the extension of D, but — especially in the case of rarely-broken colours — it does not follow that the month in which we first recovered a D is that in which D was first used on the key in question. It is very likely — to cite examples — that Skunk, Marmoset, Indigo and Gentian used D before the dates given above. Also, the general tendency towards more use of D was sometimes reversed. For example, Gadfly, which used D in August, was again all on B from December 1944 onwards. German cipher clerks reverted to use of B whenever the pressure of security officers was relaxed. Thus there was a constant fluctuation in the use of D which, over any given period, would decrease in some localities and increase in others. However, the overall tendency was towards increase.

Effects on breaking

While at the end of the first week of August we could not but feel that we had escaped more easily than we might, the long-term effects of the extension of D soon became apparent and – from this and other causes

– from August until the end of the war there was a steady increase in the difficulty of breaking most GAF keys.

First, the problem of recovering the D even when the rest of the key was known was no longer the formality it had been on Red, which was a large key with at most times a plethora of reasonable cribs — most other keys were in a less happy state. One might break into one day of a key on B and find no suitable crib on which to recover the D. One solution was to break another day in the same period, but this was not always easy, and also involved delay. To meet this case, various ingenious methods of breaking a D on a known key without a crib were devised, and sometimes deployed with success. The first occasion was in September when a Gorilla D was broken by 'Bobbery'. This was invented by Robert Roseveare, and was a method of recovering D wirings when the wheel order, ringstellung and stecker of the key are known, but no crib is available on a message encoded with D. But all these methods were fairly laborious and none so certain as breaking on a crib. Again, apart from difficulties caused by lack of cribs, complicated technical problems were raised when a key was broken on B and virtually all the remaining traffic was on D and Uhr. Moreover, the difficulties of key identification caused by the general absence of discriminants, call sign encoding, key compromises and, in the East, the endemic uncertainty of the key distribution, added to the effect of the technical snags. It was often impossible to know whether a message dud on one key was on that key plus D or on another key used in the same neighbourhood. No cryptographer worth his salt is dismayed by a tricky technical job if he is reasonably sure of his ground, but it is a daunting prospect to embark on a laborious attempt to break a D when the odds may be against the message you are working on being on the assumed key. Thanks to the cumulative effect of all these considerations, it would sometimes happen that a D would not be broken despite B breaks in the period, even when a D was believed or known to have been used.

Second, special problems were provided by 'nearly D' or 'wholly D' keys. A 'nearly D' key may be defined as one on which the bulk of the traffic and all, or most of the best cribs, are habitually on D. It was necessary, on these keys, to secure an entry on a B crib – not an easy task as they were by definition inferior or fewer – or on a stray B re-encodement. Exploitation of a break was often easy enough, as on good D cribs the

D could be found and more days in the period broken quickly. But the initial break was the real problem, and because of the time required to effect the first entry, exploitation was often far from current. It is thus not uncommon on these keys to find breaks clustering. After a blank period, seven or eight Wasps would come out in a few days due to a fortunate initial break. Typical examples of 'nearly D' keys were Wasp, Lion, Hyena and Ocelot. The last began using D in December 1944 and, as from then to the end of the war, it remained a key of the first importance, there was a constant series of alarms and excursions at the possibility that, at any moment, Ocelot might become 'wholly D'. Each break of a new Ocelot D was heralded as a major triumph, but thanks to German errors, we just held on until the third period of April.

'Nearly D' keys were in constant danger of crossing the line and becoming 'wholly D'. Once this fatal line had been crossed, nothing could be done except by hand SKO or by a D-breaking machine. In general, the labour could not be spared for hand attempts. Greenshank was already known as a 'wholly D' key and was joined by Puma on 20 November 1944 (orders were issued on Puma to start the use of D on that day, and as it ceased coming out, the inference was obvious), and at least one Eastern Front Air key — Skunk — was 'wholly D' in February 1945. Our biggest fear was that a vital operational Western Air key would become 'wholly D', but (except perhaps for Wasp at some periods) we were spared this dreaded blow.

D-breaks

The progress of the D-breaking machines under construction in Britain and America was thus watched with keen interest, and no sooner were the machines in working order than their services were called for on operational jobs. We were compelled by sheer necessity to use highly complicated machinery which was still really in an experimental stage, and in all the circumstances, the 18 breaks achieved (this is the number of Ds broken — the number of days that came out in consequence is much higher) by the monstrous triad Giant, Duenna and Autoscritcher (the war ended before the fourth monster — Ogre — could be used operationally) is highly creditable to all concerned.

A full list of the Ds broken in this way will be found at the end of the chapter. Here it must suffice to mention some of the highlights of the story. Giant – an ingenious makeshift – was the hero of the early days and

German Security Devices -2

D120, Puma of the third period of November, was the first mechanically broken D. Considering that Giant demanded a crib of 200 letters, his total of four D breaks is a remarkable achievement. The Autoscritcher was not ready until the last few months, but in a short working life showed its merits by four quick D breaks.

Duenna was steadiest and the most successful machine. She began working operationally in December, was joined in a few months by a sister machine and further reinforced by a third sister towards the end. The Duennas jointly effected 10 breaks – mostly on Puma.

The breaks of these machines were nearly all on Puma, Greenshank and Skunk – all of which were 'wholly D' as was proved by the decodes of broken days. As we had so few D-breaking machines, it was necessary to use them to the utmost advantage, so the principle was adopted of confining them to 'wholly D' keys where D breaks offered the only chance. 'Nearly D' keys which gave even a slight prospect of bombe breaks were tried on the bombe. As a precaution, any job to be sent to a D-breaker was first run on a bombe.

In December and January, Puma and Greenshank were the competitors for Duenna's favours. (Giant demanded a much longer crib, so any really long REs were sent to Giant. CY (a security device by which the position of the left-hand wheel was altered during the encoding of a message, the new position being indicated to the decoder by the letters CY followed by the setting). Puma was the easier to exploit if broken and if reasonably current was preferred by the intelligence authorities. Greenshank, as relatively virgin soil, was the cryptographer's choice. On balance, however, Puma, which gave a better chance of success, was usually rated higher. The net result was that seven Puma and five Greenshank Ds were broken by mechanical means. (In addition, another Greenshank D was broken by SKO, Major Babbage repeating Lionel Clarke's achievement).

It was known that several Eastern Air keys were largely or wholly on D, but at first the prior claims of Greenshank and Puma made it difficult to give them their chance. However, Giant's second triumph was the Mosquito D of the first period of February, and in the last months of the war, Skunk got a good innings and four Ds were broken. However, the break of the Jaguar D for the first period of April is the most spectacular use made of our D-breaking machines. It was the one achievement which had immediate high operational value.

What happened was that on 1 April, Ocelot was broken early and a RE to Jaguar D wrote through three teile [a part of a message] without alteration. All available machinery was massed in an unprecedented concentration for the attack, and at midnight on the 2nd both Duenna and the Autostitcher were starting up, Giant menus were being prepared and a hand attempt here was already in progress. In less than 24 hours – by tea-time on the 3rd – Duenna produced the answer (D 280) shortly before it would have been reached by the hand attempt. This was by far and away our most successful attempt at the operational use of D-breakers, but the possible snags were shown by a similar attempt on the second Jaguar D when our whole machinery was tied up fruitlessly for days on end. The trouble was that when the D-breakers failed they took so long to put the job down – which is just another way of saying we had too few machines.

D captures

In the closing months of the war the military situation led to the capture of many key sheets with their accompanying Ds. A large number of these were Ds we should never have broken on our own, e.g., the Marmoset Ds of March and a whole series of Indigo Ds in February and March. Most sensational discovery of all was the capture of a series of daily changing Ds on a slip of paper separate from the key-sheet. The keys involved were soon identified as March and May Grouse (an offshoot of Greenshank). This capture, plus the strong evidence of our breaks (e.g., the Ds in use on 6 and 7 March were different) was accepted as final proof that Greenshank changed its D daily.

D Rules

The dates when new Ds came into force showed considerable variation. From November on, every key had 4 Ds a month as opposed to the earlier three. In September and October the practice varies strangely from key to key.

Summary of the German use of D

On the general question of cipher security, in the special case of the use of D, their cardinal error sticks out a mile. It was a capital blunder for the Germans to have 'mixed keys' using both B and D. Any individual key should have been wholly D or not to have used it at all. It is the more surprising that the Germans made this error as the Army – which must

German Security Devices -2

have used D on Greenshank in 1943 – used the device correctly. The GAF cipher authorities adopted and misused the excellent invention of the Army. D should have been considered an integral part of the key, not an extra.

It may be that in January 1944 the Germans may not have had enough Ds available to cover all the Red system. But, in that event, they should have adopted one of two courses — either to introduce D on a part of Red, but at the same time to equip these stations with a separate key – or to wait patiently until at one blow Red could be made an all-D key. The effect of a sudden wholesale introduction of D on to selected keys would have been a much more crushing blow to Hut 6 than the slow and piecemeal changes that the Germans preferred. In warfare, a new weapon should be first employed in massive strength, not in penny numbers.

Even with all the warning the Germans gave us by their snail-like progress, the case of Puma shows what damage a wholly D key could inflict on us. Puma adopted the use of D on 20 November, as it said it would, and subsequent breaks showed it was 100% D – later indeed, 100% plus Uhr. From the beginning of August to 19 November our success percentage was 96: from 20 November to the end of February it was 35. (The fall in success would be even more striking if we included March and April when no Puma was broken). Possibly not all this decline is due to D – Uhr played its part and the crib situation also became less favourable. Still, the D situation was certainly the main cause.

So, if after months of warning (needlessly given to us) of the D menace so that we had the chance of getting D-breakers to work, if even then the Germans, by the universal use of D on a key which we had been breaking steadily for months, and which we were prepared to run with top priority on our D-breakers could cut down our success ratio by 60%, what could they not have achieved by an unheralded universal use of D on a chosen key. (This is what happened on Greenshank. We believe that D was in use on Greenshank in 1943, and in view of the German tendency to make important changes on New Year's Day, then 1 January 1943 seems a plausible date for its introduction. If so, D was in use on Greenshank months before we even suspected anything odd, and it is at least doubtful whether the Greenshank mystery would ever have been solved had not the GAF done so much to give the game away.)

D STATISTICS KEY BY KEY

Key	Total number of Ds recovered
Red	57
Jaguar	38
Hyena	27
Cockroach	20
Mosquito	20
Gadfly	13
Wasp	12
Lion	9
Cricket	7
Beetle	13
Gorilla	7
Leopard	16
Puma	7
Ocelot	19
Wallflower	13
Indigo	16
Mustard	5
Pink	5
Aster	5
Skunk	4
Marmoset	3
Moth	3
Narcissus	3
Snowdrop	2
Daffodil	2
Lily	1
Yak	1
Gentian	1
Air total	**330**
Greenshank	7
Grouse	62
D for NOT-keys	1
GRAND TOTAL	**400**

German Security Devices -2

[In this table the order of Air keys is determined, firstly, by their order of adopting D (so far as we know), and secondly, by the number of Ds we recovered.]

CHRONOLOGICAL LIST OF Ds BROKEN WITHOUT A PRIOR BREAK ON REFLECTOR B

D No.	Key and Date	Broken by	Date of Break
194	Greenshank (27 April 1944)	L E Clarke	30 May 1944
120	Puma (3 Nov period)	Giant	28 Nov 1944
150	Puma (3 Dec period)	Duenna	26 Dec 1944
160	Mosquito (4 Dec period)	Giant	2 Jan 1945
163	Puma (4 Dec period)	Duenna	3 Jan 1945
165	Puma (1 Jan period)	Giant	5 Jan 1945
185	Greenshank (14 Jan)	Major D Babbage	24 Jan 1945
193	Greenshank (5 Jan)	Duenna	30 Jan 1945
196	Puma (4 Jan period)	Duenna	1 Feb 1945
226	Puma (3 Feb period)	Duenna	28 Feb 1945
228	Skunk (3 Feb period)	Giant	1 March 1945
236	Skunk (4 Feb period)	Autoscritcher	6 March 1945
238	Greenshank (17 Jan)	Autoscritcher	7 March 1945
241	Greenshank (7 Jan)	Autoscritcher	9 March 1945
250	Greenshank (6 March)	Duenna	11 March 1945
253	Puma (4 Feb period)	Duenna	13 March 1945
266	Greenshank (7 March)	Autoscritcher	25 March 1945
280	Jaguar IIA (1 April period)	Duenna	3 April 1945
326	Skunk (3 April period)	Duenna	30 April 1945
333	Skunk (4 April period)	Duenna	6 May 1945

Breaks classified by method and by key

Hand SKO	2	Puma	7
Giant	4	Greenshank	7
Duenna	10	Skunk	4
Autoscritcher	4	Mosquito	1
		Jaguar	1
TOTAL OF BREAKS	**20**		**20**

Chapter 13
German Security Devices - 3

Enigma Uhr, Zusatz Stecker and NOT-Schlüssel

The problem

What is most remarkable about Enigma Uhr is that the enemy succeeded for once in springing a complete surprise on us. The first we knew of it was that, on 10 July Jaguar, certain messages began with a number (it was soon seen that the numbers ran from 1 to 39) and then went off into nonsense. Also, a decode referred to one of these messages as enciphered with 'Enigma Uhr'. It was clear that the nonsense represented an additional re-encoding of some kind on top of the normal Enigma, almost certainly performed by a mechanical gadget.

The first step in solving this problem was clearly to break into one of the Uhr messages and this would have been by no means easy had not the Fusion Room been able to produce a re-encipherment between a 'plain' Enigma message and an Uhr message. This re-encipherment led to the breaking of the first Uhr substitution — a reciprocal stecker different from the basic stecker. How, in the next 48 hours, substitution after substitution was recovered (some reciprocal, some non-reciprocal), how the relationship between the various substitutions was worked out and codified, and how eventually a mechanical gadget was devised top attach to the Decoding Room machines and perform automatically the variations on the basic stecker, will be found elsewhere. To the participants in the rugger scrum in the Qwatch, when the complete mathematical theory was being elaborated, the whole episode will remain as one of the most tense in the history of Hut 6.

Routine adopted

A simple routine was at once adopted (some inessential modifications were made later) by which the Decoding Room, on discovering the message, marked them 'P' (later 'H'). The Decoding Room, for convenience in breaking the Uhr, decoded the rest of the message and then passed the message back to the Registration Room, who entered them on a central 'Plist'. A small party in the Qwatch was detailed for breaking the substitutions and passing on the solution to the Decoding Room.

Extension of Enigma Uhr

Uhr was always an Air gadget and never used by an Army key. Originally used by Jaguar and Cricket only, it was later extended to 15 Air keys in all (see table below on Uhr statistics). Jaguar, which soon after the first introduction was encoding nearly half its messages with Uhr, remained throughout the chief Uhr key – the Jaguar Uhr breaks surpass all others put together. For a period in August Jaguar, Snowdrop and Cricket appear regularly in the book of Uhr breaks, then in September Jaguar is the sole survivor, and in October even Jaguar deserts Uhr. But in November the use of Uhr starts anew on Jaguar and spreads to other keys. In 1945 the highlights of Uhr's extending kingdom were its first appearance on an Eastern Front key (Beetle) and its appearance with D on Puma and Aster.

Effect on breaking

Uhr alone had little influence on our breaking of keys although it did mean that there was sometimes a lot of technical work to be done after the basic key was broken. (For the Germans, the Uhr substitution was determined automatically by the order of the stecker pairings on the key sheet. As we did not know this arbitrary order, we had to break the Uhr apart from the basic key). Serious complications arose only when it was necessary to break a key on an Uhr message or when Uhr was combined with D. In running on the bombe, Uhr created no serious difficulties in principle, for it was possible, by using closures only, to allow for the probable non-reciprocity of the stecker. But, longer cribs were required, and this meant that a colour which used Uhr very extensively and had rather short cribs, was made more difficult to break. It is probable that this was one of the reasons why we failed to exploit our last two breaks of Puma reflectors. But if long cribs or REs were available, Uhr was not a major cryptographic obstacle.

Uhr notation

The Germans originally indicated the Uhr number by encoding it with the basic key at the beginning of the message. But in November a method of encoding the number was introduced by which the number was represented by four letters encoded in the basic key at the start of the message according to a simple bigram code. The manner in which this new notation was discovered is interesting. On Jaguar of November there were some inexplicable duds, especially on the Abdulla fag (FAG = Frequency Allocation Group). It was thought these might be on a separate key, but several cribs failed. Fortunately, someone had the bright idea that the message might be on Jaguar Uhr with a new method of indicating the number, and a message was tried on all 40 sets of stecker. It came out on 28 and showed up the four dummy letters and the rest was easy. So, but for an inspired guess, we might not have discovered this new notation for several days. Once discovered, on balance the change helped us for, although it made the recovering of the basic key from an initial Uhr break more difficult, it simplified running on an Uhr message as the message had to begin in the fifth place.

A captured document on Enigma Uhr which we subsequently obtained shows that this second notation was that originally intended by the Germans. They made a great security mistake in adopting the inferior method of starting off with the number encoded in the basic key as this drew our attention to the problem, and told us that some transformation of the Jaguar stecker was the answer. If the Germans had adopted their pre-arranged system, the messages would have been considered dud and probably ascribed to a separate key. We would eventually have broken on a crib – when we had run a correct crib on a *reciprocal* Uhr — and then the connection with the basic stecker would have been noticed, but this might have taken a considerable time. The Germans, by departing from the explicit instructions of the devisers of this gadget, greatly weakened its security value.

Summary

Enigma Uhr was a highly ingenious device and gave full entertainment value to the machine experts of Hut 6. It was regarded by the Germans as increasing markedly the security of the Enigma machine. This was not done in fact, partly due to two German mistakes. Had they concentrated the use of Uhr more – e.g., had they made Jaguar, the key where they used it most, an all-Uhr key — and had they used the alphabetical notation from the start, they would have made our initial Uhr break much more difficult. As so often, the Germans' piecemeal methods were their ruin. Even so, Enigma Uhr remains a highly complicated and intricate device, which yet does not from the security angle come within a thousand miles of the mechanically much simpler Reflector D.

In order to make Enigma Uhr a really dangerous device — something that would have upset our breaking technique — its basic principle of stecker transformation should have been carried further. For example, what would have been the effect of Enigma Uhr if the Uhr had been used in every message and made to *move on one position for each letter encoded*, thus giving rise to a cycle of 40 stecker sets inside every message. Such a device would have necessarily involved radical changes in our bombe design, if not perhaps the invention of wholly new machines.

UHR STATISTICS

KEY	No. Of Breaks	First Break	Last Break
Jaguar	189	10 July 1944	9 April 1945
Cricket	39	10 July 1944	20 November 1944
Lily	7	16 July 1944	24 August 1944
Snowdrop	18	17 July 1944	15 August 1944
Red	31	22 July 1944	16 April 1945
Daffodil	25	18 November 1944	23 Janurary 1945
Narcissus	8	15 November 1944	22 November 1944
Lion	17	2 December 1944	27 April 1945
Gentian	1	29 December 1944	29 December 1944
Beetle	5	21 January 1945	6 March 1945
Puma	2	21 February 1945	27 February 1945
Aster	6	2 March 1945	10 April 1945
Leopard	2	4 April 1945	6 April 1945
Moth	1	14 April 1945	14 April 1945
Wasp	4	21 April 1945	26 April 1945
TOTALS	355	**10 July 1944**	**27 April 1945**

Zusatz Stecker

The May scare

In May 1944 the Germans introduced the most silly and trivial of their security devices, and yet the forewarning we received of their intention to do so caused considerable fluttering of the dovecotes. The reason was that the decode references to the impending change were — from our viewpoint — very cryptic. This was not due to intentional obscurities on the enemy's part, but in the messages we intercepted and read, he was merely making incidental references to documents not in our hands. What was abundantly clear was that on any one day, three different sets of stecker were to be in use on any one key. It was anybody's guess whether the sets were to be altogether different, or whether the transformations would be effected by some predictable rule, as in the analogous case of the wheel order change.

Hut 6 prepared for the worst — three completely different sets of stecker. This would mean that every key would have to be broken three times over, indefinitely, except for the second and third breaks one would presumably know the wheel order and ringstellung and could run on hoppity [a type of bombe or menu designed to allow for successive turnover assumptions, made possible by a knowledge of the position of the right-hand ringstellung clip] menus, which mean shorter cribs. This possibility was in one way providential as there were few, if any keys, where we could have produced, every day in the relevant periods, three full-dress cribs. However, we were faced with the necessity of a great expansion of our records as we might have to use as cribs beginners or signatures we had previously despised and hence left unrecorded. Under the superintendence of the Qwatch, an enlarged scheme of records was set on foot and all embryo cribs were carefully noted.

A damp squib
What happened was an anti-climax – although this was fortunate, as the attempt to break three separate sets of stecker daily on every Air key would have lead to immediate bottlenecks in staff and bombes. As it is very doubtful whether we could, at this late period of the war, have materially added to our cryptographic staff, we might well have been faced with the dilemma of relaxing our efforts on the Air keys through sheer deficiency of staff from the Army side, with consequent damage to the Army prospects. It is fortunate that we were spared such a Procrustean choice.

The Germans took the following action: the stecker was changed at 0300, 1500 and 2300, giving three stecker periods called by us R, S and T. In combination with the already existing wheel order periods, X, Y

German Security Devices - 3

and Z the 24 hours from 0300 to 0300 we now divided into five key periods: 0300-1059 RX, 1100-1449 RY, 1500-1859 SY, 1900-2259 SZ and 2300-0259 TZ. Each set of stecker consisted, as usual, of 10 stecker pairs plus six self-stecker, but at 1500 one of the original stecker pairs was unsteckered and two of the originally self-steckered letters were steckered together. At 2300 the same process was repeated with another of the <u>original</u> 10 stecker pairs and two more letters of the <u>original</u> six self-stecker, e.g., Red for 1 May 1944:

```
R    A/E B/Y D/G F/J H/L K/O M/R P/U S/X T/V    C I N Q W Z
S    A/E B/Y D/G F/J H/L I/Z K/O M/R S/X T/V    C N P Q U W
T    A/E B/Y F/J H/L I/Z K/O M/R N/Q S/X T/V    C D G P U W
```

It is obvious that the alteration in the stecker is so slight that it is, in general, a fairly simple matter – with some knowledge of cribs or even without – to deduce the other two sets from any given set. Serious difficulty only arose when traffic in one period was very small. Thus it was not always possible on certain keys to recover the T stecker. It is surprising that the Germans thought such a trivial alteration gave any additional cipher security worth bothering about. The Machine Room gave great assistance in working out the stecker changes.

Extent of change
The Army, characteristically, had nothing to do with this half-baked innovation, but Zusatz Stecker was employed by all Air keys until about 15 June, when it was dropped generally as suddenly as it came into use. Brown III, which characteristically had been very slow to get the scheme straight – to begin with the Brown operators simply pulled out one end of a stecker plug and stuck it in somewhere else in an unoccupied hole – was equally characteristically the last key to use this trick, keeping it on to 14 July. The abandonment was hailed with jubilation by all concerned as Zusatz Stecker had become simply an annoyance and time-wasting nuisance, the more so as its solution had not the compensating value of demanding much cryptographic skill.

The German idea
It is difficult to suggest any really satisfactory and adequate motive for the German introduction of this paltry nuisance. It may be suggested that it is in line with the remarkable German nervousness over depth (e.g., change of wheel order), and in particular that it was introduced

as a stop-gap until Enigma Uhr, a more radical stecker change idea, was ready. The whole conception suggests the ignorance of the layman: Zusatz Stecker can scarcely have been born in the brain of a professional cryptographer. It is not improbable that the Germans themselves gave it up in disgust, eventually realising that such a futile key-change was not even worth the trouble it caused to their own operators.

NOT-Schlüssel

Introduction

The use by the Germans in certain circumstances of NOT-Schlüssel (emergency keys) is, as a security measure, not quite in the same category as those already discussed. The object was not to render cryptography more difficult but to give a quick method of distributing new keys in case of compromise, particularly to isolated garrisons. The method adopted was to devise a system by which an Enigma key could be generated by a single keyword while the discriminant was found from another word. The two words could be selected from an emergency list held in reserve or, in case of need, sent over the air in Enigma. This last procedure was actually most insecure as we had captured the German instructions, and so could devise the key from the key word as well as they could – but this knowledge was hidden from them.

First system

The first system used by the Germans was employed wholly by the GAF as far as we know and was explained in two documents that came into our hands in the middle of August 1944. The procedure is best described by an example:

Let the keyword (schlüsselwort) be OSTSEEFISCH (C H, C K are not to be replaced by Q – also an umlaut is ignored). We first strike out all but the first example of any repeated letter giving the "fillet" OSTEFICH. We then write underneath this fillet in alphabetical order all the *other* letters of the alphabet thus:

6	7	8	2	3	5	1	4
O	S	T	E	F	I	C	H
A	B	D	G	J	K	L	M
N	P	Q	R	U	V	W	X
Y	Z						

and (as shown) number the letters in the fillet alphabetically. We then read off the letters by columns, in the numbered order, and arrange them to form a rectangle 13 x 2, thus:

C	L	W	E	G	R	F	J	U	H	M	X	I
K	V	O	A	N	Y	S	B	P	Z	T	D	Q
4			1	5			2				3	

We number from 1 to 5 the five letters in the bottom row that come earliest in the alphabet and then read off the key thus:

Wheelorder: 4 1 5 (the first three numbers from the left)

Ringstellung C E G (the letters of the top row above those numbered letters that give the wheelorder)

Stecker pairs: L/V W/O R/Y F/S J/B U/P H/Z M/T X/D I/Q

It should be noticed that all the normal key rules disappear. In particular, consecutive stecker are impossible. There is, however, one way of identifying a broken key as NOT – the (German) ringstellung involves letters that are self-steckered. (This one can be used as a short cut to the ringstellung of a NOT-key).

The discriminant of a NOT-key is obtained from the Kenngruppenwort by using the 1st, 3rd and 5th letters. There is thus only one discriminant a key and stutters are quite possible.

First appearance of the NOTS

These emergency keys were first used towards the end of August when a number of unidentified discriminants appeared on the Snowdrop frequency 4560. Nigel Forward was able to demonstrate that the key was the first of the NOTS by deducing the generating word NORDLIGHT. This and all later NOT-keys were entered in a special NOT key book. (This was because in principle NOT-keys were independent of date and our normal key book was arranged by date. However, the NOT Guernsey keys did change daily and were usually entered in our regular key book as well as in the special NOT key book).

Guernsey saga or the Qwatch and the Forty NOTS

Now we arrive at the great NOT period. From the beginning of September 1944 onwards Row 70 of the Jaguar star A began using NOT-keys, used by the unfortunate 'General der L.W. Kanalinseln', whose HQ was in Germany and was now completely cut off. He had no regular key and could not get one, hence his constant use of emergency keys. A list of the discriminant cycle from 1 September to 10 October is shown below. The discriminants from 1 to 5 September are bracketed, as no traffic was actually passed on these keys, but it is known that these are the discriminants that would have been used:

Sept		Sept		Sept		Oct	
1	(OEN)	11	HSL	21	FIC	1	HSL
2	(TAE)	12	ASR	22	KSM	2	ASR
3	(PED)	13	TBK	23	LPO	3	TBK
4	(KKO)	14	BGE	24	EHB	4	BGE
5	(TAS)	15	NBN	25	BHS	5	NBN
6	TBK	16	PRE	26	DEK	6	PRE
7	ASH	17	NRL	27	TCR	7	NRL
8	TEN	18	OTE	28	TIH	8	OTE
9	HRE	19	NMO	29	ERH	9	NMO
10	DNN	20	DNN	30	TAC	10	RNG

In this unimpressive list of trigrams is locked the secret of the forty NOTS. The keywords from 8 to 10 September were given as follows:

	Schlüsselwort	Kenngruppenwort
8	Ostseefisch	Trennschnitt
9	Nimrod	Harfe
10	Randgebiet	Duenenlandschaft

and this was the beginning of our building up the series of 'forty code words'. Some other keys were also broken on re-encipherments and NOT/ASH, with its codeword NORDLICHT, was already known.

From now on the situation got steadily more complicated. First, it became clear that the "one discriminant, one key" theory was not universally true. It will be noticed that up to 30 September there are two cases of repeated discriminants in the list, namely, TBK on 6 and 13 September, DNN on 10 and 20 September. Now, on 10 and 20 September the same key decoded all the traffic. It did not decode anyone else's TBK traffic, nor even Row 70's traffic on 6 September. It was fortunately possible to disprove the theory that the key E/TBK had been worked out wrongly by the Germans, for we were able to recover the generating word PFERDEKOPPEL (= paddock).

In October the mystery deepened. As will have been noticed, the discriminant from 1 to 9 October traffic did not come out on the September keys, several of which had been broken. Fortunately, we were quickly able to break NOT-Guernsey of 4 October on a re-encipherment from Raster [a hand cipher which replaced Double Playfair as the type of non-machine cipher most closely associated in use and content with Enigma]. The General continued to use a Raster key in happy ignorance that it was already at Bletchley Park. The key was found to be completely different from NOT/BGE key used on 14 September. Once again we tried to break the keyword and soon arrived at the fillet ENHOBAK, which did not look like any German word. However, about the same time there was a somewhat obscure message finally translated as follows:

> Key message from 1/10 0300 hours
> Kenngruppennworte as Schluesselworte, read backwards, beginning with Laufende Nr. 1. Kenngruppen
> from the Schluesselworte, read forwards.

With this hint of reading backwards we reversed the fillet to read KABOHNE. This suggested KAKAOBOIINE, which read forward gave the fillet KAOBHNE (which generated the key of 14 September) and read backwards the fillet ENHOBAK (note that the fillet from a backward word is not necessarily a backward fillet) – which generated the key of 4 October. Also, KAKAOBOHNE is clearly one of the original discriminant words – see KKO on 4 September.

It was by this time clear that the General had been given a list of 10 pairs of code words which he had used straight from 1-10 September and afterwards in several varied ways. It is possible to derive 40 keys from 10 pairs of words by using each word in turn as the keyword and using it first forwards and then backwards. The General's scheme was soon discovered to be as follows, if we denote the original Schluesselwort by S and the original Kenngruppenwort by K:

	Schlüsselwort	Kenngruppenwort
1-10 September	S forwards	K forwards
11-20 September	K forwards	S forwards
21-30 September	S backwards	K backwards
1-10 October	K backwards	S forwards
11-20 October	S backwards	K backwards

(from no. 10 to 1)

It was possible to deduce the scheme up to 10 October from the keys already broken and the scheme from the 11th to the 20th was given to us in a message of the 10th. It will be seen that only 40 keys are possible and are all used in the period 1 September to 10 October, so, in order to have NOT-Guernsey out until the General got a new set of words, we had merely to find the 40 code words. A number were already known by analysis from the keys and from source, but the attack was now pressed forward more systematically under the guidance of the Qwatch. It was now much easier to find the keyword for broken keys, for in every case we could say "the discriminant formed from the keyword for which we are looking is (say) TAE, therefore the word is T.A.E..." In this way, keyword after keyword was discovered and more and more keys written out.

It was also possible to discover keywords even when the key had not been broken. For example on 25 September the discriminant was BHS and on 5 September TAS. Hence the generating word must be T.A.S...... .....S.H.B., the central dots representing an unknown number of letters. Another skeleton crossword clue was A.S.H.........R.C.T. Both of these were solved by fortunate inspirations and the aid of dictionaries, and we were ultimately successful in hammering out the complete list which is printed below.

FINAL LIST OF KEYWORDS AND DISCRIMINANT WORDS

Lfd. Nr.	Schlüsselwort	Kenngruppenwort
1	HASELRUTE	OZEANSCHIFF
2	ANSTRICHFARBE	TRAUERMUSIK
3	TABAKPFEIFE	PFERDEKOPPEL
4	BAGGERSCHIFF	KAKAOBOHNE
5	NEBENHAUS	TRANSPORTNACHSCHUB
6	PFRIEM	TABAKFELD
7	NORDLICHT	ANSCHAUUNGSUNTERRICHT
8	OSTSEEFISCH	TRENNSCHNITT
9	NIMROD	HARFE
10	RANDGEBIET	DUNENLANDSCHAFT

It will be noticed that this list clears up the mystery of the two E/TBK keys referred to above, as there are two words that give the discriminant TRK.

It is perhaps worth noting as a minor point that, while the key derived from a word written backwards is in general quite different from the

German Security Devices - 3

straight key, in certain special cases there is a good deal of similarity. One such is when the keyword has six different letters and the column numbers differ by three on columns 1, 2, 3 and 4, 5 and 6 (reading from left to right). An example is the word PFRIEM, where the similarity of the two 13 x 2 rectangles is noteworthy, e.g.

```
       5  2  6  3  1  4        4  1  3  6  2  5
       P  F  R  I  E  M        M  E  I  R  F  P
       A  B  C  D  G  H        A  B  C  D  G  H
       J  K  L  N  O  Q        J  K  L  N  O  Q
       S  T  U  V  W  X        S  T  U  V  W  X
       Y  Z                    Y  Z

    E GOWFB KTZIDNV          E B KTZFGOW I CL U
    MHQ XPA JSYRCLU          MA J SYPHQX RDNV
    3        1 4      2 5    5 1 4       3        2
```

give the keys:

         314 GBK   C/D E/M F/P I/R L/N O/Q S/T U/V W/X Y/Z
and   514 EBK   C/D F/P G/H I/R L/N O/Q S/T U/V W/X Y/Z

with two wheels, two ringstellung letters and nine stecker pairs in common.

To conclude the Guernsey saga we should give an example of deriving the keyword from the broken key. The following example was broken with no information as to the word. Later, normally three letters of the word were known, which is, naturally, a great help. The general process is a mixture of logical deduction plus trial and error.

<u>EXAMPLE</u>: Given a key, to find the keyword.

    NOT/ASH   4 5 1   AVC   (German CYD)
    B/H E/I F/Q J/U K/W L/P M/S O/V R/Z T/X
          A C D G N Y

We must have: C Y D
                 G N A
                 4 5 1

Hence no letter between G and N is on bottom line, so that
            H I J K L M

BEUWPS

are all that way up. This fixes B as 2, E as 3 and makes HB and IE to the right of DA in the 13 x 2 block. Also from the numbering FQ is that way up.

Now A, B, E are not in the word (or they would be in the top row in the 13 x 2 block) and if D is, it is not the first letter alphabetically, i.e., if D is, C is also. From our knowledge of German it is almost certain that if C is, H is also. Let us suppose as a reasonable guess that C and H are both in the word. The letter preceding A in the 13 x 2 block must be in the word. If there is nothing between YN and DA this letter is N, which is by no means improbable. If we are right so far, D is the word, otherwise Y, an unlikely letter, would be. Thus (bracketing letters known to be in the word) we now have as our skeleton for the 13 x 2 block:

(C)	Y	(D)	(H)
G	(N)	A	B

Now what is to follow D?
A, B, C, G, H are impossible from the figure and E because I are the right way up. F is E the first possibility we come to and we know F is in the top row. Also (N) A Q is a reasonable collection as A must begin the second row of the original block and Q is about where we might be in the last row.

So let us try:

(C)	Y	(D)	F	(H)
G	(N)	A	Q	B

The letter after B must be soon after Q in the alphabet. It cannot be R which would imply (H) Z – impossible. Let us try S – this implies that R is in the word and we observe a good place for (R) is after S, which gives the plausible combination (H) M Z on top, thus:

(C)	Y	(D)	F	(H)	M	Z
G	(N)	A	Q	B	S	(R)

and

N		D		C	H
A	B	E	F	G		M
Q	S				Y	Z

C and H coming together is equivalent to a confirmation – the rest is easy. From the second diagram the original fillet must be nine letters, so

German Security Devices - 3

there are two more columns to be filled in apart from the obvious spaces. We must have:

```
N  ?  ?  D  ?  ?  C  H  ?
A  B  E  F  G  ?  ?  M  ?
Q  S  ?  ?  ?  ?  Y  Z
```

We know R is the word and <u>one</u> of the letters T, U, V, W, X must be – T and U are the most likely. Two of I, J, K, L are also in the word and one of O P. I C H seems irresistible and we see the light – the answer is NORDLICHT. The completed blocks are as under:

```
6 7 8 2 5 4 1 3 9
N O R D L I C H T      (C) K  Y (D) F V (H) M Z (I) J X (L)
A B E F G J K M P      G W (N) A  Q (O) B  S (R) E U (T) P
Q S U V W X Y Z
```

While hardly falling under the category of machine cryptography, exercises of this nature were a pleasant pastime for Hut 6, and by no means of academic importance, as has been shown. It could, perhaps, be mentioned that the above example is, as it happens, easier than the general rule.

The plague of NOTS

NOT-Guernsey was regularly broken up to the end of the year and on a few days later. The General, incidentally, eventually got a new set of codewords, but kindly told us how he intended to use them, so the cryptographic interest was ended. The GAF, however, continued to use this NOT-system whenever necessary, in particular from 12-16 January a perfect plague of NOTS raged on the Ocelot system during a compromise. No fewer than 24 NOT-keys were broken, mostly on re-encipherments. In few, if any, was an attempt made to find the keyword, as this was an academic exercise when there was no reason to suppose that the word was going to be used again.

New-style NOT-keys

In December 1944 the Germans gave full details of a new style of NOT-keys in a document *Anleitung zum Ableiten des Notschlüssels für die Schlüsselmachine Enigma* — full details of a new style of NOT-keys.

This was definitely an improvement – a pair of code-words gave keys for a month, and yet there was perfect security, as the codeword is virtually unbreakable from a given key. The following is a translation of the document:

NOTSCHLÜSSEL

1. What it consists of:
   The Notschlüssel consists of two key words (Lösungswörter) of different lengths. From the longer, the Schlüsselwort, are deduced machine set-ups which change from day to day, and from the shorter, the Kennwort, is deduced the Kenngruppe.

2. Period of validity
   The same Lösungswörter (i.e., Schlüsselwort and Kennwort) are to be used for not more than 30 days, including the day when they first come into force. Its use may be continued over the end of the month in which it is issued within the limit of 30 days. A Notschlüssel which has come into force should, as soon as possible, be replaced by an Ersatz Schlüssel.

3. Choice of the Lösungswörter
   The Schlüsselwort must be at least 12 letters long. The Kennwort must be at least 5 and should at the most be 10 letters long. Both Lösungswörter should be part of the normal vocabulary of the Funktruppführer and should admit of no ambiguity in spelling. In the Lösungswörter, ch and ck should not be replaced by q. Similarly, j should not be replaced by i. ä, ö, ü should be written ae, oe, ue. The two Lösungswörter should have no affinity of meaning (e.g., strassenbahn (tramway) and Schaffner (conductor)). There should be no limitation to a particular class of word in their choice (e.g., nouns).

4. Process for the deduction of the Notschlüssel
   From the schlüsselwort a machine-setting (wheelorder, ringstellung and stecker) is constructed. This is called the Hilfsschlüssel. A table in the lid of the Enigma gives 31 different grundstellungen for the different days of the month. With

the Enigma set up according to the Hilfsschlüssel and the Grundstellung, the schlüsselwort must be tapped out four times. From the resulting succession of encoded letters (different every day), the Notschlüssel (stecker, ringstellung and wheelorder) is constructed. Considered separately, the Hilfsschlüssel and the Notschlüssel are constructed in the following way:

5. Construction of the Hilfsschlüssel

    Wheelorder: Always 1 2 3 (on the evidence of a prisoner of war, this rule has been superseded and the wheelorder now changes every three days).
    Ringstellung: Last three letters of the Schlüsselwort.
    Stecker: The different letters of the Schlüsselwort, in their order in the Schlüsselwort, are collected in pairs from the beginning of the word, provided that in the process new and consistent pairs result. These pairs are to be steckered. If there are less than 10 pairs, the stecker process should *not* be extended to the customary 10 pairs.
    Uncle D: If used, always to be alphabetically plugged:

    AB CD EF GH IK LM NO PQ RS TU VW XZ

6. Grundstellung

    Fixed table in the lid of the Enigma:

1	2	3	4		26	27	28	29	30	31
01	02	03	04		26	01	02	03	04	05
01	02	03	04		26	02	03	04	05	06
01	02	03	04		26	03	04	05	06	07

Use of the table

Look for the number of the day of the month in the first row of the table. The three numbers underneath are the Grundstellung for the encoding of the Schlüsselwort.

7. Construction of the Notschlüssel

    The Hilfsschlüssel and Grundstellung to be set up according to para 5 and 6 and the Schlüsselwort tapped out four times.

8. From the succession of encoded letters obtained according to para 7, the following is deduced:

Stecker
Different letters in succession are to be steckered together, therefore the letters in the given order should be immediately steckered. The first three letters which occur more than once and are therefore no longer "steckerable" are to be ringed round. If there are less than 10 pairs, the stecker process should not be extended to the usual 10 pairs, but only the existing pairs are to be steckered. If there are ten or more pairs, the first ten should be steckered. If there is an uneven number of different letters, the last of these is to be ignored.

Ringstellung
The first three repeated (ringed) letters.

Wheelorder
The last five letters (corresponding to the number of wheels) are to be numbered 1 to 5 according to their position in the alphabet. If a letter occurs more than once, the numbering is done according to the position of the letters within the five-letter group, e.g.:

a	m	c	m	p	
1	3	2	4	5	= wheelorder

The last three of these numbers gives the wheelorder.
Uncle D: If used, always alphabetically plugged: AB, CD, EF, GH, IK, LM, NO, PQ, RS, TU, VW, XZ.

9. Kenngruppe
The first, third and fifth letters of the Kennwort from the Kenngruppe. The Kenngruppe does not change daily but remains the same as long as the Notschlüssel remains valid. It is to be used as seldom as possible.

10. If it is necessary to write down the key deduced, each letter of the pair should be put in alphabetical order, and then the pairs written down in alphabetical order according to the first letter of the pair. All other workings involved in the deduction of Notschlüssel are to be destroyed without a trace.

EXAMPLE (illustrating preceding paragraphs)

1. Notschlüssel
   Landerziehungsheim   (= Schlüsselwort)
   Rutschen   (= Kennwort

German Security Devices - 3

2. Notschlüssel for March is used from 27 March to 9 April (in any case not after 25 April).

3. <u>Hilfsschlüssel</u>
   Wheelorder: I   II   III
   Ringstellung   EIM = 05 09 13

   Stecker:

   L A N D E R Z I (E) H U (N) G S (H) (E) (I) (M)

   LA ND ER ZI HU GS (M)

4. 28.3.45 = date 28
   Corresponding Grundstellung: 02 03 04

5. L   A   N   D   E   R   Z   I   E   H   U   N   G   S   H   E   I   M
    z   o   m (m) a   p   j   v   d (p) l   r   k (m) f   t   k   k
    f   t   m   c   n   s   o   o   g   x   d   c   u   m   r   a   l   x
    c   s   g   x   g   f   c   d   g   t   o   m   x   f   t   g   o   t
    m   j   d   r   k   v   x   t   d   r   l   u   v   a   m   c   m   p
   (cipher text invented)

6. <u>Stecker</u>

   ZO MA PJ VD LR KF TC NS GX ?

   <u>Ringstellung</u>   (ringed in the example)

   (m) (p) (m) = 13 16 13

   <u>Wheelorder</u>
   a m c m p
   1 3 <u>2</u> <u>4</u> <u>5</u>   =   II IV V

7. <u>Kenngruppe</u>

   <u>r</u> u <u>t</u> s <u>c</u> h e n

8. AM CT DV FK GX JP LR NS OZ

It will be seen that it is (unless one is extremely fortunate) impossible to deduce the Schlüsselwort from the key and so generate the remaining keys. Also, that keys so made up are unrecognisable externally except for the unchanging discriminant (which is to be used as little as possible) and the chance that they may have less than ten stecker pairs. The scheme was not, so far as we know, used by the GAF – to the end their NOTS were of the original type. But one Army key NOT/AFE was of this class, as the discriminant lasted for about a month. The key was broken on 19 March and was:

234 XDP
B/Y D/W F/S G/V K/N L/P M/O Q/Z R/U T/X A C E H I J
(German)

If he relishes the task, the reader is invited to beat Hut 6 by finding the codeword! One peculiarity about this new system should be mentioned. It will have been noticed that provision was made for D – and the NOT D was duly entered as D 307 in our records. But it is clear that on a mixed B and D key, construction of the NOT-key as directed means that the key as used with B and as used with D will be different. This can hardly have been intended. Either it is an oversight or the compiler disregarded the possibility of mixed keys, taking it for granted that a NOT-key would be all-B or all-D.

Conclusions

The two systems of constructing NOT-keys were equally ingenious, but the second is preferable on security grounds as it gives a month's keys from a pair of words while keeping the codewords inviolate. These systems were only intended for use in emergencies. However, NOT-keys have certain advantages over keys made up in the normal way owing to their freedom from rules of keys which may help the enemy cryptographer. They would, however, have the fatal objection for regular use that, if the actual key is generated from one word, the number of possible keys is limited so drastically that some kind of key index becomes possible. For instance, on the second system, the number of keys is determined by the number of German words at least 12 letters long – which must surely be much less than 100,000.

It would appear that the regular use of any system of deriving keys from key-words could never be secure unless two conditions were satisfied:

1. that the method adopted did not, in itself, give rise to any peculiarity or rule in the keys; and

2. that the number of possible keys was not substantially reduced by the method of derivation. In practice, to satisfy the second condition, it would be necessary to derive each key from more than one keyword.

Chapter 14
German Security Devices - 4

C Y, Random Indicators, Wahlworts, The Mosse Code and Double Encoding

Introduction:
About the middle of September 1944 a new German security device was noticed, first on a few Jaguar and Barnyard links. A number of messages were observed to go off into nonsense in the middle and it was quickly noticed hat this always happened just after the decode read CY followed by two consecutive letters, e.g., RS. It was soon discovered that the left-hand wheel could be decoded if immediately after CYRS the left-hand wheel was set to the first of the two consecutive letters (in this case R). While the consecutive letters were not always the same, the CY was invariable.

Extension of the practice
Apart from the Jaguar messages mentioned above – and these were very few in number – CY was purely an Army idea and it spread fairly quickly to all Army keys and SS keys. It was later discovered that the Police key – Roulette – was the first key to use CY, as the device appeared in one early September day that came out rather late. By October, CY was in practically universal use on all Army and SS keys except on short messages.

The German regulations
In October 1944 we captured a German document entitled *Anderungen bei Schlüsseln mit Maschinenschlüssel*. The second section of this document dealt with CY and a translation follows:

RESETTING WHEELS WITHIN MESSAGES

1. The cipher clerk will interrupt the ciphering of the text of the message in all messages of 150-250 letters (250 letters was the length limit for German Enigma messages. This regulation, at least, was well observed) once between the 70th And 130th letters, e.g., at the 93rd letter.

2. The interruption will occur at a place chosen at random. In no circumstances may the interruption take place regularly at the same place, e.g., the 100th letter, or always at the end of a five-letter group. It is recommended to introduce it at the end of a word or sentence of the Klartext.

3. After interrupting the enciphering, the cipher clerk will read off the position reached at the left-hand wheel, e.g., 21, and will choose, at random, without at first altering the positions of the left-hand wheel, a new position which must be at least five stages removed from the position reached.

4. The cipher clerk then establishes in the usual manner which letter corresponds to the new value, e.g., 06 = F. He will then encipher, still without previously altering the position of the left-hand wheel, first as a <u>Weisergruppe</u> CY, and then the letter showing the new value and the letter immediately following it alphabetically, in the example F and G. He will add the four resultant enciphered letters to the cipher text so far written out.

5. The cipher clerk will then set the left-hand wheel at the new position (in the example 06) and will continue to encipher the message in the usual way.

6. In deciphering, the reverse process is to be carried out. Messages or message parts with a length of 150 messages or more are to be given particular attention between the 70th and 130th letters. Should the Weisergruppe CY appear, deciphering is to be stopped after tapping out the next two letters of the cipher text. The "clear" letter after the Weisergruppe CY is to be converted to a two-figure number in the usual manner. The left-hand wheel is to be set at this number and the deciphering continued.

These German regulations were ordered to come into force on 15 September 1944, and on the whole were strictly obeyed by the Army. Occasionally CY would be omitted in a long message or used in a message less than 150 letters long.

German Security Devices - 4

Effect on breaking

The most important result of CY was that it effectively ruled out cillying, which was now (if it occurred at all) very hard to spot. Whether from this cause or from the concomitant introduction of random indicators, cillying virtually ceased on Army traffic and SS keys, a loss that would have been more serious had not cillies already been very rare (except on Orange).

Other difficulties were that the insertion of the four dummy letters at an unknown spot upset cribs – particularly top and tail shots – and more especially re-encodements. It was a help to have the German regulations so that we knew when to expect CY and most cribs did not run into the danger zone. Greenshank re-encipherments were especially affected as (because of the presence of D) it was necessary to write out <u>at the very least</u> 80 letters correctly and (even apart from CY) this was by no means easy. Yet it is surprising how often these difficulties were overcome, and the position of CY fixed, at least approximately (sometimes exactly because of the usual tendency to insert CY after a break in the sense). While a distinct nuisance to the investigator of re-encipherments, CY did not overthrow our matured technique.

In one minor aspect CY was an advantage. On occasion – particularly when a day came out on the beginning of a message – it provided a short cut to the ringstellung, which was often taken advantage of by Army cryptographers. (If CY had been widely used on Air keys it would have increased the difficulty of breaking on Uhr substitution on a dottery).

Conclusion

CY is probably best thought of as a device for removing (if only to a slight degree) one of the main theoretical defects of the Enigma – the extreme regularity of its wheel motion. In default of a mechanical method of producing a more irregular motion (the Germans had planned to introduce this later) the idea of breaking the continual uniformity by an unpredictable change once in each message is not without merit, although it is essentially only a makeshift.

Random Indicators: The Regulations

The German document printed above contained in the first half, regulations for the security device Hut 6 named 'Random Indicators'. It will be convenient to quote the salient parts of this document:

CHOICE AND USE OF THE INDICATOR (SPRUCHSCHLÜSSEL)

I. Definitions

1. The six letters inserted in the preamble of a message enciphered with Enigma after the number of letters or, as the case may be, after the discriminant group denote (according to H.Dv.g.14 – *Introduction to Cipher Machine Enigma*) the Grundstellung and the Spruchschlüssel, previously chosen at random by the cipher clerk. In the following instruction, terms will be used as follows:

a. "Grundstellung" has the same meaning as hitherto.
b. "Spruchstellung" will replace what has previously been called "Spruchschlüssel".
c. "Spruchschlüssel" will denote "Grundstellung" and "Spruchstellung" together.

2. The "Spruchschlüsselliste" contains the "Spruchschlüssel" for one day. It is to be made up by the Funkleiter or his deputy (Funktruppführer). It changes daily at 0300 hours.

II. Procedure for arriving at the Spruchschlüssel

3. The Funkleiter or his deputy must:

 a. choose a random Klartext of general content (texts from books, songs, letters etc., but not texts of service or official content).

 b. set a cipher machine Enigma as follows:

  (aa) Wheelorder: I II III
  (bb) Ringstellung: 01 01 01
  (cc) Stecker connections: 10 stecker connections, chosen completely at random, are to be plugged. The stecker connections of any day's key must not be used.
  (dd) Grundstellung: at random, e.g., 13 07 21

 c. The Klartext chosen according to (a) is to be tapped

out on the cipher machine set according to (b). The resultant enciphered letters are to be entered in the Spruchschlüsselliste consecutively in groups of six letters. Each group is a Spruchschlüssel. As many groups are to be obtained as will cover the daily requirements in Spruchschlüssel.

III. Spruchschlüsselliste

4. Spruchschlüssellisten are to be prepared in duplicate – they are to be marked with the date of compilation and signed by the compiler.

5. The Spruchschlüsselliste is in general to be compiled daily. It is, however, permitted to compile Spruchschlüssellisten at slack times for several (at the most ten) days in advance. These are, like cipher instructions, to be kept by the Funksbearbeiter who will issue a new list daily to the Funkleiter.

6. The original of the Spruchschlüsselliste is to be handed to the cipher clerk shortly before the change of the daily key. If it is handed over earlier it must be in an envelope or otherwise sealed. The envelope may only be opened by the cipher clerk shortly before the change of the daily key.

7. The second copy of a Spruchschlüsselliste is to be handed by the compiler to his immediate superior immediately after completion. In a duplicate copy the stecker connections, the selected Grundstellung and Klartext used to obtain the Spruchschlüsselliste must be detailed:

e.g., Duplicate copy of Spruchschlüsselliste No. 10

Stecker connections: KC GO RX DA MP TW HB LN SF VZ
Grundstellung: 3 07 21
Klartext: Gottfried Keller, der gruene Heinrich,
S.23, Absatz 2 ff.
(Sgd) Meier, Wachtmeister and deputy Funkleiter

8. Should all the Spruchschlüssel not be used up on the day for which the Spruchschlüsselliste has been compiled, those not used can be taken over unchanged in the Spruchschlüsselliste of another

day. In this case it must be clearly shown (in coloured pencil) on the duplicate copy of the Spruchschlüsselliste which Spruchschlüssel have been taken over and from which Spruchschlüsselliste.

9. On receiving the duplicate copy the station which monitors the W/T station concerned, is to carry out frequent tests to see whether the compilation of the Spruchschlüssel and its use is in accordance with the regulations. Offences are to be dealt with by taking disciplinary action.

IV. Handling the Spruchschlüssel

10. In enciphering

a. Set the Enigma on the new day's key.

b. Put the 1st Spruchschlüssel (= 1st six-letter group of theSpruchschlüsselliste) at the head of the message (part) to be enciphered.

c. Set the Enigma at the Grundstellung (Grundstellung = three letters at the right of the Spruchschlüssel).

d. Tap out the Spruchstellung (Spruchstellung = three letters at the right of the Spruchschlüssel).

e. Set the Enigma at the three letters resulting from tapping out the Spruchschlüssel.

f. Encipher the message.

g. Delete the Spruchschlüssel employed from the Spruchschlüsselliste.

h. On the message pad note the number of the Spruchschlüsselliste (No. = date).

11. The next Spruchschlüssel in order is to be used for each message (part) to be enciphered. In no circumstances may one and the same Spruchschlüssel be used again.

12. In deciphering

a. Enigma to be set at the day's key of the message to be deciphered.

b. Set the Enigma at the Grundstellung in the preamble of message to be deciphered.

c. Tap out on the Enigma the Spruchstellung in the preamble of the message to be deciphered.

d. Set the resultant letters on the Enigma.

e. Decipher message.

Extension of the system

It will be noticed that (as opposed to such devices as CY), there is no external indication of the use of the random indicators, but from various small scraps of evidence it seems not unlikely that it was used fairly extensively, at least on Army and SS keys. The evidence is:

1. These keys used CY punctiliously and thus might be expected to use the companion devices.

2. The sudden cessation of cillies on Orange and (to a lesser degree) Roulette is most easily explained by random indicators (in the case of Orange at least CY is not adequate in itself. In August 1944 long strings of keyboards had appeared and the use of CY will not conceal an absolutely first class cilli story, though it will camouflage a weak one).

3. The fairly frequent use of repeated indicators on Army keys is best explained by inadvertent breaches of rule 11 (caused, one imagines, by an omission to delete a used Spruchschlüssel).

4. The actual use of the device is proved by the capture of at least one Enigma set-up with wheelorder 1 2 3, ringstellung A A A (German) – see paragraph 3(b) – and by the later capture of more than one Spruchschlüsselliste.

Conclusion

It is impossible to interpret 'Random Indicators' as anything but an anti-cilli device – a far more radical one than CY. It does kill cillies and it is clear that the Germans had at least become conscious of this possible danger. The answer they now found to the danger of cillies was as effective as anything that could have been devised – short of a complete change of the indicating system – and it did lose us Orange. The only possible criticism we can make of the German action is that (as so often) it was too late. Cillies were dying when they were killed. The history of Hut 6 would have been different had the Germans, in the full flush of their 1940 triumphs, been able to spare a thought for the suppression of cillies.

Wahlworts

Introduction

A wahlwort (the German word quickly became naturalised in Hut 6 parlance and the attempt to introduce 'nonsense word' as an English equivalent never caught on) is a word, chosen at random by the encoder of a message and placed at the beginning or end for the sole purpose of defeating enemy cryptographers. This particular device has a long history prior to 1944. The first occurrence of wahlworts was on the African Army keys (the Finches) in December 1942. Early that month the Germans sent in Chaffinch a strong anti-crib warning to the effect that:

1. addresses and signatures were to be buried in messages, preceded by a warning signal, e.g., 'Here follows address'; and

2. addresses (if of standard length) were to be altered by the prefixing of nonsense words.

Long before the month was out the second instruction had been carried into effect (the proviso being disregarded), and a plague of wahlworts had infected all the African keys with the providential exception of Phoenix.

The effect on the breaking position was immediately serious. This first great wahlwort crisis was possibly not in itself much worse than subsequent crises on other colours, but for two reasons it produced a much greater impact on the Hut as a whole.

Firstly, the colours concerned were among the most important operational keys then being broken. They could not be laid aside if necessary (as could be done to a certain extent with wahlwort-ridden keys later on), and hence the increased bombe time they required had an immediate effect on the fortunes of other keys. Secondly, our bombe resources were still so limited that a prolonged crisis of this nature might (and at its worst moments did) rule out running of Research jobs altogether, a result that would not have been arrived at had a similar crisis occurred a year later when we had more bombes here as well as American resources.

Extension of wahlworts

Wahlworts were never used on SS keys and until the closing months of the war were mainly an Army device. It is difficult to describe their extension in terms of keys both accurately and briefly as there were many fluctuations, and throughout their use depended entirely on the habits of individual encoders. Moreover, when it is stated that a certain key at a certain time used wahlworts, this does not mean that every message on the key had a wahlwort. The cryptographer had to consider each individual case on its merits and try to assess, on the latest available evidence, whether the particular crib message on which he was working was likely to have a wahlwort or not. We can only trace extensions in general terms. On Army keys, from December 1942 to the end of the campaign in May 1943 wahlworts were freely and widely used on all African Army keys except Phoenix. But during the rest of 1943 it became clear – that in theory at least – the use of wahlworts was a general Army security measure. There was hardly any Army key that might not use wahlworts, although at this stage there were few that employed them as thoroughly as the African keys had done.

To cite examples, Raven used wahlworts in May, Buzzard, Cormorant and (to a lesser extent) Albatross in June, while Vulture (pronounced free of the plague in July 1943) had succumbed when the next break was made in August. In autumn 1943 and early 1944 wahlworts appeared on Bullfinch, Shrike and even Sparrow, which had originally been free of the nuisance. Wryneck (another victim of the epidemic) had, on the Rundspruch, one of its principal cribs, an interesting cycle which shows how everything depended on the encoder's habits. On day 1 the crib started and finished flat, i.e., without wahlwort or even signature and address. On day 2 it began with a wahlwort, followed by the address and ended with a signature, possibly followed by another wahlwort. Finally, on day 23, the crib began with wahlwort, address, signature and ended flat.

In the last year of the war, wahlworts were very fortunately not used to a predominant extent on Western Army keys with the exception of the general key Puffin. (OKH [Army High Command], who used wahlworts regularly, was particularly liable to speak on Puffin). However, the Eastern and Balkan keys had become more and more addicted to wahlworts. In fact, Avocet surpassed all other keys in consistency and thoroughness in this respect. So, by the end of the war, wahlworts were fairly universal on Army keys. Greenshank, however, was to the end a distinguished exception.

A few Air keys used wahlworts from an early date. Locust, for example, impaired the value of its excellent crib, the Synoptic Weather, by prefixing wahlworts in April 1943. At the same time Mustard, the key of the German Y service – a point not without significance – introduced the same device. Mustard remained faithful to wahlworts ever after, and in a short paper written on Mustard in March 1944, this was selected as one of the general characteristics of the key. While, in this case, the introduction of wahlworts did not shake off our hold completely, breaking certainly became more intermittent. It was not until 1944 that the situation was again satisfactory.

Apart from these exceptional cases, Air keys generally remained free of wahlworts until the closing months of the war. (The occasional use of nonsense words to fill up tuning messages is closely analogous to the wahlwort proper, but these messages are a special case). From December 1944 onwards the use of wahlworts spread rapidly from the Luftgau keys to Puma and Red until, eventually, virtually all the Air was infected. The effects in breaking varied greatly according to the strength of the existing cribs on the colour in question.

German use of wahlworts
The usual German practice was to use wahlworts at the beginning and end of each message, i.e., in part messages the wahlworts were at the beginning of the first part and the end of the last part. Occasionally, as on the Finches from January 1943 onwards, a more radical method was adopted by which wahlworts were used at the beginning and end of every part. It was fortunate that this extension of the practice was not universally adopted for (as was keenly realised at the time), it virtually eliminated the popular teil-break technique of solving re-encodements, and this made still harder the already sufficiently difficult African re-encipherments.

The length of the wahlworts might vary considerably and it was an important part of crib records to note each encoder's favourite length and hence to fix the limits within which cribs should be staggered. As a general rule (although in such a matter general rules are not much good) four to 14 letters was normal. Rare alike were wahlworts of three letters and the freaks of about 40. Two of the latter deserve to be handed down to the admiration of posterity. The first is the classic:

DONAUDAMPSSQUIFFAHRTGESELLSQAFTSKAPITAEN

used on a Locus Synoptic and on several occasions on the Finches, and the other is the remarkable tongue-twister:

HOTTENTOTENPOTENTATENTANTENATTENTAETER

(used on a Gadfly tuning message), which can be translated as "would-be-murderers-of-the-Hottentot-potentates'-aunts". It must be admitted that no other language than German would express the above idea in a single word!

The wahlwort might – and often was – immediately followed by the text of the message proper. However, some form of punctuation such as X or YY could be inserted. In the last month it became the rule on both Air and Army keys to mark out the wahlwort clearly by doubling the last two letters of the initial wahlwort and the first two letters of the final wahlwort and (assuming no intermediate punctuation) it was possible to use this doubling in making up menus. Thus, on Avocet II, which was often broken on GEHEIMEKOMMANDOSAQE, staggered to allow for an initial wahlwort, we could, if necessary, run (??) (??) GEHEIMEKOMMANDOSAQE, secure in the knowledge that each pair of queries would represent the same letter.

Finally, a word on the choice of wahlworts. In theory, this should have been purely random – in practice it was not. Nouns were almost invariably chosen. Individual operators had their favourite wahlworts, and some, e.g., SOMMER, WINTER and HUNGER occurred again and again. Sometimes the initial and final wahlworts in a message were connected in a sense, e.g., MUSIK ... TANZ, or in some other way there was an obvious appropriateness. Thus a long part message on Mustard once ended with the wahlwort In this case a misnomer as a phrase was used): GOTT SEI DANK.

But, in general, such peculiarities were not sufficiently consistent to be predictable and hence usable. There was one instructive exception to this rule. A Mustard operator became so attached to the wahlworts Guten ... Morgen, Guten ... Abend (each at the appropriate time of day), that it was reckoned at one time, viz., January 1944, that it was better than an even chance that these wahlworts were correct. This was of considerable assistance in reducing the crib versions worth running, and on several occasions the initial wahlwort 'Guten' was used successfully to eke out the otherwise brief crib (the Einsatz Mark I).

Effect on breaking

Such an exceptional tour de force, however, cannot outweigh the generally prejudicial effect of wahlworts on our success. It is evident that at best, i.e., when one has good cribs, the introduction of wahlworts may mean the running of three or four versions instead of one. With poor cribs that have several variant forms, the case is still worse. Moreover, if there are no real cribs at all, one can still do something even with 10-versional addresses if one has to try them in <u>one position only</u>, but otherwise the cost is prohibitive. It is for this reason that an address key like Gentian was ruined by wahlworts. As Lincoln might have said, you can run one variant in all positions or all variants in one position, but you can't run all variants in all positions. (Of course, such a statement is false in theory, but it is true in practice, as we never had so many bombes that we could ignore the cost in bombe-hours of breaking a key. This meant that for every key there was a limit of costliness beyond which breaks would be made at too extravagant a cost – i.e., at the expense of more valuable colours).

Thus the thorough use of wahlworts will, on almost any key, make breaking more expensive and on a key with a weak crib position may make it unbreakable except at extravagant cost. This is what eventually happened on the Finches, and what would very likely have happened on Avocet in the last months of the war had we not by then, in the light of the wahlwort peril and other dangers, increased our bombe resources to what would, at one time, have been considered wildly extravagant excess. It was only owing to this free bombe position that we were able to take the wahlwort strain as well as we did in these last months. Indeed, if the Germans had suddenly eliminated wahlworts and started their messages flat again, it is possible that, like Frankenstein, we should have proved unable to satisfy the monsters we had created.

Value of wahlworts

In wahlworts the Germans hit on a simple and effective method of making cribbing more difficult. It would have been still more effective but for the eternal German blunder of 'too little and too late'. Introduced in 1940 on a wholesale scale, wahlworts might have knocked out the infant Crib Room before it had got properly on its feet. But the Germans did not use the system at all until halfway through the war and not until the last few months used it on anything approaching a universal scale.

Yet, while a good anti-crib measure, the wahlwort is not the best possible prophylactic. It tends to make cribbing harder – but not impossible. The rival system (used on Roulette) of burying addresses and signatures in the middle of the message is perhaps preferable, although much depends on the nature of the traffic. But best of all such methods is the radical device of the cut. By this, any message is arbitrarily divided into two parts and the second part encoded first. This simple but effective proceeding should make cribbing quite impossible, except perhaps in the case of short messages where the complete text can be guessed. The final judgment on wahlworts must be that the Germans discovered a useful weapon against cribbery – but not a complete answer.

The Mosse Code
The Mosse Code – named after its author, Rudolf Mosse – was invented before the war as a purely commercial code. The code-words were adopted by the GAF and given new meanings. It was used by the Germans on Air keys – never on Army and SS keys – from early 1944 onwards, but it was not until 1945 that (in consequence of certain changes in its nature) it became a factor of some importance as an anti-crib measure. In origin it probably was not intended as such, but was meant (like most internal codes in a cipher) to secure brevity in encoding and perhaps to serve as a measure of internal security.

The meanings of some of the codewords were soon discovered from their context, but in September 1944, Hut 3 was able to publish, from captured documents, the complete code as used in March. It then consisted of about 500 five-letter codewords, the vast majority denoting individual units or commands in the GAF. Even then, a few codewords represented recurrent phrases, e.g.,

PAPIC = FEHLANZEIGE

and it was this element that was destined to become more pronounced. In 1945 the code was largely altered and its character changed. It was again possible to build it up from messages, and in April 1945 there was published a final revised list of the reconstructed code. It still consisted –

as always – of five-letter codewords, but now a far greater number stood for recurrent phrases as opposed to formations of the GAF. A few selected examples follow:

> FLYMI = FEHLANZEIGE
> GUFWY = VOLLZUGSMELDUNG
> JERRO = TAGESABSCHLUSSMELDUNG
> JIJUS = ABENDMELDUNG
> NEPER = EINSATZBEREITSCHAFTSMELDUNG
> ORHAF = LUFTLAGEBERICHT

And, in addition, dates, times and numbers could be represented by words beginning with T, U and Z respectively. Whether by deliberate intention or not, Mosse certainly discovered a sound security measure. It can be readily understood that the replacement of EINSATZBEREITSCHAFTSMELDUNG by NEPER (while technically merely the substitution of one crib for another) is decidedly a change for the worse, for, given reasonable consistency of form the value of a crib depends on its length. Whether by deliberate intention or not, Mosse certainly discovered a sound security measure. Indeed, the replacement of regularly occurring phrases by brief codewords (preferably a range of alternative codewords for each phrase) must always be regarded as a useful ancillary to more radical anti-crib precautions. Yet, on the other hand, some cribs were actually improved by the use of the Mosse Code. This happened when several alternative abbreviations were replaced by the standard codeword.

Double encoding

Double encoding, in contra-distinction to the devices already described, was essentially provisional in nature. The object was apparently, by a change of encoding procedure, to use, without danger, a key believed to be compromised but which, for some reason, could not be immediately replaced. It was a cumbrous procedure and very laborious to the Germans. Hence, it is not surprising that it was used only two keys – Raven and Gadfly – and in each case on only a small portion of the traffic. Raven only used the device on a single day – 16 March 1944 – at least so far as we were aware.

Raven
Double encoding on Raven was made known to us by a fortunate reference in another message on the same day, and by an examination of the duds,

a few doubly encoded messages were found. These messages had to be decoded in two stages. First, one found the message setting in the usual way and decoded the Enigma text. This came out apparently still in Enigma (as indeed it was), but the first 12 letters had the pattern ABC ABC DEF DEF. The next step was to treat ABC DEF as a new preamble, find the message setting and then decode the rest of the message starting at this setting. The encoding method must be obvious from the above account of the converse process.

Gadfly

The method as used on Gadfly was somewhat different. It gave rise to apparent duds. But, to the credit of Hut 6, the solution was discovered by the Chief Cryptographer before we were told of it by a full explanation in a message. The method is best explained from the encoder's standpoint.

The encoder chose his message setting, say A B C, and enciphered his message in the normal way. Let us assume the message is 234 letters long and he consequently ends at A K C. (We take it that neither wheel 2 nor 4 is in the middle). Then, without moving the wheels, the operator proceeds to encode in Enigma again the already encoded cipher text. For the encoder this is simple enough if twice as laborious as usual. For the decoder, matters are much more difficult. In the normal way he finds the setting A B C, then he must determine the closing position A K C either by calculation in Hut 6-style or by the German-recommended method, unutterably tedious but foolproof, of tapping out the message. Having discovered A K C he then decodes the Enigma text to Enigma text and then has to decode <u>this</u> with the original setting A B C, truly a case of "Double, double, toil and trouble" if ever there was one!

To complete the subject it need only be said that it is possible with a little ingenuity to run a crib on a doubly encoded message (Gadfly style). Assume, for instance, we have a crib starting TAGESMELDUNG VOM and that the length of the message is 234 as above – then, in the simplest case, if the doubly encoded Enigma text is P X Z C P ... ... we have a menu starting as follows:

T <u>ZZA</u> ? <u>ZIA</u> P <u>ZID</u> ? <u>ZZD</u> E

Thus we can build up query menus. These, of course, have to be run to allow for all probable turnover assumptions, so the whole process is by no means inexpensive. Yet this method was on several occasions successful in securing breaks.

Summary

Double Encoding was used on too small a scale to have any effect worth mentioning on Hut 6 breaking. On the scale on which it was used, it must have been no less a nuisance to the German cipher clerks as it was to Hut 6.

Chapter 15
Change from Watch/Research to Air/Army

Introduction

In 1944, the most important change in the organisation of the principal cryptographic sections was the alteration of the whole set-up from a Watch/Research to an Air/Army basis. This change was preceded by a precisely similar alteration on the traffic analysis side by which TIS1 (Air) and TIS2 (Army) were remodelled to deal with Air and Army keys respectively (instead of, as previously, Watch and Research keys), and it was thus accompanied by a similar reform in the Registration Rooms. Thus the cryptographic change-over was only one aspect of a profound internal revolution in the whole Hut. While, in what follows, the cryptographic side only will be considered, the influence of the change already made in TIS must not be forgotten. From the administrative standpoint it was obviously neater and more convenient, that one set of traffic analysis should deal with one set of cryptographers that the reorganisation of TIS virtually made inevitable a similar reorganisation of Watch and Research.

Stages of the change

The changeover was made in two stages. First, at the beginning of October 1944, Air Research was abolished and the whole Air cryptographic effort was amalgamated under one head (Major Manisty). Second, at the beginning of November, Research — now Army Research only — came to an end — and Major Manisty took charge of the whole breaking effort. The set-up before October 1944 can be expressed as follows:

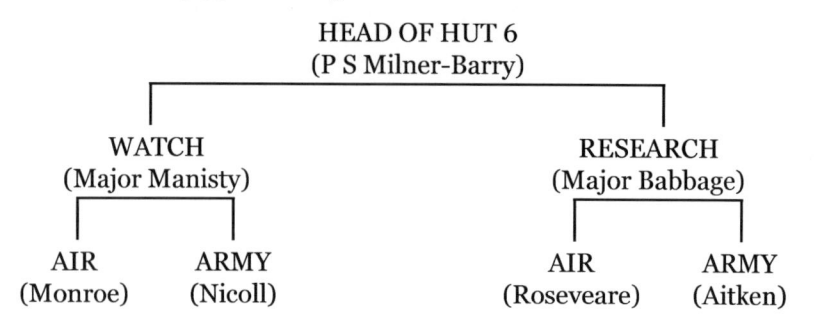

```
                    HEAD OF HUT 6
                   (P S Milner-Barry)
        ┌─────────────────┴─────────────────┐
       WATCH                              RESEARCH
   (Major Manisty)                     (Major Babbage)
     ┌────┴────┐                         ┌────┴────┐
    AIR      ARMY                       AIR      ARMY
  (Monroe)  (Nicoll)                 (Roseveare) (Aitken)
```

The internal constitution of the four sub-sections, their personnel and general methods of working remained to a great degree unaltered by the administrative change. The essential difference between the two set-ups is that the sub-sections were paired together in a new way – this involved changes of locations for some sections – and that, in the later set-up, there was a definite unity of control (apart from the general co-ordination exercised by the Head of the Hut on all activities).

Reasons for the change
These were broadly the same on Air and Army alike. The general contraction of the war into an even smaller circle around the Third Reich while the Nazis, in a terrible fulfilment of Poe's fantasy, were being driven relentlessly into the pit of doom, made all the fronts more and more mixed up with one another, and this process was inevitably cumulative. It became harder and harder to justify our neat geographical divisions of Western Front, Eastern Front and so on. Constant liaison was necessary between Watch and Research cryptographers (particularly on the Air side), and it became clear that integration was the only satisfactory answer to our problems. Furthermore, on the Air side, the number of keys dealt with by Research had for some time decreased as the Western keys had been transferred to the Watch some months earlier in anticipation of D-Day. If we excluded a few hopeless keys, a substantial number of the remainder were in a position to be broken fairly regularly and currently. In short, Research had become to some extent a misnomer and the very success of the section was an argument in favour of its abolition in its old form.

On the Army side, the case for change was not so strong in October 1944 as, at that time, the Watch and Research Army keys were still – on the whole – in watertight compartments. Moreover, there were geographical difficulties to be considered, for it was seen that the integration of the Army effort could not be a reality unless the two sub-sections – Army Watch and Army Qwatch – worked in adjacent rooms. This was bound to involve moving the Army Watch (the people engaged in breaking some of the most urgent traffic) further from the operational nerve centre of the Hut – which was the point where Air Watch, Machine Room and Decoding Room converged and there was direct tube and telephonic communication with the bombes.

Change from Watch/Research to Air/Army

However, the success of the Air fusion made the logical case for the Army fusion irresistible, as links now appeared between Army Watch and Research keys – particularly Puffin and the Balkan keys – that were hard to deal with by liaison between two sections working in separate rooms. So the final step was taken at the end of November 1944, and the geographic remoteness of the Army Watch's new quarters was alleviated by the construction of two new conveyor belts, one to bring the decodes to the Army EPer (EP = En Passant. To note cribs or potential cribs among messages on their way from the Decoding Room to Hut 3, and to enter details of decodes on EP sheets) and the other, to send them back again without delay on the first stage of their journey to Hut 3.

Results of the change

Some difficulties had been foreseen, chiefly in the sphere of technique, for Watch and Research had developed different methods for dealing with the material presented to them. It was felt, however, that the best elements of the Research technique – careful bulk entering and systematic study of difficult keys and special problems – could be combined with the alertness, speed of action and taking of snap chances necessitated and developed by Watch work. The fusion was successfully accomplished and this was made much easier by the fact that the Qwatch had already developed a technique intermediate between Watch and Research. So the best of Air Research lived on in the Qwatch and the Qwatch Annexe (Room 76), working, however, on more current traffic than had been the case formerly.

On the Army side the fusion also worked well. Quince, the Research key most regularly broken, was made a Watch key at once and Avocet was transferred later. In December 1944 the innovation was adopted of blistering (or sorting) all Army keys currently (current dealing with all traffic had been in force on the Air side for some time). This step showed how far the Hut had moved from old conceptions. In earlier days, when it was regarded as essential to blist difficult keys with great care when all the traffic was in, to blist everything currently would have been – quite rightly – considered a waste of time. The examination of all traffic currently is thus one measure of our general conquest of the Enigma. Yet to the end the Army Qwatch retained much of the old Research atmosphere. This was because virtually all the breakable Army keys were transferred to the Watch and only those difficult or impossible to break were left to the Qwatch. This is just what is apt to happen on the Watch/Qwatch system and everyone understands this. But it happened rather more on the Army rather than the Air side just because there were so many more breakable Air keys – and of such varying intelligence value – that the Air Watch could not have annexed them all had it desired to do so. And – again because of the greater number of keys – the Air Qwatch worked on Watch keys in a manner that was never necessary on the Army side.

Timing of the change
The final set-up reached was more logical than its predecessor, and the integration of Air and Army effort could in neither case have been longer delayed without harm to our breaking success – but should it have been made earlier?

The answer is bound up with the previous organisational changes of Hut 6. It seems quite possible, for instance, that had we not made the error of separating the Machine Room from the Crib Room we might have reached, at an earlier date, the final solution of our problems in this direction. But it was not until February 1943 that the initial error was corrected, and it would certainly have been unwise to complicate the re-organisation then undertaken by attempting to combine it with a change to an Air/Army set-up. It may also be maintained that while it was obvious from 1942 on that, in almost every respect, there was a great gulf fixed between Air and Army, it was not until discriminants were dropped in November 1943 that it was clear that the Air/Army division was going to be absolutely fundamental for traffic analysis. So, on the whole, there was no case for effecting the change to an Air/Army set-up before November 1943, and the question becomes whether we should have realised the inevitable trend of events and taken appropriate action between that date and October 1944.

On a difficult question like this opinions may differ. Logically there was a case for the change at any date after November 1943, but logic is not always a safe guide in matters of administration. From a practical standpoint it is arguable that we were so involved in crisis after crisis in these fateful months that it was the path of true prudence not to complicate the issue by far-reaching measures of reorganisation until a change was clearly indicated. This was the line followed by the Head of the Hut, and doubtless it coincided with the general conservative sentiment which comes so easily to human nature, and which was of very noticeable strength even in so recently formed an institution as Hut 6. Changes were never welcome unless they were not only desirable, but were *clearly* seen to be so.

Unity of control
The other side of the change effected in October-November 1944 — the unity of control over the whole breaking process — was no doubt also a logical and practical gain. We might have made this change earlier without any other alteration to our set-up, as suggested by Mr Milner-Barry in his introduction. However, in Hut 6 (as in every institution which has grown up from humble beginnings in a natural manner) arrangements that were logically indefensible often worked very well, and the dual control of breaking was one of these. The liaison between the personalities concerned was so intimate and close through the daily Lage Conference (a daily meeting held to discuss priorities on the Lage — a list of jobs waiting to be run on the bombe) and other means that the disadvantages one might have anticipated did not arise.

Organisation of the Watch

Introduction
The historical development of the Watch and the detailed technical processes involved are fully discussed elsewhere. This section attempts only to describe the organisation as it was in March/April 1945. Numbers given are approximate, as distribution between the various sub-sections varied as far as possible with the state of the work. The total strength of the Watch was 65, divided broadly as follows (see end of chapter for a more detailed distribution):

Air	37
Army	23
Admin and Signals	5

Function of the Watch
The Watch was sometimes called the cryptographic section of Hut 6. This is a false description, as the whole process of Hut 6 was cryptography and the Watch was responsible for only one stage of this process. The

primary job of the Watch was to examine the traffic already sorted by the traffic analysts and the Registration Room, to find cribs (in the widest sense) on this traffic, to prepare these cribs in a manner suitable for handling by the Machine Room or for despatch to Washington, to keep the records and do the research necessary to carry out these functions effectively, and to carry out any technical work on the completion of keys that could not be handled by the Machine Room. The Watch was also responsible for the current running policy on the bombes under the direction of Milner-Barry, acting through the Head of the Watch, and guided by the machinery on bombe control. It was responsible for all signals connected with jobs run in Washington. A borderline task was menu-making. This was for some time a Watch responsibility, but it had latterly become primarily the function of one or two menu-makers drawn from the Machine Room and sitting in the Watch. The Watch still assisted as necessary, particularly when a number of urgent jobs were prepared at once.

Basic organisation

The Watch was divided into two main groups – Air and Army – and a third small group – BOVO – whose main function was the handling of signals to and from Washington. The Air and Army Watches were each further subdivided into an operational and non-operational Watch (or Qwatch – a Quiet Watch). The nomenclature may be represented as follows:

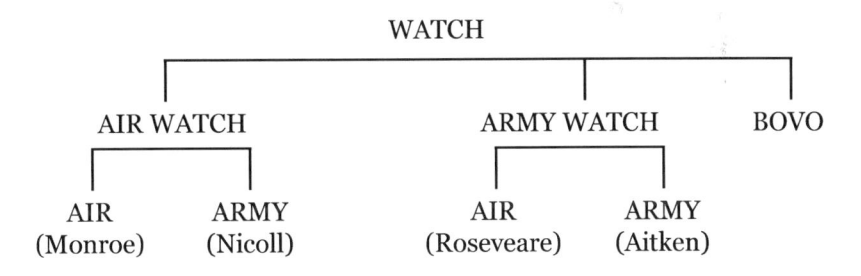

```
                          WATCH
        ┌───────────────────┼───────────────────┐
    AIR WATCH           ARMY WATCH            BOVO
   ┌─────┴─────┐       ┌─────┴─────┐
  AIR        ARMY      AIR        ARMY
(Monroe)   (Nicoll)  (Roseveare) (Aitken)
```

The descriptions 'Watch A' etc., were never in general use, but are used here for precision. In normal usage 'The Watch' could mean the whole Watch, the Air Watch or just Watch A, according to context. This was due to the way in which the organisation grew up and to a certain innate conservatism. Each member of the Watch belonged to a definite subsection. Transfers were made as the situation demanded, but transfers between Air Watch and Army Watch were on a long-term rather than on a day-to-day basis. Short-term loans were frequently made from an operational Watch to its corresponding Qwatch. Loans in the reverse direction were rare, as it takes some time for a non-operational Watch to become used to operational working.

Division of keys between Watches
The division of keys between the Air and Army Watches was simple and rigid – Air keys were handled by the Air Watch, Army and SS keys by the Army Watch. But the division between operational and non-operational Watches was much less clear-cut, particularly with Air keys. The basic principle was that if a key was of sufficient operational importance to justify the greater extravagance of current breaking, and if there was a reasonable chance of breaking it with some regularity (not necessarily every day), then it was handled partially or entirely by an operational Watch, otherwise it was handled entirely by a Qwatch. There were many exceptions to this basic principle, usually in the direction of handling in an operational Watch for a key which appeared on general principles to be more suitable for complete Qwatch treatment. These exceptions arose for two main reasons:

1. It was often more satisfactory to handle together a number of keys in the same theatre which were liable to be connected by re-encodement, even if some of them had no operational urgency; and

2. It was sometimes administratively easier to make a sensible division of work between Watches by handling some non-operational keys in operational Watches than by transferring members from one Watch to another.

Each key had its 'parent' or 'parents', drawn from the Watch primarily responsible for it. The amount of special attention given a key by its parents varied from an almost nominal supervision in the case of some operational keys, to complete charge in the case of some non-operational keys. The system of parentage has been considered more fully elsewhere.

Watch A (three shifts)
Watch A was responsible for breaking the operational Air keys. In

addition, the Head of Shift of Watch A was responsible for the general control of current bombe policy. The latter duty arose mainly for geographical reasons — Watch A adjoined the Machine Room — and the Watch Head of Shift was advised by Watch M on the priority of current Army jobs. The normal shift was five strong, of whom one was designated on the shift-list as Head of Shift. Apart from his responsibility for current bombe policy he was responsible for the distribution of work among his shift and for making sure that the most important tasks were tackled first. He took over from his predecessor a 'lage' (distinct from the more elaborate i/c Ops lage) which gave him a summary of the current position on all keys and a note of any special events. He handed over a similar lage to his successor at the end of his shift.

Apart from the finding and preparing of cribs on unbroken keys and the handling of any special machine problems (e.g. breaking a D), there were three routine tasks to be undertaken by a Watch A shift, and each was usually done by a different member. These were:

a. <u>EP entering</u>: the examination of all decodes en route from the Decoding Room to Hut 3, and entering of cribs and other worthwhile messages in folders;

b. <u>Kissing</u>: investigation of the potential re-encodements thrown up by the sheets of kiss-pairings prepared by the Registration Room;

c. <u>WLP (Watch Liaison Party)</u>: two-way liaison with Control, ICI (In Charge of Identification — name given to the person in charge of the current sorting of traffic in Registration Room Air after 1 February 1945), and other sources of information on matters of cover and identification. This task was a recent addition caused by the new call sign and frequency system.

None of these tasks was necessarily full-time, and it was usually possible for the member concerned to assist in the finding of cribs. The Head of Shift distributed these three tasks and the handling of the various unbroken keys to the members of his shift. He took a share of the work himself, but was wise to leave himself sufficient free time to keep general control of the proceedings. An unbroken key of first importance might well be looked at by more than one person, and by tradition anyone was

Change from Watch/Research to Air/Army

at liberty to look at a key which had not been allotted to him without any feeling of 'poaching'.

In addition to the five Watch members of the shift, there were also in the same room two or three members of the Machine Room, working under the general guidance of the Watch A Head of Shift. These were the i/c Ops, who handled the bombing of individual jobs and kept the necessary lages, and one or two menu-makers. In addition to manning the three routine shifts, three members of Watch A were usually working in Watch Q, and it was often possible for other members to have a few days off shift in order to deal with particular problems or to give special attention to the keys of which they were parents. Otherwise, parental duties had to be carried out during slack time on a routine shift or in spare time.

Watch Q

Watch Q is the most complicated sub-section to describe. The simplest method is to split it up into its component parts and give the primary functions of each of these parts. The distinctions were not at all rigid – the great merit of Watch Q was its flexibility and ability to turn its quite considerable strength wherever required. Watch Q worked in two rooms – Room 64 adjoining Watch A – and Room 78, not far away, but quite distinct.

Room 64

Head of Watch Q (Taunt): Responsible for the work of Watch Q as a whole, particularly for co-ordinating all activities in Room 64, and keeping in touch with Heads of Shift of Watch A.

Kiss clearance (two strong, two shifts): Responsible for checking kiss lages dealt with by Watch A, for investigating any re-encodements not fully dealt with by Watch A, and for checking and investigating re-encodement information supplied by Sixta.

QEP (Qwatch Entering Party) (five strong – three shifts): Originally started when thrice-daily stecker was threatened as a Qwatch Entering Party to maintain fuller records of keys than could be done by the regular entering system. This was still their primary responsibility on keys which it was found necessary, and the party was available for any special entering projects. But the members trained in other jobs and two at least of them had become very useful general hands. QEP night shift handled the Washington signals, a job performed by BOVO on the other two shifts.

Watch A Party (three strong – two shifts): This party, which included a Head of Shift from Watch A, worked in co-operation with Taunt on recalcitrant Watch A keys which needed more sustained treatment than could be given on normal shifts.

Room 78 (five strong – one shift): In charge of Roseveare, who also acted as deputy to Taunt. Responsible for most keys not handled by Watch A (a few were sometimes handled in Room 64 when state of work permitted), notably Eastern Front keys at the end. This was the only really non-operational part of the Air Watch.

Watch M (three shifts) and Watch R (one shift): Watch M was responsible for breaking the operational Army keys and worked with a shift of four, of whom one was designated as a Head of Shift. The responsibility of a Watch M shift was similar to that of a Watch A shift, with the exception of control over bombe policy. However, the Head of Shift in Watch M advised on the priority of current Army jobs. In Watch M advised there was no special job of WLP, but any necessary liaison was normally carried out by the Head of Shift.

The division of work between Watch M and Watch R was much more rigid than that between Watch A and Watch Q. Something analogous to QEP and to the Watch A party in Watch Q did exist, but was considered part of Watch M. One member of Watch M – working normally on Day shift – was particularly responsible for keeping records, but often had time to assist with the current work of the day shift. Another member, usually of Head of Shift status, was designated on the shift-list to work 'non-routine'. He had no responsibility for current breaking, but concentrated on recalcitrant keys and any problems on Watch M keys that needed research.

Watch R was entirely responsible for the Army and SS keys not handled in Watch M. The regular members of Watch R were supported by one visitor from Watch M on a weekly changing basis. In Watch R there was also one specialist enterer analogous to QEP.

BOVO (two shifts): The first responsibility of BOVO was the handling of signals concerning Hut 6 jobs in America and the maintenance of all necessary records. On the night shift, a member of QEP handled the signals. It was not a full-time job on this shift and the QEP member was able to devote part of the time to her normal duties. BOVO worked directly under Manisty, who was responsible for general relations with Washington, and it also assisted him in administrative and secretarial duties.

Administration

The only administrative member of the Watch was its Head (Manisty), who had found it necessary for the last year to keep himself clear of other work. Apart from general responsibility for the policy and organisation of the section, he controlled the arrangement of shifts and leave for the whole section. This was thought more satisfactory than dividing the responsibility up among the sub-sections, as considerable co-ordination between the various shift-lists was necessary. Semi-technical points of administration — for example, the control of special cover on crib frequencies — were delegated to members of the Watches concerned.

Monroe was Manisty's deputy. Normally he worked in Watch A, of which he was the senior Head of Shift, but was detached from normal Watch A work when Manisty was away. Each of the four Watches had, in effect, a recognised Head and Deputy Head. The technical organisation of A and Q was more directly under the central control than that of M and R. Two criticisms can be fairly levelled at this as a theoretical organisation:

1. There was no definite Head of the Air Watch (A and Q) — except Monroe in his capacity as Deputy Head of the Whole Watch — and no definite Head of the Army Watch (M and R);

2. The Head of the Watch had no administrative assistant at a high enough level to take responsibility, and so perhaps was too much involved in administration and did not see enough of the actual work of the rooms.

These defects were largely due to the way in which the section was formed and to the personalities involved. But they were also due to a reluctance to detach a competent technician from his technical work and 'waste' him as an administrator — whenever we considered doing it, we thought: "It is a bad moment just now, but perhaps in a few weeks' time ..."

DETAILED DISTRIBUTION OF MEMBERS

	Manisty	1	1
Watch A	Monroe, H F T Smith	2	
	Others normally acting as H/S	4	
	Occasionally acting as H/S	2	
	Other members	15	24
Watch Q	Taunt	1	
	Kiss clearance	2	
	QEP	5	
	Roseveare	1	
	Room 78	4	13
Watch M	Nicoll, Read	2	
	Others normally acting as H/S	4	
	Enterer	1	
	Other members	11	18
Watch R	Aitken, Gaunt	2	
	Enterer	1	
	Other members	2	5
BOVO	Members	4	4

		British	23
Men:		US	11
Women:			31
			65

Chapter 16
Final Developments of the Rules of Keys

Introduction
From January 1944 to May 1945 there were a number of interesting developments in the sphere of key rules, but most of them were simply extensions and applications already known. There were no radically new discoveries comparable in importance, for instance, to that of the Nigelian wheel orders. Hence it will be possible to deal with the subject more summarily than in previous periods and an endeavour will be made to avoid the extreme detail which is inevitable in current reports, but is confusing in a bird's-eye view. So, it is proposed to select from the reports of the Committee on Rules of Keys only the more important tendencies and the more interesting special details. It seems best to consider in order the regular Air keys, then a few special Air keys, then the Army keys with a final note on the rules of D.

Regular Air keys
Wheel orders: The Nigelian rule maintained its sway until the end unchallenged by any rival, although at times anarchic tendencies appeared to be gaining ground and there were many non-Nigelian keys. More serious, in some months an alarming number of breaches of the fundamental non-clashing rule occurred. Some lapses were the more unfortunate as now wheel order rules were the most practically useful of all key rules. The days of hand breaks were past, but any rule that saved bombe time never lost its value. However, the growing disregard of wheel order rules that was marked from spring to autumn 1944 was at least checked, and by December it was possible to say that there was a distinct improvements which mercifully continued to the end of the war.

Ringstellung: At first ringstellung rules appeared not infrequently, although owing to the decline of cillying, we were hardly ever able to turn them to practical account. Apart from the old 26-day rule, several new varieties appeared. For instance, in December 1943 and January 1944 several keys had no repeats of ringstellung letters in the last 26 days of the month, i.e., from the 6th to the 31st. More original was a new rule, first seen in March 1944, on Puma and Primrose by which the letters of the alphabet plus one repeat formed a block of nine consecutive days. (There was considerable variation in the days that formed the block. In October 1944, when this rule was popular, we find several keys that "block" 30-22, 21-13, 12-4, another that prefers 31-23, 22-14, 13-5 and another that takes the simple course 1-9, 10-18, 19-27). It will be noticed that this rule is more akin to the Army ringstellung rule than any previous Air rule, yet towards the end of the war (from January 1945 on) it was the only ringstellung rule observed by any Air key and even this rule was observed by very few. But the influence of ringstellung rules on our breaking had for long been so negligible that few even noticed their disappearance.

Stecker: As regards rules in the strict sense, nothing was added to what already known – viz., the avoidance of consecutive stecker pairings and the tendency to diagonalisation. However, from the Parkerian records, a number of stecker repeats were discovered – far fewer than in the palmy days of 1942-1943, but none-the-less not to be despised. The first of these was a hatted stecker repeat between two of our less important keys – Leek and Celery of April – which, despite its irregular nature and its occasional inexactitude, was successfully used on several occasions towards the end of the month. Later there was a new batch of stecker repeats which are listed below, some of very short duration which ended almost as soon as they were discovered, and others from 1944 to 1945 – this last was an innovation, as no previous key repeats of any kind had crossed the turn of the year. The particular stecker repeats were:

    a. Cockroach 5, 6, 8, 4/10 = Cricket 20, 22, 25, 26/10

    b. Daffodil 4, 5, 1, 2, 3/11 = Lily 22, 23, 27, 28, 29/11

    c. Red November = Red December (hatted repeat)

    d. Ermine 15-31/12/44 = Jaguar 1-17/1/45

    e. Cockroach 1-30/11 = Beetle 20-31/12, 1-3/12, 5-19/12

It is worth mentioning that by no means all these repeats were exact: in some cases as many as three stecker pairings were altered. Our system of recording sets of stecker and looking for repeats did not inevitably pick up such slightly altered repeats. And the whole matter was discussed with a view to devising a more certain method of picking up useful repeats, probably by the use of Freeborn machinery [*Hollerith punch cards*].

Final Developments of the Rules of Keys

However, before much was actually done on these lines, the partial repeats had come to an end. In fact, the only remaining stecker repeat discovered was a hatted one between certain days of February Hyena and February Daffodil.

Brown, Yak and Llama: These special keys went their own way. Yak and Llama were locally issued Fliegerführer [*an operational GAF command*] keys which did not observe the central Cipher Office rules of Nigelian and non-clashing wheel orders and avoidance of consecutive stecker. Yak, in addition, had on occasion the peculiarity of repeating its own keys. Thus in January 1944 Yak repeated the keys of December 1943 in a chopped and jumbled manner. It was possible to some extent to predict wheelorder and ringstellung, but the sets of stecker were completed hatted. Something similar occurred in November 1944. For the first 15 days of the month Yak repeated the stecker of the first 15 days of September, not day for day but in little runs of two to five. Except on 14 and 15 November, the wheelorders and ringstellung were different permutations of the corresponding September day's key. For the last 15 days of November the stecker repeated stecker of the last half of October in little runs, without any repeat of wheelorder and ringstellung.

Llama's peculiarity was the use of an unusual number of self-stecker, like Brown. When it was first broken in January 1944, the limits varied from 10 to 16 self-steckered letters. In April, however, seven stecker pairings became the rule — with I and L always self-steckered. In May and June there was more variation, but always a large number of self-stecker. Finally, in July, the normal 10 stecker came into force.

Brown by now, it will be remembered, had also the normal 10 stecker and so the characteristic stecker pairing rules was impossible. However, to compensate for their refusal to adopt the regular Air rules, Brown I and III invented some of their own. Brown I indulged in a key repeat. 15 February - 14 March 1945 repeated the keys of 15 August-14 September 1944, but unfortunately for us, not day for day. Each February-March day had the stecker of some August-September day and the wheelorder and ringstellung of the same day, possibly permuted and not necessarily in the same way. (This meant that for each set of stecker available there were 36 possible keys.) It can easily be imagined that this kind of repeat was not easy to exploit, and after the resources of rodding had been exhausted, we were reduced to a massive decoding assault in an unfortunately unsuccessful attempt to clear up the five or six missing keys.

On Brown III a useful stecker-wheel order rule had a reasonably long run. From 15 October 1943 to 14 March 1944 – i.e., five consecutive Brown months – only 30 sets of self-stecker were used and each was associated with one or two (and in one case with three) wheelorders. A permutation of an associated wheelorder was always used with each set. This rule was successfully utilised in breaking several days. Later, from 15 April to 14 May, Brown III repeated day for day the sets of self-stecker used in February-March. Brown III was also involved in the last key repeat ever discovered — Brown III of March 1945 repeated the keys of February Cockroach. This repeat seemed to imply that at long last Brown had forfeited its independence and that the GAF Cipher Office had gained control over its keys. It is, however, not quite certain that this is the true explanation. It may be that the Brown keymaker had somehow got possession of the Cockroach key and with characteristic disregard of cipher security decided simply to use it again.

Army keys

Wheel orders: From a general point of view there is little to report in this line except that, as time went on, clashing wheel orders became rare until, in March 1945, it became reasonable to give a preference for the 32 non-clashing wheel orders on nearly all Army keys. There were, however, a few oddities. One such was that the railway key, Culverin, only used wheels 1, 2 and 3 like Tricycle of old. Another peculiarity was found on Ibis of December. Out of 15 days broken, 14 had a 3 in the wheelorder, clearly not a fortuitous occurrence. There were also a number of wheelorder repeats, namely, days 1 and 12; 5 and 15; 7 and 19; 8, 20 and 30. This suggested that the compiler of the key had split the month into three sections and used roughly the same wheelorders in each period, but we were unable to test this hypothesis further. In no other month did Ibis show any comparable peculiarity.

Ringstellung: The old Army ringstellung rule was not seen after January 1944 and no new rule took its place. The increase in stuttering ringstellung has been noted elsewhere. Apart from this, we have to note only a few oddities – for instance, from February to April Wagtail, the practice key of Wehrkreis VIII had a ringstellung which only differed from that of Falcon I by being two less on the first wheel. (The rest of the key was the same as Falcon.) Again, July 1944 Nightjar repeated its ringstellung

Final Developments of the Rules of Keys

in a peculiar way. Days 11-19 repeated the ringstellung of 1, 3-10 (with an alteration of a letter in a few cases) and most of the days 20-31 had for ringstellung some permutation of a ringstellung previously used.

Stecker: Here we have to record a few cases of partial repeats within the same month and also a new form of stecker pattern. The partial repeats occurred on Nightjar of July 1944 (already mentioned under ringstellung) and Falcon I of January 1945. On Nightjar there was a repeat of sets of self-stecker at irregular intervals – out of 29 days broken only 14 self-stecker sets were used, some as often as three times, e.g.,

C E F H K M 1, 16, 28
I K M N P X 4, 11, 31

As can be readily conjectured, it was impossible to use such an irregular repeat. Falcon of January 1945 had a more predictable and hence more useful self-stecker repeat. The days fell as a rule into blocks of from 2 to 4, each block having throughout the same self-stecker or only slight variations. Thus days 4 and 5 had self-stecker D G H J V Y and days 6 to 9 A L M S W X while days 1 and 2 had I N Q W X Y and day 3 I N Q R W X. In two cases at the moment of transition from one block to the next the self-steckered letters of the first block were paired together for the first day of the next block.

The stecker pattern was found on Orange of August 1944 up to the 20th when it suddenly ceased. The days were divided into consecutive pairs with the same set of self-stecker and the stecker so altered that, for instance, A/L, D/O on the 1st became A/O, D/L on the 2nd. It was unfortunately impossible to make use of this transposition of stecker, as we had no means of telling which pair of stecker were to be transposed – this was doubtless determined by the arbitrary order on the German keysheets. However, the knowledge of the six self-stecker was very useful in making more easily runnable the short Orange cribs.

Repeats: In this last period of the war there were rather more Army repeats than previously. The Wagtail/Falcon repeat been already mentioned, but in addition there was a new feature – repeats on SS keys. Quince of March repeated Orange of January, wheelorder and stecker being repeated in reverse order, ringstellung in the same order. (In the Quince key a few ringstellung were slightly altered to avoid stutterers.)

This repeat was of inestimable cryptographic value in enabling us in a critical period in the history of the key to break and decode a whole month's Orange traffic.

About the same time, E/320, a practice key which only passed the German High Command communiqué, and had no intelligence value, was found to be using elements of SS keys – to judge from the only two breaks obtained in January 1944, this key was indulging in a hatted repeat of ringstellung and stecker from January Quince. Like most hatted repeats, this was of very little use and could not be exploited. A key repeat of an original nature, charming in its naiveté, was Penguin, a home-made division key of the 12th SS Panzer Division. From its first appearance in June 1944, Penguin only used six keys, two of which were very similar, only differing by a slight change in the ringstellung and a permutation of the wheel order. The six keys were used in regular sequence, the cycle starting anew on the 1st of every month. It did not take us long to break all six keys and thereafter Penguin was out automatically as long as it lasted.

Rule of Ds: It was discovered by August 1944 and confirmed by all subsequent breaks that consecutive pairings were avoided on Air Ds – for the present purpose, German notation is assumed. This is in line with the avoidance of consecutive stecker pairings. To the Germans there was no difference, as they styled D pairings stecker pairings in the reflector. The Army, as might have been expected, had no such inhibition and the D for NOT-keys was wholly alphabetical, i.e.:

A/B C/D E/F G/H I/K L/M N/O P/Q R/S T/U V/W X/Z

The number of Ds used each month was originally three, but after some fluctuation in October 1944, settled down to four in November. In all other respects the keymaker had a free hand in constructing Ds, except that he had to write down only 12 pairings, omitting the letters J and Y, which corresponded to the permanently fixed D pairing (BO in our terminology). The curious repeat between D wirings and stecker sets has been dealt with in a previous section.

Summary

The study of key rules never justified the more ambitious hopes of its pursuers. It was never possible, except for brief intervals on Brown I, to reduce everything to rule and write down a key from its predecessor.

Final Developments of the Rules of Keys

This was just as well – the discovery of a complete German system of key-making, however gratifying in other respects, would have meant the end of Enigma cryptography in any real sense.

Yet it cannot be denied that the study of key rules and the associated search for key repeats paid immense dividends, particularly in 1942 – hundreds of keys must have been broken by this alone. More important, we made our first entry by this means into many keys that otherwise we would never have broken, or at least much later. The experience in Hut 6 shows clearly the necessity in similar circumstances of examining all keys carefully and keeping thorough records. One must never argue that the enemy cannot be so stupid as to have key rules or repeat keys he has already used. If to underestimate one's enemy is a sure road to disaster, to overestimate his cleverness may result in overlooking that he has made the most obvious mistakes.

Chapter 17
Bombe Control

Introduction

No attempt has been made to describe the growth of the bombe control problem and the various measures taken from time to time to deal with it. Some mention of them will be found in P.S. Milner-Barry's general introduction to this volume. All that is done here is to state the problem as it existed in May 1945 and to describe the machinery that had been set up to handle it.

Largely because the way in which the sections grew up, Hut 6 and Hut 8 maintained independent machinery for bombe control. There was necessarily close contract between the two Huts, as a large proportion of the bombe strength was usable by either. The problem is considered here from the viewpoint of Hut 6 – the large number of different keys made it a much more complicated problem for Hut 6 than for Hut 8. There are two aspects of the problem which, although connected, can be considered separately. They are the policy aspect and the operational aspect. The former includes the distribution of the bombe strength between Hut 6 and Hut 8 and between the various Hut 6 keys, the latter the actual minute-to-minute handling of individual jobs.

The problem

At the beginning of May 1945, the following bombe strength was available in England and America:

England	14	four-wheel bombes usable only by Hut 8.
	42	four-wheel bombes usable by Hut 8, or by Hut 6 for delayed hoppity jobs.
	12	four-wheel bombes usable by Hut 8, or by Hut 6 for ordinary jobs.
	50	three-wheel bombes usable by Hut 6 for ordinary jobs or by Hut 8 on their only remaining three-wheel key (Bounce).
	89	three-wheel bombes usable by Hut 6 only.
America (Op-20-G)	112	four-wheel bombes usable by Hut 8, or by Hut 6 for delayed hoppity jobs.
(Arlington)	1	144-Enigma three-wheel bombe, usable only by Hut 6 and equivalent to four ordinary bombes.

"Intelligence Value"

The sole object of cryptography is to provide intelligence. Before considering the policy aspect of the bombe control problem, it is worth discussing briefly what is meant by the "intelligence value" of a break. At its simplest the intelligence value of a break means the amount of intelligence that is obtained from the decodes of traffic on the broken key. But this is an inadequate criterion of the real intelligence value of any given break. For example, with certain types of intelligence, continuity of information greatly increases its value. The break of such a key does not only have intelligence value in itself, but also increases the value of breaks of neighbouring days.

Again, distinction is sometimes made between the "intelligence value" and the "cryptographic value" of a break. This distinction is false. What is meant by saying that a break has cryptographic value is that it assists in some way – for example, by re-encodement or key repeat – in the breaking of further keys and hence in the provision of further intelligence. Thus the value of such a break is not merely judged by the intelligence provided by the decodes on the key itself.

It is in this wide sense that the expression "intelligence value" is used when considering bombe policy. But even then it is not purely quantitative. There is a distinction between "urgency" and "importance", although these two qualities cannot be completely separated. A different policy can be adopted with a key whose breaking will immediately affect current operations and a key whose breaking is important for planning, but will call for no immediate action. Certain keys of little importance, such as weather keys, may not be worth breaking at all if they cannot be broken currently.

Hut 6 – Hut 8

All sections concerned in Bletchley Park accepted and worked on the principal that the bombes should be regarded as a general pool and that the potential intelligence value (used in its widest sense) of the keys concerned, combined with the expenditure of bombe time necessary and the chance of breaking, should determine priority. The position in America was not quite so straightforward. The Op-20-G (Naval) bombes, which formed the greater part of the American bombe strength, had been built specifically for naval problems, in particular for Shark. But in practice this did not cause great difficulty, and apart from the overriding priority of Shark, Op-20-G effectively accepted the pool principle and their bombes had become a major factor in the breaking of Hut 6 keys. In order that the relative values of Hut 6 and Hut 8 keys could be discussed and general working principles laid down, there were regular weekly meetings between the parties concerned. Such meetings took place in Hut 8 and were attended by representatives from Huts 3 (3L), 6 and 8, Naval Section and Op-20-G. At these meetings a general line of policy was agreed, and it was left to the Hut 6 and Hut 8 representatives to issue the necessary administrative instructions. If a new situation suddenly arose, an emergency meeting was called.

Hut 6 keys

Responsibility
The Head of Hut 6 was finally responsible for bombe policy, and its current direction was delegated to the Watch and was the immediate responsibility of Air Watch head of shift. He negotiated with Hut 8 regarding allocation of bombes between the two Huts on the basis of the decisions of the weekly meeting. At one time these negotiations could be rather complicated, but later they presented much less difficulty, as all Hut 8 keys except Bounce were four-wheel, and only 42 bombes were therefore concerned unless Bounce was to be run. To assist the Watch in deciding the relative priority of various Hut 6 jobs, two routines had been instituted — a daily meeting with 3L (the liaison section of Hut 3), and a complete list of Hut 6 keys arranged according to intelligence priority.

Daily meeting
This meeting served not only as a guide for the Watch in its current work, but also as an opportunity for a general exchange of information. It was normally attended by Milner-Barry, Manisty, the heads of shift from the Air and Army Watches, representatives from the Air and Army Qwatches and 3L. A "lage" of non-current (more than one day old) jobs was typed and served as a rather arbitrary agenda for the meeting. The four Watch representatives gave brief accounts of the situation and answered any questions. The 3L representative mentioned any points of special intelligence interest. The Watch representatives could then withdraw, and the three remaining at the meeting graded the non-current lage, i.e., put the jobs into an order of running, which was passed on to i/c Ops.

This last procedure may sound rather illogical, as jobs run at Washington rarely came under discussion at all. The meeting was instituted at a time when there was a strong distinction between Watch and Research keys and when bombe time was heavily in demand, largely in order to ensure that the most important jobs on Research keys were given priority, if necessary over the less important Watch keys. At that time the Washington bombes were not a significant factor. But even at the end, when there was rarely much delay in running any jobs produced, the existence of the lage perhaps prevented the meeting from degenerating into vagueness by giving it actual decisions to make. Certainly, Milner-Barry, Manisty and 3L found the meeting of real use as a means of keeping themselves in touch, but the Watch representatives sometimes regarded it with some impatience.

Priority list

For the last years of the war, a list of keys arranged according to intelligence priority was issued regularly on information supplied by 3L. In its final form the list contained all Hut 6 keys being broken or likely to be broken. The keys were arranged in six classes for Importance and six classes for Urgency. It provided a very useful guide to the Watch (and to other rooms) in deciding priority of current work, and also gave a convenient classification of Hut 6 keys when the relative claims of Hut 6 and Hut 8 were under consideration. Hut 8 keys were sufficiently few in number to be considered individually in discussions.

Current bombe control

England

Three Hut 6 members were directly concerned with current bombe control:

Watch A: Head of Shift (H/S).
(Operational Air Watch): i/c Ops (a member of the MR working in the Watch for a particular shift).
Machine Room: OCB (OC Bombenlage).

OCB was in direct touch with the Controller in Hut 23 and was concerned with the placing of every bombe (except those in use by Hut 8). When a bombe finished a job she would tell the Controller what its next job was.

I/c Ops kept a complete current record ("Lage") of jobs running and available. This lage was arranged under keys (OCB, however, was fundamentally concerned with bombes) and was divided for convenience into Air and Army, each being sub-divided into current and non-current. ("Current" was arbitrarily taken as "not more than one day old"). I/c Ops advised OCB of the order in which jobs should be run, but was not concerned with the placing of individual bombes except where jobs demanded bombes of a special type.

H/S in Watch A was responsible for the general policy being carried out by i/c Ops. He could see the current position from the Lage and advised i/c Ops of the order in which she could run current jobs and on such points as whether to run more than one job at a time on the same key. The order of running non-current jobs had been decided at the meeting, but H/S was responsible for fitting in jobs produced after the meeting. The lage was rewritten by i/c Ops at the end of her shift and the old lage passed to the section of the Watch concerned for checking its records.

The detailed technique of bombe control in the Machine Room is considered in the following chapter, but two aspects of the problem are closely connected with policy and are worth discussing here. The first is the problem of how many bombes to put on a given job. The most economical method is to put one bombe on to each menu and then to avoid unnecessary plugging. This was rarely done even with non-urgent jobs unless a few wheelorders only had to be run. With urgent jobs, one bombe per menu is too slow, and with non-urgent jobs it makes for inflexibility, for the situation frequently arose of an urgent job being considered at short notice.

If this was a job requiring a large number of bombes, e.g., a crib of which several versions had to be run, or a naval job to be run on some 300 wheelorders, the only way to obtain the bombes quickly was to remove some from non-urgent jobs. If these jobs had at least two bombes per menu, it was usually possible to obtain enough bombes for the urgent job and still leave at least one on each of the non-urgent menus.

It was then necessary to strip the non-urgent job completely and to replug it at a later stage, with advantage both to the administration of the bombes and to the morale of the bombe operators. With the number of bombes in use and pressure on communications, administrative convenience in running the bombes was important. In fact, normal routine was to put two or three bombes on any menu running 60 wheelorders.

The second is the problem of the use of special bombes, in particular those English bombes that can run delayed hoppity menus which otherwise have to be sent to Washington. To run an urgent job in a reasonable time it is necessary to put at least eight of these bombes on to a 60-wheelorder menu. And, as these bombes were also in demand by Hut 8, their control was rather more a direct concern of the H/S than the control of the ordinary bombes.

Washington (Op-20-G)
The ideal would have been to apply to the control of the bombes at Washington exactly the same methods as were used in England — in fact to use them as part of the general stock. But communication difficulties made this impossible, and a much less flexible system had to be used. By means of a system of priority indications we were able to use these bombes fully operationally, although the most urgent jobs were, when possible, run here. But the bombe strength available for delayed hoppity menus at Op-20-G was much greater than that available in England, and so with the growth of short cribs, we made considerable use of Op-20-G for jobs of the first urgency. And certainly for these jobs they gave very good service indeed, delays being solely due to the inevitable difficulties of communication.

A standard form of signal was used for sending jobs, and these signals were encoded by the Cipher Office on the CCM. Signals all went through Hut 8 but were prepared in Hut 6 by a small sub-section of the Watch, known as BOVO (BOVRIL and OXO were cover names for jobs at Op-20-G and Arlington respectively). BOVO kept all records connected with jobs at Washington, and prepared, twice daily, a statement of the jobs in hand at Op-20-G together with the fate of jobs that had been run since the last report. The morning statement was circulated to all concerned, including Milner-Barry and 3L, and so gave those interested an opportunity of suggesting alterations of priority.

There were five classes: D, DE, E, F and G. D was strictly confined to jobs of high urgency and Op-20-G treated D jobs on a level with the most urgent Hut 8 jobs. C was rarely used. It was unusual for mere D and DE jobs to be sent than could be handled at one time, and so normally they were given no special priority among themselves. If pressure was heavy, a special note about priority was determined by the serial number, the lowest number being run first, and decimal sub-divisions used where necessary — for example, F45.1 was run before F46 but after all E jobs. Jobs were graded and numbered by Manisty or his deputy when on duty, and at other times by the H/S in Watch A or Watch M.

Op-20-G sent us three times a day a statement of jobs running and jobs completed since the previous statement. In addition, if a job came up in America, a clear signal was sent under the code word AUDIT, referring to the time of origin of the job signal. This gave advance information that the job was up and enabled work on the key to be stopped in England — the key itself followed in a cipher signal about an hour later. A similar procedure was used to indicate that D and DE jobs had gone down, but was not found necessary for lower priority jobs.

Washington (Arlington)

The method of control of the Arlington bombe was similar to that used with Op-20-G. Signals were prepared by BOVO, but they did not pass through Hut 8, but were sent direct to the Signals Registry by tube. The priority categories here were A, AB and C, and it was not normally found necessary to indicate priority with a class. The much smaller capacity of the Arlington bombe made the control problem simple, and only at times of high pressure was it used for urgent jobs. The only exception to this was the rare occurrence of an urgent cilli job in two or three periods — and such a job could only be run by the Arlington bombe.

Conclusion

The inconsistencies in this system of bombe control — as in many other Hut 6 routines — were largely due to the way in which it grew up. On the whole it worked, although starting from scratch something rather different would probably have been designed. In particular, the maintenance by Hut 6 and Hut 8 of independent control systems inevitably caused some loss in flexibility. But this was a consequence of the existence of the two Huts as separate units, which arose for reasons of history rather than of deliberate planning.

Chapter 18
History of the Machine Room (formerly Netz Room)

Historical Outline

Throughout every change, the general function of the Machine Room – formerly the Netz Room – in Hut 6 remained the same. It was, throughout, an ancillary cryptographic section, assisting at every stage the principal cryptographic sections – first Machine Room and Crib Room, later Watch and Research – in whatever way was most suitable at the time. In the last years this assistance was given primarily in the field of bombe control and testing of stops, and for this reason the present chapter follows on naturally from the last. Historically, the development of the Machine Room falls roughly into three parts:

1. The original Netz Room was occupied first of all in the preparation of the Netz sheets and then for the first half of 1940 in the shoving of the sheets to break keys. This work was highly important and demanded the greatest concentration. In the latter half of 1940, with the change in indicating system, this work disappeared and the members of the NR were usefully (but perhaps somewhat monotonously) occupied in performing various odd jobs for other Rooms – e.g., sticking decoded tapes on messages for the Decoding Room, or punching Banbury sheets for the Research cryptographers in attempts to break Greenshank.

2. The interim period, when the Netz Room took over from the Machine Room (but still under their supervision) the work of testing bombe stops and later finding ringstellung. The name Netz Room, though now a misnomer, was still retained for traditional and sentimental reasons.

3. The final period, after the Machine Room and the Crib Room had been combined and renamed the Watch. The Netz Room then took over completely the duties of direct bombe control and testing, and themselves became known as the Machine Room – a logical, but at first rather confusing, step.

This report deals almost wholly with this last stage of development, i.e., from 1943 to the end of the war. It should be mentioned that from April 1942, while technically the NR/MR worked closely with the cryptographic sections, administratively it was placed (along with both Registration and the Decoding Room) under the charge of Mr Fletcher.

Expansion of the Room
During the last years, the Machine Room was continually expanding and adopting new methods of organisation to meet the demands of the rapidly increasing number of bombes. It says much for the ability and personality of Mary Wilson, the head of the Room, that all the improvements and changes were carried through so smoothly and efficiently. Some idea of the vast increase in the volume of work is given by the fact that in 1942 a shift of six or seven was able to cope with the work of allotting the bombes, testing stops, finding ringstellung, registering and breaking Rocket and attempting to break dud messages. The last two jobs were always regarded as subsidiary functions of the MR and eventually they were delegated to a separate sub-section.

In 1945, a minimum of 13 was needed, and by this time Rocket and duds had been transferred, the number of stops per menu had been greatly reduced by various means to be described later, and a great deal of operational work connected with bombe running (e.g., the checking of wheelorders) had been transferred to Hut 23, the central bombe station situated in Bletchley Park, and the subsidiary outstations. At least half the members of the shift were engaged in organisation, and were kept busier than one girl had been in 1942, doing the work of all of them. The MR was the last Room to adopt the system of heads of shift, but this became necessary when the shifts became larger, and the division of work more complicated.

The first big expansion came in October 1942, when the first influx from the universities arrived, and by the time the move to Block D took place in February 1943, the rooms in Hut 6 were very overcrowded. At first the new quarters seemed luxuriously spacious. Three rooms were allotted to the MR, one for testing stops etc., one for Rocket and one for duds. Unfortunately, by the time these rooms would have been well-filled, they were taken away – first the Duds Room for the Decoding Room school, and later the Rocket Room for an extension to the DR. Room 1 in Block D was then used for Rocket, but the main testing room became very crowded, and remained so until the end.

History of the Machine Room (formerly Netz Room)

The breaking of duds

Before discussing the final set-up for bombe control, it seems best to deal with this minor function of the MR. By the end of the war it had mainly been delegated to a separate sub-section, presided over by the indefatigable Miss Eperson, an ex-member of the MR who had devoted herself to this work with the greatest enthusiasm from the day of her arrival, and after whom the various methods of getting out duds – i.e., messages which for some reason do not decode on the message setting arising from the indicators, though they were encoded on the key in question – by juggling with the indicators were collectively named "Eppery". This sub-section, however, only worked from 9am to midnight, and it was the responsibility of the MR proper to attempt to decode any duds urgently requested by Hut 3 during the night.

There were various methods of approach to the problem. If the dud was part of a message, the rest of which had been decoded, Hut 3 could often give a crib which could be tried on the rods. Failing this, the most likely reason for the message being dud was a Morse error in the indicator, and the more probable alternatives could be tried. It was often possible to get indicator corrections, or other helpful information, from the log readers, but this involved a delay of about 24 hours. Again, particularly in part messages, the possibility of cillying was worth consideration. Or again, the beginning of the text might have been missed, and by checking the number of letters it was sometimes possible to find the correct starting position. Often a comparison of the dupes would show that a combination of the different texts would provide the correct decode. Nor did the above methods exhaust all the hand methods for solving duds adopted. But it was difficult to lay down any hard and fast rules for the breaking of duds, as each case had to be considered on its merits and a lot depended on individual initiative and perseverance.

Machine methods were also available if required. One or two of the bombes were fitted to take an attachment which would try a common word, such as EINS, in all positions of the text, and the MR would test the stops produced. The Arlington dud-buster could also be used with a very good chance of success, but this was not practicable for very urgent duds, owing to the inevitable delays in signalling to Washington.

Final set-up for bombe control

Communications

Before the installation of the tube system to Hut 23, and the teleprinters to the outstations, there was great congestion on the telephones. First stops had to be checked back on every menu to ensure that the menu had reached the outstation correctly. All wheelorders were telephoned to the MR by the i/c Ops at the outstation, and at the conclusion of each job OCB (OC Bombenlage) telephoned Controller in Hut 23 – the Wren officer in charge of all bombes for the shift – to tell her that the bombe could strip, and to give her its new job. In addition, all stops were telephoned, and consequently the four – and later five – telephones were in constant use, and the two or three people who had to answer them had a rather harassing time. Bombe copies of menus had to be taken over to Hut 23, and this was quite an adventure at night. One moment one was ankle-deep in mud, the next walking into a concrete mixer left by the workmen engaged in building the new blocks. For several weeks there was a deep trench which had to be negotiated by a narrow mud-coated plank, and more than one person met a muddy fate at this point. However, the tube system and the teleprinters made life a much easier existence, and a later improvement, saving a lot of time and trouble, was the checking of wheelorders by the i/c Ops at the outstation, who informed Controller when a machine had finished its job. Controller then told OCB that the bombe had stripped.

Routine organisational jobs

The routine organising functions for each shift were shared among the following individuals:

(1) OCB: When told by Controller that a bombe had finished its job, she gave it a suitable new menu, remembering the idiosyncrasies of some machines, such as dislike of double-input menus, lack of D-boards etc., and informed Controller what wheelorders had to be run. She decided, in consultation with i/c Ops in the Watch, how many bombes were needed for each menu. The GAF keys generally ran on the Nigelian wheel orders, often reduced by the non-clashing and non-repeating rule, and the correct wheelorders for each job were worked out by OCB. The Watch Head of Shift advised when any particular menu should run more wheelorders, and the instructions were passed on to Controller.

History of the Machine Room (formerly Netz Room)

It was generally found more economical for the bombes on one menu to be taken from the same bay and in the case of delayed hoppity menus on the high-speed bombes, a complete bay would be put into one menu. With very urgent menus it was not always possible to keep the bombes together, and in these cases the first available ones were put on, regardless of station. This was very rarely necessary with the ordinary bombes as they came free at such frequent intervals. A detailed record was kept of the bombes with their times of stripping, the name of the new job and the time it was started. OCB kept a card for each menu on a large board giving details of the crib, number of wheelorders and the bombes running it. She was thus able to see at a glance how the bombes were disposed, and the state of each job.

(2) OCB's assistant: She entered the menus on a card index, numbering them consecutively according to the name of key and date, and marked the cards when a menu had failed. She made out stop-sheets for each menu as it was put on, writing the names of the bombes in colours, which were different for each station – red for Stanmore, blue for Eastcote, black for the US bay at Eastcote, green for Gayhurst, brown for Adstock and purple for the Hut 11A bombes. This made it simpler to find sheets quickly when stops came in. Key breaks were reported to the Duty Officer, to the Decoding Room and the Registration Room, and, if current, to Control, and this member checked that the completed key was entered on the various cards and in the Watch and MR key books. Another task was the keeping of a record for Mr Knight of the time taken by each bombe to complete its job, and this in itself provided her main occupation.

(3) Tube stooge: The bombe copies of the menus were sent to Hut 23 by tube. From there they were teleprinted to the appropriate outstation, and a copy of the teleprint was returned for the "tube stooge" to check that the wheelorders were sent over correctly, and that details such as B or D reflector, CSKO if necessary were inserted. She received the teleprinted good stops, and after checking the serial numbers passed these on to be written on the stop-sheets. After a bombe had stripped, i/c Ops at the outstation sent by teleprinter the list of stops which the MR should have received, and these were handed to the "Burier".

(4) Burier: She checked that all the stops had been received, that each one had been tested, and then filed the failed menus, with the appropriate stop-sheets attached. Another of her tasks was to keep a record of the reruns necessary owing to machine faults – these were sent in as discovered – and

to check periodically with Controller that these had been done.

(5) Stop stooge: This member wrote down the stops on the relevant sheets and passed them on to the testers. Stops from Hut 11A came by telephone to her, and first stops had to be checked back, as there was in this case no teleprinted copy of the menu. Any very good stop, which seemed likely to be the correct one, was also phoned to avoid any possible tube delay, and this was written down in the same way and passed to the testers. On night shift, or when the shift was short, it was sometimes possible to combine these last two jobs.

(6) I/C Ops: This, the most important job of all, was, strictly speaking, a Watch function, but was performed by a member of the MR sitting in the Watch and working in close collaboration with the Watch Head of Shift. Under his direction she was responsible for the minute-to-minute allocation of bombes to jobs in so far as this was governed by intelligence and cryptographic priorities. She kept a detailed "lage" of jobs waiting to be run arranged under keys, and gave the jobs to OCB according to the list of priorities and the instructions of Watch H/S. It should be noted that i/c Ops was concerned with keys, while OCB dealt with bombes.

The lage gave a detailed record of the jobs out, failed, running or in hand and i/c Ops kept the H/S in Air and Army Watch informed of the progress of their most urgent keys, reporting any breaks that occurred. She was also responsible for guiding those members of the MR who were engaged in menu-making, i.e., seeing that the jobs in hand were dealt with in their correct order or priority and any spare time she had from her primary duties she devoted to making up menus herself. In general, she acted as liaison between the Watch H/S and OCB.

Normal testing of stops
Of the rest of the shift, one or two sat in the Watch to make up menus, and the others tested the good stops, i.e., those stops that had successfully passed the initial examination conducted by the Wren testers at the bombe stations and were sent on for further scrutiny. At one time these became so numerous that steps had to be taken to reduce the number reaching the MR. This was done by various menus:

(1) The basic menus were made slightly stronger, e.g., a 9_3 was no longer run unless it could take CSKO and a 15_1 was run in preference to a 14_1.

(2) Whereas, previously, any stop with one contradiction had been sent over, it was decided that when the menu was made up on clean and

History of the Machine Room (formerly Netz Room)

well-duped texts, only stops with no contradictions would be tested. Stops on unduped menus with one contradiction on an outlying link were still tested, to allow for the possibility of corruption.

(3) A system of "phantom links" was introduced. These were not plugged on the bombe, but were used by the Wren testers for checking, and stops which gave contradictions on these letters were not sent over. This was the greatest labour-saving device of all, and despite the objections of the pessimists (in other sections!), who feared that the increased risks might result in the correct stop being missed, the Wren testers were by this time so efficient that this was never proved to have happened.

Special problems
Variety was added to the ordinary testing by delayed hoppity menus, which allowed for a turnover in the stretch and by H-menus (four-closures run with queries instead of letters, and without diagonal boards, on keys where Enigma Uhr was suspected). The joy of testing these latter was that there were no confirmations to suggest a good stop, and any one might be the correct answer. When this was found, the subsequent problem of finding the basic stecker and ringstellung provided exercise for the more mathematically-minded. Occasionally, too, the MR helped with the breaking of D reflectors, and had the expected wholesale conversion to D materialised in January 1944, there was a trained team ready to take part in the mass hand-breaking attack.

A development which preceded the introduction of Enigma Uhr was the thrice-daily change of stecker. The three periods were known as R, S and T – period S having four stecker different from the original R, and T having four others different from S. The MR provided one or two people per shift to work on this problem, and discover the correct variations. As a security device, this was quite futile, and proved nothing worse than an annoyance. It fortunately did not last long, the Germans evidently finding it as much of a nuisance as Hut 6.

Although the major crises of Hut 6 did not affect the MR so directly as they did most other sections, there was quite an appreciable amount of extra work involved, especially towards the end, when the keys, particularly Army keys, because very confused – partly owing to German security measures, such as the dropping of discriminants and the encoding of callsigns, and partly owing to the natural confusion caused by a rapidly moving battle. It was often impossible to identify a key until it was broken and decoded, and so some Army keys were run under a general name such as Barnyard (Western Front) or Aviary (Balkans), and only named when they were subsequently identified. This meant that if a Barnyard came out, every other job on a Western Front key of that date that was running had to be tried on it, and if, as often happened, they all decoded, OCB was flooded with as many as 70 bombes, all clamouring for new jobs. To get these all settled without too long a delay (one had always had to have an eye on Mr Knight and his bombe delay statistics) provided a hectic half-hour. Another irritating possibility was that the key might turn out to be that of the day before, and it was not unknown for someone to spend an hour or two on a difficult ringstellung, another 20 minutes or so writing out all the cards and entering the key in the key books, only to discover that it was yesterday's key which had been out all the time.

The introduction of CY into Army messages caused an added complication. This was a system by which the left-hand wheel was moved by hand in the middle of the message. The position was indicated by the letters CY followed by two consecutive letters, the first of these being the setting to which the wheel most be moved. Finding a ringstellung on one of these messages (and one was never sure whether or not the CY would appear) involved looking for this position. When found, it provided the correct clip position for the left-hand wheel and was thus a help towards obtaining the full ringstellung, but if the text was corrupt, it was often difficult to tell exactly where it "went off". If the crib was at the beginning of the message, the CY position could be ignored, but if it was a signature (the majority of Army cribs were) it was essential to find this position and this was often no easy task. The last few months provided such a haul of captured keys that it was almost a full-time job for someone to test them all, and to enter and report the breaks, and inevitably, as the war drew to a close, there was less and less to run, and bombes often had to remain idle for long periods. But, rather against expectations, the MR continued at almost full pressure right up to VE-Day – a more satisfactory finish than the gradual dying out they had been led to expect.

In conclusion, a special word of praise is due to the two American members of the MR. It must have been rather disconcerting to them to be placed in a room otherwise exclusively female, and to have a girl in charge, but they never showed the slightest resentment, and proved most cheerful and co-operative workers.

Chapter 19
Red, Blue, Pink and Brown Keys

General Introduction

Throughout the war, Hut 6 had a clear theoretical objective before it — to decode currently every message sent out by the Germans. This achievement being for long an obvious practical impossibility, it concentrated instead upon the traffic likely to give the maximum of assistance to the British or American forces engaged in the most important campaign of the moment. Thus the emphasis of the work shifted from one key or group of keys to another as the war progressed, the potentialities of a non-operational group not being overlooked, but the immediate requirements of the moment always taking pride of place.

In the following account of the breaking of individual keys or groups of keys, some attempt is made to show the correlation between the Hut 6 effort and the demands of the war situation, and the keys are therefore described in the order in which they rose to their highest breaking priority. Thus Red, although the outstanding key for so many years, comes first because it provided high-grade intelligence in the Battle of France, and Brown, which because of supreme importance during the raids on Britain, comes next. And so through the campaign to the end of the war, the Eastern Front Air and Army keys coming last in the list because, although they had provided valuable intelligence for a very long time, they only became of immediate operational assistance to our forces when the link-up between the Eastern and Western Fronts was drawing near.

Finally, sections are included on some of the types of key not covered under the previous headings, such as the GAF Y Service key Mustard, and the keys connected with the V-weapons. In all of these accounts it has been impossible to do more than indicate briefly the main lines followed in the course of breaking. The story of Red, for instance, broken steadily for more than four years, does not indicate the anxiety which it often gave the cryptographers — there was a night in 1942 when six correct cribs failed to produce the right answer — or the general relief felt when the day came out.

Even so, not all the keys broken are described. The Norwegian keys, especially the Air keys Narcissus and Lion, deserve a separate section, if only to tell of the hard battle fought by the Qwatch against the increasing use of D on Lion in 1944. Osprey, the key of the Organisation Todt, was broken on cillies so many times that Hut 3 felt compelled to detach an expert to read the traffic despite its uninteresting appearance. Then there was Stork, the key which caused a sensation in Hut 6 by decoding in Hungarian, and created a problem in Hut 3 because no one knew the language. Or Dingo, the Geschwader key with a remarkable crib 300 letters long which only appeared once in every ten days. These, with many others of short duration and minor importance, are omitted. But enough is said to show the general trends in the work of the cryptographic sections and the varying ways in which keys were broken.

Red

Red: A major Army blunder

In the opening chapters of this book it has been told how, in 1940, interception was confined to Red frequencies because this colour carried an immense volume of traffic and was being broken. At that time Red carried practically all the Air Force traffic of any importance with the exception of the specialised matters dealt with by Brown. The only other Air Force keys were Blue, the practice key, and special keys carrying small amounts of non-operational traffic. Thus, any GAF communications of importance sent over the air were almost certain to be encoded in Red, and by breaking Red, Hut 6 could probably give warning of any new Luftwaffe move in any quarter. It was a cardinal error on the part of the enemy to use a general key of this type: apart from the obvious dangers of having too many messages on the same key, it meant that the insecurity of a single operator in, say, Norway, might perhaps provide us with information of the employment of a new bomber group against Britain, or of concentration of planes for some new drive in the Balkans.

As the war progressed, the Germans introduced more and more keys which were designed to reduce the volume of traffic on Red and to increase security by the use of local keys. But the original error was never rectified and Red, the general Luftwaffe key, remained in use until the end. By this time it had been surpassed in urgency and importance by the keys dealing specifically with the Western campaign. But it was still of great interest as a potential source of information about the GAF everywhere.

Red, Blue, Pink and Brown Keys

Breaking — 1940 to 1945

The first war-time breaks of Red were made in January 1940 on the old indicating system. The change to double indicators before the Battle of France meant that hand methods alone could be used, for the first bombe did not arrive until August, but large numbers of cillies, coupled with ringstellung tips given by inspection of first message, enabled many current breaks to be made even at this stage. The completion of the bombe and a reduction in cillying generally soon led to a shift of emphasis from cillies to cribs — and cillies soon became of very minor importance in breaking Red. Useful in providing wheelorder preferences when bombes were few, they occasionally gave us a day which had failed to come out by other means. There was, for instance, for some weeks an operator at Bari who used to cilli most of his messages and usually used the indicators ELF and JUN. One day was broken on a menu consisting of seven ELFs, but more usually the day was out before these cillies began to arrive, for the group normally worked only during the night, when it forwarded traffic encoded during the evening.

Red always provided plenty of traffic — 1,000 a day during the Battle of France in 1940, sometimes over 500 in periods of simultaneous operations in the Mediterranean and Russia in 1941 and 1942, and always over 100 even in spells of comparative inactivity. There was therefore usually in the absence of any strict cipher discipline in the GAF a wide variety of cribs, and the problem was not normally to break the day but to break it early. Weather cribs were often valuable for they tended to come at regular intervals and frequently to report no change in standard form.

The first Red crib to break a day — Keine Zusätze — was a short message saying that there was nothing to add to a previous long report on the weather. The tradition thus set was maintained by the Shorter Wueb, which broke over 100 days in 1941, the Lett Wett and Czech Wueb, great stand-bys which went over to Fliegerkorps keys in 1942, and the Skunk Wetter, a crib of 1943 so good that Red parents were heard wishing that it would return to Skunk whence it came because it made the breaking of Red so childishly simple. At one time or another every type of routine message sent by the GAF was used as a crib on Red. There were operational orders like the famous pair sent out by Luftflotte 4 – "Besan", i.e.:

BESONDERE ANORDNUNGEN FUER DIE LUFTAUFKLAERUNG AM
(Date of next day)

and "Befehl", which said:

BEFEHL FUER DIE KAMPFFUEHRUNG
(Date of next day)

Year after year these messages would make spasmodic appearances, in form almost invariable. On Red, even when they were identifiable daily, they were only used in the last resort, for they did not arrive until very late in the day – one more example of the strength of the Red crib position. Then there were Tagesabschlussmeldungen — one of them, Chef, had a long career, tuners and operational reports of all kinds. Of the latter the most notable were from Fliegerkorps X, which for long provided several cribs a day, sometimes with depth on the address — known as the "Robinson fun and games". Of tuning messages, those on the Jägerleitkreis were of the greatest value, for in 1944 when they came into prominence, the crib position on Red was considerably weaker than before.

There were several Jägersprüche a day, and although the variety of forms included ABSTIMMSPRUQ ... Or simply Qatsch, there was usually one each day which began: DAS IST EIN ABSTIMMSPRUQ ... From 1 January 1944, some of the Red traffic was encoded with Reflector D, but breaking was not seriously affected because there were always some cribs using B, which gave a break into the successive D-periods. The Jägersprüche were particularly useful here, as they steadily used B throughout.

Supreme importance of Red
So Red was broken almost solidly from the middle of 1940 to the end of the war. In 1942, 1943 and 1944 not a day was missed, and in 1941 a clean sweep was probably only averted by the compromise of Red in November, when for ten days hand keys were used instead – to the general confusion of both the GAF and Bletchley Park. This compromise was no doubt one of the reasons for the introduction of Fliegerkorps keys on the following 1 January, an event which demonstrated for the first time the cryptographic hold which steady breaking of Red was giving us over the GAF. The new keys were broken on some of the old Red cribs which had now challenged their allegiance, and in the following years there were many instances of new keys being broken on REs from Red or on cribs either transferred to the new key or occasionally sent in Red. Even after the opening of the campaign in the West, when the Luftflotte 3 keys, Ocelot and Jaguar, took pride of place in intelligence importance, Red remained supreme as the key most likely to lead to breaks of others by re-encodement.

The direct intelligence value of Red must have been enormous — a steady stream of high-level information about the past and future of the GAF, with occasionally memorable messages on a variety of subjects like the routeing of *Bismarck* or the plans for the invasion of Crete. Scarcely less important was its indirect intelligence or cryptographic value in providing the means for so many other breaks.

Blue and Pink

Perhaps mention should be made of the two keys the most closely parallel to Red, both of which were of long duration and wide distribution, although Pink was confined to the most important commands. Blue — the Luftwaffenübungsmaschinenschlüssel — lasted from October 1939 almost until the end of the war. In the early days of the war the practice traffic was indistinguishable from the operational messages, and in fact before breaks revealed the distinction between Blue and Red, Blue was believed to be the operational key. As soon as the nature of the key was discovered it had very low breaking priority and was not touched at all unless there was some reason for believing that it might have more than its usual interest.

In 1942 Blue was involved in key repeats and was therefore broken to give assistance with other keys. Later, in 1943, some of the Cockroach traffic — including one crib — went over to Blue, and it was therefore broken by this means. Most of the Blue breaks were on cribs which had at some times passed on other colours such as the Daffodil Zahlsprüche or the Snowdrop Tagesabschlussmeldungen. It became a routine to break, if possible, a day a week to make certain that the traffic was still all practice. In 1944 Blue traffic totals were very high until D-Day, but thereafter most units ceased practising. The key, however, was identifiable until 1945.

It was in 1944 that the most remarkable Blue crib was discovered — the "Verena". This was a report on the work done by the pupils at the signals training school. Each unit sent one return a day, so that there were several different "Verenas", but they had the common characteristic of giving results in a figure proforma, the figures being encoded in a simple bigram letter for figure substitution. Thus a message beginning

```
VERENA    VL CH VL UR VL QF TK CH RX VL CH SG QF QF VL
=VERENA   X  1  X  6  X  0  7  1  5  X  1  9  0  0  X
```

where 1/6 is the date and 0715-1900 the time of working in the school. It can be imagined that this crib caused no little difficulty to the Machine and Decoding Rooms, who had to distinguish between the purely random letters even when the text "went off", and a string of meaningless letters when it was "on".

Pink — the Luftwaffenführungsschlüssel — was the key intended for messages of the highest secrecy sent between the highest GAF commands. It was rarely used and always difficult to identify. Apart from odd days broken on re-encodements — it often happened that a Pink message was refused because the recipient did not recognise or did not possess this rarity among keys — there was a period at the beginning of 1942 when Pink was used both in the Mediterranean and on the Auto between Berlin and the Russian Front. It was broken on an ex-Red crib, and provided for a day or two the very interesting message known as "Weisung", Berlin's daily orders to the Air Force governing the conduct of operations on the Eastern Front. It was broken on an ex-Red crib, and provided for a day or two the very interesting message known as "Weisung", Berlin's daily orders to the Air Force governing the conduct of operations on the Eastern Front.

In 1943, when the "Maxmeldung", a long-established Red crib giving the daily report of the German intelligence organisation in Sofia, went over to Pink it was usually the only message in the key. However, it enabled us to break one or two days when there was other traffic. Later the same year Kesselring showed a marked tendency to use Pink instead of Red for his high-grade messages, and a number of days were broken on re-encodements and routine Army reports such as the "Limbo" (Lage im Bereich Oberbefehlshaber Südwest), which tended to be forwarded for information to the Air Command. This was the last period in which Pink was regularly identified with certainty: twice afterwards keys appearing on the GHQ Auto were called Pink, but the likelihood is that they were not the Führungsschlüssel.

It was surprising — and fortunate for us — that no greater use was made of this key, for according to the instructions it should no doubt have carried all the Geheimekommandosache traffic which passed in Red. Red was stated to be "for secret and open matter", but actually a large volume of "top secret" traffic occurred in it also. Pink scarcely ever became fashionable in the GAF. Its imposing German name made it a sort of El Dorado to Hut 3, who found it difficult to believe that the Golden land had been reached when breaks decoded so little. But it was in line with German stupidity to give two keys — Pink and Red — a general distribution, and use one of them constantly, the other scarcely at all.

Brown

Introduction
In the days before the spectrum was exhausted and keys were still given colour names, Hut 6 made its first acquaintance with a Group that was to become a byword in Enigma history. The Brown cipher clerks demonstrated conclusively that the Enigma machine is only as secure as the men who use it. For it is difficult to think of any rule governing the use of the Enigma, or indeed of wireless procedure, that was not broken regularly by the clerks and operators of those Abteilungen of the L N Versuchs Regiment which used this key. Although the Group was known to the intercept stations very early in the war (some reports say before the war), it was not until the end of August 1940 that the attention of the cryptographers was drawn to the increasing traffic totals on Brown, which could be discerned amid the subsidising floods of Red traffic. As was soon proved, Brown was not a key capable of putting up much resistance to cryptographic attack and 2 September soon capitulated to the bombe, setting the widespread speculation about its content at rest.

The Brown Group was found to consist of a number of French stations, whose staffs were engaged on directing wireless beams for beam bombing by KG 100, and several German stations, where the original experiments on the subject had been carried out and where research was still in progress. As the war went on, this German Group with control at Köthen (HQ of the Regiment) proved a constant factor in a Brown picture which was always changing with the ephemeral appearances of other stations. The German stations supplied a continuous thread, linking the early beam bombing experiments with many other technical developments culminating in the V1 and V2 trials.

Since the Brown Group remained a compact wireless network separate from the other networks of the GAF signals organisation, and as a break of a Brown key often depended on knowing the personnel of a particular station, it was only natural that a more personal interest should be taken in Brown than in other keys. The facts that traffic totals were small, so that every message was necessary, and that hand attempts were possible on Brown, long after most other keys had become cilliless, accentuated the interest.

This history of the LN Versuchs Regiment as seen by a Brown cryptographer enters more into detail, perhaps, than the other key histories, in an attempt to convey the atmosphere and approach which seemed most suited to achieve the best results on Brown. Here then is not only the struggle to break the current operational key (Brown and Brown II), but also the efforts to maintain a hold on Brown I through a dull intelligence (although interesting cryptographic) period so that new inventions should not take us unawares. Probably any new Brown key could be broken in time, if there was any volume of traffic, but by breaking Brown I regularly, new keys could be broken quickly. It is at the birth of a new weapon when experiments go wrong, that most information about its mechanism is given, and not when the initial difficulties have been overcome and only the extent of its power remains to be determined. For this reason, it was important to break any new Brown keys as soon as they appeared. After August 1943, the activities of the Brown Group were divided between two opposite ideas – the one of attack, the other, defence. This period to the end of the war is covered by the story of Brown III.

"Target for Tonight" Phase I: September 1940-May 1941

The story begins during the period of the first Blitz on Britain – September 1940 to spring 1941 – which was the most exciting and momentous time in Hut 6 history. After the famous "Few" had swept the skies of Britain clear by day, Hut 6 played its part in the task of rendering those skies as hazardous by night. Although this is not the place for a description either of beam bombing or of the way our knowledge of it was built up on the information given in Brown, some facts are necessary so that the background to the work can be understood.

The Luftwaffe used KG 100, flying along wireless beams, as a pathfinder Group to indicate the target area for the other bombers. This was KG 100's main task, although occasionally it carried out special operations on its own. Each evening of an operation, the directions for the setting

Red, Blue, Pink and Brown Keys

of the wireless beams for the target were sent out in Brown from the HQ of KG 100 at Vannes to the beam stations at Boulogne, Cherbourg and Morlaix. It was the job of Hut 6 to send these instructions, decoded, to Hut 3 in time for action to be taken. Only if that vital information arrived in time, could the slender resources of night fighters and anti-aircraft guns be utilised to their fullest extent and concentrated on the small area through which it was known the enemy planes would pass. Later in the Blitz, when the technique of jamming and bending beams had been developed, it was even more important to have this information.

As most raids took place in the early evening, just after dark, the time factor was constantly in the thoughts of the cryptographer and a sense of urgency, such as was never felt again, permeated the whole Hut. For, never again, was the battle so close that the results of one's work had an immediate personal interest, when the difference of an hour in breaking time might mean the difference between life and death for some inhabitants of this embattled island. As the target had to be worked out from the beam settings, it was important to break every day so that the number and directions for the target were known for future reference, even if the day could not be broken in time to be of current operational use.

Sometimes there would be no Brown traffic until after midday and with the then shortage of bombes, the importance of picking the right version of a crib first time was paramount. It was about this time that the first decisions on bombe policy had to be taken, to run an early crib on 60 wheelorders or wait for cillies to reduce the wheelorders, thereby allowing other keys to run on the bombes. These decisions depended on how good the early crib was, and what keys were waiting to be run.

Now, any daily set of orders generally became stereotyped in the German signals organisation and Brown was no exception to this rule. The cribs on Brown were all connected with the beam bombing and the phases of a night's operation could be followed by the cribs. Let us take for an example of this, a day in December 1940. The beam stations were warned of an operation that night by a message – known as "Vorbereitet Betrieb [*Ready for Operation*] – about midday, giving the number of the target and notice whether there would be one or two operations. About two hours before the beams were due to be switched on, the detailed instructions on directions etc., would be transmitted. These, the beam stations concerned would have to re-encode and send back to Vannes as a check that there had been no corruption in the first transmission.

The beams were then directed and switched on, and a report to this effect – "Fertig Eingerichtet" – was sent back to Vannes as a check from each station. There was then an interval while the operation proceeded and should the day not be broken before the next crib came in, it would then be too late, for this crib was the "Betriebsschluss" to tell stations that it was all over. The final cribs in the series were the reports of the beam stations on the night's activity generally, consisting of that original German phrase and cryptographer's friend:

KEINE BESONDEREN VORKOMNISSE
[*Nothing to Report*]

These messages, known as "Boller's Betrieb" and Johanssen's Betrieb (the latter, one of those men whose name no two cipher clerks spell the same), were often sent out early the next morning and were the cribs that gave rise to the headaches of bombe policy.

This sequence of recognisable messages would be altered by another operation that night, and would be replaced if there was to be no operation, by a short (usually 32-letter) message which would give us this information as well as the Germans. The other occasion when the cryptographers could tell what a message was about, without decoding it, was when there was a slightly longer message than KEIN EINSATZ [*No Use*] the night after a raid. This would be HEUTE ZIEL WIE GESTERN [*Today as Yesterday Target*] and, as the Germans quite often raided the same place two nights running, a watch was kept for this message the night after a new target had been raided. The Duty Officer would inform Hut 3 if either of these two messages came in when the key was unbroken.

On 12 December 1940, a discovery was made which practically halved the bombe time needed for Brown. This was the famous stecker rule, which lasted on and off from 15 October 1940 to 15 July 1943 (Brown key months ran from 15th to 14th). Here it must be explained that the Brown keys did not follow the rest of the GAF keys in having ten stecker per day, but only had six or seven. There was thus always a temptation to pair the days so that letters steckered on one day were unsteckered the other, and to a neat and orderly German mind, this must have been irresistible. Anyway, the compiler of the Brown keys (who was one of our best aids to breaking) succumbed to the temptation.

After one day had been broken, the pair day could usually be rodded out, or a hand attempt made much easier. The very fact of there being 12 or 14 self-steckered letters every day was a great help in hand attempts and was responsible for a new technique of breaking — "the clonk". Roughly speaking, each constatation of a crib (of known machine setting such as cilli or cilli and signature) and encode was assumed self-steckered in turn and machine positions were examined to find the one with the largest number of these self-steckered pairings. On the paired day the actual self-steckered letters were known so that positions could be rejected which did not give the required pairings.

After this stecker rule was found, most Brown days were broken, and from the information gained the subtle method of bending the beams was developed so that German airmen bombed open fields instead of towns without realising their mistake. By the spring of 1941, the Germans had become very suspicious about these counter-measures and the speed with which they had been prepared, and a great security drive was launched. Fortunately for Hut 6, no one thought about wireless security, and we were able to read how all the past records of the German technicians had been checked and about the wild fantasies the Germans had of Allied agents signalling the target for the night across the Channel. When the invasion of Russia was imminent, the Luftwaffe withdrew its bomber squadrons from France and the first beam bombing attack had been withstood. The German scientists then retired to Germany to think again and to prepare for the second round safe, as they thought, from prying eyes and ears.

"Target for Tonight"
Phase II: December 1941-June 1942
Brown II

The results of these second thoughts began to appear in December 1941 when the Brown traffic, which had remained negligible and unbroken for the preceding five months, increased in volume and showed the key had split, presumably for security reasons. Communications about the experiments in Germany were passed in one key, named Brown (G) and the French stations used another, named Brown (F). Such simplicity in naming, however, was contrary to usual practice and these names gave way to Brown I and II respectively. The trials in Germany of the modification of the method of beam bombing followed much the same pattern in the sequence of cribs for an operation as the winter before, and the old routine of cribs, cillies and clonks was soon in full swing again. Because of the natural close liaison between experiment in Germany and preparation in France, re-encodements were often found between the two keys and Brown was in a healthy enough condition in January to be returned to the operational shifts as a current commitment.

In February, the Brown keymaker evolved another delightful method of compiling keys. This was to add one to each component (wheelorder, ringstellung and stecker), of the key of one day to get the next day's key. Unfortunately, these "stepping" keys were on Brown I, which was easier to break than Brown II, and they only lasted a month. It is perhaps as well that the bombing operations were not on the same scale as the previous year as the breaks on the operational keys were not as frequent as before. This was due not only to the two separate keys, but also to the fact that less traffic was being passed between the French stations. Still, enough was broken to help the counter-measures, and raids became too costly to a Luftwaffe whose wings stretched from Moscow to the Atlantic and from the Arctic Circle to the Egyptian desert, were weakening under the strain. At the end of June, the beam bombing stopped, the Brown II traffic sank to an unbreakable level, and Brown went back to Research.

But there was still one last kick left, and at the beginning of October, after an initial break on cillies, a few more days were broken on Betriebsschlüss [*Operational Circuit*](once or twice the only message), but there were no other signs of operations in the traffic or, indeed, always in the air activity over this country. This last mystery was coupled with a 10-stecker key, and so it was without regret, but perhaps with a sigh for past glories, that the cryptographers said goodbye to a key which had been the most important key broken in Hut 6 and was now only a shrunken remnant, often rescued from the "no colour" by a watchful parent. The beam stations were used as radio beacons for homing aircraft for a few more months And were then dismantled, the final farewell to a secret weapon which had only failed to secure the results it promised by the lack of cipher security in the men who used it.

The lull: Brown I

As has already been related above, Brown I was used by the stations in Germany for the experiments in beam bombing. When these were finished, the content of the traffic became purely administrative, and while cryptographically it was a most interesting key, the effort and time expended on breaking it was only justified as a long-term policy of keeping in touch with the Versuchs Regiment which was sure to be connected with any new weapon of war needing wireless. The German stations remained a nucleus of the Brown I network until overrun by the advancing Russian armies, and added to this nucleus were stations in occupied territories such as Paris and Kharkov. Also, from time to time, stations would be set up in places convenient for specific experiments and then disbanded when these experiments were completed. After a scarcity of breaks during summer 1942, a firm hold was taken on Brown I in September, which was not shaken off until the next autumn when, with the arrival of Brown III and IV, less time could be spent on Brown I.

There were mostly small stations on Brown I, and in such cases the staff consisted of an NCO in charge and a few men. All would take their turn in encoding and decoding messages, besides operating the wireless set, and with no activity at night, only two shifts were necessary. Their customary practice, thoroughly approved of in Hut 6, was to use the initial trigrams of their names as message settings for any Enigma messages they encoded and as a signature when chatting over the air. Nor was this the limit of their helpfulness, for the NCO would sign all the messages so that unless, as once happened to our annoyance, an officer or higher ranking NCO was visiting the station, the signature to messages would be constant and message settings limited for periods up to three months. Then there would be a General Post and another NCO and party arrive with a new signature and series of message settings. Often advance notice of any change was given by the operators enquiring in clear when they were to be relieved. In order to pass all such information, which could be obtained from the logs, to the cryptographers, a daily Brown "story" was instituted early in 1942. This was compiled by the log reader and included a list of messages (with receipts) with the account of the day's working as well as any Klartext. The Brown story was originally intended to help the breaking of Brown II and as a check that all Brown II traffic was seen by the cryptographers. Such a check is invaluable where the volume of traffic is small and one extra message may mean an extra cilli and perhaps another break.

With the limited choice of message settings, depth reading was quite a common exercise, made easier by the routine addresses used. For, apart from communications and apparatus tests of which notice would be given in clear, most messages were about the three fundamental interests of the serviceman common to every nation – pay, leave and supplies (cigarettes, chocolate, etc.). For example, about 90% of the messages from Wustrow in early 1943 would begin in one of the three following ways:

R E Q N U N G S F U E **H** R E R X **X**	(Pay clerk - Pay)
O B L T X X L I C H T **H** A R D T **X** X	(OC Company - Leave)
O F W X X P R I X X	(Sgt. Major - Supplies)

and have one of the three message settings H E L, G R I, S T E. The double Xs also illustrates one of the peculiar types of punctuation which were used at different times on Brown. After some glaring examples of misencoding, a new punctuation system would be laid down. At one time this consisted of putting a "Y" between each word. This last system was never very popular and gradually dropped out of use, although one or two operators kept it up long after the others – much to our disgust – as this meant more versions had to be run.

Most days were broken on cilli plus signature menu, if there was no ringstellung tip to make a hand attempt possible or if the constatations were unfavourable on a paired day for rodding. The amount of traffic passed, except at the end of the month, was very small and there was usually not enough traffic for the Brown cipher clerks to give us enough cillies for a menu. When Brown I had to be run on the bombe, its low intelligence priority handicapped it in the competition for bombe time, although it is only fair to say that, at first, it basked in the reflective glory of Brown II. Later, Brown I days were only run if there was a reduced wheelorder and one menu of cillies or cilli plus signature. Thus the right signature had to be found first time, which eliminated Köthen signatures as these were many and varied. At the end of each month each station had to send in three reports to Köthen and this, on Brown, meant three cribs. The first was a list of wireless apparatus at the station, which only varied from month to month in the items out of action. The others reported:

"Belegung über sabotage, spionage, und funkdisziplin durchgeführt."

"Waffenapppelle durchgeführt. Alles in ordnung."

It seems inconceivable that any Brown NCO ever thought about wireless discipline, never mind checked it. The most delightful piece of depth ever on Brown (see below) occurred when Unteroffizier Curth, then at Wendlestein, on 30 April 1943, used CUR as a message setting for all three messages. The result was that it was possible to read the two shorter messages completely and the first 100 letters of the equipment return.

There are many such interesting episodes on Brown, every station producing some tit-bit at one time or another. Oberleutnant Heuterkes, in charge of the Brown station at Kharkov, used a special Sonderschlüssel, Brown "S", for sending personal messages to Köthen. Every day the same key was used and this lasted from October 1942 to January 1943, in the course of which occurred the longest cilli subtraction on record. A message with setting D O F at 1800 hours on one day was followed by the next message at 0900 on the next day but one, an interval of 39 hours. Then there is the station at Frankfurt, set up in 1943 to listen for radar transmissions from British bombers. Every time there was an air raid near Frankfurt a report was sent in to Köthen of what had been heard. As this was generally a long part message cillying between every teil, a keen interest was taken in Bomber Command's operations.

Once, a simple substitution cipher was used by the Brown operators to send personal messages to each other, and although disguised as Enigma by means of dummy indicators, it was soon recognised in its true colours. The use of LB – lieber – as an initial bigram and other abbreviations from amateur wireless procedure held up the breaking, but the valuable intelligence that most of the operators were short of cigarettes was not kept from Hut 3 for long. This story has an amusing postscript for, after some days had elapsed, an enquiry was made of the Brown parent whether it was thought the request for cigarettes was genuine. Apparently there was a Group in Holland who were using cigarettes as a cover name for some type of weapon, and the enquiry was to see if Brown could be connected with this Group.

All idylls come to an end some time, and after a record week of 11 breaks in July 1943, 15 July was broken and produced 10 stecker. This immediately reduced the number of possible hand attempts, for the clonk method was valueless on ten stecker, which also ruled out pair days. The full seriousness of this situation was not felt at once, for a temporary easing of the bombe situation enabled more Brown I to be run on the bombe than before. So Brown I was broken regularly until October when, with the advent of Brown III and IV, all Brown bombe time was spent on these keys, only a little time being spared to run good cilli stories on Brown I. After October, Brown I dragged on a miserable existence, which even a key repeat in February 1944 failed to enliven, until the Russian armies advancing across the Elbe, and the American armies approaching Köthen wrote *finis* to this chapter.

Attack and Defence
Brown IV: This is a brief story of another Sonderschlüssel. Oberleutnant Heuterkes and his Brown "S" have already given us one example of how it is possible to break a key in use over a long period, by accumulating cillies from different days. The next example of such a key was Brown IV and here the reward for patience was much greater. For Brown IV was a key used between Brown technicians who had been lent for experiments connected with V2, and although no secrets about V2 were revealed by the Brown operators – presumably because they did not know any – the information they gave about trials and the men concerned in these trials helped to fill in the intelligence picture. The key used only one discriminant and, thanks to the regular breaking of Brown I, the cillies were recognised as those of particular Brown operators. After a week of collecting cillies, the key was run and came out and the messages could then be decoded as they arrived, the only worry being to make sure that the two or three messages a day did not get lost in the sorting.

Brown III: The policy of hanging on to Brown I was again justified when a new key – Brown III – was introduced on 15 September 1943. Some stations in Western Germany which went over to the new key, had passed traffic on Brown I and the information gained during this period was instrumental in breaking the new key quickly. This Western Kreis with control at Köthen, was joined in its use of Brown III on 15 October by a Baltic group which had been using Brown IA, the key of the previous month's Brown I. These two groups had nothing in common except the key and an allegiance to Köthen. The western stations were helping to defend the Reich by plotting the paths of British and American bombers, while the Baltic Groups were testing out the weapons with which Hitler still hoped to pluck victory out of defeat.

The Western stations that were actively engaged in radar work, besides reporting courses to the nearest fighter groups, also sent long reports to Köthen. These for some time were sent in a code without being enciphered in Enigma and were dealt with directly by the section of Hut 3 interested. From January 1944, these stations sent their reports in Enigma and this, of course, meant cribs. The series of cribs were called, picturesquely, "Life at Cuxhaven", "Tales of Hoffman" and "Schmitz's Blitz", the last two being named after the men in charge of the respective stations. Not only could the beginning of these messages be used, ENFAHRUNGEN VOM [Experiences From] but, as the reports were based on a proforma, the end could be used as a crib, for the answer to the seventh and last section of the proforma was always "Nein". Apart from these cribs, one Feldwebel, to wit, Schützendübel, possessed a name, long enough with his rank, to run as a delayed hoppity. In fact, later in the year, after Brown III had been unbroken for some time, an initial break was possible because an operator, querying a signature, received Schützendübel as a reply. This was run assuming a promotion which had been thought imminent the last time the key was broken, and out it came.

There were a few stations on the Western Kreis not on operational work and one of these, the station at Erfurt under the command of Lt. Gauss, provided a large proportion of the breaks during the period of its existence. The trials at Erfurt involved the use of an aircraft, and this led to the only weather crib ever seen on Brown being sent daily from Köthen to Erfurt. While there was no point in refusing additional aid, the fact that most messages from Erfurt were addressed ANX EINSVIERX KOMP and the others ANX EINSFUENFX KOMP and all signed by Gauss, was generally enough in itself to produce top and tail menus. The favourite message settings of the operator encoding these messages were SCH and HAU, which he used in that order, so that after a cilli to SCH could be assumed a message setting HAU. All the operators used the initial trigrams of their names in the old Brown tradition – one day was broken on seven OBEs. On another day, apparently overjoyed at being allowed to encode messages for the first time, one operator used CLA ten times.

For testing purposes, V1s were fired off from Peenemünde into a stretch of the Baltic and their courses were plotted by a series of Brown stations situated along the Baltic coast near Stolpmünde. These stations, known by their code names of "Spinne", "Ameise", "Fliege", "Hornisse" etc., were commanded by Lt. Mütze, familiarly called "Hut" by his friends both here and in Germany. Lt. Mütze spent a lot of his time travelling round the stations and as he would sign any messages emanating from the station he was visiting, it was important to keep track of this peripatetic Hut. As all Brown days were not broken, we had to supplement the announcements of his movements in decodes by references in log chat and it was rare for a Mütze signature to turn up at a station where it was not expected. Signatures were extremely important on Brown keys and it was pleasant to find another man whose name was long enough to run on its own. The Baltic counterpart to Fw. Schützendübel was Fw. Klüssendorf, who was in charge of Fliege and also deputy to Hut.

The star operator in this Kreis was a man at Spinne who used LFG as outside indicator and DER as message setting. As Spinne acted as link station between the Baltic Kreis and Köthen, appearing in both Groups, this operator had the task of passing on messages to and from Köthen. One week he decoded all the messages he received on one star and re-encoded them in the same key before passing them on in the other star. This would have been a good security and camouflage measure had he not set his seal of LFG DER on all the re-encoded messages. The Baltic stations, transmitting on frequencies in the 3000-4000 band, were always difficult to intercept – once an operator remarked that his interception was hindered by "the sound of running water" – and various "Black Market" sets were obtained to get down clean texts both of the messages and the non-Enigma traffic passed as well. These sets were either normally at stations not normally intercepting Enigma or were above the quota allotted to Enigma, and not obtained through the usual channel of Control Room. It is rumoured that there were one or two operators in Sweden taking this traffic, but whatever the unorthodox measures adopted, the distressing tendency to find cilli messages without any text to them was largely cured. Both Western and Baltic Groups passed non-Enigma traffic (generally figures-letter code of plots and reports), and as this began to go astray because Hut 6 only received Enigma messages, the step of labelling all traffic on Brown frequencies, Brown "Sexto" was taken, and all such traffic was sent to Hut 6, where the Brown parent sent on to Hut 3 the messages that were not Enigma.

The fact that Brown III had ten stecker did not prevent the keymaker from trying to help us. From October 1943 to March 1944 he only used 30 sets of self-stecker, each set being associated with one or two wheelorders, or permutations of those wheelorders. Thus it was possible to run a weak menu by assuming a set of self-stecker and running it on the wheelorders associated with the self-stecker. The sight of 96 wheel orders written on a menu, when 60 was the limit for Hut 6, was a little startling at first, but successes were achieved by this method on days that would not have been broken otherwise. In April and May, the keymaker went one better by repeating the February and March self-stecker respectively day by day.

About this time, with cribs on the Western Kreis, cillies and signatures on both Groups, and helped by these self-stecker curiosities, Brown III seemed to be in as healthy a condition as a key could be on that amount of traffic. Yet, before a month had passed, the cribs had gone, traffic, and so breaks decreased, and that annual disease of summer sickness crept over another Brown key. It was broken occasionally throughout the next six months and survived the destruction of the Western Group by the Allied armies and the transplanting of the Baltic Group to Denmark, where they continued their experiments until VE day. By February 1945, Brown III was being broken regularly again, but the Brown keymaker was not to be thwarted in his desire to help us. As the March Brown III key, he copied out the Cockroach key for February, leaving only three March days to be broken by an ungrateful cryptographer.

Conclusion
The preceding sections have shown how the Brown operators and clerks were completely lacking in any sort of security and how this was the only reason that Brown keys could be broken so consistently on such a small amount of traffic. One section in Hut 3 was accustomed to grade keys by their intelligence density, each message receiving some mark for the information it contained. The intelligence density was not always very high on Brown, but the cilli density certainly was, especially the day when there were 11 cillies in 15 messages. One further example of this total disregard of all regulations is given by the procedure in the case of a message being wrongly encoded. If only part of the message was corrupt, the clear text of the offending part would be sent, giving a crib. If the trouble was wrong wheelorder, ringstellung or stecker, so that it was

indecipherable at the receiving end, the encoder would adopt one of two courses. If he could find out what the trouble was, he would explain this in clear to save re-encoding the message. As this was usually in the form 431 NN ... ..,. 451 CC for a wrong wheelorder, the correct wheelorder was given to us as well. If forced to replace the message by pressure from the other operator, the same message setting would be used and any stecker trouble could be deduced from an examination of the two messages.

Why was it, then, that there was no cipher security on Brown and that this was not noticed? The first reason is simply that the Brown operators and cipher clerks were not primarily concerned with this part of their job, but regarded it as a sideline to their experimental work. The fact that it was a strong group on its own with little contact with the other GAF signals units, led to their being no change in personnel. No operators were posted away and the only newcomers in five years of war were the L N Helferinnen, who caused more log chat, not less. The operators always knew the recipients of their messages and chat, and were not afraid of official interference. The officers were all more interested in science than discipline, and Oblt. Lichthardt, OC 14 Kompanie, after his promotion from the ranks, still liked to operate a wireless set and sign himself LIC. Small wonder, then, that lesser ranks were not afraid to chat happily over the air with such an example before them.

As the work the Brown technicians were engaged on was so secret, it must be presumed that no security was allowed near the group, and, no doubt, the small volume of traffic that was passed, rendered it safe to minds obsessed with fears of depth from quantities of traffic. Perhaps the final comment on this lack of security is given by the news that all the records and files of the Brown group had been destroyed by the time Allied units reached them. This must be a classic example of locking the stable door after the horse has gone. Brown provided valuable information about beam bombing in the 1940 and threw light on V1 early in that terror weapon's career, yet, to one looking back on five years of Brown, the most interesting thing was the way the characters and lives of the ordinary cipher clerks and operators were revealed by the indiscretions they committed and the information they provided.

Example of Depth in Brown I

On April 30, 1943 an operator at Wendelstein used his favourite indicator CUR, for three messages. From our knowledge of the monthly cribs it was possible to read in depth as follows:

```
X K B B V D P K A D X E L H V O C T X U E F T S
S A R A M Y U N D Y K W Y E M I L Y A N T O N Y

V D S F B N P K V D H W U H Q T H J V H K Y S I K
B E L E H R U N G Y U E B E R Y S P I O N A G E Y

D O I W H Q - W R M Q P I E N G A Y C K A K N I K
A N Y O B L T Y L I C H T H A R D T Y B I T E Y
```

Chapter 20
The Mediterranean Air Keys

General

It was along the African shore of the Mediterranean that Britain had to fight back against the Germans. Libya was the testing ground for the skill of British commanders and the perseverance of British troops. And from the fall of France to the few months before D-Day, the Mediterranean was the central Allied operational zone.

The effect of this disposition of forces on the work of the cryptographers was to focus attention for many months on a batch of important Mediterranean keys. Particularly in 1942, when the work of Hut 6 was vital in covering the tank battles of the Western Desert, and when the resources of Hut 6 were inadequate to cater for all needs, we had to concentrate all our attention on the African war complex in much the same way that we had to concentrate on Red alone during the Battle of France. Research keys often had to be sacrificed to meet more urgent priorities.

During 1943, the resources of the Hut grew extremely rapidly, and both the Mediterranean picture and the other war pictures could be viewed more carefully. 1943 marked the climax of the African campaign. On 23 January our troops entered Tripoli, and by 13 May the last Axis forces in Tunisia had surrendered. The African campaign, which had ended so successfully, led naturally to the campaigns against the European mainland. The work of the cryptographers was focussed on those keys which dealt with the Allied invasion of Italy. 1944 saw the liberation of the Balkans and the firm establishment of Allied power in Italy, but just as the Allied capture of Rome on 4 June was overshadowed by the landing in Normandy two days later, so inside Hut 6 the emphasis on the Mediterranean keys was eclipsed by the rise in interest of the Western Front keys. In the days after D-Day, it became difficult to summon great enthusiasm for some of the surviving Italian keys, particularly when Puma, the most important of them, went over to Reflector D and eventually Enigma Uhr as well, thereby producing a crop of technical difficulties.

The Mediterranean Air Keys

The best way of describing the long attack of Hut 6 against the Mediterranean keys is to divide the story into phases, many of which are quite distinct, and can be treated chronologically. This account is divided into five sections:

1. The Triangle
2. The African Campaign
3. The Italian Campaign
4. The Balkans
5. The Last Months

The fourth section, on the Balkans, is not chronological. That is to say it covers a long period in itself which, while part of the Mediterranean story, is best treated as a unity. It seems natural to leave it to almost the last for simplification, though the close integration of the Balkans in German Mediterranean strategy, particularly during the African campaign, needs no emphasis.

The Triangle

Before the beginning of 1942, Light Blue (German name – Brigitte) was the major Mediterranean Air key. It first appeared in January 1941 as an offshoot of the general Red key, and was broken for the first time on cillies on 28 February. Its main content was Western Mediterranean, especially Sardinia and the islands, and traffic passing to "Italuft" in Rome. The arrival of Axis troops in Africa gave this key a wider application, but the German campaign in Greece (6-27 April) was mainly covered on Red. There were frequent re-encodements from Red to Light Blue throughout this period which were very valuable in giving experience on how to deal with this new approach to key-breaking. At the beginning of 1942, Light Blue split into Gadfly (Fliegerkorps X) and Red. A third key, Primrose (Lgau. Masch. Schl. West), also made its debut. Together, these keys provided a convenient triangle for the concentration of cryptographic effort. There were re-encodements between all three keys, particularly "Taxi" re-encodements (messages referring to the arrival or departure of aircraft), which passed in Light Blue during 1941, and now passed to Athens in Gadfly, to Rome in Red and to Africa in Primrose.

Earlier still, there were Vorausmeldung re-encodements, passing on all three keys, and many sporadic re-encodements between two corners of the triangle. The triangle was linked at first not only by re-encodements, but also by stecker repeats. The crib position was thin, and difficulties of interception added to the problems of breaking these keys operationally. Primrose began as it ended with a crop of Abstimmspruch messages. It soon acquired, in addition, Flak messages, which remained one of its characteristic forms of expression. Gadfly inherited a Light Blue crib "Chavan", but was always difficult to deal with from a crib point of view. Recce messages on both Red and Gadfly soon became the standard form of entry.

This original triangle did not take long to break up. In April 1942, Primrose split into Primrose (Lgau. Masch. Schl. Strd) and Snowdrop (Lgau. Masch. Schl. West) and, later in the same month, Gadfly split into Gadfly (Fliegerkorps X) and Scorpion (Fliegerführer Afrika). Gadfly continued to deal with the Aegean. Scorpion became a key of high importance and urgency, having links with army groups. This complication coincided with the final crisis in North Africa. On 21 June, Benghazi was captured by the Germans, and three days later they advanced 50 miles over the Egyptian frontier. On 1 July they captured El Alamein. Against such a setting, and the story of British recovery, beginning with the appointment of General Montgomery to the command of the Eighth Army on 1 August, the African keys assumed an enormous importance.

The African campaign

The main flow of German intelligence in Africa came from the Army keys. By comparison, Primrose was of very low operational priority, and methods of breaking had to be adopted which would throw least strain on the bombes. Scorpion, however, was important not only for its general information, but also for its re-encodements, particularly the invaluable Panzer Meldungs, sporadic on Scorpion, but regular on the Chaffinches. Luckily, the breaking of Scorpion was not dependent on its very inadequate cribs. Key repeats from Primrose, coming month after month, provided a potential way in. It was always difficult to fill in the missing days. Some idea of the concentration of bombe time on the Mediterranean keys during this period can best be given statistically.

In one week – the week ending 21 November 1942 – Red, Primrose and Locust took 2,205 bombe hours, almost half the maximum number of hours available for the total work of the Hut. The concentration of bombe time would have been even greater had it not been for two things: first, the key repeats; second, a spurt of re-encodements from non-Enigma keys. Short reports on the condition of aerodromes, re-encoded from Red to Primrose, were found in September 1943 to pass also in a simple June code, which could be broken almost at sight. The Crib Room was given a copy of the code, and then had the pleasant task of trying to fit the short June reports to the length of the Enigma messages.

Low grade ciphers were of great value in helping to consolidate the position of Locust, the key of Fliegerkorps II, which rose from a Research key to a key of high operational urgency, with the increasing GAF activities in Sicily and the Western Mediterranean. At first it had been of interest for its accounts of German attacks on our Mediterranean convoys, but its intelligence became more general. Synoptic weather messages, coming regularly at all hours of the day, made Locust easy instead of difficult to deal with. The figure content of the messages could be given in part at least by the Meteorological Section. Even after these synoptics had become less satisfactory, another excellent figure-code weather crib – Three GTO – enabled us to break many days. This crib is worth describing in detail. It started off with DREI, followed by the first two figures of the German Time of Origin (e.g., 05), usually followed in turn either by OOXOO or 7OXO. This consistency was maintained by reason of the stability of the Mediterranean weather. These two cribs were soon joined by yet more weather messages, Erika and Pantellaria being the chief, and a combination of both, known as Pantrika.

Re-encodements between Red and Primrose and between Red and Locust came steadily throughout the whole of the campaign, and were of particular value when the fortunes of war destroyed what had previously been good cribs. Thus, after the Allied capture of Tripoli, we waited for a Red/Primrose re-encodement before slogging hard at the latter key. In fact, throughout the whole period, great care was taken not to be over-lavish with Primrose, and in March 1943 it was taken over by a "kind of fourth Watch" (later the Qwatch) who examined likely kiss pairings, and this helped to save the work of the main Watch. Dragonfly, a new key of short duration (Fliegerkorps Masch. Schl. Tunis) was dealt with in the same way.

From April 1943 onwards, with the Allied victory in Tunisia merely a matter of time, a shift in emphasis was already beginning to take place. The final stages in the battle in Africa were, on the whole, allowed to take care of themselves. The result of this was that not only that more time could be devoted to Primrose, but more important, that many non-Mediterranean Air keys could now be dealt with such as Snowdrop in the

West and Hedgehog in the East. Keys like Primrose and Locust were now taking on a more "European" appearance, and the stage was set for the opening of the Italian campaign. One final point is worth noting about the cryptographic attack on the African keys. Interception of the messages was largely carried out in the Middle East, and this led to a certain delay in their arrival, and often to a large number of unsatisfactory or unduped texts. Despite this, the collaboration between stations as far afield as Derna or Sarafand and the central organisation at Bletchley Park was an example of effective and efficient co-operation.

The Italian campaign
The prelude to the Italian campaign came in the islands off and around the Italian mainland, and had the disastrous effect on Hut 6 of cutting down almost all the Locust cribs. The Synoptic Weathers and Pantellaria were the first to disappear, and they were followed by the Sicilian cribs which had more than adequately filled the breach. The Sardinian Recces and short reports were invaluable for several weeks, but they too disappeared with the German withdrawal from the islands.

In the meantime, three new keys had appeared as offshoots of Red, Locust and Primrose respectively. The long-range bomber groups in the Mediterranean, which had used Red until the beginning of July, began to use a key of their own – Squirrel – which, although of Watch importance, was most difficult to deal with on an operational basis. It was breakable on re-encodements from Red and Locust – intrinsically very unpleasant – but it later developed quite a spate of cillies and very many examples of depth. It never was a good crib key. The new offshoot of Primrose was Mayfly, and after a short spasm of re-encodements, it settled down to give us long-lived cribs, Hauptfunkstelle and Mayspruch. Its life as a Watch key was a short one, and it soon passed into the hands of the Qwatch and ultimately of Research. It never was a specifically Mediterranean key, and it dealt with air transport in all parts of the German occupied territories. The offshoot of Locust – Puma – fell into a very different category. At first it dealt with Army-Air co-operation in Sicily, but soon its scope was extended, so that although it temporarily disappeared, it returned to supplant Locust in Italy, and to become the Flivo key, of vital importance during the Allied operations further north. Its importance grew while that of Squirrel diminished, and most of the Squirrel frequencies either faded out or tried to cover their decline and disappearance by sending inordinate amounts of spoof traffic. Other offshoots of Primrose – Sheep and Leveret – never provided very profitable recreation.

In November 1943 there was considerable uncertainty about which keys were in use, and what was then thought to be Locust was in fact Puma, while what had been called Squirrel was Locust. From this time onwards Puma usurped the position of Locust as the leading GAF key in Italy. For a time there were valuable messages sent in Pink to cover the Italian operations, and Feindverhalten was re-encoded on many messages from Pink to Albatross, the Army key, but Pink soon disappeared also, and its traffic either passed on Red or was not sent by wireless at all. Pink was almost always broken on re-encodements, and many of the other keys depended on re-encodements, at any rate to fill in the awkward days.

With the Allied landings in Anzio Bay, considerable life was infused into the attack on the Mediterranean keys. Locust had many Recce re-encodements from Red dealing with the beachhead, but with the growth of Allied air supremacy in the Mediterranean as a whole, Fliegerkorps II was withdrawn from the Mediterranean to meet the new threat of the invasion in the west, and Locust now became a French instead of an Italian key. Its successor in Italy was Leopard, the key of Luftflotte 2, then of Komm. Gen. Italien, but the importance of this key was never as high as that of its predecessor, and by the end of the war it had degenerated almost into a Flak key. Puma, by contrast, reached its highest peak of importance and urgency at the height of the Italian campaign. It inherited some of the oldest authentic Locust cribs – Absichten and Vorhersage – and, in addition, produced a spate of short messages which were not sent over a long period, but which made early breaking possible. At first these messages were mainly weather messages. These were followed by the "Diaries", the routine reports of the liaison officers. Occasionally, from this very mixed bag, a report would stand out as a workable crib.

In the meantime, Primrose, now reduced in status to the key of Feldluftgau XXVIII, sent little of any importance other than the Platz Reports, still re-encoded into Red, and the method of breaking was both dull and uninspiring, chiefly by tuning messages. When the tuning messages disappeared, breaking became very difficult. Leopard, too, had some very black passages with the disappearance of the JG53 frequencies, but determination to hold on to it, despite the rival attractions of the new Western Front keys, was repaid when Leopard and Primrose united happily in one key in October 1944.

The Allied advance in Italy, which was far less spectacular than the sweep from Avranches to the Rhine, gave the Italian keys a long and somewhat unhealthy life. The short reports which marked periods of inactivity were far more valuable to us than the disintegrating operational traffic, sent during our advances. Our best cribs tended to come from behind the front line, Meyer-Bethling sending his reports on partisan activities from the Adriatic coast, or weather experts in Venice sending out reports to Pola. After the fall of Rome, it was very difficult to hold a grip on the keys. The Flivos who had previously sent out their battery of messages day after day, fled with their "Truppe" into the far reaches of the Gothic Line. Although Puma continued to be broken regularly, mainly on more standard and general reports and on Recce re-encodements on Red, this initial disintegration was an unwelcome foretaste of the shape of things to come. Technical security methods had already been tried in the Mediterranean (in addition to security devices like wahlworts), the chief of these being the Zusatz Stecker arrangement in the early summer of 1944. In November 1944, a much more serious blow was struck. The Flivos had already sent a wealth of messages ominously describing in detail the distribution of Reflector D. It was felt by the experts in Hut 6 that while the use of this reflector would be annoying, Reflector B would continue in use as well, and we would be able to break the key in the same way that we were breaking Jaguar or Red. However, Puma went over solidly to Reflector D in the middle of November, and the period of regular sustained breaking was at an end.

In any case, there was little doubt in November 1944 that Italy was a subsidiary theatre of operations. The Germans had been pushed back to their own borders, but still held firm in the hills of Italy, ensuring their mastery of the Lombard plains. The Allied armies were not yet ready for the final advance. Most of the attention of the Hut was rightly concentrated on the Western and German keys, although Puma and Leopard remained as Watch keys, where they still received vigilant attention from their admirers.

The Balkans

For a year from the autumn of 1942 to the autumn of 1943, Gadfly was treated as a Research key, though in its last stages, it was dealt with by the Qwatch. Messages from the Middle East arrived late, and back days were blisted, texts were often poor, cryptographically, chiefly because of lack of bombe time, the key was often neglected. This particularly applies from the period from October 1942 to July 1943, when only re-encodements were tried, and they were only exploited sporadically, mainly by visitors. Greater attention was given to the key after the end of the African campaign, and the results were immediately plain. In August 1943 a complete month's breaks was obtained. On 1 October, it became a Watch key on account of its increased intelligence importance and urgency. It was no longer the key of Fliegerkorps X, but of Luftwaffenkommando Südost. In the Watch, it received careful and sympathetic attention, and enjoyed a great run of success. It was always difficult and often tantalising, for cribs came and went in a bewildering manner, and even those that stayed saw frequent changes in their form. Thus an Aufklärungsbefehl became an Einsatzbefehl overnight, as in the case of Konsulab, Rollfeldmeldungs, Bandenlage and Krab, were the chief standbys, and though the intelligence value of such messages was not urgently important, the accumulated information given by Gadfly as a whole presented a fairly clear and often interesting picture of the complex Balkan situation, and would have been of vital importance if the forgotten Balkans had been the scene of a Third Front.

In its prime, Gadfly produced two strange and unusual offerings. The first of these – Yak – was the key of Fliegerführer Kroatien, and although it used Bird Book calls and GAF habits of punctuation, it used consecutive stecker, crashing and non-Nigelian wheelorders, and passed some of the same reports as Wryneck, the Balkan Army key. Bad interception shadowed the successful treatment of this key, which was for the most part dealt with on Research lines, though it had a short spell in the Watch. In the dim days of early 1945, with Red Army troops and armed partisans attacking the last representatives of German power in the Balkans, Yak was, if anything, of more value than its very unhealthy parent.

The dissolution of Gadfly itself is quite a long story. The isolation of the Balkans was largely responsible for the nature both of the W/T setup and of the amount and the character of the traffic sent. Balkan traffic on Gadfly remained for many months at a daily level of about 300 messages of an operational and an administrative nature. With the end of Balkan isolation – the breakaway from the Axis of Rumania and Bulgaria, the withdrawal of the Germans and the entry of the Red Army – not only did there result a considerable confusion of keys, but also keys that had been specifically Balkan became allied with keys that had been specifically

Russian. The confusion of keys became a great nuisance in September 1944. Gadfly – now using Reflector D – was compromised, and because of the isolation of lonely units and troops on the Greek islands, several keys were in use.

Although by the end of the year the position had been cleared up again, many different Gadfly keys – in hatted order, reserve keys etc – were in use during the interim period, and created a terrible mess both for the cryptographers and the traffic analysts. The growth of a Central European complex during this period is also very noticeable and is dealt with elsewhere – see the separate account of the Eastern Front and German Air keys. It had often been wondered what would be the effect of the impact of keys like Orchid and Ermine on the Balkan set-up after the Russian advances beyond their own frontiers. As early as June 1944 there was a re-encodement from Gadfly to Orchid that broke the Orchid day, As the year went by, Gorilla (the key of Luftflotte 4) came more into the centre of the cryptographic picture, which was further complicated by the arrival of Fliegerkorps II (Locust) in the same area. Gadfly began to play a varied, but on the whole diminishing role – 32 breaks were secured during 1945. Yak had 10 breaks at very heavy bombe count. The interest in the Central European keys grew, however, and reached its height during the last weeks of the war.

The last months
In addition to the last remnants of the Balkan keys, Leopard and Puma continued to be broken in 1945. The breaking of Puma was an important technical problem. The first thing necessary was to find a suitably long re-encodement from Red (there were re-encodements from Leopard also, but they were not suitable) and then to prepare it for the D-breaking machinery. Seven Ds were broken in this way on Giant and Duenna. A break on a Puma D period in January revealed that the traffic was not only on Reflector D, but almost solidly on Enigma Uhr as well. Although one other D-break was achieved, it was impossible to follow up the breaks and to secure the remaining days of the period. Previously these had come out quickly on the short weather cribs. Now those cribs had either disappeared or were too short to use for Enigma Uhr menus. From the end of February onwards, Puma had virtually to be written off, and even the Recce re-encodements from Red almost dried up.

Leopard, too, had its Reflector D, but the Flak units, which passed

The Mediterranean Air Keys

most of the traffic on the key, continued to use B. Consequently, we were able to break the Ds by cribs, bobberies and occasionally skirts, without a great many gaps, though often with a good deal of difficulty – 14 Leopard Ds were broken in all. Apart from the problem of D, Leopard had an extremely good run in 1945. The number and strength of the cribs was greater than ever before, and in March, for instance, only four Leopard days were missing. A comparison of Leopard and Puma breaks and bombe hours during 1945 is of considerable interest:

	LEOPARD			PUMA		
	Breaks	Time	Hrs/ Break	Breaks	Time	Hrs/ Break
1-27 Jan	23	1268	55	25	925	61
27 Jan-25 Feb	22	1765	80	7	756	108
25 Feb-31 Mar	31	1630	53	2	1742	871

This shows that in the last period, more time was spent trying to break Puma than was spent securing the 31 breaks on Leopard. Probably even more Leopard breaks would have secured had it not been for bad interception. Leopard was the last of the keys to have almost all its traffic intercepted in the Mediterranean, and it never received very high priority from the Italian intercepting stations, who had the Italian Army keys as their first commitment, and who and who could not spare more sets on the M/F band. Leopard, too, in the last stages of the war became bound up with the Central European keys, and re-encodements to Gorilla and similar keys began to appear. The German armies which had once been supreme from Alamein to Sicily, and held Athens, Belgrade, Rome and Tripoli were now squeezed into a small pocket, all that was left of the mastery of the Mediterranean. It was with the small pocket that the last work of the Watch was concerned.

Chapter 21
The African Army Keys

General

It is stressed throughout this history that the German Army keys were usually spasmodic in appearance and intractable to deal with because the army signals officers were schooled to construct landlines and to send as little by wireless as they could. In Africa, however, the vast distances and difficult country made intercommunication by wireless essential, while all traffic home to the mainland had to go over the air. And up to the last month of the campaign, when a Fish link to Tunis was constructed, the entire traffic had to pass in Enigma. Here then was Hut 6's chance to bring off its most spectacular coup. The prize was detailed information about the strength, disposition and intentions of every unit in the field, sidelights on the mind and character of the commanders, and glimpses of the attitude of the authorities in Berlin to their C-in-C in Africa. The Chaffinches were not all broken all the time – for periods of months none of them came out at all. But the measure of success will be judged by the volume and detail of intelligence which flowed from Hut 6 via Hut 3 to Cairo and Algiers from early in 1942 to the end of the battle in May 1943. It is surely inconceivable that any campaign had ever been conducted before with such advantages as Hut 6 was able to afford to our commanders in that period.

For those engaged in the work it was a most fascinating and exciting struggle with the odds, as always with Army keys, fairly heavily against the cryptographer. At no time was one so closely in touch with the course of the battles as when the daily report of Rommel's army provided not merely an excellent crib but also a first-rate off-the-record story.

The first breaks: 1941-1942

The breaking of the African keys fell into two distinct periods: September-November 1941 and April 1942-May 1943. Heavy traffic soon appeared in Africa following the arrival of the Germans there early in 1941. The key used, which was then known as AF5, was broken once in March and once in April on cillies without, however, showing up any cribs. One or two breaks in September were more profitable, and until mid-November there was an average of at least one Chaffinch break every two days. Of a variety of cribs the best were two day reports, one of them being the famous Bison, the Rommel Tagesmeldung which usually began: AN (X) IDA BISON (X) UEBER (X) IDA PINTSQUER, Ida Bison and Ida Pintsquer being the code names for the operational staffs in Berlin and Rome.

The British offensive in November had two repercussions in Hut 6. First, the army captured and sent home the Chaffinch I and II and Phoenix keys, together with their reserve keys, which enabled us to decode the complete Chaffinch traffic for the month up to 23 November, when the Germans brought new keys into force, and also to study for the first time the rules of Army keys. At this time they were obeying the non-clashing rule, which was of great importance to us in the days of few bombes, and also the "Army ringstellung rule" which could occasionally be of help, especially when there were cillies. Secondly, the offensive was so disturbing to all the German elements that they ceased to send any cribs, and the Chaffinches simply ceased to be broken through the period of the advance to Benghasi and the retirement to Gazala.

In March, hope of Chaffinch breaks revived with the appearance of Gadfly on many days of what was clearly the old day report of the Panzerarmee, and Sixta were able to point out that a routine re-encipherment between two of the Chaffinch keys was almost certainly the same thing. It was now clear that there were three Chaffinch keys in use – Chaffinch I and III, which were general keys and Salonika, and Chaffinch II, which was a special key for communication between Rome and Operational HQ in Africa (Sondermaschinenschlüssel Rom – Panzerarmee Afrika). Phoenix (Maschinenschlüssel Panzerarmee Afrika) was used for operational communications between Division and Corps, Corps and Army in Africa.

The re-entry into Chaffinch: April 1942
The routine re-encodements between Gadfly and Chaffinch when dealt with currently, failed, and two members of the Crib Room were therefore detailed to make a thorough investigation of the Chaffinch problem. It appeared that the message on Gadfly was routed from the Panzerarmee to Fliegerführer Afrika, while on the Army networks it went from Africa to Rome on Chaffinch III, and several days of both keys were tried without success. One day a very short report appeared saying simply:

WEGEN SANDSTURMES AUF PANZERFRONT
KEINE AENDERUNG DER LAGE

This, together with the usual address and signature and designation as the Tagesmeldung of 17 April, made up the whole message. And with the German checked by the linguists as correct and almost certainly invariable, the crib experts proceeded to stagger the stretch through the Chaffinch versions and run all the possible positions, which were few in number – but they failed. The message was then attacked by statistical methods, for a "boil" had revealed that while the Chaffinch II versions (the Bison) were certainly not in their old form, the Chaffinch III transmission had far fewer than the number of crashes expected by random on the beginner: TAGESMELDUNG (Day) X (Month) or VOM (Day) X (Month). These forms were therefore run and the day came out. It then appeared that the text of the re-encipherment had been run in the correct position, but unfortunately no-one had noticed PANZERFRONT (the tank front) was a rather odd expression. It was, of course, corrupt for GANZER FRONT (the whole front), and the single wrong letter in the crib was sufficient to fail the shot, an interesting example both of the luck of the game and the letter perfection which Hut 6 had to achieve.

Rapid exploitation of this break enabled Chaffinch to become a full operational commitment very soon afterwards, and until the end of August the general position remained substantially the same. There was the one crib on Chaffinch I or III, known as the Panzermeldung, and the same crib in its previous transmission, known as the Bison on Chaffinch II. Apart from this message there was, for a month or so, a strong alternative in the crib Marinebericht on Chaffinch III, and there were one or two weak cribs which were just good enough to break a day or two before they disappeared. In addition, occasional unexpected successes were achieved by methods such as cillies or reading in depth which, while valuable, did not alter the general outlook of the keys.

April-October: improvement in technique and increasing success
For three or four months, then, the breaking of Chaffinch proceeded by much the same methods, and with the same amount of success. At this time very little Chaffinch I was broken – it was the smallest key and we had not discovered the reason for its existence. Of the remainder, normally eight or nine out of a possible 14 keys were broken each week, with double figures occasionally when things went well, and as few as four in harder times.

The African Army Keys

In this period every success represented hours of toil by members of the Crib Room. Every break was hailed with delight by those on duty, and the incoming shift could usually tell from a glance at the faces of their predecessors whether their fortunes had prospered. There were three factors which precluded us at this time from achieving the completeness of our success which we were enjoying on the Air keys:

1. The small number of bombes
2. The poor quality of Chaffinch cribs
3. Our own experience in dealing with Army keys

The first and second of these were, of course, closely interconnected, for with so few bombes nothing could be run unless it stood a fairly good chance of being right. The Chaffinches depended on one crib, which said on its good days: TAGESMELDUNG (Day) X (Month). It was known sometimes to vary this with: TAGESMELD X (Day) X (Month) or TAGESMELDUNG VOM (day) X (Month), and normally these three forms were run. By the time they had failed, the next day's message had come in and it was time to start running the same forms all over again. We knew that sometimes it had the signature (VON PANZ X ACK X ACK X AFRIKA) at the beginning and sometimes it used forms like GEHEIM X YY TAGESMELDUNG etc. But there was simply not bombe time to run them. There can be no doubt that another 20 or 30 bombes in this period would have enabled us to come very near to completeness. The other factor which perhaps cost us several days, which we might have broken even without more bombes, was the novelty of the problem of re-encodement. Before the Chaffinch era, keys had been broken on re-encodements, but with good cribs on most Air keys, one did not usually use a re-encodement unless it produced a relatively simple and certain answer. Now every success with the Chaffinch Panzermeldung meant at least one re-encodement into Chaffinch II, and this was a key without any other crib. It was now that we perfected the technique of selecting the ideal stagger stretch, of finding the teil breaks, and of analysing the alterations in a routine re-encodement. It was to improve our tally on these messages that the card system was adopted whereby the different versions of the decoded re-encodements – Chaffinch II and III and Red or Scorpion II if they happened to appear in Air traffic – could be compared at a glance. Thus one saw the standard lengths of the addresses and signatures in the different versions and allowed for them, noted common differences in abbreviation and punctuation, and in many ways obtained an insight into the differing outlooks of the various German encoders.

Perhaps the best indication of the improvement in our methods is shown by the fact that in the first four days of August, the Panzermeldung suddenly appeared three times in Scorpion II, giving re-encodements into Chaffinch II and III each day. In spite of hours of work by all members of the Room, only one out of six possible keys was broken, whereas when we had a return of the Scorpion version at the end of September, no days at all were missed for over a week. Throughout September and October increasing bombe power and improved technique of cribbery brought us much closer to the goal of 21 Chaffinch keys a week. By this time there were enough machines to allow more expensive methods, for analysis revealed that messages with certain routeings tended to start in the same way, e.g., Mersa Matruh from Tripoli:

AN X KARPFEN X VON X UNGEHEUR

Karpfen and Ungeheur being two of the code names of which the Army in Africa was so fond. And such beginners were as good on Chaffinch I as on III, for we had by now discovered the Army use of Staff and ordinary keys. Chaffinch I was OKH Stabsmaschinenschlüssel Nummer 1, and Chaffinch III, the corresponding OKH Maschinenschlüssel, and all Geheimekommandosache traffic was sent in I while the rest came in III. This was well worth knowing, because it meant that one could recognise the grade of traffic from the outside. When, for example, the Chaffinch Panzermeldung was sent in Chaffinch I, we knew that it could begin with the Gkdos but not the Geheim forms. This was simply one example of the tightening grip we were obtaining over these keys and the success obtained inevitably led to German doubts as to their cipher security. One enquiry produced the decision that "the Enigma was safe as long as the wheelorder was changed three times" (this measure was generally introduced in the Army in July 1942). And a later order said that addresses were to be buried and nonsense words used in front of standard beginnings, and within a week or two wahlworts were in general use. This measure was a crippling blow to Hut 6 at the time with its extremely limited bombe power, but two circumstances enabled us to proceed for two or three months with success not appreciably less than before. Of these, the more important was the growing tendency for re-encodement between Chaffinch and Phoenix, which hitherto had been quite unconnected with the other Army keys.

Phoenix: the difficulties of overseas interception

The forward Army units naturally required low-power short-distance wireless transmission, and as a result the medium and low frequencies used were normally inaudible in Britain. Interception in Africa, while not up to the superlative WOYG (War Office Y Group) standard, should have been sufficient for Hut 6 requirements and in spite of errors in Morse, teleprinting and Typexing, it was usually possible to attack the traffic – when it arrived. The Typex situation in Cairo, over which Hut 6 had little control, was the weakest link in the whole Enigma organisation at this time. It is quite clear that with better arrangements for sending the traffic home, Phoenix would have been broken at an earlier date and thereafter much more often and more quickly. Furthermore, the anomalous situation would not have arisen whereby we were unable to break the key currently on a crib and unable to decode most of the traffic for very many hours because it had not arrived.

Phoenix was not actually broken until 1 June 1942, although several good cilli menus had failed through interception before that time. Other days were broken on cillies but no crib appeared except for a brief period of two or three days, when one unit suddenly began to announce "No Change" every two hours, and a day was broken on NIQTS NEUES X GIERLING X, the complete message. Many of the days broken came out very late because of the accumulation of traffic over a period of days, which meant that a message vital to a cilli menu might be one of the last to arrive. Much clever hand-breaking was done, too, with the aid of ringstellung tips and the operation of the block rule. But, it was not till near the end of August that any attempt could be made to deal with the traffic operationally, when the cilli breaks at last revealed some cribs. These were very short morning messages reporting quiet nights, e.g.:

NAQTVERLAUF RUHIG

or   NAQT RUHIG VERLAUFEN

which had the virtues of certainty and early appearance, but were sometimes too short for running as anything but single menus risking a number of turnovers. This, it must be remembered, was before the days of hoppity bombes, and various ways, therefore, had to be found to account for the days when the turnover came in the middle of the message. Ringstellung tips enabled hoppities to be run and it was presently noticed that the cribs tended to have nearness indicators which enabled turnover assumptions to be made. With cillies reducing the wheelorder on many days, breaking went on through September with scarcely any missing days. And early cribs, coupled with a speedier return of at least a part of the traffic, meant that the intelligence could be used operationally. October was an even better month than September and then Alamein and the advance brought floods of traffic, but the demise of all the cribs.

The wahlwort era – the Phoenix-Finch complex: December 1942-April 1943

By great good fortune, however, the Panzermeldung and Feindverhalten (Rommel's 1A and 1C reports) began to appear on Phoenix in transmissions to Superlibia, i.e., the Italian High Command. This enabled us to break one or two November and December days by re-encodements and keep in touch, and then at the end of December the remains of the Afrika Korps settled down to hold a line and all the old cribs returned.

Meanwhile, the introduction of nonsense-words as an anti-crib measure had been ordered in a Chaffinch message at the beginning of December, and after a brief period in which the German operators, misunderstanding their instructions, made things easier for us instead of more difficult, the entire Finch groups settled down to the new procedure. Whereas one formerly used a crib at the beginning of a message, one now had to allow for a nonsense word of from four to 14 letters long, and thus the crib (on the more unfavourable days) would have to be run in as many as ten times the number of versions. Further, breaking on straight addresses was now out of the question, for whereas a favourable address might have as few as three alternative forms of which one could eliminate one, or perhaps two, by selecting a message on which they crashed, under the new regime one would have to stagger all three forms over a range of ten, and would find at least 20 possible versions.

With the bombe power then available this innovation ought, on reasonable calculations, to have stopped us from breaking the Finches at all except by sheer luck in, say, guessing the right position in ten, or by concentrating perhaps on one day a week. However, the rebirth of the Phoenix after the fires of Alamein was Hut 6's saving dispensation. The NachtRuhig crib returned and was sometimes intercepted in Britain, while the shift in the scene of the fighting enabled WOYG regularly to intercept the Phoenix version of the Panzermeldung, which was also a good crib. It was even now very difficult to hear, and WOYG, informed of the vital importance of the message, and in particular of its first groups, put a battery of sets and ace operators on to it. Mr Walton, supervisor of the WOYG set rooms, used to take a version himself, and there was one famous occasion when the station rang to say that they had just taken ten copies of the message, of which eight had 'E' for the fourth letter and two 'I', but as Mr Walton's text was one of the two giving 'I', then 'I' was certainly correct. It was!

With Phoenix broken it was possible to proceed by re-encodement into the Finches. The Bison had now developed another leg in its journeys, for it was sent from Rome to Tunis in the new Tunis key, Bullfinch, which was first broken in November when the 21st came out on a re-encodement from Chaffinch. Crib Room Research – or CR2 – at this period made a comparison of times of origin of all Army traffic, and the break of Bullfinch was its first success. Other days were then broken by the current watch on more re-encodements, chiefly of the Lagebericht West, a general intelligence report sent from Rome to both the Afrika Korps and the army in Tunis. The 'LBW re-encodements' as they were called, were some of the most difficult which had to be faced, for the two versions were often widely different in content. That going to Tunis had a section about Rommel's army which was omitted from the other because he already possessed the information – and vice versa. The method, therefore, was to find the part common to both messages – a process difficult enough – but increasingly so when the Germans produced what could only be construed as an anti-re-encodement measure, the placing of wahlworts at the beginning and end of every teil. This virtually eliminated the teil-break as a factor in solving re-encodements, and from our point of view the only good thing about the new rule was that it was not always kept.

The first Bullfinch days, broken at the end of November, were extremely valuable later when the key was used again next month, and with these days, together with others broken on re-encodements from Phoenix, it became possible to estimate the full effect of the use of wahlworts. It was clear that they were universally used on everything except Phoenix – on which they were rare – and only on frequencies of no crib value. Occasionally some of the routine Finch messages were sent without wahlworts by the Rome station, which encoded both versions of the LBW and also the Panzermeldung. Hence it became policy to run these cribs in the first position only each day, giving an average of about one break a week. Meanwhile it was reasonable to expect five – and with luck all seven – Phoenix days out fairly quickly each week, with the Panzermeldung re-encodement to take us thence into the Finches. So then, with Phoenix as a jumping-off ground, most of the vital Finch traffic was broken in January, although reliance on chains of re-encodements meant that the last link was apt to be reached only after the lapse of some days. The score sheet of the African keys for a typical week at the end of January 1943 is listed below. It will be noted that Phoenix provides the initial entry on six out of seven days, while three of Chaffinch II were some days late in coming out.

CR1 WEEKLY REPORT: WEEK ENDING 30 JANUARY 1943

Date	Chaffinch I	Chaffinch II	Chaffinch III	Bullfinch	Phoenix
23		LBW RE	Panz	Bison RE	Morgenmeldung
24		(Phoenix RE)	Panz RE	Bison RE	Phanz
25	Panz RE	(LBW)		LBW RE	1545 Nacht Ruhig
26	Panz RE			Bison RE	1545 Nacht Ruhig
27	Panz RE	(LBW)		Bison RE	Phanz
28	Bullfinch RE	LBW RE	Panz RE	Morgenmeldung RE	Morgenmeldung
29			(Panz RE)	(Bison RE)	(Morgenmeldung)

Brackets indicate breaks since midnight 29-30 January 1943
RE = Re-encodement. LBW = Lagebericht.

At the beginning of February the Italian Command — Superlibia — was dissolved, and the Rommel reports were no longer sent on Phoenix, with the result that Finch-breaking became dependent on the rare stray re-encodements from Phoenix or on long stagger jobs on poor cribs like the LBW, Lagost or Panzermeldung. However, Rommel's counter-attack against the Americans at Gafsa caused the division of his forces into the Gafsa force — under his own command — and the Mareth force under the Italian, Messe, and both groups from 21 February began sending day reports which were re-encoded into the Finches. Thus for over a week there was a glorious revival in Army breaking, but from the Hut 6 point of view it was the last bright spell of the African campaign. March and April found even Phoenix very difficult – and there were practically no Phoenix-Finch re-encodements. At the beginning of April, long stagger jobs on the Finches were abandoned as too expensive and unprofitable. Under strong pressure from the Intelligence authorities, who even with the net drawn tight round the army in Tunis, thought the information still vital, they were resumed in the last half of the month and two breaks were quickly obtained – thereafter none. In the last week of April, five Bisons and three Lagosts were run in a total of 73 versions without a single day coming out. One more break of Chaffinch, thence of Bullfinch was obtained on a re-encodement from Fish on 9 May, and thus the battle against the African Army keys ended – quietly. The enemy's security campaign had caught up with us before the end of the fighting, but by this time the issue was no longer in doubt.

Thrush (Sonder M/S Rom-Mallemes) and other keys
One or two other keys should perhaps be mentioned in this section although they were of no real significance to the general breaking procedure. Thrush was a special key used for triangular communication between Rome, Greece and Crete, dealing in particular with supplies for the island. It lasted from July to December 1942 and was interesting to break, although with bombe time scarce, it was frequently neglected in favour of more urgent and important commitments. The first break was obtained by a re-encodement from Chaffinch on 23 July, and revealed that the operator in Crete used almost invariably indicators of the nearness type (1, 1, 2) on from the outside indicator. Subsequent breaks on indicators and other re-encodements showed two cribs – Hornschaft and Ankunft – both long supply returns, Ankunft being a statement of the material which had arrived in Crete by air during the day. Further evidence of these messages revealed a three-day cycle, which enabled the forms of both the cribs and the indicators to be predicted with accuracy, and it became policy to break a day or so a week and otherwise to only attempt to get the day out if there was a re-encodement to Chaffinch. For such re-encodements occurred from time to time, chiefly owing to the location of units of the 164th Light Division in both Crete and Africa, intercommunication taking place via Rome.

Thrush finally disappeared at the end of November, leaving some unsolved problems which probably did not receive the attention they required owing to pressure of current work. On all the latest days broken, only part of the traffic is decoded. On one of them, one or two messages came out on an illegal permutation of the wheelorder, but the remainder were still dud – and still we don't know why.

The Army in Tunis – Panzer AOK 5 – produced its own key, analogous to Phoenix, which was named Dodo in view of its approaching extinction, and broken two or three times on cillies. No crib and no more cillies came before the final surrender. And hence further breaks had to await the creation of a new and equally ill-fated 5th Panzerarmee – and hence a new Dodo – during the final Western campaign.

Falcon I and Falcon II (then known as Merlin) were each broken a few times by re-encodements from the African Army keys, owing to the variety of keys which appeared on the wireless link between Rome and Salonika. This rather happy-go-lucky state of affairs puzzled us for a long time, but it is clear now that the reason for the presence of the Falcons on the link was to enable messages to be forwarded without re-encodement on the wireless – more usually the teleprinter – link between Salonika and Athens. For Athens did not possess the Chaffinch keys, but only the Eastern OKH and the general keys Vulture and the Falcons and Mallards. Such inter-area connections were of great cryptographic significance, for thus light was brought to the lands of darkness, but in this instance they were of more importance from the point of view of the Balkan and European keys than of the African group, and hence will be considered in a separate section.

Chapter 22
The Italian Army and Balkan Army Keys

Italian Army Keys

General
The campaign in Sicily and Italy, with its long periods of static warfare and consequent facilities for landline communications, offered Hut 6 but poor material for exploitation in comparison with the fight along the southern shores of the Mediterranean. Traffic came sometimes in floods and sometimes not at all, but most commonly in trickles, wireless links being kept open in case of need and used as an overflow for the teleprinters. Brief spells of heavy traffic sometimes led to breaks which could not be followed up because the flow dried up as suddenly as it had begun. For the cryptographer this was dispiriting. For Hut 3 it meant that intelligence from Italian Army keys tended to be fragmentary and mostly of a low grade. Fortunately, the Fish section was able to fill the breach by continuous and complete breaking of Bream, so that it was left for Hut 6 to act on the assumption that "what is worth encoding on the Enigma is worth decoding", and do what it could with anything that came to hand. The result was normally a grey picture of difficult breaking and low-grade intelligence, brightened occasionally by spectacular flashes of brilliant success and priceless information.

Before the surrender of Italy: May-September 1943
The Italian campaign from the Hut 6 point of view began some time before the landings in Sicily. With rapid movement of German troops into Italy and the islands during May 1943, following the surrender in Tunisia, new keys at once appeared — Albatross I and II — which were later identified as the key and staff key of the 10th Army, and Cormorant, a special cipher used for communication between Rome and one of the German units in Sardinia. These keys were examined by the newly-formed Army Research Section, and a Cormorant break on a re-encodement from Primrose was one of the first successes. This key was broken once or

Solving Enigma's Secrets - The Official History of Bletchley Park's Hut 6

twice afterwards on re-encodements from Albatross, but never showed any sign of producing any cribs or cillies, and with wahlworts used on all messages, was normally quite unbreakable. It finally disappeared with the evacuation of Sardinia.

Albatross I, with an average of 150 messages a day at the end of June and the beginning of July, was obviously of the first urgency and importance with the invasion of Sicily drawing near. By good fortune cillies appeared from a station in Sardinia and a number of days were broken, disclosing no crib but an interesting stecker pattern in the July days, whereby the pairings were at a fixed distance each day, the distance going up one a day. Thus, on Day 1, the stecker would be three apart, e.g. A/D, B/E, C/F etc.), and on Day 2, four apart: A/E, B/F, D/G. With this assistance it was possible to break nearly all the July days on short cribs or, in many cases, on cillies by hand. The invasion of Sicily was followed a few days later by the transference of Albatross from the Research Section to the Watch, for it could be seen that breaking could be attempted currently while the stecker rule was in operation, and it was hoped that in due course cribs would make their appearance. Albatross I was occasionally broken in this period, too, but entirely by re-encodement. Nile (Mediterranean Naval), Locust and Cormorant all gave re-encodements, but none of them revealed a crib.

The turn of the month brought the end of the stecker patterns and breaking in August depended on the occasional bursts of cillies and such cribs as had appeared during July. Of these, the only one of any value was a Tagesmeldung from Sardinia, and that was probably the most unreliable crib ever regularly to be run on any key. And yet it broke several days, including the one when the form written out was entirely wrong but happened to be made into menus of which one had letters in common with the actual text! Presently another and better crib appeared — a report on mine-laying — and later a really good crib dealing with the oil supply in the islands. One way or another three or four days were broken each week until the surrender of the Italians at the beginning of September, whereupon the islands were evacuated and two of the cribs disappeared. From now on for many months, Albatross I was broken only very occasionally on cillies or re-encodements from Bream. The cillies came from a unit which used the trigram ENG as both a fixed call sign and the indicator of many of its messages.

Surrender of Italy and rise of Shrike and Bullfinch: September 1943-February 1944

The impending Italian collapse near the end of August caused the German High Command to send large forces through the Brenner, and Heeresgruppe B, the staff of which had been moved from the Russian Front, established itself in Munich to take charge of the new divisions. Its arrival was immediately reflected in the W/T picture, and a short morning message which soon appeared rapidly presented us with our first break of the new key, Shrike I, on the guessed beginner MORGENMELDUNG (VOM) (Day) X (Month).

After an initial spurt of breaks in the course of which most days at the end of August and the beginning of September succumbed, and the key was transferred from the Research Section to the Watch, there was a long blank period when the crib was not heard. However, after a gap of three weeks it came back, and thereafter one crib appeared as its predecessor vanished, so that four or five days a week were broken steadily until the traffic finally petered out in February 1944. Shrike, although originally used by Heeresgruppe B and all its subordinates, was almost certainly the key of the army in the north, AOK 14. When AOK 14 moved south, it left part of its forces, together with its key, behind, the northern portion being named after its commander "Armeegruppe von Zangen". Hence, there was later a new key of AOK 14, which was named Kingfisher.

Shrike was an interesting key to break and the decodes made good reading. It was fortunate that wahlworts were not commonly used on this key, and very rarely on the crib messages. Thus Hut 6 was able to provide a fairly complete intelligence picture of the Italian front for a spell of over a month at the beginning of 1944. For, while Shrike dealt with forces in the north, a key had been discovered and broken which adequately covered the fighting front in the south. A very long daily routine message was observed in November and December passing from a station in Italy, thought to be AOK 10, to OKH, and after speculative shots based on the evidence of crash analyses had failed, a stagger of the date EINS FUENF X EINS ZWO was sent on the message for 15 December to be run on the Washington bombes. This succeeded early in January, the message proving to be the Tagesmeldung of AOK 10. In spite of the use of wahlworts, the message was a good crib on the stretch TAGESMELDUNG (VOM) (Date) X (Month), which had to be staggered over a short range at the beginning. On most days, too, there was also a Morgenmeldung, and sometimes a Zwischenmeldung, so once the original break had been achieved nearly every day came out until the disappearance of the group early in February.

This was traffic at the highest level of urgency and importance, and its similarity in these respects to the Bullfinch of the Tunisian campaign- the two keys had nothing else in common — led to the second use of the name. Bullfinch and Shrike were the cases in the desert of the Italian Army keys. They were regularly breakable over period, and in intelligence content they compared with the Chaffinches of Africa and the Puffins and Bantams of the days to come in the West.

Kingfisher: May-August 1944

From the end of January to early May 1944, traffic from the Italian front was at its lowest ebb. Then there was a marked increase, and several keys appeared, of which one began to come out regularly for the first time. This was Kingfisher, the key of AOK 14, which was now at the front although the traffic was of supply rather than operational content. It was broken for several days on re-encodements from the associated Playfair, and then on cribs. In spite of some blank patches, a certain amount of Kingfisher was broken from this time forward until the end of August. Breaking was mainly dependant on cribs sent by the 26th Panzer Division, which withdrew from the line in August and reappeared a few months later under AOK 10. The cribs were thus transferred from Kingfisher to Albatross, and they were of sufficient reliability to ensure fairly regular breaking. The best of these was a message signed by a certain Hauptmann Krupinski dealing with available storage space (Freier Nutzraum). Perhaps the Hauptmann did his own encoding, or maybe it is that a man can be a hero to his own cipher clerk. At any rate, the indicator of the message was always part of the name Krupinski. At first it was always KRU, but later, for variety's sake, I suppose, our friend indulged in obscurer portions, using either forwards or backwards, such as PIN, SKI, RUP, PUR and even KSN. While the indicator remained KRU, it was possible to run a shorter crib with the assistance of the three extra constatations and known turnover, but afterwards it was only of assistance in finding the ringstellung.

Revival of Albatross: October 1944-April 1945

In August Kingfisher breaks became rare and finally stopped altogether. Meanwhile, a break had been made into Albatross by re-encodement from Sparrow, and more than a week's steady breaking achieved on a crib, but then the crib died and Albatross was lost again. But better things were to come. During September Mediterranean traffic rose in volume, and early in October routine re-encodements of reconnaissance reports between Puma and Albatross were spotted by Sixta. Success with some of these revealed good cribs which enabled breaking to proceed until the Allied breakthrough in the final offensive in April. In this final phase traffic was steadily rising in volume and in intelligence value in the last two months. Before that time it dealt with many minor matters and the content was rated very low. Yet — this happened with many keys — there were anxious enquiries from Hut 3 whenever Albatross failed to come out for a few days. Actually, in this last period of about six months, there were few big gaps, the only notable one being about Christmas, when all the old cribs disappeared and the great power of a message which had just been intercepted for the first time had not been realised. This was a crib of almost invariable form for about 80 letters, and for many weeks it made the breaking of Albatross purely a matter of routine.

The Puffins
Albatross and Kingfisher were keys designed for use by AOK 10 and AOK 14 and their subordinates. At the higher level Army — Heeresgruppe — OKH, there was normally very little traffic in the Italian theatre. However, the W/T links were there if required, and when they were used the keys were obviously well worth breaking. At this level the keys used were most commonly Puffin I and II (originally called Jay and Puffin) and sometimes the Armee keys of the Army involved, or its staff equivalent. There were spells when Albatross II or Puffin II were broken on the IA and IC reports of OB Südwest, known from their contents as the "Limbo" (Lage im Bereich OBSW) and the Feindverhalten. Unfortunately, they were poor cribs and very expensive to use, so that most of the breaks made on them were by re-encodement, for this pair sometimes appeared in the Air keys, Red or Pink, and frequently on Fish.

After D-Day the Puffins were used in the West as well as in Italy, and in fact the first two Western Army messages decoded were on Puffin II on 7 June, which was broken on one of the few cribs which ever appeared on this key – the Hunter. This was a Y intelligence report on Tito's activities, sent from Heeresgruppe F in the Balkans to Heeresgruppe C in Italy, and it ended with a serial number which could sometimes be predicted.

But as Western traffic increased, the Puffins, from the breaking point of view, became entirely Western keys. Italian traffic was decoded on them, but it had little crib value. Even so, the veterans Feindverhalten and "Obswag" (descendant of the Limbo) are recorded as each scoring once on Barnyard keys of August 1944, thus possibly giving us some consolation for their previous shortcomings. Normally, then, there was very little high-level traffic from Italy, and when it appeared it was expensive and disheartening to break.

Sparrow

One other Army key was in general use in Italy, that used for communication between Y-intercept stations. It was broken first on cillies in April 1943 and subsequently on cillies and cribs. In the early months the cillies tended to be short-lived, and continuity was with difficulty maintained on spasmodic outbursts of pronounceable cillying, such as the sequence which a thirsty operator produced in April 1943: VIN, GIN, COG, NAC, WAS, SER. But in September the two-hourly D/F reports, which earlier had been used as cribs, returned in a new form and made Sparrow-breaking a simple matter for a long time afterwards. The messages began with the times during which the bearings were taken, e.g. VON JJJJCCJJ BIS JJBBCCJJ, i.e. von 0030 bis 0230, the letters A-J being used for the figures 1-0. This crib was called "J" for obvious reasons, and while it lasted, Sparrow was dealt with in the Watch as an operational key. This was partly because it sometimes produced an urgent message, and partly because there were very occasionally re-encodements into Albatross.

The "Js" were liable to disappear from time to time and in February 1944 an alternative crib, a long report about the Allied Order of Battle was successfully used for the first time. It began FULA (date), Fula being an abbreviation for Funklagemeldung and was easily recognisable from the great length of each teil – often 400-500 letters. "J", with support from Fula, broke a very large number of days until July 1944, when both finally vanished. Re-entry was made in November by running the beginnings of messages of a known type in a very large number of versions. These were Allied low-grade reports, decoded and translated, which either began with the time of origin of the Allied message or in one of several common forms, e.g.: EINSFUENF (X) FUENFVIER (X) UHR, BOMBARDIERUNGSAUFTRAG, FDLX AUFKLX MELDET, etc. By choosing a message which rejected well, one or two days were broken without undue expenditure of bombe hours, and it was then seen that the old Fula was still present under a new name – Nalm – which stands for Nachrichtenaufklärungslagemeldung or "Y-situation report". There were two versions of this, one on the general key Sparrow II, while the other was the only message on the other key, Sparrow I. The two encodings differed in certain respects – one had the figures in German, while the other used the letter for figure substitution of the "Js", but it was very difficult to account for the existence of a separate key. From our point of view this process had the advantage that, if the Nalm failed on Sparrow II, we could run it on Sparrow I, and if it came out, proceed to II by re-encodement.

The Nalm continued to appear almost until the end of the Italian campaign, but in the closing stages it did not come out. The last day broken was an odd one in February 1945, but isolated breaks of a key of this type were valuable as a check on the enemy Y activity, and Sparrow had by this time played its small part in the maintenance of Allied security.

The Balkan Army Keys

General
The Balkan theatre throughout the war was full of the excitement which one expects from this turbulent corner of Europe, but the fact that it never became a major Anglo-American land front like North Africa and Italy meant that Balkan affairs took a secondary place to weightier and more urgent commitments. In 1941 and 1942 following the German occupation of Greece and Yugoslavia a considerable volume of Army traffic was intercepted from these regions, but it was not till February 1942 that some cillies gave decode evidence that this activity was in connection with operations against the partisans. A single day's traffic was to readers hardened to cynicism by constant press and radio reports of guerrilla activity quite sensationally illuminating. In one day German units had been engaged in half a dozen areas of Yugoslavia: bridges had been blown, trains derailed. It was obvious that large Axis forces were being used, and that with battle, ambush and frostbite taking their toll, they were having a most uncomfortable time. The early breaks provided a good example of the type of traffic which the Balkans produced almost until the end of the war. Clearly it could not compete in importance with

material dealing, for instance, with Rommel's African army. So then, when resources in bombes and cryptographers were small, the Balkan keys were run only when fairly cheap and certain shots offered themselves.

Before the Italian surrender: February 1942-September 1943
A penchant for nearness cillying by some of the Balkan stations was noticed in February 1942 and skilful exploitation – particularly difficult with this type of cilli – led to an average of four to five breaks a month on cillies, cillies plus beginners, and in one or two cases, on cribs, throughout March, April, May and June. The last of this series of cillies appeared at the beginning of July, and thereafter cillying ceased. In this period no first-class crib had been observed, and bombe time did not permit of weaker shots. The Ravens, as the Balkan keys were generically named, were therefore lost to us from early in July. The precise distribution and function of the keys was not at the time clear, but it is fairly certain now that Raven I was the key of AOK 12, with Raven II as the associated Staff key, while Raven III, which was actually the first of the group to be broken, was perhaps some special key for an operation.

Raven I and Raven II retained their importance as the keys of the senior unit in the area until the surrender of the Italians in September 1943, although AOK 12 during this period turned into Heeresgruppe E, and the key name presumably changed, too. With the institution of a permanent Crib Room Research Section and the arrival of numerous bombes at the end of 1942, the stage was set for the breaking of Raven on cribs. And the appearance of a very long message every day from OBSO (Oberbefehlshaber Südost) suggested a possible means of entry. A number of examples of the OBSO Tagesmeldung had been seen on the days broken in the March- June period, and it then began with a long and highly variable address. However, on a November Mallard day, which owing to a compromise carried some of the Raven traffic, it was seen to begin: GEHEIM X TAGESMELDUNG VOM (Date).

It was thought, therefore, not improbable that on some days it might begin flat with the Tagesmeldung, and a "directed boil" was carried out on the messages of December and the first week of January. The number of crashes was less than the random expectation, and one or two shots on different days soon resulted in a break. Two cribs were then revealed, both more reliable than the OBSO Tagesmeldung, the Supersloda Tagesmeldung, and even better, the Lagemeldung. Both these were

The Italian Army and Balkan Army Keys

daily reports from German liaison officers with Italian formations, and together with the OBSO Tagesmeldung enabled a grip to be kept on Raven for many months. None of these were reliable, and when they were all out of form, many days passed without a break, but they always came back again to the known variations. The OBSO Tagesmeldung had the additional merit of occasionally being sent in Codfish, which offered the possibility of breaking by re-encodement. Such re-encodements were always technically difficult on account of the punctuation differences between the ciphers, and in this case particularly so, because the Enigma version sometimes omitted portions which appeared in the Fish. However, analysis and practice led to increasing success, which became even more pronounced when the message began to appear on a new Balkan key, Buzzard.

Buzzard was broken on cillies almost on its first appearance on 11 April 1943, but traffic was very small in quantity until May, when a few more days were broken on cillies and revealed the daily OBSO Tagesmeldung re-encodement into Raven. The reason for the introduction of the Buzzard key never became clear, and its German name was not discovered. Buzzard tended to be used in the northern Balkans – mostly in Italian occupation – while Raven remained popular in the south. But all major German formations throughout the area apparently possessed both keys – the commanders in Crete and Rhodes, for instance, possessed Buzzard although normally using Raven – and the only plausible theory advanced was that Buzzard was intended for liaison with the Italians, while Raven was only issued to German staffs. At any rate, Buzzard mostly came from German liaison officers with Italian groups, while Raven surely could not have been in Italian hands when it contained such uncomplimentary remarks about them as: "It is deplorable that again the Italians are trying --- --- to make fools out of us and get what they want behind our backs " (Raven II, 13/5). Whatever the reason for its use, Buzzard throughout May and June passed a large volume of traffic and was a most interesting problem, with occasional cillies, one or two cribs which could be attacked in different ways, and sometimes re-encodements from Raven or Codfish.

The cribs by this time, both on Raven and Buzzard, mostly began with wahlworts and therefore were less expensive when the ending could be used instead. Hence much ingenuity was employed in attempts to forecast the serial number at the end of the OBSO Tagesmeldung and its companion mid-day report, the Mittagsmeldung. If a version appeared on Fish, then the number would be known, and a plausible shot on both the Buzzard and Raven would be the popular ending, as: DREISEQSSIEBENFUENF GEHX or DREISEQSSIEBENFUENF STRIQ VIERDREI GEHX. If the number was unknown, one could at least forecast with some degree of probability the first two figures, and then make use of the standard end of the signature immediately preceding. One would then stagger ROEM EINS ANTON STRIQ OTTO EINS NUMX DREI SEQS and run it in the positions which required a reasonable number of letters following, to account for the other two figures and the variations of GEHEIM.

With the disappearance of Buzzard, the amount of traffic on Raven naturally increased, and early in July new cribs from Rhodes began to score, so that July and August both saw most days broken. "Rhodes C" and "Rhodes A" were the IC and IA reports from the German staff on the island. Normally there was nothing to say and the IC report was in the form: (Address) MORGENMELDUNG VOM (Date) KEINE BESONDEREN VORKOMMNISSE (Signature). Thus a plausible attempt could be made at writing out the whole message.

Raven I, then, was broken with increasing frequency as the year progressed. Meanwhile, the more secret traffic was difficult to deal with because more than one key was involved. By analogy it should all have been sent in Raven II, but in practice many of the stations preferred Merlin (later known as Falcon II). Merlin was broken for the first time in May, when it was realised it was a Staff key, by the process of running a number of messages from Susak on the beginner GEHEIMEKOMMANDOSAQE. The evidence of a crash analysis suggested that this was the best station, and so it proved. Occasional Merlin days from May to September were broken in this way, whenever there was enough traffic to make an attempt worthwhile, shots were made with normally about 20% of success. Raven II was treated at first as a rather different problem, for in June it gave us our first manifestation of a peculiar rule of the German Army Cipher Office which lasted until the end of the war, namely, that all Armee Staff keys should have the same discriminants. When traffic with Albatross II discriminants first appeared in the Balkans and failed to decode on the Albatross key, it was assumed that the two keys were basically the same with some minor difference such as a changed ringstellung, and great efforts were made to break into a message on such assumptions. Eventually Albatross II (Balkans) – i.e. Raven II of 5 September was broken on the bombe on the beginner GEHEIMEKOMMANDOSAQE and the key was found to bear no resemblance to that of Albatross II of the same day, which fortunately was also out. It was soon realised that all Army Staff keys were being allotted the same discriminants, and in future the fact enabled us to recognise Staff traffic more easily.

Surrender of Italy: appearance of Wryneck: September 1943-November 1944

The imminent surrender of Italy at the end of August caused the Germans to reorganise their Balkan forces and Panzer AOK 2 was brought from Russia to direct the divisions of Yugoslavia, while Heeresgruppe E was left in charge of Greece and the islands, both groups being subordinate to the C-in-C with his staff, Heeresgruppe F, at Belgrade. In spite of these precautions, the situation caused by the announcement of the Italian surrender was chaotic. In most places the Germans took charge according to plan. But at Tirana, the Italians took the German liaison staff prisoner, while on Rhodes there was severe fighting before the Germans finally took charge. These two events made the key situation extremely complicated, for all the existing keys were believed compromised at Tirana, while the best Raven crib was no longer sent because there was now something to report from Rhodes. Raven therefore became very much smaller in quantity and throughout September it resisted all attacks. Meanwhile, Wryneck, the key of the new northern army – Panzer AOK 2 – had been identified, and broken on a short morning routine message which had been correctly guessed on 21 September to say in 27 letters: KEINE BESONDEREN EREIGNISSE YY.

Other days were broken on variations of this form, including more than once the solecistic KEINER BESONDERE EREIGNISSE – sometimes with the addition of some form of the signature ROEM EINS ANTON, and some days early in October were broken on cillies when one operator, for a period, used the setting PAU for every message. Meanwhile Raven I (30/9) was broken on keyboard cillies, and revealed the form of the Rundspruch, a daily broadcast from Belgrade in both Raven and Wryneck giving details of Allied preparation for the invasion of the Balkans.

From this point the Raven-Wryneck position became increasingly stronger. Both keys developed excellent cribs, Tagesmeldungen from the 114th Jaeger Division and the 118th Infantry Division being particularly good on Wryneck, while the old Rhodes IC Morgenmeldung and a similar "Nothing to Report" message from Cephallonia could be expected to break most Raven days. The Rundspruch re-encodement was easy when one of the keys was broken, and the Rundspruch itself was a possible crib in three-day cyclic form. To make things simpler still, the Raven and Wryneck keys indulged in some odd repeats, almost the only examples of this form of laziness which were ever found in Army keys. Raven in October and November repeated its stecker with some small alterations after 15 days. Wryneck did the same in October, November and December and in addition, in these months the wheelorder and ringstellung repeated themselves in blocks in such a way that by December it was possible to predict the wheelorder nearly every day and also the letters of the ringstellung. With a stecker repeat for the last half of the month, it was possible to write down the wheelorder and stecker and to find the ringstellung by trying the six possible permutations of the known three letters, and therefore, for a short spell, Wryneck was passed from Research to the Watch so that the traffic could be handled currently.

Raven was broken nearly every day in November, and then in December most annoyingly split into three keys. Of these, one – E/6315A – passed the Rundspruch and nothing else, another – E/3730A – consisted of the Cephallonia crib and other traffic on the same frequency, while the third contained the bulk of the traffic, and clearly from this point was the key referred to as Maschinenschlüssel Aegaeis Süd. The loss of two of the best cribs left Raven breakable only on weak cribs and only a day or two each week came out. There was a revival in March, when a third report from Rhodes broke several days, but this faded away, and from the beginning of May no traffic was read on the key for many months.

Meanwhile, Wryneck I went from strength to strength throughout January, on three days the two best cribs, the Paulmeldung and the Monikameldung, which by this time both began TAGESMELDUNG, coming in depth. This remarkable occurrence, which gave us 100% certain cribs on all three days, was due to the extraordinary coincidence that two different operators both became attached to the same message setting LOS. On 31 January, the Monikameldung was sent in Wryneck II, which gave us our first break of the Staff key. Three routine messages turned out to be useless as cribs, though interesting, since they provided Y Intelligence derived from decodes of Tito's traffic. Cryptographically they were not entirely valueless, for during June and July they were occasionally re-encoded into Puffin II for the benefit of the armies in Italy. And, when there was no information to give, a short message was

The Italian Army and Balkan Army Keys

sent in Wryneck saying something like: SIE HOEREN UNS WIEDER UM ... ... UHR. The re-encodements, however, were fiendishly difficult, while the little messages giving the QRX – times employed so many variant forms that they could rarely be used. The initial Wryneck II break was nevertheless not unprofitable, for it showed that at least some of the messages ended with the standard G-tails:

STRIQ VIERVIER GKDOS

GEH(X)KDOS

which had been tried before, but not apparently on a sufficiently large scale. Henceforward a certain amount of Wryneck II was broken by the G-tail method until the final disappearance of the key late in 1944. Wryneck I, with its heavy traffic, was usually breakable too if enough messages were run on Geheim Teile, and from time to time when the cribs had bad patches this method had to be employed, notably in May and June. The June break restored the position, and from then on until December, four or five days were broken nearly every week on various cribs, mostly operational reports from the Corps under Panzer AOK 2.

Arrival of Russians and new Balkan set-up: November 1944

In November 1944 the Army, with some of its Corps, turned to face the advancing Russians and was subordinated to Heeresgruppe Süd, so that Wryneck became an Eastern Front key rather than a Balkan key. The result was that the traffic dropped to only a few messages a day, and only a few Wryneck days were broken in 1945.

Large parts of the forces which had been under AOK 2 were now subordinated to Heeresgruppe E, which in consequence was once more allotted an Armee key and Staff key. These were given a new name – Quail – as the old name Raven was still in use for the Aegean key. December saw the gradual transference of some of the cribs from Wryneck to Quail, as units were re-subordinated. Annoyingly, one very good one went over to the little used general area key, Emu II – the Heeresstabsmaschinenschlüssel Süd. However, there was yet some semblance of order before the end. Wryneck and Emu II virtually disappeared, while Quail, with often as many as 100 messages a day, was broken with increasing regularity in January and February 1945 until finally the engulfing Allied armies overwhelmed the area and all the Quails and Wrynecks in it. The last Balkan break was an April Raven day, but it was like the many Ravens broken in December and

January, a bird of tattered plumage, a skeleton of its former self. In 1942 and 1943 we had read of ambush and reprisal from Hungary to Greece, from the Aegean to the Adriatic. In 1944 and 1945 Raven told of the two small beleaguered garrisons of Crete and Rhodes, well-provisioned and comfortable, disturbed only by the fear that unsympathetic islanders might resent the ease in which they were quietly waiting for the end of the war.

Chapter 23
The Western Air and Army Keys

Western Air Keys

General
The story of the breaking of the Western Air keys is in general one of the most interesting examples of the ability of the cryptographers to exploit changing military circumstances with the minimum of delay. Allied war plans and Hut 6 successes moved side by side. The period between the fall of France and the beginning of the great air offensive of 1944 saw no breaking of Western Air keys except Red and Snowdrop (Masch. Schl. West, later Lgau West Frankreich). The whole emphasis of operational work was on the Mediterranean. Western keys were, for the most part, problems of Research, and it was realised that an Allied landing in the West would lead to a remarkable growth and shift of keys, and that the changes could not be completely predicted. It was only in the period February 1944 to D-Day that our plans for exploiting the Western keys could become a little clearer, and it was felt that we should have to start afresh on D-Day itself, hoping for large numbers of re-encodements, and being prepared to see the relative decline and fall of Snowdrop within a short period of the beginning of the offensive. Snowdrop and Red had been the objectives of our attack on the Western keys before D-Day. It was realised that the former would go as the main cryptographic pivot, and that Jaguar – the key of Luftflotte 3 in Paris – would usurp its place. The assistance of Sixta was invaluable at this point – they had a much clearer idea of probabilities than we did.

D-Day brought the expected change in emphasis in the Watch from Mediterranean to Western Air keys, and it had many surprises as well. The Flivo key – Ocelot – began to claim prior attention from the early days of the Normandy bridgehead, and soon jumped right ahead of Locust, the key of Fliegerkorps II, just as Puma had leapt forward in Italy. From the first landings to the drive across the Rhine, the number of German Air keys and the volume of German Air traffic never reached the same proportions as it did on the days immediately after D-Day. Many keys were transformed or absorbed – Cricket and Ocelot, and Wasp and Cockroach being the chief. Towards the end of the war, there was a further shift in the emphasis in the work of the cryptographers towards the Luftgau keys of Germany itself.

The work on the Western Air keys can be treated as a coherent whole, in much the same way as the work on the African Army keys. It was always the chief operational GAF task of the period. To undertake it, large reserves of staff were built up in 1943. To carry it through, internal changes of organisation were frequently made. Towards the end, the strain of Reflector D and Enigma Uhr made this job particularly hard, but the fight continued until the end of hostilities solved many imminent difficulties, and released the cryptographers from a problem which was becoming very awkward to handle.

The breaking of Snowdrop
Snowdrop, the key of Luftgau West, was the only specifically Western Air key broken regularly before and after D-Day, until the days of the German collapse. In 1942, despite many black patches, its battery of short reports provided useful material for Research, and in April 1943 it was considered to be in a sufficiently flourishing condition to be handed over to the Watch. Its heyday was short-lived. In June, a wireless standstill order was imposed in France, and this killed most of the cribs, most of the practice messages, and all the operational traffic. Snowdrop went back to Research via the Qwatch, to be broken intermittently until it was ready to be returned to the Watch in March 1944. Its return was facilitated by the sending of a good crib alternately in Red and Snowdrop, and by a surprising increase in the number of routine Tagesabschlussmeldungen. Its value in the events around D-Day was surprisingly high, but the prophesies that it would not outlive the successful onslaught of the Allied armies proved substantially correct. From being the key of Luftgau West Frankreich it eventually became the key of Luftgau V with headquarters at Stuttgart, and the key persisted, on a small scale and of minor importance, almost until the end. The last break was 15 April 1945.

The history of Snowdrop spans the change from the period of German supremacy in the West to its final eclipse. The routine Seenots, Zahlsprüche, and Tagesabschlussmeldungen coming in clusters over long periods of time were the cribs of a nation resting on its laurels, the symbols of the serenity of an Air Force in comfortable occupation of a conquered land. One of the longest known cribs came from the Channel Islands. "Flak Jersey" never was a good crib, but its continuity in face of external changes was of considerable use. The turn of the tide in the West was marked by the German wireless silence, and then with the Allied landings, Snowdrop became virtually operational, passing as many as 820 messages on one day – 9 June. The Raffs – messages describing the state of aerodrome runways – were the swansong of the key, and in its Stuttgart days, little was left except re-encodements from other Luftgau keys.

The pivotal importance of Red
Before D-Day the main pivot of the cryptographic exploitation of the Western Air keys was, as in so many other cases, Red. As a general key, it provided frequent re-encodements into Snowdrop, and both W/T experts and cryptographers realised that the chances of getting into other Western keys were essentially dependent on re-encodements from it. The preparations for D-Day in the Air Watch were mainly concerned with the refinement and development of kissing technique. The growth of a re-encodement complex was noted and exploited some months before D-Day. On 16 February 1944, Jaguar – the key of Luftflotte 3 – was broken on a re-encodement from Red. This was the beginning.

February saw an entry into Tulip and Lily from Jaguar, and in March a slightly firmer hold was secured on Jaguar by the discovery that one of the small German LN units in the Vosges was using Snowdrop and Jaguar on alternate days for the transmission of its small battery of cribs. The value of this Zoo group (so-called because the codenames used on it were Hippo, Maus and Muffel) was proved – not for the first time. It had already enabled us to break many Red days early and cheaply, despite the queer habits it occasionally acquired, such as using its own key Aster, or using Aster and Red on alternate days. Now its peculiarities could be put to real use, and Snowdrop and Jaguar were both sent from Research to the Watch. In this way experience on Red was utilised to break other keys. Quite apart from this information and the value of re-encodements into Red, Red was a Western Air key in its own right. Two days after the first landing in Normandy, the Red traffic total went up to 809 messages.

The further growth of the re-encodement complex
In the days before the invasion much of the W/T picture was sketchy,

and in particular the existence of some keys was regarded as problematical. This particularly applied to Cricket, the key of Jagdkorps II. Its existence was in doubt, and traffic was closely tied up with Blue, the general practice key, which was thought to be part operational. This problem was cleared up by re-encodements, which enabled us to get the situation in hand on the eve of the offensive. Blue was broken on 18 March on a re-encodement from Jaguar. In April, a series of Tagesabschlussmeldungen on Lily, Snowdrop and Cricket were sent out in consolidated form in Jaguar. This unique form of re-encodement was of considerable value. On 27 April, Wasp, the key of Fliegerkorps IX, came out on a re-encodement from Legation Fag to Red. These various breaks justified the transfer of Cricket, Wasp, Lily and Locust to the Watch in May 1944, though Locust was impossible and Wasp unamenable, and the rest of the keys entirely dependant on re-encodements.

D-Day

The effect of D-Day on the keys in France was much as had been expected. There was first a vast increase in the amount of traffic:

	5th	6th	7th	8th	9th	10th	11th
Red	324	459	501	546	809	611	462
Snowdrop	209	357	611	706	820	678	785
Jaguar	129	180	231	356	584	625	491
Cricket	31	168	219	239	328	271	249
Wasp	17	23	28	72	49	118	31
Locust	19	110	221	81	167	218	215
Ocelot	---	---	---	152	179	122	123
TOTALS	729	1297	1811	2152	2936	2643	2356

Expressing it more colourfully, the Red total on the 9th or the Snowdrop total on the 9th were each higher than the total traffic of all these groups on the day before the invasion. There were other changes too. The Tabs messages, which had been the backbone of the previous attack, disappeared overnight. Snowdrop was far more important and urgent than had been thought likely. Locust, the key of Fliegerkorps II, proved to be not one key but two, a large proportion of the identified traffic passing on Ocelot, the Flivo key of Luftflotte 3.

For some time the only profitable line of attack on the keys lay in re-encodement. The task of comparing over 3,000 daily kiss pairings became the chief task of the Watch, and when a key was broken, quite frantic efforts had to be made to secure complete entering, and to prepare the way for the discovery of new cribs. The crib position remained obscure throughout those early days, but there were sufficiently numerous re-encodements to give us samples of all the important keys (including Gnat and Wasp), and there were reasonable grounds for the hope that many of them would prove tractable after more evidence had been obtained.

The period of regular breaking
By the end of June 1944, the Western Air keys as a whole were in a very healthy state, and all major Air keys were being broken on cribs. The change was most marked on Lily, which was entirely dependant on re-encodements for the fortnight after D-Day, but during the last ten days of the month, all days broken fell to cribs. Ocelot, Jaguar and Cricket all produced short messages of crib value, while Wasp developed a veritable battery of cribs. The shadow of D was not yet hanging over the West, and the successes in the routine Watch enabled the Qwatch party to deal with more difficult keys like Firefly, the key of the German paratroop army, and with minor and somewhat curious keys like Armadillo (a home-made Sonderschlüssel with consecutive stecker and non-Nigelian wheelorders) and Platypus (the key of Flak Korps 3 dealing with air security). The successes on the major keys in the period between 6 June and the end of the month are worthy of quotation:

Snowdrop:	all days broken (25 breaks)
Wasp:	all days broken except 7th and 11th
Lily:	all days broken except 17th and 27th
Jaguar:	all days broken except 14th
Cricket:	all days broken except 7th
Ocelot:	all days broken except 9th

The total score was 143 breaks out of a possible 150. In the last six days of the month on the keys mentioned above, 24 breaks were made before 0100 GMT on the following day. The average times of breaking were in some cases extremely early: Ocelot (1055) and Snowdrop (1030) being outstanding.

In a sense this was the peak month of our successes on the Western Air keys, for although many major successes were to lie ahead, the elements which were to upset the hold on the West were already beginning to be noticeable in July. On 10 July, the first messages to be sent on Enigma Uhr came on Jaguar and Cricket without warning, and they certainly slowed down the breaking of Jaguar, which had never been the best of keys to deal with. On 1 August, regarded as crisis day, the first use of Reflector D on the Western keys affected Jaguar again in particular, and many other keys as well. On 5 August, Wasp appeared to go over entirely to D, and even though B messages on the Nosegay Fag enabled us to recover the days at the end of the month without much difficulty, nonetheless the circumstances inspired little confidence in the future. On 1 August, Ocelot changed its Funkplan, and though this W/T change had little effect on breaking, it was an unpleasant foretaste of things to come. And these changes – technical and otherwise – came at a time when a rapid and all-sweeping Allied advance was having a very bad effect on the stability of both cribs and keys. Many cribs went about this time, the most lamented of all being the Zoo cribs on Snowdrop. Snowdrop itself as a key was compromised in the second week of August, and two or three keys were put into use. Although Snowdrop traffic was to reach high levels again with the landings in the south of France, the position of Luftgau West Frankreich had been settled for good and all with the breakthrough at Avranches.

These elements of doubt and uncertainty were mainly incipient however. Some of the most valuable work of Hut 6 was done in this period of Allied drive and advance. Ocelot was broken regularly – mainly currently – for every day in July, and all days but one in August. Its message totals were high, and its intelligence value high also. Time tests were taken at this period to make sure that the messages went through to Hut 3 with the minimum of delay. The average times of breaking are worth quoting:

Week ending 8 July:	1430	Week ending 5 August:	1310
Week ending 15 July:	1245	Week ending 12 August:	1500
Week ending 22 July:	1905	Week ending 19 August:	1640
Week ending 29 July:	1330	Week ending 26 August:	1650

Despite a considerable amount of Jaguar traffic on D and Enigma

The Western Air and Army Keys

Uhr, every Jaguar day in July and August was broken, 33 of them currently – only 11 Wasp days, despite the period of universal D, remained unbroken. Taking into account the Snowdrop compromise, the position on that key was as good as it could have been: 42 Firefly days were broken. None of them were easy, cribs were few, and cillies marked the best line of attack. A firm grip was maintained on Gnat until it disappeared with the Allied advance from Angers to Rheims: 26 breaks were made on Lily, many of them of considerable value because of the connection of Lily with V-weapon supply. In fact, this was the period when Hut 6 was able to supply all the important operational intelligence to the Allied commanders. After September, the German Air Force itself was effectively finished as a major factor in holding back the Allies or securing the safety of the Reich.

Changes in emphasis

With the Allied advance to the German frontier, the work of the Watch began to be based more and more on the German keys (see separate section). The W/T position of the Western keys was itself radically changing. Luftflotte 3 (Jaguar) moved from Paris to Rheims, from Rheims to the Coblenz area, from the Coblenz area to near Limburg. Its title changed to Lufwaffen Kdo. West. Luftgau West Frankreich (Snowdrop) and Luftgau Belgien-Nord Frankreich (Lily) were absorbed into the Reich structure by the division of Luftgau VII. They became Luftgau V and Luftgau XIV respectively. The remaining Dutch airfields were subordinated to Luftgau VI. Luftflotte Reich (Hyena) grew rapidly in importance. It was a re-encodement between Jaguar and Hyena that cleared the air after Jaguar had become particularly difficult during the early weeks of September. At the end of the month, Daffodil seemed to be taking a more important place at the cryptographic centre with re-encodements to Lily and Snowdrop as well as to Hyena, Cockroach and Gorilla.

With the withdrawal to Germany, the numerous Festungen, left behind by the Germans as strong points in the rear, began to use hand-made NOT-Schlüssel. Snowdrop cast off a number of such offshoots. NOT-Guernsey, for instance, made its first appearance at the beginning of October. The system was to spread to all sectors, both Air and Army, but it began in the West. On 1 December, Daffodil split into its constituent Luftgau keys, a natural and somewhat surprisingly delayed change, which finally placed Lily, Snowdrop and Aster (Luftgau VII) in the German orbit. This left only two of the original Western keys, for one of the welcome changes of the beginning of November had been the amalgamation of Cricket and Ocelot. Jaguar and Ocelot were now left as the two basic keys. Wasp, mainly on D, was broken from time to time (e.g. 28 October), but until Jagdkorps I was disbanded and some of its networks taken over by Fliegerkorps IX on 1 March 1945, there was no long period of breaking.

The decline of the West
Until the end of 1944 and the beginning of the new Allied offensive into Germany, the Western operational keys, now properly including Cockroach (Jagdkorps I), were in good operational trim, despite technical difficulties like Reflector D and Enigma Uhr, and despite a growing number of key compromises, which at times made the W/T position very complicated. At other times, they helped us much more than they helped the enemy. For instance, Jaguar of January 1945 repeated the Jaguar B key of December, and though this was not solidly broken then, there was little difficulty in filling in the gaps left. Similarly, one subscriber on Ocelot in January 1945 had not got the new month's key, and obligingly used the previous month's key backwards, giving daily letter-to-letter re-encodements into the current key. Such mistakes on the part of the enemy were frequent in 1945, and together with the capture of key-sheets, enabled us to keep a precarious hold on keys, which might otherwise have slipped from our grasp. By such improvised methods we were compelled to live through the few months before the great link-up of Russians and Americans and the final victory of the Allies. Nonetheless, in 1945 there were 108 breaks of Jaguar and 105 breaks of Ocelot out of a possible total of about 120 days. Only one Cockroach day was missing until it became known as Wasp at the beginning of March, and thereafter 39 Wasps were broken. Breaks of Ocelot were becoming increasingly expensive. An examination of bombe-hour figures on the key at different periods throws up some interesting results:

	Breaks	Bombe Hours	Hours per break
2-29 July	28	1150	41
29 July-2 Sept	33	2410	73
28 Jan-24 Feb	28	6609	236
25 Feb-31 March	33	8892	269

All these figures only count one key break per day, e.g. when there was a

The Western Air and Army Keys

Jaguar I, a Jaguar C and a Jaguar IIA, Jaguar IIA is counted because it was the main Jaguar key. The same applies to the counting of Ocelot II and Wasp II. These breaks were accomplished against a fluid war picture, in which the decline in the importance of the Luftwaffe had greatly reduced the intelligence value of the operational keys. Traffic totals reflected the changing fortunes of war, and towards the end dropped phenomenally – Jaguar, for instance, from a daily average of 233 messages at the end of March to 81 messages at the end of April, and 24 messages for the week ending 5 May.

The main cryptographic theme of this period was the hard fight against D. When the Allied troops landed in Normandy in June 1944, D15 was in use – by May 1945 we had reached D333. Early in March 1945 it seemed that because of the use of D, and the scarcity of satisfactory B cribs, Ocelot was certain to go. A stray re-encodement from Jaguar into a key that was hoped to be Ocelot providentially came out. It revealed new cribs and a considerable amount of B traffic. The Jaguar which gave the re-encodement was itself a captured key. By the end of March, Jaguar, Wasp and Ocelot were almost wholly on D, and the future seemed very black indeed. April saw a precarious but happy start. Ocelot was broken on B traffic, the D recovered, and a re-encodement into Jaguar came out on Duenna. Each new D period in April came as a critical turning point. The three keys were now hanging together as they had never done before. Operational messages like Erdlages and Aufklärungen were re-encoded freely between all three keys, but they had a habit of not being there when they were most required.

The May prospects for breaking seemed depressing, but the difficulties we had to face were paralleled by those of the Germans. Faced with the problem of distributing fresh cipher material, the Germans were having to rely increasingly on rehashes of old keys. In May, part of the Ocelot network was to use the April keys over again in a hatted order. May Jaguar was used in April by units of Flieger Division 14, and re-encoded into Ocelot and Wasp. Wasp itself was mainly on D, its two bad cribs were both D, and it was dependant on occasional re-encodements from Raster. Despite all the difficulties, the way in through new lines of attack in May was clear, and there is little doubt that if we had once made an initial entry, a break into the other two keys would have been possible.

Western Army Keys

General

The German army was well trained in the first golden rule of cipher security, that no traffic should be sent over the air unless it is absolutely necessary. Consequently, the history of Army keys everywhere is a story of spasmodic bursts of activity with long periods of silence, and often no continuity between the traffic of one period of activity and another.

The Western campaigns thus provided three glorious periods – the initial landings, the drive through France, and the final battles on both sides of the Rhine – in which most of the Heeresgruppen and Armies engaged were on the move and had to use wireless communication. In such times the Army Watch spared no effort to make hay while the sun shone, and the supreme importance of the intelligence given meant that bombe time was always available if required. The stress and movement of these times was the exact reverse of the conditions in which one usually found cribs, for normally these came from units which were settled for long periods in one place, and had fallen into a groove. Consequently, the breaking of Western Army keys was a hand-to-mouth affair, dependant upon the closest inspection of current decodes, and allowing plenty of scope for ingenuity.

The number of keys issued to units in the West was normally out of all proportion to the amount of traffic actually sent over the air. In addition to the general operational keys, the Bantams and Puffins, and the general supply key, Peewit, every Army had its own key and Staff key. As there were always at least five armies in the West, and in the later stages seven or eight, it might be thought that the Armee keys alone would present a formidable problem from sheer weight of numbers. In fact, there was rarely any great volume of traffic on any one Armee key, and apart from the very early days of the invasion, when there was plenty of Duck from AOK 7, and after Avranches, when Panzer AOK 5 began to send Dodo, we scarcely saw any Armee traffic. When the current keys of AOK 19 and AOK 1 (Gosling and Swan) were captured in August, it was unusual to see more than a single message decoded, and sometimes there was not even that, and this was when the two armies were heavily engaged and on the move. Panzer AOK 6 (Whimbrel) was more forthcoming after von Rundstedt had launched his counter-offensive in December, and with

30 or so messages a day of high urgency, it was well worth having. In this case the first two breaks were the last, for no sooner had they been achieved than the offensive ended and the army was withdrawn and sent east – a typical example of triumph and disappointment for the Army cryptographers.

Before D-Day
Unlike the Air keys, the Western Army keys passed virtually no traffic of significance before D-Day. The keys were in existence – we had reference to them in other traffic from time to time – and were occasionally used in large-scale W/T practices which were some times coincident with army manoeuvres. During these practices, which usually lasted for a week or rather less, numerous frequencies appeared passing quantities of traffic in several different keys, the messages mostly being days of discriminants, it was fairly easy to identify the Armee keys by area and it was recognised that there was more than one general key in use. After dropping of discriminants, identification of the keys was very difficult, a state of affairs which persisted throughout the subsequent history of the Western Army keys.

The first break in the West was in January 1944 when a routine message from Brussels had a cilli to MIX with TOM outside, and the day was broken on MIX plus a stagger of the date. Disappointingly little traffic decoded, and all of it was clearly practice. The routine message proved simply to be the German High Command communiqué, encoded and transmitted presumably for practice, and one other day was broken as a result of this discovery. An interesting point about the first 320 Group break was the fact that the key had the same stecker as one of the broken Quince days of the same month, suggesting that the key was an SS key, for SS keys sometimes bore a relationship to each other, but were never known to be connected with Army keys.

A big W/T practice in February led to the first genuine break of an Army key. "Chicken" 27 February was broken on some cillies plus a stagger of VIERVIER, and proved to have a quantity of operational practice, i.e. traffic which looked in every way like the real thing, except that somewhere in the text appeared the words X UEBUNGSSPRUCH X or X UEB X. In addition there was a little genuine traffic and the whole dealt with supply matters. It is quite clear now that "Chicken" 27 February was the first break of the key which was later known as Peewit, the supply key in the West.

Although this exercise lasted for over a week, and the Chicken decodes seemed to hold good crib prospects, no other days were broken at this time. No further successes were scored until the beginning of May, when the procedure of running the standard Geheim and Gkdos Tails on multi-teile messages brought breaks of Bantam I 3 May and Bantam II 5 May. The traffic was at the highest level, signatories including OBW, Heeresgruppe B, AOK 7 and AOK 15, and it included genuine as well as operational practice material. This was our first intimation of the fondness of OBW for the standard G-Tails, but we received confirmation of it in yet another big exercise at the turn of the month, when a Bantam II and a Bantam I came out on these endings. Another Bantam I day – 30 May – came out on cillies.

These, then, were the only glimpses we had of Western Army traffic prior to the invasion, although there was one special purpose key which was being broken fairly regularly, namely Nightjar, the key of the military occupation authorities, who had a big wireless network throughout France. Prior to the invasion, the traffic passed was mostly practice, but even then it was clear that the object of it was speedy reporting of sabotage to communications, especially landlines, so that alternative routes could be quickly devised and repairs set under way.

Nightjar was first broken in April when a March day came out on a Geheim Tail run on a long routine message which proved to be a LAGEORIENTIERUNG. Incidentally, the first break was extremely lucky, for the message scarcely ever ended in this way again. However it was quite a good crib at the beginning, and broke many days until it finally disappeared two days after D-Day.

D-Day and the first breaks

Thus, when D-Day finally came, bringing with it floods of traffic, we had a very good idea of what to expect, but very little notion of what they would be saying. It was fairly clear at once that two or three keys were in use and that there was a good deal of re-encoding going on, and it was very disappointing, therefore, when the first key broken proved to be a Y key having but little connection with the others. This was Pullet (8 June), which was the only key ever to be broken by a "Banbury Stagger", a method used where the same text was encoded at different positions of the machine at known relative distances.

However, success was not long delayed. Heeresgruppe B tried to send

The Western Air and Army Keys

Bantam on the Jaguar star, which quickly resulted in a re-encodement from Jaguar as Luftflotte 3 possessed no Army key. A break of Duck I, the key of AOK 7, on a re-encodement from the Bantam, followed a few hours later, and Duck II, the Staff key, succumbed in its turn. All these were keys of 9 June broken very quickly after the Jaguar had come out during the afternoon of the 10th. One promising day into other leads appeared, a 1C Abendmeldung from AOK 7 which scored on the 11th and then not again till the 17th. From the 17th, the breaking of most days of Bantam I and Duck I and some days Duck II, proceeded until the fall of Cherbourg on the 25th. There were re-encodements between Bantam and the Ducks every day, and it was a case of scoring one break on a day and then exploiting the re-encodements. Bantam had a crib from the 1st SS Panzer Corps, while Kampfgruppe Schlieben in Cherbourg, which had lost all its keys except Duck and Dolphin – the Naval key – obliged by providing the re-encodements from Dolphin and also by being sent several days Pullet keys in Duck II messages.

The first lull
With the fall of Cherbourg on 25 June, traffic which had fallen off considerably since the first few days of the invasion dropped to not much more than a trickle. However, there were still one or two keys to be broken, for Nightjar was providing plenty of traffic and produced some cribs which enabled us to break almost every day in July. Meantime, a break of Peewit, the Western supply key, had been achieved on a depth-reading, and several long supply reports, coupled with a considerable amount of cillying, enabled us to break nearly every day in July. This was a most valuable key, for apart from the obvious uses of supply intelligence in a period of static warfare, there was a tendency for the enemy to fall back on his supply key when the operational keys were compromised, and thus at various times, Peewit breaks decoded much that was normally on operational keys like the Bantams.

Two minor oddities were Penguin and Diver, which provided innocent amusement for the cryptographers without, one feels, greatly increasing Hut 3's knowledge of the German Army. Diver was the special key used by the 319th Division in the Channel Islands, and was sometimes broken on its short nil returns. Penguin was one of the few divisional keys which was ever identified. It was quite clearly an ad hoc cipher for use between the operational and supply HQ of the 12th SS Panzer Division, and was remarkable in that there were only six different keys – and two of those were very similar – which were used again and again. By the end of the third or fourth period of six days all but one of the keys had been broken on re-encodements from Non-Indicator traffic or on cillies, and eventually enough cillies were collected from different dates to break the last day. Penguin lasted from the middle of June to the end of August, and for most of that time nearly all the messages were being read currently.

The breakthrough
On 26 July the American offensive in the direction of Avranches and the resumption of open warfare caused traffic totals to rocket to unprecedented levels. Some of the signatures of the Corps of which we had collected evidence in June gave some quick breaks, and re-encodements from Bantam to Duck and day-to-day re-encodements helped by carrying most of the traffic on the last two days of the month when most of the other keys had been compromised.

From now on two features stand out in the general confusion which followed the German defeat in France. First, it became quite impossible to sort out the various keys in use, and therefore the Barnyard cover name was introduced, the first key to be broken on a day being called Barnyard I, the second Barnyard II and so on. Generally, all the traffic was tried on each key broken which, while a heavy burden on the Decoding Room, was the only way of ensuring a minimum of delay in sending urgent material to Hut 3. Secondly, from the breaking point of view, it now became possible to exploit the tendency of OBW (C-in-C West) to use the standard secret endings to his messages, for OBW was now consistently on the air passing traffic to the Heeresgruppen and Armeen. Meanwhile, the landing in southern France had brought Armeegruppe, or, as it was later called, Heeresgruppe C, on the air, and it soon became apparent that this station had a strong tendency to end his messages with the current day's date. From this point until the end of the war, OBW and Heeresgruppe G were fairly reliable stand-bys whenever they appeared on the air.

With the spread of the war more general keys came into use, Bantam, Wehrmacht Maschinenschlüssel West, remained in use between the main Western stations, but there was a tendency to use Puffin as an alternative. This was probably because OKH was frequently on the air at this time, and although possessing Bantam, showed a strong preference

The Western Air and Army Keys

for Puffin, which was indeed his own key (OKH Maschinenschlüssel B). Falcon, too, began to be concerned with the western fighting, for as the exact counterparts of Bantam for the Home War Area, it was possessed by units such as Heeresgruppe C, who had now retreated right into Germany. With frequent compromise and a rapidly changing battle front, it was usually impossible to tell which of these keys one was trying to break. Puffin was sometimes obvious when there was some Mediterranean traffic on the key, but this theatre was liable to the same fluctuations in traffic as the western, and days would pass without a single message being taken.

The second lull: October
With the completion of the occupation of France and the reversion to static warfare, traffic dropped once more, but the successes of August and September left us with two or three breakable keys which continued to pass a fair volume of traffic.

E/Lorient was steadily broken until near the end of October, when the Fortress was transferred to the Naval Command, and the operational military traffic disappeared. Occasional breaks were secured afterwards on a long report on losses which was sent once or twice a month, but the interest of such a local key was never great. It was one of those keys which were broken because they were cheap and easy to break rather than because their intelligence value gave them a high priority.

Bantam I soon dropped to a trickle but was breaking most days owing to a routine re-encodement from Ocelot, sent on an Air frequency. This died at the end of October, but it lasted just long enough to give us one or two re-encodements into Blunderbuss, the Western Railway key, upon which we were then able to obtain some sort of hold.

Blunderbuss (formerly known as Rocket II) traffic was first read in August, when four days keys were given us by a deserting cipher clerk. The decodes were unpromising and no progress was made, but the re-encodements from Bantam at the end of October revealed one or two cribs which, before they disappeared, sufficed to break a few days and show the power of the ends of messages from Essen. From now on until the end of the war all messages from Essen were run on the ending SPRUQ ESSEN NUM (serial number), and many days in most months were accounted for. Obviously, steady breaking was essential here, for otherwise one soon lost track of the serial number.

Culverin (first called Stephenson) was another Railway key which made its appearance at this time. A group was intercepted in Holland for a few days, passing Non-Indicator traffic, of which one day was broken. Enigma was passed from the beginning of October and a break was obtained on the evidences of the NI decodes. The key was soon seen to be very easy to break, since only wheels I, II and III were used, and nearly all the messages said either:

    DURQLAUFXBENTHEIMXRIQTUNGXHOLLAND

or

    DURQLAUFXBENTHEIMXRIQTUNGXREIQ

according to the direction in which the train in question happened to be going.

All these keys, however, were of minor importance compared with Falcon II, which was the great legacy of the breakthrough period. In some of the Barnyard breaks of that time, multi-teile messages decoded which were routed from Berlin to the western Wehrkreis centres on the main Greenshank network. These messages discriminated to distinguish them from the normal Greenshank traffic, and it was fairly obvious that Falcon II was being used as the Staff key to Greenshank as there was no Greenshank II. This was extremely fortunate from out point of view, as Greenshank itself was almost unbreakable owing to the daily changing Reflector D, but Falcon II possessed cribs and was on Reflector B. A proportion of the messages in this key emanating from Berlin began with some variant of:

    GEHEIMEKOMMANDOSAQE AN STELLV GEN KDO ROEM

or

    AN WEHRKR(EIS) KDO ROEM

The large number of variations of this beginner, coupled with the fact that much of the traffic had quite different and completely unpredictable beginnings, made the breaking of Falcon II extremely expensive in bombe time, but the very high level of intelligence proved made it worth breaking at almost any cost. Falcon II remained in this state of breakability until traffic finally disappeared at the end of March. There were periods of days and sometimes weeks when there was little or no traffic. But as soon as Berlin obliged by sending a few messages, the "Secret Head" method of breaking usually sufficed.

Parallel to Falcon II, but with a different function, was Falcon I, a key of wide distribution but chiefly used for communications within Wehrkreis VI. Long before D-Day this key was being broken regularly on addresses, but interception was seriously affected by the introduction of encoding callsigns, and cover on the groups was dropped after D-Day in favour of M/F traffic more closely connected with the battle. In August and September it was realised that some of the keys which were being broken as Barnyard were in fact Falcon I – odd messages taken on search from the Wehrkreis VI stations decoded – and a drive was instituted to improve interception. With encoded callsigns it was difficult to identify the stations on the group, and breaking, which had formerly been exclusively on addresses, would depend on correct identification. By taking the best of the old addresses and running them on messages having a large number of different routeings, some breaks were obtained and it became possible from a combination of D/F, log-reading, callsign continuities from breaks and observation of station idiosyncrasies, to identify some of the main stations and thus make breaking not prohibitively expensive.

Falcon I was broken on most days from November onwards until the end of March. For the last two months or so we were permitted the luxury of two genuine cribs – an evening report on the position of the Allied armies, sent out by Münster to all stations, which had a useful address as well as a good signature, and a series of CQ messages from Münster, giving information on a variety of subjects, but most commonly on action in the event of landings from the air or signals matters. The messages were recognised by procedure and at either the beginning or end announced themselves as SAMMELSPRUQ NUM (number). With good interception it was fairly easy to calculate the number, which went up one for every message. At the end of March, Münster was evacuated and the administration of Wehrkreis VI finally broke down. The key gave steady if unexciting intelligence concerning administrative supply matters in the vital Ruhr area over a long period, and was of great cryptographic value in that it gave re-encodements into Greenshank on the one hand and Bantam on the other.

Bantam, as the main operational Western key, still appeared spasmodically in bulk, but normally consisted of a steady stream of from 20 to 30 messages a day, mostly on a star controlled by OBW, with the main active outstation at Münster, hence the Falcon-Bantam re-encodements which arose when one of the subordinate stations in

Wehkreis VI wished to send a message to OBW, and did via Münster. Both Bantam I and II were broken from time to time on the endings of messages from OBW, while there was a period in January and February when Bantam even had a crib, a short nil return of many variant forms which came from a forward supply dump of Heeresgruppe B. The sender quite clearly tried to produce a different form of the message every day, and it was amusing to attempt to guess each one as it was used.

One other key was broken in this period. A break into Pigeon, the Western Y key for communications between German intercept stations and breaking centres, enabled us to maintain valuable information on our own ciphers. The tightening up in our own security which followed resulted in the disappearance of the Pigeon crib messages, which gave lists of Allied frequencies or announced breaks of our low grade ciphers.

The final battles: heavy traffic once again

The long lull in Army W/T activity, which had lasted – apart from occasional short bursts of traffic – since September, was finally broken with the offensive to clear the left bank of the Rhine, and with the Rhine crossings and the subsequent open warfare, the totals rose to their highest levels once again. As before, OBW and Heeresgruppe G were normally expected to provide us with at least one break, and other keys were broken by re-encodements. In this period, as before, keys did not remain in force long owing to frequent capture – or suspected capture – by our forces. The resulting chaos meant more keys to break than would otherwise have been necessary, for usually some of the stations went on using the compromised keys, while others obtained new ones, and others used some available substitute. It is somewhat ironical to recall that in most of these supposed compromises the keys must have first been destroyed by the Germans. At any rate, they did not normally reach us. But on one famous occasion when the Canadians captured the current Bantam I and Dodo I and II keys in August and sent them back in time for us to decode half the month's traffic currently, the Germans specifically stated that these keys were quite safe!

Puffin finally came into its own in the last days. This, the general OKH key for use in the West (including the Mediterranean and the Balkans), was used to a considerable extent in August and September when Puffin I, II and even III (the key used for Chefsachen messages of the very highest grade of secrecy) were included among the many Barnyard breaks. In the period of quiescence there were several occasions when Puffin had enough traffic from the various fronts to make it worth breaking, and considerable bombe time was then expended on numerous versions of the cribs from Crete, the Morgenmeldung, Abendmeldung and Tagesmeldung which were sometimes sent from Crete to OKH in the special Cretan key, Flycatcher, and thence to Heeresgruppe E in Puffin. A dozen versions on any one of these messages might offer no better than a 25% chance of success, which was not encouraging to the cryptographer, but nevertheless yielded success to the persevering. There were long periods, too, when most of the Puffin traffic consisted of those broadcast Y reports which were such a feature of the German intelligence system in the West. This type of traffic would occasionally succumb to a heavy exhaustive attack, for all the messages contained a serial number, usually in the middle but sometimes at the beginning or the end. But at least one break very close to the day under attack was necessary, for otherwise the number would have lain within too big a range.

But the Crete reports and the Y messages were the cribs used in the quiet periods. Perhaps some of the most valuable Army intelligence came from the efforts of these times – from Falcon II, for instance, which outlined the building up of the new 6th SS Panzer Army for the December offensive and was a continual source of information on German defensive policy. But the exciting moments for the Army Watch were in the periods of traffic, with their crescendos just after D-Day, again in August and finally in March and April. In these times, the unit on which we worked was the message, or, if it discriminated, on its discriminant. We ran on the bombes anything which any of the messages might plausibly say, and when one came out, the others were tested on it. Some did not decode because they were on other keys and they were left to run until another key was broken. Thus, in August and September, on some days as many as nine or ten keys were broken – nameless keys – because they were simply called Barnyards I, II, III ... IX. Most of them came out on re-encodements from key to key, which meant that those last in the chain tended to be broken two or three days late. But it also meant continuously exciting and interesting work for all concerned, with its aim to get a glimpse into the mind of a German commander, or cipher clerk, or both, and do it in time to assist our own command.

Chapter 24
German Air and Eastern Air Keys

German Air Keys

General

It is difficult to write the history of the German Air keys except in the reflected light of the Allied advance of 1944 and 1945. Yet in 1942 and 1943, such advances were very remote. When the Germans were battling towards the Nile Estuary and fighting along the banks of the Volga, Greater Germany was still secure, miles away. At that time, the German Air keys were distinctly a research proposition, occasionally providing some intelligence about night fighter defences or aircraft dispositions. Such was the case in January 1942, when Cockroach was wanted for radar information. The demand for this key soon went down, and it became a routine research commitment. Daffodil was, as a rule, even less valuable, and traffic totals were low over long periods. Both Daffodil and Cockroach (along with Hyena, the key of Luftflotte Reich, which first appeared in 1944) were not transferred to the Watch until the eve of the Second Front, and Daffodil did not soar to really high intelligence value until the end of September. From that time onwards until the end of the war, the cryptographic exploitation of the German keys was made more difficult by disintegration, compromise and increasing technical complexities.

Research

The long period of research breaking of Daffodil and Cockroach in 1942 and 1943 can be told very briefly. Cockroach appeared at the beginning of 1942, after the splitting up of Red. At first it was the key of Fliegerkorps III, which it remained until October of the same year when Fliegerkorps III was renamed Jagdkorps I, the first Jagdkorps that appeared. In Research, it fell into the category of Cilli Keys, and the number of cillies and occasional examples of depth gave it a fairly interesting life. From the crib point of view it was chiefly distinguished for its "Spruch" messages, although by 1943 it had acquired some of the standard cribs

– particularly Gefechtsberichte – which were to serve until late in the war. On the whole, breaking was steady and unspectacular and we were helped considerably by key repeats. Daffodil appeared rather later than Cockroach. On 1 May 1942, Snowdrop (Lgau. Masch. Schl. West) was restricted to France, Belgium and Holland, and a new key was introduced for North Germany and Scandinavia. For a month it was known as Snowdrop II, then it was given the name of Daffodil. Two months later a separate key was introduced for Norway, named Narcissus. Some Norwegian traffic continued to be sent on Daffodil in November 1942, but in general its use was now restricted to Germany and Denmark. On 1 March 1943 each Luftgau was allotted a separate key, and Daffodil became the key of Luftgau XI. (There had been a Luftgau II key issued in 1941 – Daisy – but it was never broken by Hut 6), but two months later all the German Luftgau groups, with one or two exceptions, went back to Daffodil again, which remained the general key until 1 December 1944, when it split up into seven components.

Over this long period, Daffodil traffic totals fluctuated considerably. In 1942 and 1943 totals were usually low, but a heavy air attack would lead to a great increase in the volume of traffic. Early in October 1943, for instance, there were heavy air attacks on Hanover and the Hamburg region. Traffic totals rose enormously, the intelligence value of the key rising also, and the cryptographic interest of Daffodil was enlivened by a bout of cillying on the part of the German operators. This was somewhat exceptional. For the most part, the breaking of the key was not a thrilling or particularly rewarding cryptographic experience. Re-encodements were few, although now and again re-encodements from Red were useful, particularly when cribs were difficult. The first Daffodil crib —the Zahlspruch – was a day report on the number of practice messages sent and received. Luftlage, first used as a crib in the early days of 1943, was the foundation stone of almost all regular breaking, and remained so until the end of the war. Its cyclical habits were a later development. Early in 1943 new cribs appeared on Daffodil, of which the best known were the Luftparks, and a spate of stecker and other key repeats gave some scope for breaking on these new messages. When Daffodil was transferred to the Watch in May 1944, it had already had a long history, and round about that time was being used throughout the area of Greater Germany.

One other point of interest was the periodical interchanges between Daffodil and Blue, the GAF practice key (Luftwaffenübungsmaschinenschlüssel). Occasionally Daffodil cribs, like the Luftlage, would pass in Blue, and Blue Quatsch messages would pass in Daffodil. It was useful to break occasional Blue days to clarify the W/T picture.

Hyena, the key of Luftflotte Reich, was first broken in March 1944. At first it was thought to be merely an offshoot of Cockroach, passing on the Jagd. Div. 7 links, but later it was discovered that the key also decoded messages on Luftflotte Reich stars. Eight breaks of Hyena in the first week was perhaps the summit of Hyena's success. It was never so easy again to break as it was in March 1944, when the Cockroach Luftlage and the Zudet 3 both passed on the key as well as its own cribs, the weekly Tuning Programme and the daily Reichspruch. By the end of May, when Hyena was transferred to the Watch, it was in a much more tricky and unyielding condition.

The Watch

The treatment of German Air keys in the Watch and the Qwatch falls into three phases:

i. From late May 1944 to 1 August
This was the period when the keys were absorbed into the operational system of Watch and Qwatch-breaking, when they were given Watch parents and Watch folders, and when they were examined currently by the routine shifts.

ii. From 1 August to 1 December
1 August marked the first use of Reflector D on the German keys, and this radically affected their prospects and exploitation, particularly in the case of Hyena.

iii. From 1 December until the end of the war
1 December saw a split of Daffodil into its component Luftgau keys (Luftgau XI – Daffodil, Luftgau VI – Wallflower, Luftgau VII – Aster, Luftgau III – Gentian, Luftgau VIII – Violet, Luftgau XVII – Foxglove). From this date until the end of the war, the exploitation of the German keys, which now, properly speaking, included the Western Keys as well (see the History of Western Air Keys for further details), became progressively more difficult. This was not merely due to key complications and compromises, but also to the security measures and devices of the Germans.

The first phase

Cockroach was soon added to the list of those keys which the Watch broke currently and usually inexpensively as matter of day-to-day routine. Daffodil was more unwieldy, and tended to be neglected a little after the opening of the Second Front, but it too soon became recognised as a bona fide Watch key. Traffic totals were enormous, and new groups of cribs appeared, including a vast family of Flubels (Flugzeugbelegungsmeldungen) from different aerodromes scattered about the Reich. Daffodil breakers were divided into two classes – those who plunged deep into the blists to pick out such messages, and those who were content to take the cautious but stubborn line of exploring morning and evening Predictions – cribs that could be identified with some certainty – and could be worked on with little imagination. The total amount of labour involved in breaking Daffodil was high, but then the measure of success achieved was high also.

Unfortunately this success did not spread to Hyena, which was examined from the start mainly in the Qwatch. We expected to be able to break an average of two days a week, with a few extras at times when Red was compromised and when Red cribs would pass on the Luftflotte key. The only Hyena crib during this period was the Reichspruch, and this was so dingy over long periods that re-encodements provided the best way in. Re-encodements had been investigated for the first time as early as April 1944, when messages passing out of the Luftgau XI area on the Luftflotte Reich stars, were systematically examined. Re-encodements did not have the same time of origin, the Red or Hyena messages coming as late as 24 hours after the Daffodil. This meant that a Daffodil version of a Red or Hyena message could only be identified by length and routeing. The idea was at this time to break recalcitrant Daffodil days via Red, and then to break Hyena via Daffodil. By the end of July, Daffodil was easy to break and the first step in the process could be eliminated.

The second phase

The introduction of Reflector D on the German Air keys on 1 August did not affect Daffodil at all, and the position on Cockroach was no more difficult than before, with the Gefechtsberichte remaining firmly on Reflector B. The position on Hyena was made much worse, however, since the Hyena versions of the Daffodil re-encodements were almost all on Reflector D. Luftgau VII still continued to use B on the Luftflotte

Reich star, and by dint of much sweat and tears, the Hyena D for the first period was broken on a Travemünde signature, but this luck was too good to last, and we could not expect it to be repeated every time. Even when the D was recovered after the Hyena key had been broken on the Reichspruch, the Daffodil re-encodements were very difficult to deal with, and new cribs like the "Burbelsatz", which appeared at the end of September, had a very short life.

In October, after many ominous threats, Daffodil produced its own Reflector D, but the amount of traffic sent on D was never very high. There was also some Enigma Uhr traffic, but here again owing to its sparse distribution, the problem was kept well in hand. Cockroach remained steady despite a fair amount of D and Uhr. On the whole, therefore, by the beginning of December, the problems of D seemed well in hand, except on Hyena, which was difficult enough anyway, but despite our successes no one was foolish enough to paint pictures of a rosy future.

The third phase
The split of Daffodil into its constituent Luftgau keys on 1 December was a natural development, which was only surprising in that it had not happened before. Even after the change Daffodil remained much the biggest key, accounting for 500 messages or so each day, Of the Luftgau keys, four – Wallflower, Gentian, Lily (which had been in existence the previous month as well) and Aster – were soon under control. Wallflower in particular proved very amenable to Watch treatment. Snowdrop, Violet and Foxglove never passed out of the research stage, and all proved very difficult. Little was known about Clover, the key of Luftgau I. The Snowdrop of these days had little continuity with the Snowdrop which had been broken so regularly earlier in the war. Unfortunately, no sooner had this group of Luftgau keys begun to look exploitable, than the Germans began to use wahlworts in a far more systematic and formidable way than ever before. This was particularly serious in its effects on the breaking of keys like Gentian, where the only lines of attack was via short addresses or signatures, usually multi-versional, which became prohibitively expensive when allowance had to be made for wahlworts of uncertain length.

Re-encodements went up in value. Hyena was given quite a new lease of life by regular re-encodements from Wallflower, and some of the dingy, cribless Luftgau keys like Violet or Foxglove came out occasionally on re-encodements, usually discovered by Sixta. Early in January a determined effort was made to spot and tie up re-encodements in a combined operation between the Watch EPer and the Qwatch. Likely re-encodement candidates on Daffodil were marked by the EPer and returned to Hut 3 as quickly as possible. They were then looked at by the Watch, if they were operationally important, and passed on to the Qwatch (usually the Watch party in the Qwatch, which paid special attention to these re-encodements) if the Watch had no time to deal with them. The scheme resulted in some gratifying successes, and was just beginning to get really underway when the W/T complications of 1 February added to the problems of Hut 6.

Even without this new horror, the Luftgau keys were becoming sufficiently difficult to test our resources to the maximum. In February, almost the whole of Lily went over to Reflector D, Gentian took to using Enigma Uhr, Aster went over to D and Uhr on 10 February, while the frozen runways, which had given us our only Snowdrop crib, thawed with the promise of an early spring. By dint of strenuous effort, hold was kept on Aster and Wallflower, and re-encodements from Wallflower to Hyena provided plenty of work for plenty of hands without producing much in the way of reward. Gentian, which had increased in volume as a result of the Russian drive on Berlin, was broken for two days at the beginning of March, but this was its swan-song. Wallflower ended with a flourish, passing a group of quite powerful Wasp cribs, before the Allies overran the area of Luftgau VI.

The final fortnight of the war saw the total disintegration of Hyena. Several keys were in use – the compromised key, two replacement keys, and some emergency keys. Genuine Hyena was a very small remnant at the beginning of May, and only Aster, of the Daffodil offshoots, ended the war in a blaze of glory. A re-encodement broke the second April D period, and a windfall arrived at the end of the month in the shape of a complete week's keys in a Jaguar message.

The story of Cockroach and Daffodil in this last phase of the war is not quite so gloomy, but marks quite a sharp decline in our fortunes before 1 December. Daffodil was made far more difficult to deal with by the encoding of callsigns on 1 February. The identification of the Flubel messages became very difficult without callsign help, and though we built up a detailed picture of the distinction between the different aerodrome reports (length, gap between GTO and TOI, average GTO etc), it was always changing, and impossible to keep up-to-date. Daffodil provided considerable interest for the cryptographers in the final period. Although the Allies poured into Central and Northern Germany, and overran the German aerodromes one by one, two Danish stations, Husum and Hürnum provided a long run of Daffodil breaks until, on 3 May, the crib frequency died and was heard no more. The story of Cockroach is more complicated. An increase in the use of Reflector D in the early days of 1945 was serious but did not affect our breaking powers. At the beginning of March Cockroach was renamed Wasp because Fliegerkorps IX had taken control of the Jagdkorps I network, and its history is told more fully in the section on the Western Air keys.

One new arrival in this latest phase was Chimpanzee, the key of Luftflotte X, an organisation mainly concerned with the training of Air units. It was broken for the first time on a crib which had previously passed on Blue, a break which revealed the wide distribution of the key. A number of successes were scored until it, too, fell a victim to wahlworts and dingy and dying cribs, not, however, before it had provided a welcome re-entry into Foxglove. An odd re-encodement from Red in February did not clear the crib position, and by March the Germans had more to think about inside their own country than the training of new GAF units.

The Eastern Air Keys

General

The invasion of the Soviet Union, forecast by Enigma decodes on Rocket and Red, led to a great increase of traffic on the general GAF key. The percentage of Eastern Front traffic was high, and continued high even after the splitting up of the key in January 1942. The amount of Eastern Front traffic relative to the total amount of Enigma traffic remained high until the end of the war, for it was now on the Eastern Front that the largest German armies were contained and driven back until the end of the struggle. The importance and urgency of breaking this mass of Russian traffic varied greatly at different periods of the war. At some stages in the war the traffic was regarded as being operationally important. Beetle was broken in CR1 currently with a high sense of urgency. In the last weeks of 1944 Mosquito was given a lot of careful attention, and profited from the use of new D-breaking machinery. In 1945, the last phase of cryptographic activity was centred on Ermine, and other remnants of the Eastern Front keys. But on the whole, the Eastern front, from the viewpoint of Hut 6, was a subsidiary front. It never claimed the attention given to the African or to the Western Air keys, and the weight of Allied bombing on Germany obviously gave the German Air keys a more direct significance.

The same general story that applies to the other fronts applies to the Eastern Front as well, the story of increasing difficulties due to the German use of Reflector D and similar technical devices, and also to the increasing complexities of the German W/T and callsign system. Mosquito, a large and important key in 1945 suffered especially from Reflector D. The callsign problem made it very difficult to sort out the continuities of the Eastern groups, and the result of the mix-up was the wide range of keys, named after Counties or American States, which could not finally be identified. The keys were compressed into the relatively small area, which was the sole remains of the vast empire of the Third Reich.

Although the general story holds, there were certain other difficulties in dealing with the Eastern Front as a unity when they were driving forward and carrying everything before them. The Russian Marshals were able eventually to carve up the front into sectors by their swift and sharp drives towards the German and Polish borders, while the Red Armies in the South burst across the Balkans to Czechoslovakia and Austria. At the end of the war, we were dealing with two different sets of Eastern Front keys, those concerned with the Northern (Germany and East Prussia) sector and those concerned with the Balkan and Austrian sector. Ermine had touched Gadfly in the South, Mosquito had touched Hyena and Lion in the North. Because of the size of the front, units were constantly being moved from one area to another, and this led to a certain amount of confusion about keys. Beetle began, for instance, by being the key of Fliegerkorps VIII, but when Fliegerkorps VIII was withdrawn in May 1942 from the Moscow Front to the Crimea, Beetle became the key of Luftwaffenkommando Ost (later changing again in May 1943 to become the key of Luftflotte 6) while Skunk, first broken in May 1942, became the Fliegerkorps VIII key. Keys would "amalgamate" for a month and then separate again – such as Hornet and Ermine in 1943 or Gorilla and Ermine in 1944. Keys would flourish and disappear. Hedgehog, the special operational key in South Russia, was perhaps the most important key to do this. On the other hand, new keys came into operation quite late. Luftflotte 4 did not use its own key, Gorilla, until September 1944. It had previously passed mainly Red. The deadline and fall of Red in the late summer of 1944 produced quite a spate of new Russian keys.

It was difficult to keep hold of all the keys at the same time. For some reason it was particularly difficult to break both Beetle (Luftflotte 6) and Mosquito (Luftflotte 1) at the same time. Some keys were never broken at all. These included not only small and unimportant Geschwader keys like Rabbit or Badger, which abounded on this Front, but at least one quite important GAF key on the Central Front (Puce), which passed quite a lot of traffic in 1944. Our hold on the East was never as complete as our hold on the West. Interception difficulties were perhaps the most important reason for this, but in addition, volumes of traffic would fluctuate alarmingly, and continuity over a period of years was very difficult to establish. Nearly all the keys had surprising changes of fortune, particularly the two most important, Beetle and Mosquito. Our record on the Luftgau keys, Foxglove and Orchid, was much better, though there were more re-encodements in these cases to assist our efforts.

It was not only keys that changed and fluctuated. Cribs had a fantastic butterfly life, some of them being very good for short periods, then dying ignominiously, others were there for the duration, but moved disconcertingly from one key to another. The famous Befehl and Besan, archetypal cribs, were usually sent on Red, but they appeared in half a dozen or so other keys as well. Zusauf was a steady crib, but always inclined to be fickle in its loyalties. In 1942 and 1943, Skunk Wetter had passed indiscriminately on Red and Skunk, and had broken both keys, not always breaking the one that was intended. Flak MVM moved in August 1943 from Orchid to Weasel. In February 1944, Vordere Linie, a Beetle crib, passed on Skunk every fourth day, and eventually appeared on Skunk regularly. Such "crib vagrancy" was often as valuable in breaking keys as were re-encodements, though the value of the latter in the overall picture, particularly in 1945, cannot be over-estimated. Standard cribs, re-encodements, and the short messages which were sent when all was quiet on the Eastern Front, or at any rate on a very small part of it, were our chief standbys.

Because of these changes there had to be particularly close collaboration between Hut 6 and Sixta in dealing with the Eastern Front. Sixta experts kept the study of the Front alive at a time when broken days were few. And there were times when the whole front seemed to be stricken with decay. This was particularly so in June 1944, when traffic totals were falling catastrophically, and frequencies disappearing chaotically. A Sixta re-encodement was one of the few hopes left to the cryptographer. It was only when traffic totals were really high that a sturdy independence could be maintained, and such periods never lasted for long.

The German advance

During 1941, there were many Eastern Front cribs on Red, and in the split of keys in January 1942, some of the cribs survived. Hornet, the key of Fliegerkorps IV, passed two such cribs – Czech Wueb and Befehl. In January, a stecker repeat made Hornet particularly easy to break, 26 days being a very good total. Hornet continued to be easy in February and March.

Beetle, the key of Fliegerkorps VIII, was first broken on a chancy re-encodement from Red on 7 March 1942, which won a close race from a weather crib that had previously passed on Red, and whose continuity had on that very day been noticed by both cryptographers and Control. "Beetle Weather" thereafter broke many days, and was the standard crib until Fliegerkorps VIII left the Moscow Front for the Crimea in May 1942. This withdrawal led to the change of key distribution mentioned earlier. Skunk, the new Fliegerkorps VIII key, was broken for the first time in May 1942. it fitted into the Southern and not the Central sector.

Mosquito, the other Central Front key (Fliegerkorps I, later Luftflotte 1) was not attacked very strenuously, even though it passed one old Red crib, Lett Wett. The reason was that traffic totals were very low.

Foxglove, the key of Luftgau Ost, later Luftgau XVII, was not broken until March 1942, when a providential stecker repeat revealed a number of tuners, of which the most likely crib was the "Glovespruch". There were signs of other cribs, however, though Foxglove was quite important, it could not be given high enough priority to compete with the African and Mediterranean keys, which had then reached their peak demand.

Key repeats

In the same month that Fliegerkorps VIII left for the Crimea, Hornet became terribly difficult, and was banished in disgrace from CR1. The Eastern Front seemed to be becoming impossible. A great recovery in the East came about from a wealth of key repeats, which not only enabled us to make up ground on the slipping keys, but paid handsome dividends

Solving Enigma's Secrets - The Official History of Bletchley Park's Hut 6

in opening up the way to the breaking of new keys. What was perhaps most important of all, it was now possible to break solid blocks of days, whereas running on the limited number of bombes available could have produced at best only a limited number of breaks on this Front.

In June, for instance, it was possible to get into Skunk, the new key of Fliegerkorps VIII by using the wheelorder and ringstellung of May Hornet, and the stecker of May Snowdrop. To get into May Hornet, it was necessary first to break the June Primrose, which was repeating wheelorders and ringstellung. In such a roundabout way, driving at keys of both months, it was possible to break a new key. Other keys to be broken on key repeats were Mosquito, broken on a key repeat from Cockroach, and Weasel, the key of Flak Korps I, on a key repeat from Daffodil.

August was the dominating month for key repeats, and without them the Eastern Front keys were much of a Research proposition. There was a lull until December. This was the time of the fierce German onslaught on Stalingrad and the Caucasus. By December, when we had full use of key repeats again, the Russians had started their great counter-offensive, and the war had turned. We also reaped a rich harvest in December when Foxglove, Primrose, Celery and Beetle formed a useful quadrilateral. The grip on Beetle did not long outlast the repeat, and the only other breaks on Weasel and Skunk were gained after great effort and perseverance. There were occasional cillies on Mosquito, which kept the key alive, and a new key appeared in the region of Luftwaffenkommando Don. It was first broken in February 1943 and was called Ermine. It proved in effect to be the key of Fliegerkorps I, Mosquito now having been taken over by Luftflotte I.

Odd breaks were made on these keys in Research during the early months of 1943, but cribbery on the Eastern Front was always difficult because of interception difficulties, however much cover was put on, and also because of lack of bombe time for Research keys. There were, however, striking changes, which began on 1 March, when the Luftgau keys split up, and Foxglove produced seven components, corresponding to the different Luftgaue on the Front. This might have been a mortal blow had it not been noticed that different Luftgau keys came out in groups, even though they had different discriminants. Clover, Foxglove and Narcissus came out on the same key, and Orchid was partnered with Daffodil. Clover was the key of Luftgau I, Orchid the key of Luftgau XXV.

The investigation of this tangled set of twins and even quadruplets is described more fully elsewhere. Certainly it gave new life to the Russian Front.

Hedgehog
The last burst of Watch activity on the Eastern Front as a whole came from their exploitation of Hedgehog, used as a general operational key on the whole of the Eastern Front, and replacing in most cases the local key of the Fliegerkorps. This key, along with Porcupine, a similar animal, was exploited at first by Research, but in May 1943 it was sent to the Watch. It stayed there until the end of August, when it split up again into its constituent Fliegerkorps keys. It was a very interesting key to deal with, offering a battery of short reports, most of them routines, known as the "Storchs", and what was much more valuable, a regular daily re-encodement from Red, known as the Luftflotte 4 Re-encodement. Even when the message did not turn up on Red, the Watch could recognise the message on Hedgehog, and fit in the various beginnings – Luftflotte 4 unterstützte, bekämpfte or merely führte. The re-encodement began to be sent also on Orchid, which was in consequence transferred to the Qwatch, and even on other small groups as well. All the June Orchid days were broken by this means. On one occasion at least, Hedgehog was rather less monotonous. It obeyed the GAF ringstellung rule, and on 24 July was broken by hand, with a good cilli to make the going. It was with a good deal of regret that the Watch said goodbye to the Eastern Front, when on 1 August the re-encodement was sent on Hornet and Ermine. From this time onwards, with one short exception, the breaking of the Eastern Front keys was a Research proposition.

The heyday of Research
As a Research proposition the situation was made a good deal easier by the disappearance of Hedgehog and the continued sending of the re-encodement on Red and the different Fliegerkorps keys. So long as this lasted, the fortunes of the whole group were high. There were also Flugsi re-encodements from Red to Orchid, and Rundspruche which passed in Hornet and Red. A good measure of the success that Research achieved at this time is seen in the week ending 27 August 1943. Nine Hornets, three Weasels, eight Orchids, six Foxgloves, five Ermines and three Skunks were broken. If there had been more bombe time these figures would have

been repeated more often. Difficulties of traffic analysis arose with the abandonment of discriminants on 1 November 1943 and the experiment was started of a composite Eastern Front blist sector by sector. This was valuable also in view of the increasing coalescence of the Southern and Central Fronts. It had been impossible earlier in the year to make a concentrated attack on Beetle and Mosquito, but now the Germans began to assemble some of the forces of Luftflotte 6 (Beetle) and the Hornet-Skunk set-up. The two most active Beetle groups passed a considerable amount of Skunk. Beetle itself was broken on a re-encodement from Red on 27 October 1943, and it was possible, with the help of cribs, to get into a few of the other days. Mosquito remained an unsolved problem until a re-encodement from Beetle, a four-teile message on 5 December, broke the key for the first time for over six months, and revealed enough cribs to prepare the way for further exploitation. Traffic soared with the Leningrad offensive. Eventually decodes produced one valuable and interesting crib, called at different times Deck, Knob o'Garlic and Ventriloquist. These names were codenames (Decknamen), which represented numbers and references chosen from a list of about one thousand words. Two of the earliest to be chosen were Knoblauch (Knob o'Garlic) and Bauchredner (Ventriloquist). The validity of cover names lasted approximately for a month, so that with each change of allocation the name of the crib had to be altered, until it got the composite name, Deck. Code names formed the bulk of the messages, and considerable ingenuity was required in breaking them. The crib had previously passed in Red, a characteristic example of "crib vagrancy". Other Mosquito cribs were found, but successes faded out by the early summer of 1944. At the time of D-Day all the cribs were dead, and Beetle, too, was in an unbreakable condition. A good deal of attention was paid to the two keys in view of the possibilities of a large-scale Russian drive in the East to synchronise with the Allied landings in the West, but June 1944 was a singularly black month for the Eastern Front as a whole, the lack of success contrasting strongly with the striking exploitation of the Western Front keys.

In the meantime, the period 1943-1944 saw many other changes in the anatomy of the German W/T system in the East. On 1 September 1943, Foxglove (Luftgau XVIII) disappeared, and the bulk of Luftgau traffic now passed on Orchid, Gadfly and Red. Orchid was for the most part easy until interception difficulties ruined effective breaking. The highlight was a memorable 48 hours in October 1943 when seven breaks were accounted for. As the months went by, the alignments of Orchid became more interesting. It became bound up with the Balkan keys, and had occasional re-encodements into Gadfly. Finally, it was swallowed up in the autumn of 1944 into the maelstrom of Central Europe. Attempts to get into Puce, or Gorse (Luftgau XXVI) were much less successful despite occasional bursts of powerful but abortive cillying. Weasel was broken in patches. The Fliegerkorps keys had varying fortunes. Hornet disappeared early in 1944, and Ermine was broken quite regularly in the spring of that year. In fact, it was the only Eastern Front key to be well in hand at the time of the opening of the Second Front in the West.

The problem of the Luftflotten
On 1 July 1944, Red was compromised and the different Luftflotten took to their own keys. The Luftflotten on the Eastern Front were:

Luftflotte 1:	Mosquito
Luftflotte 4:	No key of its own as far as was known
Luftflotte 6:	Beetle

This compromise of Red marked the beginning of the break-up of Red as a general key, for although there was a recovery, a further compromise two months later left lasting disintegration. In July, the traffic of Luftflotte 4 was sent out on the Skunk key, and the veteran crib Zusauf enabled us to make our breaks. In September, Luftflotte 4 used its own key – Gorilla – which was in use until the end of the war. The Luftflotten were closely inter-connected, and all passed a fair but varying amount of Red traffic. Mosquito was at first more tractable than Beetle owing to the occasional appearance of old cribs like "Einsatz". In August, however, the tables were turned. A re-encodement from Red broke Beetle of the 16th and revealed some grounds for increased confidence. Traffic from Luftflotte 1 to Luftflotte 6 had addresses which were cribbable, though only temporary in nature, and there was a residue of Flivo traffic which, while sporadic in appearance, was workable in content. It was on re-encodements from Beetle that we were able to get into Mosquito and Gorilla early in September. Both keys had their individual lines of attack – Gorilla by the Zusauf, Mosquito by the use of ex-Red cribs – but the re-encodements from Beetle were essential preliminaries to further cryptographic drives.

The really complicated factor was the appearance of Reflector D on the Eastern Front. By the end of September (the date of the disappearance of Air Research as a separate body and its absorption into the Watch), all the old Red cribs on Mosquito were sent with Reflector D. Gorilla too had its D, and the first Gorilla D was broken without a crib by the new Bobbery method. Beetle alone seemed entirely on B, and could be handed over to the Watch for current breaking, chiefly on routine Gefechtsberichte. Gorilla too became a Watch key. Mosquito sulked behind the scenes and was never amenable to current treatment. However, like all situations on the Eastern Front, this situation did not last for long. Mosquito revived at the end of October, and because of the Russian offensive, became of more operational urgency. By the law of compensation, Beetle relapsed, and the standard Geraeteklarmeldung disappeared. This time, however, the law of compensation did not bring about perfect equilibrium. Relapses, revivals and short spurts of success on both keys continued until the end of the war. Mosquito profited from the development of the new D-breaking machinery, and the Erdlage re-encodements from Lion or Red were suitable fodder. The link-up with Lion shows the complete reversal of fortune on the Eastern Front.

At the same period, Gorilla was linking up with Gadfly and Ermine in the lakes and mountains of Hungary and the approaches to the Austrian borders. The fortunes of Gorilla were variable, but on the whole sound. In September 1944 it absorbed Ermine, but had to compete with Red II, which was also used in the Luftflotte 4 area. Competition with Red persisted: Gorilla was sound when it passed Zusauf, tricky when Red took the crib over. Even Zusauf was not missed when Befehl and Besan made their sporadic appearances on Gorilla, and the cobwebs were dusted from their folders, which had long lain buried in forgotten files. Between Luftflotte 4 in the South and Luftflotte 1 in the North, Luftflotte 6 (Beetle) fluctuated both in traffic totals and in exploitability. It was just kept alive in December by a mysterious stecker repeat with Cockroach, and afterwards began to use Reflector D. By the end of January 1945, Reflector D was the big bogey everywhere.

The end

On 1 February the Germans introduced the system of encoded callsigns and changing frequencies, and although some of the Eastern Front keys

German Air and Eastern Air Keys

continued to use the old routines, the general effects of the W/T picture in the East were very depressing. In particular, a number of groups now existed which had recognisable continuity (chiefly by discriminants), but which could not be precisely identified. Such groups took County names (e.g. E/Suffolk) and later the names of American States (e.g. E/Ohio or E/Maryland). Frequent compromises on the Eastern Front and the extensive use of Reflector D made the position very complex, but it is true to say that much of the cryptographic interest of 1945 centred on this very difficult field. Properly speaking, we were faced with two complexes: first, the South-Eastern complex, consisting of Luftflotte 4, with Fliegerkorps I and II attached, and second, the Eastern complex, consisting of Luftflotten 1 and 6 with Fliegerkorps VIII.

The South-Eastern complex represented the remains of German Balkans power: the three units, formerly so powerful, were now squeezed into a relatively small area. The communications of Luftflotte 4 were complicated in February by the use of "Pink" – identification dubious – for communications to Luftflotte 4 from the higher authorities. Gorilla was still used in the dealings of the Luftflotte with its subordinates, and it decoded also the last remnants of the Gadfly network (see the report on the Mediterranean keys). Locust was used by Fliegerkorps II and took over the remains of Yak. Ermine, the key of Fliegerkorps I, had had a very varied recent history, but it was breakable on its ancient weather message, whenever it appeared. On the whole, some hold was maintained on this South-Eastern complex until the end of the war, and if the war had been prolonged, we could still have registered some successes. In May 1945, Gorilla and Locust were both repeating the April key for part of their traffic, while the last key to be broken by Hut 6 was Ermine. Even after Grand Admiral Dönitz had agreed to unconditional surrender, a small party of cryptographers still wrestled with this small but interesting tangle of keys.

The Eastern complex proper was so complicated that it could only be tentatively mapped out in the broadest outlines. Beetle, the key of Luftflotte 6, was broken by D-breaking machinery, and Skunk, the key of Fliegerkorps VIII, dependant on Luftflotte 6, followed shortly afterwards. Skunk was almost 100% D, and partially Enigma Uhr as well, but it ended in a blaze of glory. Both the third and fourth D periods of April were broken, and as May repeated the April key backwards, we should have been able to read the traffic for as long as the Germans continued to oppose the Red Army. Mosquito was less fortunate, and was mixed up with both Beetle and the County keys. A new key – Moth – made its debut when Fliegerkorps II left the South-East for the Northern sector. This wealth of keys produced a welter of re-encodements, providing far more work in April and early May than Hut 6 was capable of dealing with. The extent of Reflector D on the minor keys made all shots on the bombes something of a gamble. And in the last days "crib vagrancy" was particularly marked. Cribs would be searched for on any Eastern key blist, and in the confusion no one quite knew which key was being broken. Even re-encodements from Army keys came into their own, and Avocet-Skunk re-encodements appeared on several occasions. Despite all the havoc, the efforts and the patience of the cryptographers were still not quite exhausted on 8 May 1945.

Chapter 25
The Eastern Army Keys Greenshank and Allied Keys

The Eastern Army Keys

General

The ebb and flow of battle on the Eastern Front was rarely the sole reason for the great fluctuations in the volume of wireless activity which were the most marked feature of interception in this campaign. There were periods of static warfare when traffic was passed over the air in some quantity, and there were great and fierce battles which produced no W/T reaction whatever. The reason lies in the extensive landlines which the Germans kept as far as possible constantly in working order, and also in the Fish links from OKH to the Armies and Heeresgruppen which were set up at a fairly early date.

Initial advances: June-December 1941

When Hitler invaded Russia on 22 June 1941, traffic began at once to be intercepted in some quantity and before the end of the month one of the two maiu keys, which were named Vulture I and II, was broken on cillies. In the following months there were occasional breaks until a big increase in cillying in September led to frequent and early breaks for a long period. Cribs soon appeared, for the Heeresgruppen and the Armies were all sending their operational reports by wireless, and there were often cillies on the crib messages. The Vultures provided traffic at the highest level, which would have been of great operational urgency had it been dealing with a front on which British troops were engaged. As it was, it was of extreme interest but not of great urgency.

Other keys of less importance but with some volume of traffic were also identified at this time. There was Kite, a general supply key, of which one day was broken before the end of 1941, and Kestrel I, II and III, and later IV, the broadcast keys (Rundspruchmaschinenschlüssel) for the four Heeresgruppen on the front. It is clear now that a key of this type was part of the recognised equipment of each Heeresgruppe, but the use to which they were put changed in the course of the war. At the end, in the West they were used for broadcasting intelligence of general interest derived from Y, but in the early stages of the Eastern campaign much of the traffic dealing with Army-Air Force co-operation, which later passed in the Air Flivo keys, was sent in these Army broadcasts. In the autumn of 1941 many days of these keys were broken on cillies and on cribs. In fact, with sufficient bombe time, all days would have been broken without much difficulty, for on all the keys there were early cribs reporting on the number of messages sent and received during the previous 24 hours. During the early months of 1942 Kestrel traffic continued to appear in fairly small quantities, and the policy was adopted of breaking – if possible – at least one day per week, to make sure that the cribs remained unchanged in form.

Quiescence: 1942-1943

In January 1942 Vulture traffic dwindled to nothing as a consequence of some stabilisation of the front and widespread construction of landlines. The system of wireless communication was still available if required but it was only used when all other methods had failed. Presumably as a security measure, the W/T network was radically altered to the exclusion of the series of stars used in the opening phases of the campaign. Instead, the GHQ net was extended, by which each Army and Heeresgruppe was allotted a receiving frequency and was thus enabled to communicate with OKH or any other unit in the system by use of the appropriate frequency. Throughout 1942 activity on the Netz was very low. In a burst of traffic one day in July there were enough cillies to break the day, and the same thing happened again in December. Then traffic totals in general rose steadily, and in particular there was daily a large amount from the beleaguered Sixth Army at Stalingrad. Another break on cillies showed us the form of some of the routine reports from this Army, and it then became possible to break on cribs a number of days before the eventual surrender early in February.

This was a good example of the opportunist methods that had to be used to exploit the unpredictable appearances of Eastern Front traffic. It was impossible to tell how long these bursts would last, and therefore one member of the Research Section always had the investigation of the Eastern Front traffic as his primary responsibility, in order that no chances of obtaining such valuable intelligence should be missed.

Thus, in March 1943 the Vulture parent observed a KR message with time of origin 0500 passing on the same frequency on four successive days and broke a day on the assumed beginning MORGENMELDUNG. This was the first of a spell of breaks of Central Front traffic, the units engaged being Heeresgruppe Mitte, AOK2 and Panzer AOK 2. AOK2 sent several routine reports of which the Morgenmeldung was the simplest to recognise and the most standard in form, and a remarkable feature was the fact that the range of forms used on these messages in March-April 1943 was precisely the same as when they had previously been seen in autumn 1941.

Spread of use of local keys: July 1943 – December 1944
July and August 1943 saw a steady level of traffic from OKH with a marked tendency to keyboard cillies which gave us several days. This time, however, the traffic provided no crib, and when next a Russian Front break was achieved in October, on one of the old AOK 2 cribs sent over the air on one single day, it was apparent that some changes in the normal key usage had taken place. Only traffic passing between Heeresgruppe Mitte and AOK 2 decoded, whereas in July similar messages were coming out on the general key.

The tendency to use a local instead of a general key was seen again when, in February 1944, a break was made into Owl, the key of AOK 17 in the Crimea. At the same time there were signs that the old Netz system of working was not proving entirely satisfactory, most of the units regularly active on the air using fixed line frequencies, although they had still their Netz frequencies available if required. This was a general development not confined to the Russian Front. Thus AOK 10 in Italy had special frequencies for communication with OKH, and a special key – Bullfinch – for use on those frequencies in addition to its normal Armee key – Albatross. Similarly, AOK 17 had line frequencies and a special key – E/8532 – for traffic to OKH, while there was a fixed frequency for communication between the Army and its controlling Heeresgruppe, HGA, on which the Armee key Owl was used.

Owl was an interesting colour to break, with several cribs of variable forms which required considerable judgment if they were to be employed successfully and inexpensively. Owl I was broken more often than not until 8 May 1944, the day before the German surrender in the Crimea. Old days of the Staff key, Owl II, were obtained by the standard G-Tail technique. Traffic still came in bursts from different parts of the Front, but if two Armies began using W/T at the same time, it is now more than likely that they would be using different keys. The general key was still in existence, for some cillies from Panzer AOK I at the end of March gave four or five breaks, of which some were obviously the Armee key Pelican, while some decoded traffic from other parts of the Front.

In late June, July and August there was heavy traffic from the Northern sector of the Front, with a number of different keys in use. In the resulting difficulty of identification, keys were known as "Vulture 2924" or "Vulture 5393" according to the frequency on which they were used. The genuine Vulture key – the OKH key for use in the East – was renamed Avocet to distinguish it from the many pseudo-Vultures. The Geheim Tail method of attack brought a number of breaks, which in due course revealed the key distribution and usage. Avocet, by far the largest, was used for communications between Heeresgruppe Nord and Heeresgruppe Mitte as well as among their subordinate Armies. Flamingo was used between OKH and Panzer AOK 3, which gave us several days early in August on cillies. And several smaller keys, which were not given separate names, were connected with different Armies on other parts of the Front.

The final spurt
Traffic fell suddenly for a week or two but rose again in September, and for two months continued heavy but very difficult to break. Drives on Geheim Tails sometimes staggered to allow for a final wahlwort, produced only isolated breaks, and it was not till the end of December that progress began to be made by means of routine messages. At the same time an entry was made into Avocet II, which proved to have a daily routine message of some value as a crib in spite of its addiction to wahlworts. This was the Feindbeurteilung, a 1C report from Heeresgruppe Nord giving an appreciation of Russian dispositions and intentions. During 1945 occasional breaks of Avocet II were made on this message, while Avocet I was broken with steadily increasing regularity, the routine reports from the isolated Heeresgruppe Kurland being the best of a large number of possible cribs.

The last fortnight of the war saw Avocet being broken as a full Watch colour by the Army Watch, the Fronts being by then so confused that some of the units seemed to be facing East and West at the same time. By a turn of the wheel full circle, the German campaign ended as it began with nearly all active units on the air and using one general key, so that Hut 6 was able to provide a commentary on the last days as on the first.

Greenshank and Allied keys

The main feature of Greenshank
There were times in the history of Hut 6 when we felt that the enemy was delivering himself into our hands, when one simply had to write out a crib which said the same thing every day, it all seemed a little too easy. One group of keys, however, never produced this reaction. They were under the direction of a signals officer who was clearly pitting his brains against those of the Allied Y Service and Hut 6 welcomed the challenge. For years Greenshank stood as a massive peak inviting assault, surrounded by lower hills which were surmounted in turn in the hope that they would prove steps to the path of success.

Greenshank – or Green as it was called in 1939 and 1940 – was the key of the German Home Administration. Germany, even before the war, was divided into about 20 military districts (Wehrkreise), each with its HQ. Each district was responsible for the recruitment of a Corps, which in time of war would be reinforced from its home area, and so the Wehrkreis administration was regarded as standing in place of the Corps. Hence the quality of nomenclature, whereby the home HQs were referred to as simply "Wehrkreiskommando I, II etc.," or as "Stellvertretendes Generalkommando I, II etc., Armeekorps".

The Wehrkreis stations were linked by a wireless system which was extremely complicated long before the war. The operators were highly trained and well-versed in each others' foibles – "eingespielt" – as they themselves neatly put it, so that traffic was dealt with speedily and with a minimum of queries and delay. The W/T system was designed to make interception as difficult as possible, consisting of a high-frequency Netz in which each station had one receiving frequency out of a possible 26, which were allotted to a clever daily-changing table, and a simple low-frequency network in which five or six frequencies served the need of all the stations. The changeover from high to low frequency was often carried out at short notice in the middle of a message. And the initial success of these tactics may be judged from Mr Welchman's discovery early in the war that while SYG had been unable to intercept most of the

L/F traffic for lack of L/F sets, the French had been concentrating on the L/F and were quite unaware of even the existence of a H/F network!

The complexity of the frequency system was one indication of the competence and discipline of the Wehrkreis wireless operators. There was some evidence that their cipher clerks were of the same standard, for there was a rule, normally not adhered to, that the length of one part of a message should not be more than 250 letters. Throughout the war it is believed that not a single Greenshank message was intercepted with more than 250 letters, and usually each part was as near 250 letters exactly as it could be. It was no uncommon thing to see a teil-message with a very short last teil – e.g. 3 Tle. 1T 249. 2T 250. 3T 6., where on any other network the operator would have committed a very venial breach of the rules. Other remarkable features about the Greenshank traffic was its bulk – a steady average of 200-300 messages a day – and its obviously non-operational character. Most of the Wehrkreis stations did not work at night, there was little KR traffic, and many messages were sent several days late. Greenshank was not a key likely to provide information of an operational urgency. No single message was likely to be of much importance, but it was hopped that steady breaking would give a wealth of intelligence on minor matters of administration and supply which could enable a clear picture to be drawn of conditions and troop movements inside the Greater Reich, just as Falcon in 1943 and 1944 accurately sketched affairs in Wehrkreis VI.

Breaks: 1939-1942
Green was broken on the old indicating system in October 1939 and several times afterwards until the change of indicators in May 1940. At this time the traffic was largely practice, and it was not till 19 November 1940, a day which was broken by hand on cillies, that a good sample of Wehrkreis traffic was read. This break revealed no crib, and no more cillies appeared, so that no advance was made. During 1941 there were periods when the Wehrkreis network was not intercepted owing to lack of sets, but towards the end of the year traffic totals were high again and a number of attempts were made to break on what were later called Berlinismus menus – from the habit of the Berlin station of stepping its outside indicators alphabetically or along the keyboard with gaps of one, the intervening letters presumably being the inside indicators. Thus one would find such sequences as:

The Eastern Army Keys, Greenshank and Allied Keys

1. AJS	QJR		1. QAY	LTA
2. CLU	ZOL	or	2. EDC	KGO
3. ENW	HHG		3. TGB	BYL

the inside indicators in the first case being assumed to be BKT, DMV, FOX, and in the second WSX, RFV, ZHN. None of these shots succeeded, and strong though they seemed, the impression grew that the basic assumption must be wrong.

During 1941 the Wehrkreis traffic stopped discriminating, and when, therefore, some cillies began to appear on a small extension of the Wehrkreis network in Czechoslovakia, there was considerable doubt as to whether they were on the main Green key. One day was broken and the key failed to decode any of several samples of traffic taken on the main network, and it was therefore assumed that the Villach extension used a separate key. Two months later, however, it was discovered that the Orange and Mustard keys had a variable ringstellung, and a Green message was therefore decoded on the Test-Plate in all positions of the March key. It came out – and proved to have the original ringstellung! The remainder of the traffic was then tried and about half decoded on all six permutations of the wheelorder. The rest had to be left unbroken.

From an analysis of the decodes and duds it appeared that there were two keys, the identity of the key being revealed by summing the last two figures of the time of origin. Further, the day had been split into six unequal periods in such a way that roughly the same volume of traffic would be encoded in each permutation of the wheelorder. The permutations were not in any obvious order like the ABC, CAB, BCA order which later came into general use. And there for the first time the matter rested. The decodes were most unpromising, for there were no routine messages and the addresses and signatures were usually buried in the text of the message. This no doubt accounted for the failure of a programme of addresses produced on the evidence of the 1940 break, coupled with a crash analysis of the traffic from each station taken over a period of several months. From this it had seemed that the beginner AN STELLV (X) GEN (X) KDO (X) ROEM was most likely on messages from Berlin, and a programme of 20 or 30 such shots had been run in the early part of 1942 without success. Further, the failure of the Berlinismus attempts was probably due to the fact that some of the messages used in each shot had been in a different wheelorder or key from the others.

A blank wall

From this time until the middle of 1943, Greenshanks remained a problem offering no hope – no glimmer of hope of solution. Then re-encodements, thrown up by a general comparison of times of origin, began to appear, first from Mallard, which was very rarely broken, and then in the autumn from Falcon, which was coming out with fair regularity. Clearly the re-encodements were not straightforward, but nevertheless some quite good shots were produced which aroused some suspicions by not coming out. Then, on 10 October 1943, a re-encodement appeared which gave a first-class answer, and when several consistent versions had been failed, it was assumed that some change had been introduced into the machine. Versions were thereafter run assuming, in turn, a twist of Reflector B, Reflector C and the wheels and Reflector combination of the naval machine, all without success.

Then, on Christmas Day, came the news in a Red message of the intended introduction of Reflector D on Red on 1 January, 1944. Perhaps the new Reflector was already in use on the Wehrkreis? At this point came information that a Pole had deserted to us in Italy who had at one time served as a cipher clerk in some of the Wehrkreis stations, and an interview was arranged in the hope that he might be able to give us the answer.

Inside information

On 15 January 1944 – the date of the interrogation – two wirings of the new Reflector had been recovered and there was considerable speculation as to its nature. Gefreiter Pziuara, however, could tell us nothing of the new invention, for he had been moved from Hanover in October 1942, after spending some months there and in Berlin. But he gave us some interesting details of the Wehrkreis practice. Each encoder had two Enigma machines set up to two quite different keys called A and B. He decided which key to use by adding together the last two figures of the time of origin, and referring to a table on the key-sheet of the form:

A	2	3	5	7	8	9	10	11
B	0	1	4	6	12	13	14	

Thus a message with a time of origin 0721 would give the answer 2 + 1 = 3, therefore key A, and time of origin 1259 would imply key B. This table formed part of the key and changed every day. The basic wheelorder and ringstellung for the day were given in charts in the form:

The Eastern Army Keys, Greenshank and Allied Keys

	I	II	III	IV	V
1		14	03		23
2	07		01	19	
3	24	16	15		
4	13			11	20
5			08	17	11
31	...	...	...	...	...
...	...	...	...	...	...
	14	01			25

Thus the basic wheelorder for the first of the month would in this case be 235 and the ringstellung 14, 03, 23, or as we preferred to say – NCW. The day was divided into six periods: 0000-1115, 1115-1330, 1330-1500, 1500-1700, 1700-1800, 1800-2400. The six wheelorder permutations were lettered:

a = abc = basic wheelorder   d = acb
b = cab   e = bac
c = bca   f = cba

One of these letters was allocated to each period by means of a further daily-changing table, e.g.:

Day	0000-1115	1115-1330	1330-1500	1500-1700	1700-1800	1800-2400
1	a	c	e	d	f	b
2	f	d	b	a	e	c

These measures ensured an even distribution of traffic between the two keys and among the wheelorder permutations, and made it quite impossible for anyone to tell from the outside either the key or the wheelorder of any particular message. The main points of the system had been guessed at following the break of March 1942, but the details were enlightening and perhaps rather depressing. If the Wehkreis authorities had made such clever use of the standard Enigma, they would surely show no weakness in their employment of the new device which they had presumably introduced.

The mystery solved

Re-encodements from Falcon came in a steady stream in the early months of 1944, and occasionally good shots were run on the ordinary bombes, and Reflector B "just in case". There was also at this time a revival of Berlinismus and of a similar indicator habit named after the station which developed it – Viennismus. Both types scored successes on Nuthatch, the key used on the southern extension of the Wehrkreis to Belgrade, and therefore the underlying assumption on which our menus were produced was proved correct. Early in February there was a day on which the Berlin operator excelled himself by producing at least 15 different indicators of this type in the same period, and proved to be on the same key by various repeats both of indicators and text. The failure of menus on these indicators removed any lingering doubts there may have been that our inability to break the Greenshank was due to a change in the machine.

It remained for Lionel Clarke, the relentless pursuer of the Greenshank, to demonstrate what that damage was. On 27 April 1944 there was a re-encodement from Falcon to which a fairly complete and plausible solution had been fitted. He attacked this by the stecker knock-out method and broke the key in about a week's work, a well-deserved success after his years of labour. The break showed that Greenshank was now using Reflector D, as we had suspected, for the Reflector recovered had the fixed BO pairing. The next stage was to discover the period of validity of each wiring. On the Air keys one wiring lasted for ten days, and if this were the case on Greenshank, then with the arrival of D-breaking machinery it might be possible for Greenshank to come out fairly regularly. Several shots were therefore run on days near the 27th, assuming the D wiring of that day. The only success was Greenshank B on the 27th, which showed that only one Reflector wiring was used for both keys on any one day. The shots which failed were not by any means certain, and therefore the period of validity of each D wiring remained in doubt.

The last phase: statistics and summary

The completion of Duenna and Giant, the reflector-breaking machines, at the end of 1944 enabled Greenshank to be run again early in 1945, although by this time the introduction of the "CY" device by which the position of the left-hand wheel was altered in the middle of a message, meant that the maximum number of letters which could be at consecutive positions of the machine was reduced from 250 to 150. And as Giant

The Eastern Army Keys, Greenshank and Allied Keys

required 200 letters of crib, it could not be used for Greenshank menus. But its use on Air jobs meant more time for Greenshank on Duenna. In January 1945 there were routine re-encodements between Falcon and Greenshank, and in spite of the tricks of alteration employed by Münster, which was normally the re-transmitting station, Major Babbage, Lionel Clarke and others developed their technique of re-encodement to a point at which they could produce a stretch of over 100 letters with reasonable certainty in perhaps 20%-25% of the cases. During February the re-encodements began to dry up though two final breaks were secured in March. However, January 1945 was left as the best Greenshank month, ever since the days of the old indicating system.

The following chronological table will perhaps give some idea of the stubbornness of the opposition (dates referring to breaks are underlined):

January 1940	Green of 25 October 1939 broken (first wartime break in Hut 6).
May 1940	Change to double indicator system.
19 November 1940	Broken on cillies by hand.
1 January 1941 or 1 January 1942	Introduction of six wheelorder permutations and two-key system.
5 March 1942	Broken on cillies (one key only).
(?) 1 January 1943	Introduction of Reflector D.
27 April 1944	Broken by hand stecker knock-out by L E Clarke on Falcon re-encodement. Second key broken on bombe.
5, 7, 17 January 1945	Broken on Falcon re-encodements on Duenna or Autoscritcher (one key only in each case).
14 January 1945	Broken by stecker knock-out by Major D W Babbage on Falcon re-encodement. Second key on bombe.
6, 7 March 1945	Broken on Falcon re-encodements on Duenna or Autoscritcher (one key only in each case).

Our methods of breaking depended on the discovery of cillies, cribs or re-encodements and the Germans had orders not to send the first two of these, and to change the last in such a way as to make them unusable. It will be seen that in the five years from May 1940 to the end of the war, 11 keys were recovered from re-encodements, two from cillies and none at all from cribs. Such was the security of the Enigma when properly used.

The associated keys: Falcon, Gannet II and Mallard

A number of keys were used on groups connected with the Wehrkreis system, and throughout the war the most determined efforts were made to break them, partly for their own sake, but more especially to secure a possible means of entry by re-encodement into Greenshank. The Greenshank key was not normally used for the internal W/T system of the individual Wehrkreise, or for communication with stations outside the German Reich. Thus most of the Wehrkreise used Falcon (Heeres M/S) for their internal networks, while the extensions of the administrative network into Finland (Kemi), Eastern Poland and Russia, and Yugoslavia (Belgrade), used Gannet II, Mallard and Nuthatch respectively.

The Falcons are referred to in detail under the heading of "Western Keys". Falcon I, though a key of wide distribution, was chiefly used for traffic on the internal Wehrkreis VI network, and re-encodements into Greenshank occurred when a message from a station such as Bielefeld was sent to Berlin via Münster, the Wehrkreis VI HQ, the first transition being in Falcon and the second in Greenshank. Falcon II, the Staff key, was occasionally used as Staff key to Falcon I in Wehrkreis VI, but from July 1944, the bulk of the traffic came on the Wehkreis network proper. There was no Staff key to Greenshank, and Falcon II was generally used instead. This was extremely fortunate from our point of view as Falcon II, using Reflector B, was breakable, while Greenshank on D was not.

Gannet II was used between Berlin and Finland, and was first broken in August 1943 on a stray re-encodement from Vulture. Later breaks were made in Berlinismus, an address to the 20th Mountain Army in Finland, and on the beginning or ending known as "SIVA" – SPRUQ IST VOM Date of an earlier day – which occurred on some of Berlin's messages. The quiescent state of the Finnish front normally resulted in only small quantities of traffic of low intelligence value. There were very occasional re-encodements into Greenshank. None of them proved of any value, chiefly because Gannet II could not be broken to order. One had to wait for a day of heavy traffic and then run a number of addresses and "SIVAS".

Mallard was never broken with any regularity. There were perhaps four or five isolated breaks in the course of some years of traffic, but they revealed no way of holding the key. On 1 September 1944 the functions of Falcon and Mallard seem to have been interchanged or combined, so that perhaps the key broken under the name Falcon should more correctly be called Mallard. At any rate, one of the keys seems to have gone out of use at that time, and Gannet II disappeared too, the traffic being sent in the Falcon-Mallard key.

The breaking of Nuthatch

The Falcons, Gannet II or Mallard, in spite of their close connections with the Wehrkreis system, were Enigma keys of the normal type with the usual three wheelorder periods. Nuthatch, the key used on the triangular automatic link between Berlin, Belgrade and Vienna, followed closely the Greenshank pattern. In was stated above that in 1941 Greenshank stopped discriminating. In January 1943 the main network began to use discriminants again, but the Belgrade extension remained as before, the traffic being known for want of a better name as "Non-discriminating Greenshank". An isolated break was secured on 14 February when the outside indicators of a teil message were alternate keyboards, the inside indicators being correctly guessed to be the missing ones in the sequence. This break, the first success of Berlinismus, revealed that the "Non-discriminating Greenshank" was not using the main key, but it had little value apart from this, as very few messages decoded and they had no crib possibilities.

No progress was made for several months until three re-encodements from one of the Fish keys — Tarpon — were discovered by Sixta in the traffic of 16 September. After some difficulty, the correct solution was found to one of them, but the key decoded only the three re-encodements and one other message, the three re-encodements decoding on the same wheelorder, and the other message on a non-cyclic permutation. The remainder of the traffic — some 70-80 messages — seemed outwardly indistinguishable from the messages which did come out.

It was not until November that the solution of the mystery was found. Then, two October days were broken on re-encodements from Woodpecker – a key used in the Balkans apparently for teleprinter traffic – and broken at the time because one of the Wryneck cribs happened to be sent in it. Nuthatch, as the non-discriminating key was now called, was using two keys and six wheelorder permutations like Greenshank, with the same method of distinction by time of origin. But the Nuthatch group did not play strictly according to the rules, for the cipher clerks clearly arranged the times of origin of the messages in such a way that the vast bulk of the traffic on any day was on one key. By ill-luck, on the September day we had broken the small key. Subsequent breaks were in almost every case of the large key, decoding 70%-80% of the traffic. The residue was usually too small to be worth breaking.

From November 1943 to June 1944, when the wireless link disappeared, some days were broken each month on "SIVA", Berlinismus and QEF – an address used on some of the messages from Vienna to Berlin which said: QEF HEER RUEST UND BEF DES ERS. The proportion which began in this way was small, but the form was invariable, so that occasional breaks could be expected if enough messages were run. The intelligence value of Nuthatch was low. In spite of its close association with Greenshank, there were few re-encodements between the two keys. And an early hope that the two Nuthatch keys, which used Reflector B, might be the same as the Greenshank pair which used D, was soon effectively disproved.

Grouse and the Wehrkreis CQ key

Two other Wehrkreis keys were identified, which both used Reflector D. One, called by us Grouse, was used on an extension of the Wehrkreis system in Austria, North Yugoslavia and Czechoslovakia, and although it was never broken, near the end of the war two months' keys were captured without the Germans noticing the loss. The key had a different Reflector wiring each day, but was in other respects similar to a normal Army key, i.e. all the traffic was in one key and only three wheelorder permutations were used. The German name for Grouse was the Wehrkreis Fefu (Feste Funkstelle) Maschinenschlüssel, although as far as is known, it was only used on the southern extension of the Wehrkreis, which connected centres like Graz and Innsbruck.

Yet a third Wehrkreis key on D was that used for CQ messages sent out from Berlin. When these were Geheimekommandosachen they were encoded in Falcon II, and we read several of them in this key in the closing months of 1944. They either began or ended with a CQ serial number which said simply, e.g. SAMMELSPRUQ NUM SEQS ZWO FUENF. In dealing with such messages the Wehrkreis operators showed what, for them, was remarkably bad security, for they often referred to them in clear by the serial number. Sometimes a message would be received by Berlin

The Eastern Army Keys, Greenshank and Allied Keys

and retransmitted CQ, and in such cases there was always an addition to the last teil of the message which was, of course, the serial number. So that on several occasions we were able to fit certain cribs to such additions, but when run on the ordinary bombes they did not come out. Since they did not decode on Greenshank or Grouse, one must assume that here was a third Army key using a daily-changing Reflector D.

The role of WOYG (War Office Y Group)
It would not be fitting in any account of the Wehrkreis group to close without mentioning the magnificent work of the WOYG intercepting operators and liaison staff. Only the skill and experience of the operators enabled them to take this most difficult network, and their work was only made possible by the brilliant feats of Malcolm Spooner, who, an almost legendary figure working in the small hours of the morning in his tiny office, could be relied on to break the various complicated system of callsigns and frequency allocation which the Wehrkreis authorities from time to time devised.

Chapter 26
Police and SS Keys

General Characteristics

The SS keys formed a relatively small – there were never more than a dozen separate keys – but in many respects very interesting group. While a branch of Army keys in the wider sense, and for this reason dealt with by the Army section in the final Air/Army division of Hut 6, they showed certain peculiarities which differentiated them not only from the Air keys but from most other Army keys. These were:

   a. Specialised content and style. The keys used many contractions not commonly met with on pure Army traffic, e.g. the most common abbreviation was XSSX, which on Army keys was often indicated by SIEGFRIED SIEGFRIED. The use of "spellers" was very rare on SS keys and the use of X as a stop or after a contraction very common. YY was rare and wahlworts never used.

   b. Individual rules of keys in certain respects (see sections on the topic). It seems probable that the keys were made up and distributed by a special SS cipher office.

   c. Fixed callsigns on the bulk of the traffic throughout – normally OL, OM or DO. This made W/T research and traffic identification much simpler on SS keys than on the Army proper. And if there were cribs, there was no trouble in identifying the relevant messages.

History to the end of 1941

During the war the first SS key to be broken was Orange – known to the Germans as SS Stabsmaschinenschlüssel – though it was not a Staff key in the normal Army sense and the traffic was not as a rule "top secret". The content was SS matter of a general administrative nature, including organisation of concentration camps. The early history of the breaking of

Police and SS Keys

Orange to May 1941 has already been referred to. Up to the end of 1941 the position remained essentially unchanged – Orange still cillied occasionally and was broken at intervals on bombe menus or hand attempts. From the beginning of Machine Room 2, Orange was one of the most interesting colours and was one of the first to be formally adopted, but it must be admitted it was hard enough going.

Apart from Orange, two other SS keys had appeared before the end of 1941. The first was the famous TGD (named after the Berlin callsign at one period. Later TGD used fixed callsigns of the type SN, SO), the key of the Security Police. From information we have received this key was broken by the Poles as far back as 1937 but the only decodes Hut 6 was able to examine were on 31 July 1939, when the traffic was largely in code. The key was never broken during the war and to this day is one of the classic mysteries of Hut 6. It never cillied so far as we know and no convincing re-encodement from any other key was ever produced.

The other key was named Orange II. It first appeared in December 1941 but had not been broken by the end of the year. It used Orange-like calls but had a separate series of discriminants which, in January 1942, it began repeating day-for-day.

1942: The Orange Age

An era of discoveries was heralded in 1942. Orange I began to be broken more frequently on cillies, particularly an amusing type of cilli from one station (OMW) – the famous AAA variety. Increasing decode evidence threw up some crib possibilities of which more hereafter. On Orange II success was also gained in February and it was proved that December, January and February were all on the same key. (It was later discovered that the key was still used in March and this period was called the first cycle. The second cycle lasted from April till Orange II died out in August). This meant that one could take corresponding days together and combine both cillies and ringstellung tips, a fascinating pursuit which resulted eventually in the breaking of a substantial number of days of the first cycle. Orange II was found to deal mainly with communications between Berlin and SS divisions on the Eastern Front, with the well-known LSSAH and the Wiking Division figuring prominently.

4152: Meanwhile, an intriguing mystery was revealed on Orange I. In February 1942 a new frequency – 4152 – came up with Orange calls and discriminants but was obstinately dud on the Orange key. This

Solving Enigma's Secrets - The Official History of Bletchley Park's Hut 6

phenomenon aroused interest and some disquiet, for never previously had the same discriminant on the same day failed to decode on the same key. As nothing new was known of the new frequency, nothing could be done in the crib line, but in March 1942 two cillies turned up on 4152 on a day when the main key was broken and the cillies were rodded out on the Orange stecker. The wheelorder was the same as the main key but the ringstellung differed – no connection was ever found. But on the evidence of signatures it was almost always possible to rod out the 4152 when the main key was known, and more rarely the 4152 was broken first as a stepping-stone to the main key.

HOR-HUG reports: The contents of 4152 Orange dealt with some of the concentration camps such as Auschwitz, Dachau and Oranienburg, and the next sensational advance in SS cryptography was also connected with this frequency. For several months a number of non-Enigma messages had been sent out from some six or seven stations to Berlin early in the morning – in fact between 7am and 8am. These messages were eventually passed on to us as it was thought they might tie up in some way with the Enigma traffic. Inspection revealed the following characteristics: the messages, known as HOR-HUG reports from two frequently occurring code groups, were short, consisting of about ten groups of letters, followed by a few more or less invariable code groups. In the message proper the number of letters in any group never exceeded four, and on any one day only ten different letters were used. The last point strongly suggested a figure code and on this hypothesis one day's traffic was broken early in April 1942. The messages contained, in tabular form, the vital statistics of concentration camps – the first four columns denoted:

    (a) Number of inmates at start of previous day
    (b) New arrivals
    (c) Departures by any means
    (d) Number at end of day

Thus $A + B - C = D$, and for any station, D on one day was A on the next. Once this was known, it was generally easy to break any individual day on its own by a series of equations, and it was thus, of course, absurdly simple if the previous day's substitution was known.

The cryptographic importance of this discovery lay in the remarkable fact that the substitution was derived from the Orange stecker of the

Police and SS Keys

day by the simple process of writing the numbers 1, 2, 3 ..... 0 above the first five stecker pairings. (Each individual stecker pair was written in alphabetical order – not the whole set. Thus 2 was farther on in the alphabet than 1, 4 than 3, and so on). Fortunately, this incredible piece of enemy carelessness was noticed as soon as the first figure code had been broken, and no time was lost in exploiting it. Arrangements were made at once to have the vital messages well intercepted and the HOR-HUG key was broken as early as possible in Machine Room 1. Thereafter, the Orange stecker for the day was known.

This knowledge could be used to aid breaking in three distinct ways: (a) by rodding a crib, beginner or signature or sometimes a cillie (for the technique of rodding in general and the somewhat special problems of rodding half the stecker - instead of the complete stecker - see the appropriate chapter in the technical volume); (b) by using the known stecker in hand attempts on cillies plus ringstellung tip, or; (c) by running bombe menus on either cillies or cribs with the known stecker postulated. Method (b) was the most elegant, and the fact that, in hand attempts, one could nearly always start from a known stecker pairing, made it possible to try a far larger number of positions than would otherwise have been feasible. Other factors in favour of the hand-break method were that the HOR-HUG stecker made rejection of wrong stories easy and that the Army ringstellung rule (which Orange frequently obeyed) made it sometimes possible to guess the ringstellung even without a tip by Herivelismus.

Method (a) could be very laborious and was not as a rule adopted unless circumstances were favourable – i.e. unless there was in close proximity a number of constatations where the stecker of both letters involved was known. Method (c) was maid-of-all-work for use in cases where other lines of attack were impracticable or too laborious. It had the merit of cheapness in bombe hours as it could be run on the corner of a machine which was doing another job as well (for menus could be made up on a small number of links because of the extra closures) and it was possible to combine the method if desired with method (a) e.g. by putting down a favourable stretch on the rods and running another stretch on the bombe.

Henceforward, for about a year the HOR-HUG stecker (it should be mentioned that the HOR-HUG reports were not sent out on Sundays or public holidays such as Xmas Day – but to compensate there was hardly any Orange traffic on these days) formed the trump card of the Orange cryptographer. March and April 1942 were the best Orange months to date, but from May 1942 to January 1943, an average of 19 days per month was broken. Orange was always a colour on which we looked for signatures, as virtually every message started with an address and ended with a signature, and though few of the signatures were really good for breaking in their own right, some were serviceable enough when the whole stecker was known (as in breaking the 4152) or when half the stecker was known. One of the best was from OMG: XSPORRENBERG XSSX OBERSTUFX.

Orange Cribs: But during 1942 a few real cribs were discovered on Orange. These were never quite first-rate by the standards of easier colours, but were none-the-less very welcome on a colour so cribless as Orange and, of course, even a comparatively poor crib is greatly strengthened by the HOR-HUG stecker. The best known of the Orange cribs were the Bestand and Weather messages. The Bestände were messages similar in content to the HOR-HUG reports but enciphered in Enigma. There were two such messages – the men's and the women's Bestand – and both were summaries of the state of affairs at the concentration camp of Stutthof near Danzig. The cribs had a usable stagger stretch and quite a good signature (XKLX STUTTHOFX), and could often be used to break with the HOR-HUG stecker.

But the most famous of all Orange cribs was the Weather messages from Krakau (OLQ). The first of these messages turned up in October 1942 and they were at once recognised as high-class weather reports covering the whole of Europe. Apart from their value for our bombing operations, these reports were at that time of particular intelligence interest because of the state of the weather on the Eastern Front was then regarded as of high importance in forecasting the developments of that crucial campaign and so a morning weather report on the Eastern Front was placed daily on the Prime Minister's desk. It was suggested that if Orange could be broken more or less currently – at least before 8am the next day – the Orange Weather could be included in this report.

Fortunately the message itself was both readily identifiable and proved cribbable in an original way. It was found to end: SONNEN AUFGANG KRAKAU MORGEN ... ... UHR SONNEN UNTERGANG ... ... UHR. Consultation of the Nautical Almanac revealed that Krakau

Police and SS Keys

was an extremely fortunately situated place with a longitude of 19° 59' which counted as 20° and made it easy to calculate the times of sunrise and sunset. These were found to nearly always agree with the German times (later it was found that the Germans made occasional errors in calculating the times), and as a result, on any weather message there was a stagger stretch of average length 50 – ideal for breaking on the HOR-HUG stecker. Henceforward, the Orange Weather or Sunrise at Krakau became the main means of breaking, and to secure currency, Machine Room 1 took over partial responsibility for the key. This new crib was the more important, as in August 1942, the AAA cillier had ceased to send traffic, and though pronounceable and keyboard cillies still occurred on Orange at intervals, no single station quite took the place of the deceased OMW.

Quince: While Orange I was thus being broken on concentration camp statistics and astronomical lore – a striking example of the comic aspect of cryptography – Orange II had faded away to nothingness in the midst of its second cycle. But in August 1942 this blank began to be filled by a new SS key named Quince, destined in the latter half of the war to become the principal key of its class, though this could not have been foreseen from its modest origins. Quince was called the SS Feldnachschubmaschinenschlüssel and was primarily concerned with supply and administration of SS divisions wherever they were stationed – Eastern Front, Balkans, Italy and the West. While it never contained operational orders of the first importance, it did at times contain reports of operational interest, e.g. a flamboyant description of one of the last noteworthy German successes on the Eastern Front, the recapture of Kharkov, was sent in a long message on Quince on 13 March 1943.

The first Quince day to be broken – on straight keyboards – was 27 August 1942 and in September (which repeated discriminants and keys of August), more breaks were secured on cillies (a popular cilli in the early days was PFL followed by OCK or AUM in 2-teile messages – Pflock and Pflaum were SS officers), sometimes eked out by beginners (ANX, ANX SSX or ANX SSX FHAX – FHA = Fuehrerhauptamt), were all worth trying). From October 1942 onwards Quince had a new key every month. It continued to be broken most frequently on cillies – both pronounceables and nearnesses – but occasionally on cribs. The earliest crib was called the Dodgemeldung – a report from DOJ and DOF (Berlin), and it was first used in November 1942. In the course of the following year, as cillies declined, this crib was employed more and more frequently.

On 30 December 1942, Quince produced one of the best Banbury stories on record. From the evidence of counts, two 5-teile messages and one 6-teile had clearly used the same indicators, part for part, at least for the first four parts of each message, but it was impossible to arrive at the message settings by subtraction. The day came out on a pure Banbury menu and the settings were found to be for the 5-teile:

PRO SIT NEU JAH RXY

and for the 6-teile:

PRO SIT NEU JAH RXA HOI.

With these good wishes ringing in our ears we set forth into 1943.

1943-1945: The Quince Age

Decline of Orange: In 1943, though SS keys in general improved their position, this was mainly due to the success of the newcomer, Quince, for blow after blow was suffered by Orange, the senior SS key. The most unkindest cut of all was dealt early in the year when towards the end of January it was announced that landlines were to be used instead of the vital frequency 4152. This decision was carried into effect forthwith and by February 1943 the HOR-HUG messages were no more. The disappearance of the HOR-HUG stecker revealed the true weakness of the crib position on Orange and there was a catastrophic decline in the number of breaks. It is possible indeed that on a colour of the highest priority value, we might, by great extravagance in bombe time – e.g. by running all possible variations of the Weather – have made a supreme effort to maintain our hold. But Orange was not sufficiently important to justify such expense. When it had to compete on level terms – i.e. without the bonus of the HOR-HUG stecker – with colours of operational importance, we soon discovered that the amount we could run was severely limited. (For completeness sake it should be recorded that two minor SS keys, Orange III and Apple, existed for a comparatively brief period in 1942. Orange III dealt with the affairs of the SS Kav. Div. and was broken several times on cillies plus ANX (which was almost 100% on this key). Apple, from D/F evidence was used by SS groups in Norway. It gave a few fair cilli stories, and once even a re-encodement that was thought well of, but none-the-less never elected to come out.)

There was never any permanent recovery from this loss, though even in 1943 periods of moderate success occurred. Breaks could still

Police and SS Keys

be secured on cillies, beginners or signatures or on the weather, though even as a crib this deteriorated – latterly the times of sunrise and sunset were omitted. A new method of entry – re-encodements from Quince – was also employed whenever possible. June and July 1943 were both considered quite good months at the time. But even they only recorded nine and six breaks respectively and the monthly average of breaks from February to August 1943 was only seven – as opposed to 19 in the previous nine months. This unfortunate colour reached the nadir of its fortunes in September and October 1943 when a long-impending crisis in our cover resources came to a head and Orange had to be completely sacrificed by the removal of sets. In November it proved possible to restore cover and happily a quick break was achieved on keyboard cillies plus ANX SSX, but nonetheless, by the end of the year, Orange was far from convalescent and was indeed in a very delicate position. The few breaks that were achieved were due to cillies or re-encodements from Quince.

<u>Revival of Orange</u>: In the course of 1944 matters somewhat improved and in February a fair number of breaks was secured not only on cillies and re-encodements, but in some cases on new cribs of which the most interesting and best was the so-called 'Bomb for Terboven'. Terboven, the Reichkomissar in Norway, had a fatherly interest in Düsseldorf and liked to be informed whenever there had been a raid on that town, and the address of this message could be used as a crib. In March 1944 it was discovered that current Quince was repeating in a rather complicated pattern elements of the keys of January Orange, and this eventually led to the breaking of all January Orange. This, of course, gave much needed decode evidence, and as cillies tended to become more frequent – especially on 6535 – a good deal of Orange was broken in the summer months. It was easy to break any day with a good cilli story. It was in general very difficult and expensive to break days when there was not a good cilli story and much depended on the bombe position. Apart from a message like Bomb for Terboven, Orange crib menus were usually on signatures – not cribs in the strict sense – and these were liable to frequent alteration. In any case, owing to their shortness, these jobs generally had to run as delayed hoppities on the American naval bombes which were subject to frequent jams. Hence, Orange breaks would come in a rush due to good cilli stories, then there might be a lull due to the absence of cillies while shots on signatures piled up in America. Eventually the jam

would be released, probably a few breaks secured, and the cycle would start anew. The cilli stories – which were mainly, but not always, strings of keyboards – reached their height in July and August 1944. The piece de resistance was unquestionably this memorable sequence on 1 August: PAQ, YSW, XDE, CFR, VGT, BHZ, NJU, MKI, LKO, MJI, NHU, BGZ, VFT, CDR, XSE, YAW. Breaking in this month was also facilitated by a curious stecker pattern from which it was possible on occasions to predict the self-steckered letters for the day.

Final position: On 15 September 1944 the CY device began to be used on SS keys. As is now known by captured documents, the Germans introduced CY and random indicators at the same time. To this cause we must probably assign the sudden death of Orange cillies. From this time on Orange went into a cryptographic decline. Two fair means of breaking were left: (1) variants of AN ALLE FUNKSTELLEN on CQ messages, and (2) a good signature from OLD, known as the Teschner signature. But nothing else that was any use could be discovered, and so when these last cribs died in the course of nature (for all cribs are mortal), Orange-breaking stopped. The only remaining days broken was on a stray re-encodement from Quince and on long shots such as BETRIEBSSPRUQ in what looked like signals messages. Such isolated breaks showed no real possibilities of new progress. There was, however, to be a last glimpse of Orange before the end. The keys for April were captured and it was possible to decode the full month's traffic. Cryptographically the position was all but impossible – there were no cribs nor even reasonably good signatures – and a formal attempt to break the scanty remnants of May Orange on the evidence of April was foredoomed to failure.

Golden age of Quince: It is a relief to turn from the rather melancholy story of Orange and the anticlimax in which it ends to the happier tale of Quince – a colour which especially in the last 18 months of the war, had such consistent and uninterrupted success that at times it was almost dull. Yet happy is the key that has no history. It is, however, possible to divide the story of Quince into three successive stages which overlap to some extent but are yet broadly distinguishable. In the first period (which has already been discussed) Quince was broken mainly on cillies. But in the course of 1943 a gradual but persistent decline in the transparency of cillies took place and cribs were used more constantly, and from July to November 1943 Quince can be more fairly reckoned a crib colour. The old crib, the Dodgemeldung, was still frequently employed and a new arrival, the Eugenmeldung, a report from the SS Division Prinz Eugen, then stationed in the Balkans, to the SS FHA in Berlin, proved a valuable second string. This message has a curious and complicated history – it was at various times passed on Quince, Raven, Wryneck and Peregrine, and sometimes it was possible to break Quince on re-encodements from these keys.

The third and last stage in the history of Quince began in November 1943 when the frequency 6315/3851, which carried the Balkan and Italian Quince, suddenly packed up. This involved the disappearance of the Eugenmeldung and left Quince cribless, as the Dodgemeldung had already gone. Henceforward, apart from occasional breaks on cillies, we had to rely on beginners and signatures and Quince soon became a classic example of this type of key. It was broken almost daily to the end of the war on addresses such as ANX SSX FHAX INX SIEBENX, signatures such as the famous pair SCHEFFEL and SHAEFER, and a host of others. This was an expensive process, but Quince (which in 1944 steadily increased in quantity and quality) was counted well worth the cost and success was virtually certain to reward perseverance.

Occasional cribs would sometimes appear for a fortnight or so, but rarely for longer – there was probably no key which was broken so often that had so few genuine cribs. The paradox about Quince is that its last 18 months must have been the most interesting to Hut 3 and the dullest to Hut 6, for breaking by sledgehammer has none of the elegance and finesse dear to the cryptographer's heart. But Quince's intelligence importance was at length recognised by its promotion to full Watch status in December 1944. The Quince keys for April and May 1945 were captured in a great SS key haul towards the end of the war, and as the Germans got into a complete muddle about what was compromised and what was not, no new key was issued and we were able to decode Quince currently to the end. This was not so valuable as it may sound as traffic fell drastically and there were sometimes only one or two messages a day. But Hut 6 never looked gift horses in the mouth, and in fact the very lack of traffic made it in one sense more desirable for us to have the key, otherwise we would have had difficulty in breaking it. Like Orange – and indeed all the SS keys – Quince ends in a cryptographic anticlimax, but we could at least claim it remained breakable as long as there was any quantity of traffic. Probably no Research key (for such it was for most of its life) was more frequently or regularly broken – let this be its epitaph.

Minor SS keys: A large number of minor and sometimes more or less ephemeral keys – not always easy to identify – were thrown up by the SS system from time to time and deserve brief individual mention.

Two keys were confusingly called Quince II, though they had, in reality, no connection with each other. One was used by certain SS units in Italy and the Balkans and was first broken on a remarkable cilli story – seven HRDs – on 13 October 1942. This was probably the first appearance of the key. It was later broken a few more times on cillies or signatures, but disappeared in November with the rest of Balkan and Italian Quince.

The second Quince II was more reasonably named. It was the SS Chef Sonderschlüssel and the traffic was nearly all TOP SECRET. In fact, the orthodox and almost universal method of breaking was to run variants of the beginning GEHEIMEKOMMANDOSAQE on any message, preferably long part messages, though there were a few sporadic cribs. Quince II in this new sense was first broken on 1 April 1944 under the name of Discriminating Quince. To the end nearly all its messages discriminated, and this was indeed the only way by which either the Germans or ourselves could distinguish the messages from Quince I.

Another Balkan key (like the first Quince II) was Peregrine (this key was given a bird name before its true nature was known), which had a brief life from August to October 1943. It was used by the SS Division Prinz Eugen and passed the Eugenmeldung and usually nothing more. Its intelligence value was negligible as this message was in any case often read on other keys, but it had some cryptographic importance as a possible lead into Quince or Balkan Army keys. It was always broken on the Eugenmeldung used either as a crib or a re-encodement from some other key. One peculiarity was that in September (though not in August or October) every key broken had eleven stecker pairs - a fact which suggests that the keys were home-made. It is also worthy of note that the version of the Eugenmeldung passed on Peregrine was sent to the V SS Geb. Korps and the reason for the decease of Peregrine was that this Corps and the Prinz Eugen Division came together in the same place.

In 1944 there appeared a trio of keys named Medlar, Grapefruit and Pumpkin. Medlar was originally called the Quince-Orange link (German name: SS Querverkehrschlüssel) and was definitely intended for pass-on messages between the Quince and Orange system – presumably as a means of avoiding re-encodements. There was seldom much traffic on this key and what there was was very hard to distinguish from Quince

Police and SS Keys

and Orange, so it was never blisted separately (except in April and May 1945 when discriminants and keys were known by capture), and broken rarely, generally by accident. Medlar was first broken on 29 May 1944, and from the German key-number this month was the first in which it was used. It continued to the end of the war, and in fact Medlar, 9 May 1945, was the latest key on which traffic was decoded.

Grapefruit was a concentration camp key – a revival of 4152 Orange on the old frequency, but on this occasion with a key of its own and – alas – without the HOR-HUG stecker of the past. This key used fixed DO callsigns and appeared in April 1944. It was only broken once – on 21 August 1944 – when a double re-encipherment from Quince and Orange came out after immense efforts. The traffic was virtually uncribbable. The only line of attack was on CQ messages which, in any case, had an extensive repertory of varied forms. Grapefruit gradually declined and was practically dead sometime before the end of the war.

Pumpkin was a propaganda key connecting Rome and later North Italy with Berlin. It started in April 1944 when a break of one day on cillies revealed that the key was identical with the Quince I key of the previous month. Also, May Pumpkin used the same key as April Quince. But the repeat of keys did not continue thereafter and no more Pumpkin was broken. It must be admitted that no attempts were made – the contents of the traffic was so valueless that Hut 3 was apt to despise Pumpkin even when it was secured as a free gift. The later history of Pumpkin is like Grapefruit, except that its decline and final disappearance was even quicker.

In the closing stages of the war, a new key, Plum (SS M/S Sondersatz C), supplanted Quince I for a short period during a compromise and was broken for several days in March 1945 on Quince cribs. When a new Quince key had been distributed, however, Plum declined and indeed was only broken once more on a re-encodement from Quince when only about half a dozen messages decoded. Also in the last stages, a considerable haul of SS keys gave us the Orange, Quince I, Quince II and Medlar keys for April, and all the above (except Orange) for May (also in most cases the corresponding reserve keys – some of which were used). Of all this bunch of keys Quince II was the most useful to intelligence and indeed it produced some sensational messages in the last agony of the Reich, in particular the news of Göring's arrest (by Himmler?) and a long message of indignant expostulation sent by the

Marshal to the Führer. Incidentally, the capture of these keys with their discriminants immeasurably simplified the sorting problem. For some time past we had been reduced to a composite SS Discriminating blist which contained a large number of keys – Quince II, Quince I Discriminating if any, Orange Discriminating if any, Plum, Medlar and so on. Apart from the keys already referred to, there were broken from time to time odd unidentifiable keys to which were given such names as Quince III, Orange II for want of better and two keys that are referred to in the Western Army section (E/320 and Penguin) had something of an SS flavour. There was, in addition, the class of Police keys which deserve separate treatment.

Police keys: The German Police was characteristically much more closely related to the Army than we should think fitting. In particular, it was closely bound up with the SS and high functionaries often held rank in both services. But for most of the war the Police, as such, had no machine ciphers. (Perhaps one should except the Secret Police (Gestapo). It is generally considered that TGD was in a sense their key. Roulette was the key of the Regular Police – Ordnungspolizei or Orpo). They made do with hand systems such as Double Playfair, which were successfully dealt with in another section of Bletchley Park. It thus happened that when, in February 1944, the Germans at last decided to introduce an Enigma key for the higher police officials in occupied Europe, there followed a close collaboration between two different cryptographic sections to break this key named Roulette (Polchi M/S). This kind of collaboration was not unique in the history of Hut 6, but there were few, if any, keys on which we were so dependant on outside aid for breaking as in the case of Roulette.

The introduction of Roulette did not result in the disappearance of Double Playfair which remained the vehicle for most of the Police traffic. The first breaks of Roulette (10 and 16 February 1944) were made on re-encodements from Double Playfair. (Throughout the whole history of Roulette most breaks were made on re-encodements – probably not far short of 45 days out of a total of about 60). These initial breaks showed that Roulette followed almost universally the Double Playfair practice of burying addresses in the middle of a message. Even had this not been done it is unlikely that the very varied addresses and signatures would have proved cribbable, but the universal burying made it impossible even to consider attempts.

Police and SS Keys

Roulette is a standing example of how easily the Germans could have defeated cribbery by sufficiently thorough measures. The burying of addresses and signatures in the middle of the message is an even more effective measure than the alternative system of wahlworts, which they did eventually use very extensively on the Army and to a slighter extent on the GAF. It has only one serious weakness – if there is in the traffic a routine Tagesmeldung, Lagebericht or the like, by burying the address one may actually make the message a better crib, as it then starts with the Tagesmeldung part. For a short time Roulette had quite a good crib of this nature, the "Routag" (a report on anti-partisan activities in Albania) that flourished in the last week of March and the first week of April. But this crib had a short life and its successors were still more ephemeral. Roulette largely escaped the dangers mentioned above for two reasons: (a) there were no routine messages that lasted for any length of time, and (b) those routine messages that did occasionally turn up and were sometimes spotted on evidence of past police decodes were largely spoilt as cribs by the odd contractions they might use, e.g. TAGESM VX for TAGESMELDUNG VOM. Roulette was notorious (even among keys of its class) for the frequency and strangeness of its abbreviations – for instance, any word ending in DUNG could be contracted to DGX.

A few Roulette keys could be broken on cillies and these entertaining stories are worth recording. On 6 April we had two messages with the following sequence of outside indicators: WIR, UCH, IGA, TEN and the same message settings. The blanks were filled up thus: WIR-BRA UCH-ENZ IGA-RET TEN (= we want cigarettes) and the day was broken on this missing word combination. Again, on 11 July, the day was broken on cillies from DRT (Laibac) and the full list of settings used is worth mentioning – WIG (5), SPI (3), PAU (3), PAM (2), HOE (2), HER, HOH, HAH (the indices denote the number of times the message setting occurred – not all were cillied), while a few days later a key was broken on WIG (3) plus BETRX. However, these cilli stories were exceptions and the CY system (which was introduced on Roulette somewhat earlier than generally – viz. at the beginning of September) effectively rules out the possibility of cillies.

So, with a few exceptions, Roulette was broken on re-encodements. Of these, the supply was fluctuating and not all succeeded. The success attained was probably about 60%. In August 1944 the supply of re-encodements reached its peak and no fewer than 12 days were broken during the month. But in September this supply suddenly dried up owing to the replacement of Double Playfair by a much superior hand system known as Rasterschlüssel. This led to an awkward situation, for much the best means of breaking Roulette was on Police re-encodements, but with this new system in force, Hut 6 was now asked to break Roulette on its own in order to give re-encodements into Raster.

We promised to do our best but the situation was very difficult. We had kept full records of anything that looked like a crib, but when all this material was put together in order, it was hardly possible for the most optimistic cryptographer to feel confident of success. Besides, any attempt would be most expensive in bombe time, and there were severe limits to the time we could spend on Roulette even when full allowance was made for the increased cryptographic importance of Roulette as a lead into Raster.

Our utmost efforts were not entirely useless, for we succeeded in breaking Roulette of 7 October on a vast stagger job and this break was a distinct help to the Raster party. But it must be admitted that in the main the Raster cryptographers had to fight their own battle, and indeed we had from the beginning of the crisis warned them that salvation could only come from their own efforts. In the end the Raster system was largely mastered and the supply of re-encodements started again, though never quite on the same scale as before. The course of the crisis is well mirrored in the monthly figures of Roulette breaks:

August 1944	12
September 1944	2
October 1944	1
November 1944	0
December 1944	7
January 1945	2
February 1945	2
March 1945	3
April 1945	6

These breaks were mostly effected on the old re-encodement lines, but it is worth noting that the last breaks in April 1945 were partly due to a few tolerably indifferent cribs of which the most amusing was the "Letter to Rauter", a short report from the notorious (Arthur) Seys-Inquart

Police and SS Keys

(Reichskommissar of the Netherlands) to Frau Rauter, wife of a high police official in Holland. Incidentally, these messages often appeared to us to be written in an absurdly optimistic vein.

Roulette was, in general, broken late. This was because we were so dependent on the re-encodements which in turn – especially in Raster days – were broken far from currently. So, more often than not, we were running about a month behind on breaks. Thus, it is not surprising that some of the last breaks scored by Hut 6 were of this key – no fewer than four April breaks were actually chalked up after VE-Day. It should be stated, to conclude this account, that to begin with Roulette had certain peculiarities (such as the discriminant in the first group and the use of only one wheelorder per day) that were old-fashioned by the standards of other keys. But in April 1944 Roulette began putting discriminants in the preamble, while by December it was using three wheelorders per day. This brought it into line with other keys except that all Roulette messages discriminated. In the matter of routeing, Roulette was treated differently from any other Hut 6 key. The traffic came to the Police Section, was there blisted and afterwards brought down to Hut 6 for examination. The decodes, in their turn, went back to the Police Section, not to Hut 3, as was the case with other keys.

The discovery of re-encodements between Police ciphers and Roulette was not done by Hut 6. These were reported by our colleagues in Lt.-Col. Evans' section and were often in fact first noticed by the Police log readers. Our task was confined to working the re-encodements that were discovered. In other respects, also, the Police Section helped us, e.g. by looking for any routines known on their keys. It is thus obvious that Roulette cryptography (to a greater degree than any other key) was only partially in the hands of Hut 6, and we must unreservedly acknowledge the great assistance we received throughout from our Police colleagues. It was fortunate that, owing to the highly intractable nature of Roulette in its own right, we remained to the end so dependant on a lead from them. It only remains to add that a few minor Roulette keys appeared from time to time – the so-called Roulette II – which used the Red key and had useful cribs; Roulette III, dealing with electricity supplies in the Ruhr (and only once broken) and Roulette IV, which was really Quail, used sporadically by a few police stations in the Balkans. Of these, only Roulette II had any cryptographic importance.

Summary

The exploitation of the SS and Police keys can definitely be said to have been cryptographically successful. The most important key – Quince – was broken almost daily for long periods on end and every key that passed any quantity of traffic was broken frequently, with the exception of TGD. With respect to this last failure, it must be remembered that the pressure of other commitments made it impossible to maintain adequate and continuous cover on TGD, so it was never subjected to concentrated and long-sustained cryptographic assault. But honesty compels the admission that the key always seemed so unpromising that no one can say whether even a full-scale attack would have succeeded. But apart from TGD, there were no serious failures in our attack on the SS keys. On the whole the success attained was satisfactory in view of the intelligence rating of the colours. (It must be remembered that the SS keys were never operational. Their importance did tend to increase towards the end of the war, but even Quince I or Quince II – the best keys for intelligence – were never considered better than good second-class keys at their peak – though it must be remembered that this was a respectable rating, as five or six classes were recognised). Any increased success could only have been secured, if at all, at the expense of more important and urgent commitments.

Chapter 27
Mustard

Introduction

Mustard was one of the last keys to be named before the rigid application of class distinction was made and the name arose by natural association with Mr Colman, the head of the Control Room. Whether the namers had also in mind the arguments about mustard in Alice in Wonderland or whether the name was merely happy foresight, the fact remains that the Mustard organisation, in the first instance, at least had no links with other GAF units and so would have been difficult to classify under the headings adopted.

The Horchmaschinenschlüssel – or key of the GAF Y Service – first appeared in June 1941 on the invasion of Russia and was used by those Signals units with Y duties for sending intelligence reports on Russian wireless activity back to centres where these reports could be collated, codes broken and the intelligence issued to interested parties. As active fronts appeared in the Mediterranean and the West, so did Mustard networks and keys. Behind each front there was usually one main centre to which all information, reports and D/Fs were sent. These centres – at Warsaw, Rome, Athens and Paris – forwarded, when necessary, items of interest to the head office in Berlin.

Mustard provided the first example of one key being used with four sets of discriminants – a device presumably adopted to camouflage the use of one key over a wide area. This meant that, for security reasons here, Mustard was divided into I and IV on the Eastern Front, II in the Mediterranean and III in the Balkans. The Mustard networks in the West did not come active until after D-Day when the other Mustards had been reduced to Mustard II, covering Italy and the Balkans. Western GAF Y messages were sent in an assortment of keys including Jaguar and Red, but Mustard I and Cress were the normal keys. Each Mustard, in turn, was responsible for the breaks recorded, for Russian Mustard was the source of practically all breaks until 1943, when the Mediterranean Y services took over the task of keeping us informed of what the Germans knew about the Allies.

Russian Mustard: Mustard I, IV

The initial break into Mustard was made in June 1941 on cillies, and keyboard cillies (favourites were PAQ, PAP, QAP) supplemented by the beginner ANX WX EINSNULL (W10 was the cover name for the Warsaw office) accounted for most of the 12 other breaks in August and September. The strength of the few cribs shown by the evidence of these broken days can be judged by the fact that no break was effected on them after the cillier had gone. Indeed, the rest of the year was a blank, and this unhappy state of affairs continued until 9 April 1942 was broken on pronounceable cillies. Even here there was a disappointment for, while some of the Mediterranean Mustard decoded, one frequency – 9840 – remained obstinately dud. But this was to be the last misfortune for a year, as a few days later the first of the quadrilateral key repeats was discovered, and for the rest of the year Mustard was involved in these repeats.

March Mustard keys were known when both April Red and Foxglove were out, and could generally be broken if only one of the components was known. Moreover, once the significance of a discriminant repeat had been established, it was possible to delve into the unblisted masses of January Mustard and rod out a day on the stecker of February Red. When it was found that January Mustard had the wheelorder and ringstellung of February Primrose, most of the January days only needed blisting and decoding. Incidentally, one reason why Mustard was not infrequently a victim of pressure of work in RR 2 (Registration Room, Research) was that at this time the traffic consisted of long messages (up to 60 teile a message) giving the Russian Order of Battle and other information intercepted. As these messages could be subtracted on the register, there was not the same urgency for blisting as on other keys.

Fortunately, the key repeats in 1942 coincided with an outburst of cillying on these long messages, and the combination of these two factors often made breaking an academic exercise. In June, the operator at Shitomir realised that the whole business of encoding and decoding might be enlivened by the use as message settings of sentences chopped up into three-letter groups. So, appropriately enough, he started on 15 June with the cilli sequence: WIR/LIE/GEN/INX/SHI/TOM/IRX, which was the first time intelligence had been derived from message settings. The idea was taken up by other operators and greetings and good wishes were popular, especially at Christmas time. Apart from sentences, such a cilli sequence as ANF/MIT/MUT/GOT/END (used in January 1943) was very typical. ANF and END were particular favourites. A more unusual sequence for a German operator – OLD/BOY/HOW/ARE/YOU – was used more than once in the year of cillies and repeats, and indicator habits in general became so well-known that it was possible sometimes to make correct guesses at message settings even when the operator had attempted to disguise his favourites by twiddling three or four on every wheel. With the large number of breaks, cribs were established which helped to fill in cilliless days. After the end of the great period of key repeats in December 1942, Mustard was still broken regularly for some time, naturally not so often as before, but as frequently as was necessary for the intelligence sections to keep their Russian Order of Battle up-to-date. However, the introduction of wahlworts in February 1943 was speedily followed by the decay of Russian Mustard, and although thereafter some long messages did appear – and even cillied once or twice – the cryptographic centre of Mustard moved permanently to the Mediterranean area.

Mediterranean Mustard: Mustard II, III

Although the story of this region does not really start until the cryptographers were forced to scratch around for cribs after the end of the Russian cillies and cribs, there is a prologue in the shape of 9840 Mustard left dud in the last section. With the recent precedent of Orange 4152 it was only natural that attempts should be made to rod out 9840 Mustard. There were no cribs, but various beginners were tried without success. Finally, in a mood of considerable scepticism, a Test Plate job was prepared and produced on one message the beginner ANX WILLIX EINSNULL. Then it was discovered that every message on the frequency had a *different* ringstellung which was determined by a daily changing figure code on the last three figures of the GTO, while the key otherwise was ordinary Mustard. Thus, e.g. on 10 March 1942 the code was:

1	2	3	4	5	6	7	8	9	0
B	T	K	P	C	G	J	E	U	M

So a message at 1943 had German ringstellung UPK. It was necessary first to break the normal Mustard key and then to rod a number of 0940 messages until the full substitution for the day had been discovered.

This device only lasted for a month or two and was then abandoned, presumably as being too much nuisance from the German standpoint.

When, however, the decline of Russian Mustard turned our attention anew to the Mediterranean Mustard, useful cribs were discovered, and though all used wahlworts, these were generally limited to from four to six letters. The cribs at this time all originated from Crete, the best being Jagdflugtätigkeit, and the others the long-lived Einsatz Eins and Einsatz Drei, all of which were named from their initial words. The first of these disappeared in July, and for some time after that the breaking of Mustard was less frequent and more expensive as the other cribs were shorter, and subject to occasional irregularities of form. Mustard certainly suffered also by its expense in bombe hours and its comparatively low intelligence rating.

By September 1943 the position had become so bad that not even the unexpected evidence of a week's Mediterranean Mustard traffic on Red (due to a capture of Mustard keys by the Italians) helped us to continue breaking and the ephemeral reappearance of cillies on Russian Mustard gave us a couple of days in October and one in November without influencing the long-term prospects appreciably. But in December 1943 a new type of traffic appeared on Mustard which led to a remarkable improvement in the situation. On 14 December 1943, a string of short KR messages appeared on the Balkan Mustard and, as these messages cillied to keyboards, the day was soon broken. These messages continued to appear on other days in December and January and continued to cilli to keyboards or pronounceables, and with the knowledge of the message contents, it was possible to use them as cribs and sometimes to read them in depth as the message settings were known. It was discovered that the messages were "H" reports, originating from Durazzo, giving details of our air penetrations into enemy territory and there might be any number from 8 to 60 a day. They consisted of a reference number and a string of code names which changed monthly but could, in general, be predicted with fair accuracy. A report on Mustard published in January 1944 gives us a current example of a typical "H" message: H X VIER X MUMIE X PIRAT X JU WEL X LEUTE X PRIMA X PEDAL X INDER X HEQT, where the predictable code names are underlined. As a good example of the possibilities of depth reading we may cite 8 January, when two messages cillied to PAT and PAR and fitted thus:

Mustard

```
      R Y X V - - F S M S K X F
      H X E I N S X F R A N Z X
P M Y M E X F C F S M S K X F
Z U X H X Z W O X F R A N Z X
```

Of course, such gifts from the gods did not last for long, but the current crib situation on Mustard was clarified. The Einsatz cribs were still to the fore in somewhat changed guise. In our notation, there was the Einsatz Mark I, sent from Athens to Belgrade three times a day, about 0500, 1400 and 1800. Early in 1944 the wahlworts used were exclusively three to six letters long and at the appropriate hours of day it was better than an even money chance that they would be GUTEN ... MORGEN and GUTEN ... ABEND. In January 1944, the wahlwort GUTEN was used successfully for the first time but not the last time to eke out the otherwise short crib.

With the Einsatz cribs and a few inferior second strings, Mustard was broken happily and regularly throughout the summer of 1944 – in fact from 8 June to 15 July there were only two missing days. Latterly much of the damage was done by the Einsatz Mark II, a crib sent out several times a day from Durazzo. In January this crib, which had a long variable address, is described as "dingy", but it improved considerably from April onwards and eventually supplanted the Einsatz Mark I as the standard means of breaking Mustard.

After August 1944 there were fears that the Mustard position might be ruined by the spread of Reflector D. It was not, however, until October that Mustard used D and our breaking was hardly affected as the Balkan Mustard remained on B. In November, however, there was a sharp deterioration in the crib position due mainly to the confused Balkan situation, and on 1 December Mustard split at last into two keys, Mustard I for the West (on D and unbreakable), and Mustard II for the South, the Italian stations using D and the Balkan stations B. Several breaks of Mustard II were made in the first half of December, but the veteran cribs were now on their last legs, and in fact, 15 December 1944 was the last Mustard of any kind broken in Hut 6.

Western Mustard and Cress

A brief note should be added about Mustard in the West. Until after D-Day there was very little Western Mustard. Just after it for some time there was a good deal, but it came out until December on the same key as Mediterranean Mustard, so we were relieved of the hopeless task of trying to break it in its own right. Indeed, for some time after D-Day, Mustard became to some extent of operational importance, as the Western Mustard was giving re-encodements to Jaguar, one of the principal GAF Western keys. A second Y Air key that appeared in the West – Cress – was also much mixed up with Jaguar, and was broken several times on cribs that had migrated from Jaguar, or on re-encodements. We can never, however, be said to have got a firm hold of this minor key.

The end of the story

Little, indeed, can be said of Mustard in the last months of the war. Increasing preoccupation with more significant keys and the general problem of encoded callsigns had driven it more and more into the background, and the last reference in the Hut 6 weekly reports in January 1945 merely notes that it is in a very poor way. So far, indeed, had Mustard become a wraith of its former self that it hardly needed the last blow of encoded callsigns to banish it to oblivion – if, indeed, that word can ever be fittingly applied to a key that throughout its history did so much to enhance the gaiety of Hut 6.

Chapter 28
The V-Keys

General Introduction

Compared with the themes of other chapters, the present subject is very restricted and well-defined. It is concerned with three keys only – Corncrake, Ibis and Jerboa – which all flourished within the period March 1944 to the end of the war and were all concerned to a greater or lesser extent with the V1 and V2 weapons and the attacks on this country. Jerboa – an Air key – was concerned with V1 attacks, Corncrake and Ibis with V2. The difference was that Corncrake dealt with the experimental and preparatory side, while Ibis appeared in the period of rocket attacks and referred to the actual operations.

It seems convenient to treat these three keys within the same section, but they will be discussed in separate sub-sections. This can be the more easily done because there is no real geographic or cryptographic connection as has been the case with most groups of keys previously discussed. Corncrake, Ibis and Jerba have no point in common beyond the general subject with which they dealt. The keys are indeed not a regional or cryptographic but an intelligence unity – as such they were dealt with by the same section in Hut 3. In Hut 6 the keys were all treated on a Research basis – no attempt was made to break them currently by the Watch. Neither their intelligence importance nor their cryptographic stability demanded or justified such an attempt. Corncrake was dealt with by Army Research and Jerba by Air Research. Ibis, which only came into being after the abolition of Research, was a key of the Army Qwatch.

One other point should be mentioned before we discuss the keys in turn. The grouping of these three keys as V-keys should not allow us to forget that there were other keys that gave us valuable information about V-weapons. Brown, in particular gave, over a long period, hints on the developments of V1, and other keys such as Lily, Orange and Falcon gave more occasionally useful sidelights on these topics. But in the latter case the information was usually given incidentally in keys mainly concerned with other matters, while Brown (which in any case is fully dealt with in a separate section) covers the whole period of the war – not merely what we may call the "V-period". So now that due acknowledgement has been made of the contribution of these other keys we can still, with a clear conscience, style Corncrake, Ibis and Jerboa the V-keys par excellence.

Corncrake

The history of the breaking of Corncrake is so brief, and yet so full of interesting points while it lasted, that it is both possible and desirable to treat it in rather more detail than can generally be done in this history. In most cases our important colours were relatively long-lived and breaking extended over a period of many months or even years. In the case of Corncrake, the breaking period is from the middle of May 1944 to the end of July. The story really began about the middle of May 1944 when, in accordance with what was then established practice, a long message – actually a 7-teile – was brought into Army Research (this then contained all the Army cryptographers. The Army Watch was not set up till D-Day and the Watch was at this moment wholly concerned with Air keys) by a member of the TIS (Traffic Identification Section) for routine examination for cillies. This was a standard precaution specially intended for new and obscure groups so that no chance of a snap break should be missed, and ninety-nine times out of a hundred nothing came of it – the message was tossed aside after a hasty inspection. But this was the hundredth time. The delighted cryptographer discovered the cilli sequence FRI, FRA, FRE, FRO, FRU – settings that were amply confirmed by counts – and the day was quickly out on a bombe menu.

This initial break – E/6245 of 13 May – was a virtually unknown group. We had no reason to suspect it was of any unusual importance and the break was effected simply in the normal line of business. The motto of Hut 6 was to break everything possible whether it was considered important or not – a principle whose ultimate validity even on intelligence grounds was proved again and again, perhaps never more so than in the case of Corncrake (as E/6245 was soon named). The contents of Corncrake created an intelligence sensation in Hut 3. The exact significance of much of it was obscure but it clearly referred to scientific artillery experiments of importance and was described as an "Army equivalent of Brown III". Strong representations were made from the highest quarters in the Park in favour of a determined drive to break more days, and the work was at once set under foot, the new key being assigned to a parent, as was our usual practice.

The V-Keys

Enquiry from Sixta – who were always referred to on the emergence of new and obscure groups – showed that Corncrake had been known as a W/T group since December 1943 but could not be said to have passed traffic in any quantity at all till March 1944, and even in the early part of March traffic was very low. Signs of cillying had been received from time to time, and in fact one or two keys had been run unsuccessfully before the breakthrough in May. As often happens in such cases, one break was quickly followed by another – the 19 April came out on cillies plus STRIQ VIER VIER GEHEIM (which had appeared on 13 May).

The W/T system of Corncrake was simple. There were three stations – Heidelager, which acted as control, i.e. the messages fell by routeing into four classes under which the traffic was entered. The original couple of breaks, however, revealed nothing that could be regarded as a crib (a small compact system is unfavourable to the rise of cribs – e.g. Brown for most of its life. Brown's good crib period was when it was fully operational), and the possibilities of "cilli plus" menus were soon exhausted. So as a last resort we decided to run the Secret Tail – STRIQ VIER VIER GEHEIM – on all promising messages. This was a recognised line of attack on Army keys in general. In the case of Corncrake it was known to occur sometimes, it was also known to be very bad, but it was still considered worth running on the grounds that a large number of shots might break one or two days and so get us going. This is a line of attack that can only be practised with considerable reserves of bombe power such as we had in 1944.

The Secret Tail drive proved successful after a blank week. Out of approximately two dozen days run, two May days came out (later evidence showed that this was just about the percentage of the success we were entitled to expect). On this further evidence two more days were broken on cillies plus an address AN VERSUQSSTAB. It was only at this stage, i.e. when some half-dozen days had been broken, that what was to prove the best line of attack appeared. It was discovered that a number of messages to Kooslin started off with the "Wagnerian address": AN KDO STELLE SIEGFRIED and this was broken three days in the week ending 10 June and no fewer than eight days in the following week.

We had now secured a good entry into Corncrake and exploitation went forward rapidly. From the nature of this key, back days were as valuable as current breaks, and the traffic back to March (prior to which it was all too scrappy) was examined and produced on concurrently with the new traffic that came in. In all 33 Corncrake days were broken (2 March, 5 April, 11 May, 10 June, 5 July) of which precisely two-thirds were on cillies plus. A couple of days were even broken on a sporadic crib – numbered BESTANDSMELDUNG – which must have been sent out daily but was rarely passed on the air. It will thus be seen that Corncrake provided, in a peculiarly pointed form, an illustration of the fact that the best means of exploiting a key are not always obvious until a number of days have been broken on inferior and laborious methods. Corncrake met a sudden death with the evacuation of Heidelager on 23 July, and no traffic was passed after this date. Possibly this quick death was preferable to the slow decline of other keys. It is true indeed that in September a key was captured (Sonder Maschinenschlüssel P-W Kdo II) which decoded traffic on a couple of days that was Corncrake in content. But it proved impossible to break this revived Corncrake and traffic swiftly declined to lowest levels. The friends of Corncrake will prefer to forget this ineffectual ghost and to date the funeral obsequies of the true bird to the fateful 23 July.

Ibis

The history of the breaking of Ibis is even more highly concentrated than in the case of Corncrake. Apart from one belated success, all the breaks occurred in a period of about six weeks from 12 February to 24 March 1945. The traffic was, however, being examined for a considerable period before the initial break was secured. This traffic was in fact passed in small quantities as early as October 1944 (it will be remembered that the rocket attacks on London began in September), but it was not at first recognised as a separate group, and was blisted along with other miscellaneous scraps on a section of the composite Western Front blist. In November, however, the separate identity of Ibis became clear and the key was named and blisted separately.

From the W/T standpoint, Ibis (or the Z2 complex in the Sixta technical nomenclature) was a somewhat complicated study. At various times no fewer than ten stars were recognised which passed not only Enigma but quite large quantities of traffic in other ciphers. (Actually only three stars – 2, 4 and 8 – ever passed Enigma in any quantity). In fact, one method of identifying the Enigma traffic as Ibis was the appearance of the stations concerned passing these other ciphers, some of least at which were readily identifiable at sight. It was soon suspected – mainly by coincidence of messages with times of rockets – that the non-Enigma traffic at least in the Ibis system was concerned with the launching of rockets and this was eventually confirmed by breaks. This traffic, known as VERA, was dealt with by Major Owen's section – then in Block F.

As soon as it was established early in December that in all probability Ibis dealt with the V2 attacks it was recognised that it was highly desirable and might be most important to break the traffic. In complete contrast to the case of Corncrake, Ibis was attacked in full knowledge of its nature. But while this knowledge gave the cryptographer an added incentive to break the traffic, it did not give him the means to do so – cillying was non-existent, re-encodements could not be expected, and while certain possible routine messages did appear, too little was known in details of the units and personnel involved to make anything like cribbery possible We seemed indeed to be up against a blank wall, and in sheer desperation after the failure of several G-tails and the like, a mammoth 63-versional stagger was produced in a January day – the stagger being the number of a unit which it was thought might appear in a message. Fortunately it was not necessary to run this drive through to the end, as on later evidence it would certainly have failed.

But when the outlook was at its blackest, light shone out of the darkness. Towards the end of January we received information that a part of the VERA system had used Double Playfair that month, and that a number of days – eventually nine or ten – had been broken. Examination of these decodes revealed that they were all on Star 8 and consisted of messages to and from the launching batteries in Holland. What was still more important, the batteries were in the habit of each sending in an evening message to the control of the group, a list of the rocket launchings and some of these reports appeared cribbable. Finally, it was clear from the traffic on Ibis that while in January these reports (for some reason unknown to us) had passed on Double Playfair (because of this there was very little January Ibis, and as the cribs to be now described were absent, January Ibis was never broken and in fact not much tried), in November-December 1944 and January 1945 they had passed and were passing on Enigma.

Immediately a campaign was opened on these reports – Rocket Bradshaws as they were called – and on 12 February success was attained by the breaking of 4 February on one of these messages. This success was soon followed by others, and by the beginning of March 17 days had been broken on the Bradshaws, three February days and the rest December 1944. The reason for this preponderance of December days is rooted in the nature of the crib. The title "Rocket Bradshaw" must not be regarded as the name for a specific message, like most crib titles. It is rather a generic title for a group of messages from different stations and in many diverse forms and agreeing only in their general content, viz. that they all gave times for the departure of rockets from Holland. The times of arrival in England – four minutes later – were not given. These messages generally began with a "framework" which was followed by the times in the correct sequence. Now some of the stations involved varied the framework considerably, but one particular station was most consistent in using the form START AM day (x) month (x) UM time, and most days were broken on this. (Of course, the original evidence for forms used was the Playfair messages for January. The assumption was made that these would be the same as the Enigma forms in December and February. Fortunately this proved to be correct). The station in question was far more active in December than in February and this was the principal cause for the larger number of December breaks.

It was possible to obtain from Major Owen's section the times of rocket launchings as given by the various batteries in their low-grade ciphers, and in fact this information was passed on to us regularly. As these times ought in theory to be – and often were in practice – the same as those enciphered in the Rocket Bradshaw messages, it might have been thought that at least sometimes the whole message could be written out as a re-encodement, but for various reasons this was impossible. First, the times as given to us were not always precisely the same as in Enigma (this was apparently due to corruptions in the low-grade ciphers), and secondly, it was in practice impossible to make allowances for such parenthetic remarks in the fate of a particular rocket (e.g. "faulty start", "bursts where it stood" and similar misadventures) as did occur in Enigma, but were normally absent in the other ciphers. The first time of launch, however, was quite often used to eke out what would have been an insufficient menu: the hour (which was pretty safe) was generally all that was employed.

Also, towards the end of February and the beginning of March when what we have called the framework of Bradshaw had become uncribbable from the variety of forms, we tried the experiment of running the Time at End, i.e. trying the last time given to us at the end of the message. This usually failed, but did succeed in breaking three days – and every day counted on Ibis and indeed the V-keys generally. It was, however, sometimes possible on "nil return" days to write out the whole Rocket Bradshaw and several days were broken on: AM FUENF X EINS ZWO KEIN START and the like. There were also examples of a 14-letter message saying: HEUTE KEIN START or KEIN START HEUTE, but on broken days this, as a rule, gave us the cryptographer's hoodoo – a certain crib that is too short to run.

The breaking of one particular Ibis day – 1 February – is worth recalling. For the first four days of the month some of the traffic was in a curious "code" which was in fact little more than a kind of shorthand. The message consisted mainly of a string of numbers represented by their first letters (or in a few cases a letter when the initial letter would have led to ambiguity), i.e. L = 0, E = 1, Z = 2, D = 3, V = 4, F = 5, S = 6, I = 7, A = 8, N = 9, with X, Y and T as punctuation. It was possible on the evidence of the 2nd to the 4th to build up a rather stereotyped framework which was true for at any rate a fair number of messages, and this curious crib "XY" was run on two messages on the 1st and broke the day at the second attempt. The crib ran something like this (unusual as this was, it was not quite unprecedented – "Code Cribs" were not unknown on Blue and Brown):

PL ... X.Y..X.T..X.Y..X.T..X.Y..X.T..X.Y..X.T..X.Y..XYMSD..X

By 24 March, 22 Ibis days had been broken, 15 being in December, six in February and one in March. But the course of Ibis was now almost run. Traffic which had reached its flood at the beginning of February with 80 messages a day had declined to a trickle in March and vanished altogether in the last week of that month – a development not unconnected with the German collapse in the West and the consequent discontinuance of the rocket attacks. It was thus possible to write at the end of March: "To Ibis we hope to have bidden farewell". Yet this was not quite the end. From the nature of the traffic, the date of Ibis decodes was largely immaterial and in fact some of the best intelligence came from the December breaks. It was now admitted that the period December to March had been cryptographically exhausted, but little had been run on earlier days, and during April Hut 6 was approached by the intelligence experts of Hut 3 with a request for a drive on those early days.

An investigation was accordingly made and it was at once apparent that nothing could be done with the scraps of traffic in October, but November seemed to offer some possibilities and contact was made anew with Major Owen's section to secure the necessary information of continuity of callsigns and rocket-launching times. (It will have been noted that in the case of Ibis – as in that of Roulette – we were greatly indebted to external assistance in the preparation of material to run. On Ibis our dependence was not on the whole so great, though it must be admitted that the initial break would never have been secured without the crib evidence supplied by the work of Major Owen's section). A drive was prepared on the best days and sent to the American bombes, which throughout did invaluable work on Ibis. Honour was satisfied by the break of one day, 28 November, on 8 May 1945. Symbolically at least it was not unfitting that the final break of a V-key should be effected on V-Day.

Jerboa
The history of breaking Jerboa has analogies to both of the preceding stories. Like Ibis, Jerboa yielded all its breaks – 20 days in all – in a very short period, less than three weeks from 13 August to 2 September 1944. Like Ibis, again, Jerboa was only broken at all on evidence supplied by breaking a low-grade cipher while, like Corncrake, it had a second birth which was a sad anticlimax to its great days.

Jerboa first attracted notice as an Air group in Western Europe in July 1944 and a few G-tails were run. It was known from three-letter traffic (known as KLAVIER) passed by the same systems that it was connected with the launching of flying bombs but for some weeks there was no good line of attack. Eventually, however, an early morning routine message appeared which was thought on Klavier evidence to give the time of the next tuning message. We had had experience of this type of message on various Air keys and knew roughly the sort of forms to try, and on 13 August the 26 July Jerboa came out on the beginning: DER NAEQSTE ABSTIMMSPRUQ WIRD AM. In the following weeks this form broke many other days and several other forms were discovered by trial and error. To the end we were never able to claim that we could break any day – the Spruq did nor reveal all its twists and turns – but the final result of a swift campaign was that 20 days in July and August were broken on the Spruq and 1 September on a stray re-encodement from Jaguar. Traffic was always very low, sometimes, indeed consisting of the crib message only.

The V-Keys

Early in September Jerboa disappeared in consequence of the Allied advance through Belgium and France. Its absence was hardly regretted as the Spruq, the only means of breaking, had disappeared a few days earlier. By October even the name Jerboa had disappeared from our traffic statistics. In December again and in February-March 1945 there was a recrudescence of Jerboa traffic which reached its peak in the week ending 24 February with an average of 51 messages per day. In the next week this fell to 15 and then vanished for ever. It was quite impossible to find any entry into this revived Jerboa. The only ray of hope discovered was that there was some reason to believe that March Jerboa might be using Indigo, the GAF teleprinter key. But this proved a will-o'-the-wisp – the Indigo key was captured and did not work.

Importance of the V-keys

It was not in general the business of Hut 6 to form opinions on the relative intelligence importance of various keys. While, of course, in decisions of bombe policy, regard had to he paid to the intelligence rating of keys, we had recourse to the gradings periodically published by 3L. In accordance with this limitation of Hut 6's responsibility, the present history does not normally discuss in any detail the intelligence value of keys. But in the special case of the V-keys, their importance was of such a peculiar and unusual nature that it seems justifiable to pass beyond our usual limits and discuss the matter briefly and in general terms.

It would hardly be untrue to say that <u>in their own way</u> the V-keys were among the most important broken in Hut 6, but such a statement would be open to serious misapprehensions unless the nature of their importance was understood. The importance of other keys lay in the degree of their relevance to operations that were already in progress or impending. In general, the most important and urgent keys (as e.g. Ocelot and Jaguar among Air keys, Bantam and Puffin among Army keys) were those that were <u>immediately and tactically</u> concerned with current operations or <u>strategically</u> relevant to the conduct of future operations. The V-keys had none of this kind of importance, not even in the case of Ibis, which gave the times of rocket launches. This was because their reports were historical – so that even if the key could have been broken currently – the decoding of these messages would only have told us what rockets <u>had been</u> launched against England – a fact presumably already known. (Had the reports been of intentions to launch rockets at future times, the case might well have been different.) For this reason there was no special advantage in current breaking.

The breaking of V-keys was thus not of immediate operational significance, nor was it on the whole (once the attacks had started) of significance so far as counter-measures were concerned. The problem of defence against V1 had to be, and was, worked out in the practical field of action. The contributions of our intelligence to this lay in forecasting the probable scale and manner of the attacks before they took place. Against V2 there was from the nature of the weapon no effective defence (apart, of course, from the clearance of the rocket sites). The true significance of the V-keys lay in a longer issue – in their general relevance to the future of warfare.

It may be truly said that in the last year of the war the Germans were endeavouring – with such measures of success as the increasing pressure of the Allies permitted – to change over from one type of war to another. It has doubtless been true from the beginning that this has been the most scientific war in history, but it is clear that the Germans, towards the end, were finding their way to a kind of war that would be scientific in a still fuller sense – a type of war in which the scientist and the weapons he invents and develops will be the decisive factor, and no longer generals, admirals, armies and fleets. It may be claimed indeed that in their obsession with this new type of war – an obsession fully proved not only by the V-weapons they used, but even more so by those they planned – the Germans lost their sense of reality, that in reaching out after the future they sacrificed the present. But, however that may be, no one can doubt that the V1 and the V2 (to mention nothing more) are true forerunners of the weapons of a new war.

If it is admitted that the achievements and visions of the Germans in this last phase foreshadow the future lines of the advance of the art of war, then the true significance of the V-keys become apparent. It is obviously essential for our present and future research that we should know, in as precise detail as possible, exactly what the Germans have accomplished in these highly technical fields. Now that the war is over we have other means – e.g. interrogation of prisoners – available to discover the exact position reached by German practice and theory. But before the war ended the V-keys represented the best means of obtaining the necessary insight into German scientific progress. This is especially true of Corncrake, which dealt with matters on a higher level than the other keys.

The V-Keys

This peculiarly long-term importance explains how date and currency were largely irrelevant. There was a certain timelessness in the scientific context of much of these keys. Also, the matter was so technical that it was desirable to break as many days (of whatever date) as possible, as any new break might explain hitherto hopeless obscurities in a day already broken. Old days were at times indeed specially desired so that one might catch the beginning of some scientific argument. The difference between the importance of the V-keys and other keys broken by Hut 6 is illustrated by the fact that for most keys priority of decoding ran in backward order of date, while for the V-keys the converse was true.

To sum up in a sentence – while the importance of most Hut 6 keys was in the degree of their immediate relevance to current military operations, the ultimate significance of the V-keys lay in their long-term connection with the probable future of developments of science as applied to war. (To avoid any misapprehension of the writer's position, it should be stated that the above is not meant to convey any fatalistic acceptance of the inevitability of future wars. It merely involves what must surely be considered a justified conclusion about the nature of future wars (if these arise), and a belief that until the very possibility of future conflict is excluded forever, common prudence for the safety of our country demands that we take steps to ensure that our science is not behindhand in these technical developments – which in turn underlines the necessity for full knowledge about the scientific progress of our enemies.)

Chapter 29
Summary and Conclusions

General

"It may well be doubted whether human ingenuity can construct an enigma of the kind which human ingenuity may not, by proper application, resolve."

The celebrated dictum of Edgar Allan Poe, quoted above, was certainly proved true in the special case of German Enigma. Its universal truth, however, is most questionable except, indeed, in the general sense that what one human mind has conceived can hardly be essentially insoluble by another mind. But from the practical standpoint it is certainly possible to construct an unbreakable Enigma. What follows is an attempt to analyse the general concept of cipher security with illustrations from the Enigma and then to explain why the Germans so signally failed to attain it.

The first part of the discussion will, for the sake of universality, deal with the subject on the most general lines. Two assumptions only are made: (1) that the cipher system is high-grade, i.e. intended to resist cryptographic assault indefinitely, and (2) that the enemy cryptographer knows the construction of the permanent elements in the cipher system, i.e. in the case of a machine cipher the elements of the machine that cannot be changed every day are assumed known. In the special case of the German Enigma as used by the GAF and Army we postulate a knowledge of the wiring of wheels 1 to 5 and of Reflector B.

This second assumption is not unreasonable. Hut 6 possessed this knowledge from October 1939 and in warfare it is fairly certain that sooner or later the enemy will capture any machine that is used extensively. Hence no machine is secure unless messages enciphered by it are still unbreakable even after the machine has been captured. It is, of course, desirable that the machine itself should not be breakable on the material that can be expected to be available to the enemy. The German Enigma, as used in 1939, fulfilled this condition, as is made clear in the early part of this history.

Summary and Conclusions

How breaks are secured

If a cipher that is meant to be invulnerable to cryptographic attack is in fact broken, this must be due to a mistake or series of mistakes on the part of one of three classes of people:

1. The cipher may be broken through an error made by those people who originally invented the system, i.e. there has been an unnoticed fatal flaw in a system regarded as theoretically secure. (More will be said\ later on this concept of theoretical security).

2. The cipher may be broken through an error made by the people who made up the keys, e.g. by a non-random construction of keys. The most flagrant instance of error in Enigma was the key repeats in 1942. It must be noted that this type of error can scarcely give an initial break, but once discovered, it can help to give a whole series of subsequent breaks.

3. The cipher, even if secure in the above respects, may still be broken by errors on the part of the cipher clerks. An "error" in this case means any avoidable action by the clerk which permits the break. In the case of the Enigma, the most important such error was the providing of a crib or cilli. Other possibilities were the provision of ringstellung tips or depths. To exploit such errors, constant decode evidence is necessary, hence the maxim "Continued success depends on continued success".

How breaks can be prevented

The three desiderata
The general methods of preventing breaks, i.e. achieving full cipher security, are obvious from the foregoing analysis. All the above classes of mistakes must be avoided, and this gives us three conditions for the security of a cipher:

1. The cipher must be theoretically secure, i.e. unbreakable if no errors are made in the construction of keys and encoding of messages.

2. The construction of keys must be wholly random, i.e. there must be no rules of keys or key repeats (other than such repeats as can occur by chance).

3. The effect of possible errors by the cipher clerks must be obviated.

Of these conditions, the first two are the easiest to achieve. The Enigma machine, provided it is used with an adequate indicating system, does fulfil the first criterion. But the proviso is important: the first two indicating systems employed by the Germans were quite inadequate. In both cases the bombe provides an easy theoretical solution on a small amount of traffic, apart from the other methods that were used. It was not till May 1940 that the Germans, by introducing an adequate indicating system, made the Enigma theoretically unbreakable. The second proposition is largely independent of the exact cipher system employed. The Germans could have easily kept this condition – in fact they lamentably failed to do so, particularly on the Air keys. But in practice the third condition is the hardest to keep, and the main reason why theoretical security of the Enigma in May 1940 did not give practical security is that the Germans failed so badly to control their cipher clerks.

The two roads
How can the effect of possible errors by cipher clerks be obviated? There are, broadly speaking, two methods, but an essential preliminary to using either method effectively is for the men responsible for inventing the system to ask themselves what errors the cipher clerks can make, i.e. what he can do which will assist the enemy cryptographers to break the theoretically secure cipher (we are assuming that the first condition is satisfied). When, by an effort of imagination, this question has been answered, there remains the choice of two roads either to make the committing of these mistakes difficult or preferably impossible, or to make the machine so much more complicated that the mistakes of cipher clerks will not now be sufficient to break the cipher. An illustration from Enigma history will make this clearer.

To break the Enigma after May 1940 it was necessary to obtain a crib in the widest sense of the term. This was done through errors on the part of cipher clerks and we broke on cillies, cribs in the narrower sense and re-encodements. To stop this breaking the Germans had two policies – either to prevent their cipher clerks providing us with cillies, cribs or re-encodements or to complicate the machine so that it should become unbreakable on the material provided. In fact, they adopted both courses, the first by various anti-crib and anti-cilli devices (re-encodements were a blind spot throughout), and the second by the use of Reflector D which (if used universally on a key) made cillies and cribs of normal length unusable for breaking.

The principle of over-protection
If it is asked what is the best method to adopt to neutralise the effect of the encoders' mistakes – the method of prevention or the method of further complication – the writer's personal bias would be to answer "try both". Logically it may be answered that this is unnecessary – if one has so complicated the cipher that it cannot be broken on the length of crib that can be expected to be given as a result of encoders' errors, then it is, strictly speaking, a work of supererogation to eliminate cribs. But in practice it is very difficult to be certain that one has fully allowed for all the mechanical cryptographic aids the enemy may invent (it does not appear from our interrogations of German cryptographers that they had conceived the possibility of the bombe), and so nothing can be lost and much may be gained by making assurance doubly sure. Thus, for example, if one had a cipher which – as far as one knew – could not broken on a crib of less than one thousand letters, it would still be a useful precaution to try and eliminate cribs of 30 or 40.

The German Enigma

Theoretical and practical security
The Germans attained theoretical security in their use of the Enigma in May 1940, but on most keys they never attained practical security. The German experience provides for all posterity a classic demonstration of the yawning gulf between these two objectives.

The failure of German efforts
Of the three conditions of cipher security the Germans achieved the first, never properly realised the importance of the second, and failed despite great efforts and a wealth of ingenuity to achieve the third. The particular errors they made in their use (or often misuse) of the security devices they adopted have been pointed out previously, and it is noteworthy how

often one type of error occurs. Again and again, the Germans introduced new devices in a piecemeal and half-hearted way = "too little and too late" should be found engraved on the heart of the German cryptographer. Such diverse devices as wahlworts and Reflector D all suffered from this radical fault.

Air and Army security
It is only fair to say, however, that certain parts of the German Enigma complex were more security conscious than others, and by their relative successes, show up badly the weaknesses of other sections. In particular, Army keys were more secure than Air and hence were, for most of the war, harder to break. This was due to the following reasons:

1. Army keys in general obeyed much better than Air keys the obvious precaution of keeping traffic down to a minimum by the use of landlines, omission of unnecessary reports and other measures.

2. Army keys avoided many of the Air type of cribs – especially the longer lived weather cribs such as the Czech Wueb.

3. Compared to Air keys, Army keys were usually constructed in a random manner. Their rules and repeats were much fewer.

4. While the Army did not use some of the Air security devices, such as Enigma Uhr, it made much better use of the devices it did employ. One need only contrast the correct use of Reflector D by the Army with its misuse by the GAF.

It is true that something can be said on behalf of the GAF. The air was much more continually in progress than the war on land, and the generally wider distribution of GAF units made the Army reliance on landlines impossible. Moreover, weather reports were much more important for the GAF than for the Army, and the larger number of Air keys that had to be made up was certainly one reason for the labour-saving devices of their keymakers. While these considerations cannot be regarded as a valid defence for the GAF against the charge of cipher insecurity, they may justly be pleaded in mitigation of sentence. But perhaps the fairest moral to draw is that the more any Service is continually involved in operations, the more vital is the necessity for constant supervision of cipher usage if security is to be preserved.

Summary and Conclusions

The special case of Greenshank

In particular, Greenshank shows how secure the Enigma could be made. If we do not reckon as two, the breaking of the A and B keys on the same day, only nine days were broken on the double indicating system – nine breaks in five years – and seven of these were re-encodements. So, if the Germans had changed the Time of Origin on re-encodements – one of the security measures they never thought of – we might have had only two breaks in five years!

How to achieve security

Before summing up the results reached, two subsidiary points should be mentioned – the value of W/T camouflage measures and the possibility of radical improvements to the Enigma machine. On the first point, W/T camouflage, while in the writer's opinion such matters are not of absolutely primary importance in defeating enemy cryptographers – not, that is, in comparison with cryptographic terrors like a new reflector – they are nonetheless useful in a subsidiary way. Every measure which makes accurate key identification of messages from the outside difficult or impossible should be adopted as a matter of course as a supplement to the measures to be described.

On the second point, it is certainly possible to introduce very radical improvements to the Enigma machine as used by the Germans, In particular, the use of a more irregular motion for the wheels and the abandonment of the reciprocal property of the machine would enhance its security value. The first reform at least was definitely contemplated by the Germans, as is shown by an interesting interrogation of Dr. Fricke, one of their cryptographers – he evidently considered the uniformity of the wheel motion as one of the weaknesses of the Enigma machine. But I think it may be claimed that such extensive changes alter the very type of the machine. Of course, this is purely a matter of definition, but an Enigma-type machine is generally held to be (1) a machine with a uniform motion consisting of the right-hand wheel turning over constantly and the other wheels moving at regular intervals, and (2) a machine where the text is encoded by a there-and-back process, i.e. by the enciphering proceeding through the wheels from right to left and back again via a reflector, possibly (but not necessarily) with a stecker substitution at each end. Such a machine is necessarily reciprocal.

So, in what follows, I propose to ignore the more fundamental improvements mentioned above, and to consider the more restricted problem of how any Enigma-type machine can be made secure. The recommendations I will make underline clearly where the Germans went wrong.

1. The security of the machine should be such that even if cribs of normal length are available it should be unbreakable – for this purpose the German Enigma of 1939 is inadequate. The Enigma plus a pluggable reflector is a good answer provided the reflector plugging is an integral part of the key and no fixed reflector is still used. Pluggable wheels might be an even better solution in theory, though possibly too complicated for actual use. Any such plugging should be changed daily.

2. As a safeguard against underestimation of the enemy's mechanical ingenuity, stringent anti-crib measures should be enforced. These should include:

    a. Prevention of cillies, preferably by an indicating system which makes this form of carelessness impossible;

    b. Prevention of cribs by a definite attempt to eliminate as far as possible all routine messages (particularly nil returns) and by use of the "cut" in all messages (see the discussion on wahlworts);

    c. Prevention of the discovery and use of re-encodements by their elimination as far as possible through a carefully planned system of key distribution and the systematic camouflage of such as must remain by changing the Time of Origin, altering the form etc.;

3. All keys must be constructed in a random manner.

The Necessity of Supervision

It only remains in concluding this subject to emphasise the absolute necessity of a strict system of supervision over keymakers and cipher clerks alike, if the second and third recommendations are to be carried out. It was here that the Germans failed so badly. They had a system of supervi-

Summary and Conclusions

sion, certainly, and from time to time an exceptionally zealous Security Officer issued an anti-crib regulation or rapped a negligent operator over the knuckles. But it is clear from the German failure on the subject of cribs that their supervisory system was not thorough enough or sufficiently co-ordinated.

One distinct weakness was that their cryptographers were kept too much in the dark. They were never allowed to inspect genuine traffic or keys, according to Dr. Fricke – consequently they could not check whether the second and third recommendations were being obeyed, and they often were not. It may be shrewdly suspected that the German cryptographers would have been horrified at their cipher clerks' neglect of security and their frequent misuse of the Enigma, but as they were not permitted to inspect genuine traffic they could not discover the mistakes actually made. Hence, no doubt, their frequent barking up a wrong tree. Note the German obsession on the subject of depth, which occurred so seldom that it was not an important factor in breaking. Also, many of the mistakes for which we criticised the German cryptographers were probably due not so much to their errors, but to the disregard by the German authorities of their experts' advice.

The general moral seems to be that it is a mistake on fancied grounds of security to keep your own cryptographers in the dark. If they are to be sure that the systems they have invented give not merely theoretical security but actual security as used, they must be allowed to inspect occasionally, at least, actual keys and encodes. Theoretical security is not enough, and practical security can only be attained by a constant intelligent supervision of practice.

NOTE TO THE APPENDICES ON KEYS
ENGLISH KEY NAMES OF AIR AND ARMY KEYS

The early days
In the early days of Hut 6 the number of Air and Army groups intercepted was so small that the provision of English covernames was a very minor problem. As soon as the continuity of a group was established it was named after a colour – thus the GAF groups in December 1939 were Red and Blue and the Army group, Green. Colour names were chosen because messages could then be identified by marking them with correct coloured pencil. Before a definite long-term continuity had been established, groups were distinguished by frequency names, e.g. E/4700 Group, E/5420 Group. Certain groups, because their function was known, were given a purely functional name, e.g. Police, Railway, AF 5 (Army Formation 5).

This method of naming was considered adequate until early in 1941, but by this time the number of keys had already greatly increased and the extension of the North African and Russian theatres promised many more. The position was carefully reviewed and the authority for naming all Hut 6 keys vested in a single individual, whose task it was to keep liaison with other sections to prevent any possible confusion arising from the duplication of key names. Later, a central Government Code and Cypher School authority was set up and the naming of Hut 6 keys became part of its commitment. The realms of ornithology were allotted to the Army and bird names became the distinguishing mark of Army keys until the end of the war. Air keys were more strictly categorised, the divisions being distinguished by the names of colours, flowers, vegetables, insects, mammals and jungle animals.

Air keys

    a. **Colours**: Colour names were retained for GAF keys of the "general" class. At the time of the change there were only Red,

Blue and Pink, though later it was necessary to add Indigo and Puce. The old Army key, Green, was renamed Greenshank, but Brown, the key of the "beam bombers", retained its original name, partly for sentimental reasons, but mostly because source information had been passed on for some time under that name and confusion in intelligence circles might have resulted from a change.

b. **Flowers**: Flower names were given to the Luftgau keys because the principal Luftgau key had formerly been called Violet – a colour name.

c. **Vegetables**: Vegetable names were allotted to the weather keys and also to certain technical keys such as Mustard, the key of the GAF Y Service.

d. **Insects**: Insect names were given to Fliegerkorps keys, introduced by the Germans in January 1942.

e. **Mammals**: Mammal names were reserved for Geschwader keys, which had a most disconcerting habit of appearing and disappearing – again at short notice – a trait which made the correct identification and naming of such keys a rather tricky business.

f. **Jungle Animals**: The names of jungle animals were assigned to the Luftflotte keys, a fairly late key division in the GAF. The choice of this type of key arose in the following manner. A key appeared in Norway on the stars of Fliegerführer Luftflotte 5 and was named Lobster to bring it into line with the only other known Fliegerführer key, Scorpion, the key of Fliegerführer Afrika. (Fliegerführer keys as such were never distinctly recognised as a separate category since they were Sonderschlüssel, and when later two more Fliegerführer keys appeared, they were called Yak and Llama, names having no relation to Scorpion). The name Lobster was objected to by the Naval Section on the grounds that it would lead to confusion with their "marine" classes for naval keys. About the same time it was discovered that Lobster had a wider scope than was originally thought, and was in fact more likely to be the key of Luftflotte 5 itself. The name was therefore altered to Lion and a new key category started.

There were certain exceptions to the system as it has been outlined above, for, although this was in essence the theoretical basis upon which all GAF keys were named, in practice various inconsistencies developed, the result either of identification to the wrong category by us, or a German alteration in the status of a unit after its key had received an English covername. In either case it was difficult to change an established name without threatening to disrupt intelligence continuity. In all fairness to those responsible for identifying keys, it should be noted that discrepancies were for the most part the result of German changes and not of misidentification. The two examples which follow will make the exact nature of the problem clearer:

1. When the system of nomenclature was originally drawn up, all Luftflotten used Red – the general key. In January 1942 the key of Fliegerkorps I, in the North Prussian sector, was named Mosquito, but in July of the same year Fliegerkorps I was transferred to the south and given the title of Luftwaffen Kdo. Don. As, however, it left its key, callsigns and frequencies behind with Luftflotte 1, it was necessary to retain the name Mosquito in the north and introduce a new name – Ermine – in the south. The matter was further complicated by the fact that in February 1943, Luftwaffen Kdo. Don. reverted to its old status and was again known as Fliegerkorps I. This meant that, by then, both Mosquito and Ermine were inconsistent as regards name categories, with the original schedule. They remained so to the end of the war.

2. The key known as Skunk, when it first appeared, was on a Geschwader network and was named on that basis. Later it was shown that the key was really the property of Fliegerkorps VIII, but at the special request of Hut 3 the name was retained. When, on 1 February 1945, the Germans introduced changing frequencies and encoded callsigns in the GAF, it was realised that some new system of temporary nomenclature would have

Appendices

to be introduced to deal with groups for which a discriminant repeat had been established, but which were otherwise unidentified. It was decided to issue such predictions under "County" names, i.e. E/York, E/Kent, to the stations and Sixta until a more definite identification could be suggested on the strength of new source and W/T evidence. The supposition was that such names would be shortlived, but in actual practice it soon became apparent that many of the groups (or keys) so named were "new" keys in the sense that they had no counterpart under the old key categories. They were in fact mainly keys issued by local units to bridge gaps in key distribution caused by the general disorganisation of the German lines of communication during the last few months of the war. English county names were used for the month of February, Scottish for March, American states (by a polite extension of the term) for April, and Irish for May.

The use of numeral and letter suffixes with Air key names requires a word of explanation. With very few exceptions (e.g. Brown I, II and III, Mustard I and II) Roman numerals were used to distinguish the Ersatz key from the Gebrauch in the cases of a compromise (Jaguar I = Gebrauch key, Jaguar II = Ersatz key). Letter suffixes were used as follows:

A = last month's key (i.e. Jaguar of March used in April = Jaguar A).

B = Ersatz key of current month likely to be used as a Gebrauch key of following month.

C = Either a compromised current key, or the key intended as the Ersatz of the following month, used as the Gebrauch key of the current month.

X = Any key used in a hatted order.

Army keys

It has been stated that Army key nomenclature was based wholly on bird names. In the following discussion, however, SS keys and the Railway keys are, for the sake of compactness, being considered in the same category. Although all Army keys were named under the single category of bird names, there was some attempt made to associate keys in certain areas with definite classes of birds. For example, birds of prey were used for the Eastern Front (e.g. Vulture, Kite, Kestrel) and "Barnyard" names for the Western Front (e.g. Duck, Bantam, Chicken).

It may be observed in connection with Army key nomenclature that certain types of key (Armee, Heeres, Wehrmacht) had two or more "versions". One, the **M/S** for **Geheim** traffic; two, the **Stabs M/S** for **Geheimekommandosache** or Chefsache; and three, rarely used, the OKH or **Offizier** key, the highest grade Army Enigma key. As it would only have complicated matters to have assigned a different name to each "version", it became the convention to refer to them as I, II and III respectively (e.g. Puffin I, Puffin II and Puffin III). Various exceptions to this general rule crept in from time to time, so that I and II following an Army key name might occasionally have reference to some purely functional association (e.g. Osprey I and II and the Railway key Rocket I and II). An attempt was made, however, to remove the confusion wherever possible, unless the type of key involved (as in Rocket I and II) made any real confusion unlikely. The Army use of Roman numerals with key names must thus be sharply distinguished from Air usage.

The first SS key – intercepted from early in 1939 – was finally named Orange in April 1940. It was thus originally a colour key. With the appearance of other SS keys, however, it was found more constructive to look upon Orange as a fruit and to name the other SS keys by fruit names (e.g. Quince, Medlar, Apple). The key originally known as Railway retained its name until October 1943, when it became Rocket. As Rocket, however, soon after became paired with another Railway key called Stephenson, it was considered that the association was too obvious to be secure. As a result, the railway keys were renamed after weapons (e.g. Culverin, Blunderbuss), Rocket retaining its original name as being equally proper in the new category. The key known as TGD, probably the key of the Reichsicherungsdienst, was named from one of its early fixed callsigns, a name which was left as undisturbed as the key was unbroken throughout the war.

Towards the close of the war, when the tide was turning more and more seriously against the Germans, two types of special key were brought into common use in both GAF and Army. The first – **Sondermaschinenschlüssel** – already noticed in the discussion of "County" covernames in the Air, likewise appeared in the Army, and were most usually allotted to isolated units garrisoning fortresses. The second – **NOT-keys** – were for units, both Air and Army, in

Appendices

similar circumstances or for units with no other machine key available. Sondermaschinenschlüssel were in all respects quite normal keys, but as their days of validity were generally considered to be numbered, they did not – if Army – receive a bird name but were distinguished by geographical location (e.g. E/Lorient, E/Dunkirk). In the Air, the use of County names has already been noted, and before 1 February covernames based on frequency were quite usual. If, however, any Air or Army Sonder key was expected to function permanently, it was given a regular covername (e.g. Armadillo, a Flugsicherungs key, Corncrake – the key of P.W.Kdo.II. NOT-keys, both in the Air and Army, were named from their single discriminant (e.g. NOT/HNG). There was one exception to this rule – NOT/Guernsey.

Note to Appendix I
First Break of Keys

It seems fitting to conclude the series of key histories with a chronological list of the first breaks of every key that was given an individual key name. This will give a picture of the constant expansion of the field of our breaking, for instance, up to the end of 1940 we had broken eight different keys, by the end of 1941 the figure was 25, and in the subsequent years it rose to 61, 108, 170 and finally 181. It will be realised that a number of difficult points have arisen in compiling this list and it has seemed best, for consistency, to adhere rigidly to certain rules.

Dates: The date given is that of the key broken, not the date when the break was effected – this was usually later, sometimes much later. Also, it is not necessarily the first day we broke of the key in question, but the earliest date among the full tale of broken days. Probably in most cases one would get the same answer, but on keys like Corncrake and Ibis there is a distinct difference. Moreover, the few breaks prior to 1940 are ignored – this is because of some uncertainty in identification, as breaks prior to 1940 are not given key names in our records.

Breaks excluded: On the principle of only including named keys in the list, breaks of numbered groups, NOT-keys, Barnyards and County keys have been excluded (except in a few cases where, e.g. a numbered group has, since the first break, been given a definite name). Rocket I and Tricycle breaks are also omitted – the former because Rocket I is being dealt with in Mr Twinn's History, the latter because Tricycle keys were never recognised as proper Hut 6 keys and were eventually taken over by Mr Twinn's section. Furthermore, suffixes (which on Air keys at least meant usually a replacement of a compromised key) are not regarded as a different key – i.e. no separate account is taken of Red II, Gadfly IIA and the like. On Army keys, I and II are naturally counted as different, but no account is taken of III etc., which could merely indicate a replacement except, of course, in such clear cases as Chaffinch III and Kestrel III, which were quite distinct keys. These omitted breaks are very numerous indeed, particularly in the last year of the war. Had they all been included, the following list would have been double its present length.

Breaks included: The breaks include breaks by capture – this is sometimes mentioned in the last column, but not necessarily always. This list was compiled from our key books which made no separate mention of captured keys.

Composite breaks: During 1943 it was discovered that certain normally separate keys were using the same machine settings for a month at a time. Such composite breaks are here only reckoned as new if none of the components had previously been broken. If a composite break is reckoned, later independent breaks of one component are not reckoned as new.

Comment: Under this head there are only inserted points of special interest with regard to number of breaks or duplication of a key name. More general details of the key must be sought in the separate key histories or in the lists of Air and Army keys identified (see Appendices II, III and IV).

Authority: The authority from which this list is compiled is the series of keybooks kept currently by Hut 6 – ultimately the sole authority on such matters. It is thus almost inevitable that any errors made in this current record – e.g. in identification or naming of keys – will be transferred to the present list, but the wholesale exclusion of unnamed keys does at least remove the most doubtful category.

APPENDIX I:
FIRST BREAK OF KEYS

	DATE	KEY NAME	COMMENT
1	6-Jan-40	Red	
2	18-Jan-40	Green	Later called Greenshank
3	29-Jan-40	Blue	
4	10-Apr-40	Yellow	
5	26-May-40	Purple	Not broken again
6	2-Sep-40	Brown	
7	10-Dec-40	Orange	
8	24-Dec-40	Violet	
9	28-Feb-41	Light Blue	
10	26-Mar-41	A F 5	Later called Chaffinch
11	8-May-41	Onion	
12	27-Jun-41	Vulture	
13	27-Jun-41	Mustard	
14	9-Jul-41	Kestrel	Later split into four keys as under
15	31-Jul-41	Leek	
16	10-Aug-41	Kestrel III	
17	16-Aug-41	Kestrel I	
18	20-Aug-41	Kestrel II	
19	21-Oct-41	Vulture II	
20	12-Nov-41	Chaffinch II	
21	14-Nov-41	Chaffinch I	
22	23-Nov-41	Phoenix	By capture
23	27-Nov-41	Kestrel IV	
24	1-Dec-41	Orange II	
25	17-Dec-41	Brown II	
26	1-Jan-42	Hornet	First day of key's existence
27	1-Jan-42	Wasp	First day of key's existence

Appendices

	DATE	KEY NAME	COMMENT
28	1-Jan-42	Pink	
29	1-Jan-42	Gadfly	First day of key's existence
30	2-Jan-42	Kite	
31	7-Jan-42	Cockroach	
32	12-Jan-42	Foxglove	
33	12-Jan-42	Locust	
34	17-Jan-42	Primrose	
35	22-Jan-42	Gannet I	Not broken again
36	20-Feb-42	Raven III	Not broken again
37	3-Mar-42	Orange III	
38	4-Mar-42	Beetle	
39	8-Mar-42	Raven I	
40	7-Apr-42	Snowdrop	
41	8-Apr-42	Garlic	
42	13-Apr-42	Chaffinch III	
43	22-Apr-42	Scorpion	
44	9-May-42	Daffodil	
45	11-May-42	Raven II	
46	18-May-42	Skylark	
47	8-Jun-42	Mosquito	
48	16-Jun-42	Skunk	
49	15-Jul-42	Weasel	
50	23-Jul-42	Thrush	
51	10-Aug-42	Narcissus	
52	14-Aug-42	Quince I	
53	24-Aug-42	Rook I	Not broken again
54	2-Sep-42	Celery	
55	24-Sep-42	Crab	
56	30-Sep-42	Osprey	
57	20-Nov-42	Bullfinch	
58	28-Nov-42	Mallard	
59	2-Dec-42	Goldfinch	Really Bullfinch A

	DATE	KEY NAME	COMMENT
60	16-Dec-42	Robin	No broken again
61	31-Dec-42	Brown "S"	
62	2-Jan-43	Hawfinch	Really Chaffinch I
63	8-Jan-43	Dodo	
64	21-Jan-43	Porcupine	
65	10-Feb-43	Bullfinch II	
66	12-Feb-43	Merlin	
67	13-Feb-43	Nuthatch	Called at the time E/8738
68	21-Feb-43	Hedgehog	
69	22-Feb-43	Falcon I	
70	25-Feb-43	Ermine	
71	1-Mar-43	Orchid + Tulip + Clover	
72	5-Mar-43	Dragonfly	
73	9-Mar-43	Shamrock	
74	6-Apr-43	Sparrow	
75	1-May-43	Lily	
76	8-May-43	Cormorant	Only broken a few times
77	12-May-43	Aster	
78	13-May-43	Lobster	
79	16-May-43	Buzzard	
80	2-Jun-43	Albatross	
81	2-Jun-43	Albatross II	
82	14-Jun-43	Lion	
83	30-Jun-43	Mayfly	
84	3-Jul-43	Squirrel	
85	23-Jul-43	Puffin II	Called at the time Puffin
86	1-Aug-43	Puma	
87	2-Aug-43	Gannet II	
88	4-Aug-43	Sheep	Really Primrose B
89	13-Aug-43	Dingo	
90	23-Aug-43	Shrike I	
91	24-Aug-43	Peregrine	

Appendices

	DATE	KEY NAME	COMMENT
92	2-Sep-43	Goshawk	Later found to equal Kite
93	9-Sep-43	Firefly	
94	13-Sep-43	Poppy	
95	15-Sep-43	Puffin I	Called at the time Jay
96	18-Sep-43	Wryneck I	
97	20-Sep-43	Gorse	
98	22-Sep-43	Brown III	
99	3-Oct-43	Indigo	
100	3-Oct-43	Shrike II	
101	11 Oct 43 onwards	Brown IV	
102	13-Oct-43	Stork	
103	22-Oct-43	Yak	
104	23-Oct-43	Quince II (Italian)	See section on the SS keys
105	16-Nov-43	Leveret	
106	16-Nov-43	Woodpecker	
107	29-Nov-43	Magpie	
108	15-Dec-43	Bullfinch (Italian)	See section on Italian Army Keys
109	31-Jan-44	Wryneck II	
110	9-Feb-44	Llama	
111	10-Feb-44	Roulette I	
112	5-Feb-44	Leopard	
113	11-Feb-44	Jaguar	
114	14-Feb-44	Owl	
115	27-Feb-44	Chicken I	
116	1-Mar-44	Bantam I	
117	3-Mar-44	Owl II	
118	5-Mar-44	Wagtail	
119	17-Mar-44	Nightjar	
120	23-Mar-44	Corncrake	
121	27-Mar-44	Pelican	
122	1-Apr-44	Quince II	

	DATE	KEY NAME	COMMENT
123	1-Apr-44	Pumpkin	
124	3-Apr-44	Coot	Possibly the same as Kite
125	17-Apr-44	Avocet	
126	24-Apr-44	Cricket	
127	1-May-44	Gnat	
128	30-May-44	Bantam II	
129	30-May-44	Kingfisher II	
130	31-May-44	Ocelot	
131	6-Jun-44	Medlar	
132	9-Jun-44	Duck I	
133	9-Jun-44	Duck II	
134	9-Jun-44	Armadillo	By capture
135	11-Jun-44	Raccoon	
136	11-Jun-44	Pullet	
137	13-Jun-44	Cress	
138	15-Jun-44	Penguin	
139	16-Jun-44	Platypus	
140	19-Jun-44	Peewit	
141	29-Jun-44	Kingfisher	
142	5-Jul-44	Jerboa	
143	7-Jul-44	Nightjar	
144	16-Jul-44	Glowworm	
145	1-Aug-44	Emu I	
146	1-Aug-44	Emu II	
147	2-Aug-44	Chipmunk	Not broken again
148	3-Aug-44	Flamingo	
149	6-Aug-44	Blunderbuss	Called at the time Rocket II
150	10-Aug-44	Dodo II	
151	21-Aug-44	Grapefruit	Not broken again
152	5-Sep-44	Gorilla	
153	8-Sep-44	Gosling	
154	12-Sep-44	Quail	Called at the time Vulture G

Appendices

	DATE	KEY NAME	COMMENT
155	2-Oct-44	Lorient	
156	2-Oct-44	Culverin	Called at the time Stephenson
157	5-Oct-44	Falcon II	
158	10-Oct-44	Pigeon	
159	16-Oct-44	Diver	
160	21-Oct-44	Sparrow I	
161	21-Oct-44	Sparrow II	
162	2-Nov-44	Quail II	
163	8-Nov-44	Egret	
164	21-Nov-44	Flycatcher	
165	28-Nov-44	Ibis	
166	1-Dec-44		Wallflower
167	2-Dec-44	Gentian	
168	8-Dec-44	Avocet II	
169	10-Dec-44	Violet	Not same key as Violet 1940-1941
170	15-Dec-44	Chimpanzee	
171	15-Jan-45	Whimbrel	
172	1-Feb-45		Oriole
173	16-Feb-45	Roulette III	Not broken again
174	1-Mar-45	Grouse	By capture
175	1-Mar-45	Marmoset	By capture
176	14-Mar-45	Plum	
177	17-Mar-45	Hummingbird	
178	11-Apr-45	Moth	
179	23-Apr-45	Monkey	
180	26-Apr-45	Whinchat	
181	28-Apr-45	Goat	

NOTE TO APPENDICES II - IV
GENERAL USE AND DISTRIBUTION OF GAF KEYS

Luftwaffenführungschlüssel: Pink. It was used for encoding messages of secret content on the Führungsnetz, and was strictly for the use of officers. It was identified periodically on the Autos and very occasionally elsewhere, e.g. the Jägerleitkreis and the S E Recce following a compromise of Red. But, generally speaking, its distribution was confined to Luftflotten and other Auto subscribers.

Luftwaffenmaschinenschlüssel: Red. Also referred to as **Luftwaffenmaschinenschlüssel allgemeinbereich** or **gesamtbereich**. According to GAF signals regulations it was for "secret and open W/T messages on the Führungsnetz and on the Befehlsnetz of a Luftflottenkommando where a special key had not been issued." Actually, its distribution was wider than that – it was recognised to be in use by OKL down to Flughafenbereiche and Geschwader, and originally to Fliegerhorste and Gruppen. In the winter of 1939-1940, it became the general operational key and was used for major campaigns, e.g. in the Balkans and France. For the North African campaign, however, a special key was issued, known as **Brigitte (Light Blue)** which lasted until the end of 1941. After 1 January 1942, Red was normally restricted to Luftflotten as Fliegerkorps were issued with separate keys. Its importance and bulk dropped when Luftflotten keys began to appear largely on the Autos in September 1944, and in the last few months it was replaced to a considerable extent by Sonderschlüssel, owing to compromises and difficulties in distributing the new keys.

The use of Red outside the Autos was widespread and may be classified as follows. It was used by:

i. Units subordinate to or operating for O.B.d.L. – the Courier Service and KG 200.

ii. Y Service, for administrative matters on the network of IV LN Regiment 351 in the West.

iii. The other branches of the armed forces, e.g. Fallschirm AOK 1 after the demise of Firefly, when the normal key was believed to be an Army one, and naval stations in the Mediterranean.

Appendices

iv. The Hermann Göring Division.
v. Fags, e.g. Abdulla – LG1 and Astoria – KG 4.

After the introduction of Luftflotten keys in 1943 Red did not often appear on the Befehlssterne, except in the case of Luftflotte Reich, where no differentiation could be observed between the use of Red and Hyena. It remained, however, the normal key on the Recce stars and appeared from time to time on the Luftgau stars.

Luftflottemaschinenschlüssel. Two types of key must be considered in this category – (a) the ordinary key for general purposes, and (b) the Fliegerverbindungsschlüssel:

1. (1) These were introduced about the beginning of 1943 – originally there was no place for them in the key set-up. They were used on the Autos, the Befehlsterne and by subordinate units not possessing a key of their own – i.e. Fliegerkorps and Luftgau. Thus Gefechtsverband Kowalewski used Jaguar, the general key of Luftflotte 3, to which it was subordinated. The distribution, however, included Luftgaue and Flughafenbereiche, and sometimes Luftflotte keys were identified by discriminants on the Luftgau stars. Certain units used the Luftflotte key irrespective of subordination, e.g. the use of Jaguar by Versuchsverband O.B.d.L. in March 1945. In Italy and Norway after October 1944 one key only was valid each month in each area, in which both operational and administrative messages were encoded. Though in the first place they were the keys intended by the Cipher Office for Luftgaue, in later distributions the keys belonged to the LW Kdo. class. When some of the Luftflotten were regraded, Luftflotte 3 to LW Kdo. West (September 1944), Luftflotte 2 to Komm. Gen. Italien and Luftflotte 5 to Komm. Gen. Norwegen, a new class of key was formed, recognised as the "LW Kdo. class". There were instances of upgrading which altered Fliegerkorps keys into LW Kdo. or Luftflotte keys – Fliegerkorps VIII (original key Beetle) was replaced by the staff of Fliegerkorps V, which was upgraded to LW Kdo. Ost, and in May 1943 to Luftflotte 6. The W/T organisation and cipher material remained, so Beetle became, in actual fact, a Luftflotte instead of a Fliegerkorps key. Further

examples are the regrading of Fliegerkorps X to LW Kdo. Süd Ost in the same month, and the assumption of Mosquito, key of Fliegerkorps I, by Luftflotte 1.

2. (2) Fliegerverbindungsschlüssel was used by liaison officers with Army formations, and by close Recce units, and was introduced in March 1943. It was classed by the OKL Cipher Office with the ordinary Luftflotte or LW Kdo. key. Ocelot, Flivo key of Luftflotte 3, was issued as the adjacent key to Jaguar (i.e. they had consecutive key numbers), both before and after the regrading to LW Kdo. West – sufficient evidence to disprove the original theory that it constituted a type of Fliegerkorps key, In addition to normal distribution and use, Puma and Ocelot both passed on the Autos in considerable quantity for rapid notifications to OKL, and the latter occasionally on Western Army links.

Fliegerkorpsmaschinenschlüssel was generally confined to Fliegerkorpstars, but was identified now and then on the Autos, when its appearance caused much confusion. Occasionally it was used on the Flugsicherung network, and widely by fags. Where subordinated to a Fliegerkorps, Fliegerführer and Jafue used the Fliegerkorpsschlüssel, otherwise the appropriate Luftgau key, or in some cases, a Sonderschlüssel. The peculiarity of Fliegerdivision 9 possessing a key of its own in the Fliegerkorps class is explained by the fact that it was really the key of Fliegerkorps IX, whose function and cipher material it assumed after Fliegerkorps IX moved north to replace Jagdkorps I.

Jagdkorpsmaschinenschlüssel. Once again, this class of key did not appear in the original key set-up, but was formed from the Fliegerkorps class when Jagdkorps I and II came into being. Distribution was to all subordinate units down to Gruppen and to authorities to whom the Jagdkorps was itself subordinate or with whom it co-operated. Thus **Cockroach** (JK 1) was used frequently by Luftflotte Reich and LW Kdo. West. It was employed extensively by fags. A peculiar usage occurred in April 1945 when IV LN Versuchs Regiment (Brown) used the previous month's Cockroach key.

Flakkorpsmaschinenschlüssel – for "secret and open W/T messages on Flakkorpsbefehlsnetze". This class was first identified in the summer of 1942. Very few messages were seen on these keys as there was little activity on the few Flak frequencies intercepted. Most of the traffic identified consisted of discriminating messages appearing on the Luftflottebefehlsterne from Flakkorps and Flakdivision. Where Flakartillerie was administered by the Luftgau, traffic of Flak content passed in Luftgau and Flakkorps keys. **Goat** (Flakkorps VI) was first identified in April 1945 as a Sonderschlüssel, but fell into line in the cipher distribution of May.

Luftgaumaschinenschlüssel – "for secret and open W/T messages within the area of individual Luftgaukommandos, including Flakartillerie (except Flakkorps), aerodromes and safety service ships, also Fliegerführer and Jafue." Distribution followed strictly the above regulations, and examples may be given of such usage. Before D-Day, Fliegerführer Atlantik normally used Snowdrop (Luftgau Westfrankreich), safety service units **Lily**, **Daffodil** and **Snowdrop** according to their respective locations, and the Italian Flak stars, **Primrose**. Capstan, KG 53 and other Geschwader used Luftgau keys, in this instance originally **Gorse** and later **Daffodil**. When operational keys were compromised it was a frequent practice to rely upon the Luftgau key of the area. Similarly, when a unit on the move was separated from its headquarters, it was natural to pass any message in the key most readily available, normally the aerodrome key and therefore a Luftgau key.

The history of this category of key has been extremely chequered. Up to 1 November 1940 Luftgau traffic passed in Red, but then a separate general Luftgau key was issued – **Violet**. During the first half of 1941 each Luftgau was given a key of its own. Those identified were:

Luftgau I:	Gorse
Luftgau II:	Violet
Luftgau VIII:	Foxglove
Luftgau XI:	Daisy
Norway:	Heather
Süd Ost:	Speedwell

On 1 January 1942 Luftgau keys were restricted to two: Luftgau Ost (**Foxglove**) and Luftgau West (**Primrose**). On 1 January 1942 a new key was introduced in the Mediterranean, and the Western key, hitherto valid in Italy as well, was confined to West and North Europe.

Mediterranean area:	Primrose
West and North Europe:	Snowdrop

The latter, in its turn, was divided into two on 1 May 1942. The original key served Luftgau Westfrankreich, Belgien-Nordfrankreich and Holland, while the new one was used in North Germany, Denmark and Norway – (**Daffodil**). On 1 August 1942 a separate key was issued for Norway named by us **Narcissus**, a continuation of **Heather**. From 1 March 1943 until 1 May 1944 each Luftgau had a separate key, then all Luftgau within the area of Greater Germany used one key – **Daffodil**. By this time Luftgau Holland (**Tulip**) had been absorbed into Luftgau Belgien-Nordfrankreich, and the following disbanded:

Luftgau Moskau:	Daisy
Luftgau Süd Ost:	Speedwell
Luftgau XII/XIII:	Poppy

By the end of November, Luftgau XXV (**Orchid**) had been absorbed by Luftgaue VIII, now named Violet, and XVII (**Foxglove**), and Luftgau Riga (**Gorse**) by Luftgau I (**Clover**). On 1 December 1944 separate keys were issued for Luftgau in Greater Germany:

Luftgau I:	Clover
Luftgau III:	Gentian
Luftgau V:	Snowdrop (originally Westfrankreich)
Luftgau VI:	Wallflower
Luftgau VII:	Aster
Luftgau VIII:	Violet
Luftgau XI:	Daffodil
Luftgau XIV:	Lily (originally Belgien-Nordfrankreich)
Luftgau XVII:	Foxglove

This distribution remained until the end. From this brief historical outline it will be appreciated that frequent changes, added to the comparative failure to intercept these networks or identify the units in the early days, has greatly confused the naming of the keys.

Sondermaschinenschlüssel – "for use within company areas of Flugmelde, Flugsicherung and Funkhorchkompanien." That these were not only uses will be apparent from the following table:

i. **Safety Service Armadillo** was active for a few months during the summer of 1944 and its distribution was extremely limited. It was not known to have discriminants and had consecutive stecker. A key known as "RCN" was also used and had a long career. Unlike **Armadillo** it did occasionally appear on outside links, notably on the Befehlssterne of Luftflotte Reich.

ii. **Y Service**

a. **Horchmaschinenschlüssel**: **Mustard** monthly sheets were numbered consecutively from one upwards. In February 1943 there were three sets of discriminants but only one key – in March the number of sets of discriminants rose to four. After June 1944 there were two sets of discriminants and two separate keys – **Mustard I** on the Western Front and **Mustard II** in the Balkans and on the Eastern Front. Until the last few months of the war it was confined to Y Service networks, but then it began to appear spasmodically on the stars of Fliegerkorps IX and Luftflotte Reich.

b. **Aufklärungsschlüssel**. One only was identified, namely Cress, belonging to Luftflotte 3 in the summer of 1944. It was not, however, considered by the GAF as a Luftflotte key, and was issued in conjunction with other Y Service keys. It was closely associated with **Jaguar**, but also appeared on Army Y Service links. Some units, however, did not use a Sonderschlüssel. IV LN Regiment 351 in the West used **Red** and **Wallflower**, and LN Regiment 351 itself regularly used **Jaguar** instead of **Mustard I**.

iii. **Weather: Luftwaffenmaschinenwettersonderschlüssel.**
There were four weather keys:

Celery:	Deutschland West
Endive:	Deutschland Zentrale
Garlic:	Süd
Leek:	Ost

By February 1945 **Celery** died, and **Endive** was used instead for the whole German area, the stations being as far apart as Stettin, Munich and Hamburg. It was not certain whether both the other keys were still alive, though they were referred to in source.

iv. **Geschwader: Geschwader Sondermaschinenschlüssel**.
These first appeared in April 1942. As their use was generally

of short duration and distribution was restricted, they may well have been issued for specific operations. **Otter**, used by KG 200 in April 1945 was later referred to as "Sonderschlüssel Eisenhammer" – Eisenhammer being the codename for an operation. **Opossum**, used by KG 100, was probably of similar nature. **Chipmunk**, though used by Versuchsverband O.B.d.L., is included in this category.

v. **Fliegerführer:** As mentioned above, it is irregular for a Sonderschlüssel to be issued to a unit of this authority, but from November 1943 until the end of 1944 Fliegerführer Kroatien used a special key. His neighbour, Fliegerführer Albanien, was similarly equipped. **Yak** and **Llama**, the two keys concerned, had consecutive stecker and alphabetical discriminants, characteristics of true Sonderschlüssel. As far back as August 1942, Fliegerführer Luftflotte 1 had been identified as using a special key.

vi. **Substitutes for ordinary keys**: In March 1945 the GAF introduced a system of shuffling two or more keysheets to form one new Sonderschlüssel. This practice was an emergency one forced upon them by the difficulty of distributing new keys from the OKL Cipher Office. The various versions known as **Maryland I, II and III**, belong to this category and another – **Ohio** – was referred to as "Sonderschlüssel Kurfürst 1." They were only used on the Autos as far as is known, Notschlüssel apparently being preferred elsewhere.

vii. **Special Services**. To this section belong such keys as **Jerboa** (Flak Regiment 155) for the launching of flying bombs, **Brown** (IV LN Versuchs Regiment) for navigational beam experiments and **Leveret** (LN Regiment 200).

viii. **Maxschlüssel: Puce**. This key, identified at the beginning of 1944, was used to encode a resumé of reports of German agents on the Russian Air Force. These reports were transmitted to Robinson Ost from Luftflotte 4 at Vienna on an Abwehr link. There were naturally two types of Sonderschlüssel: (a) those issued by Luftgaukommandos from blocks allocated to them by OKL, to Geschwader and other units not automatically issued by OKL with their own keys by virtue of their rank or authority. They possessed consecutive stecker and alphabetical discriminants, and were the true Sonderschlüssel as recognised by Hut 6. (b) The second type comprised keys issued by the OKL Cipher Office in the normal routine distribution to such services as Hut 6 classified as "non-operational oddments".

Type (a) includes the following keys: Yak, Llama, Armadillo, RCN, Goat 4/45, Hyena in the first few months of its existence, Otter, Badger, Civet and Mole.

Type (b) includes: Mustard I and II, Jerboa, Celery, Gibbon, Chipmunk etc. It will be noted that Geschwaderschlüssel can belong to either type.

Uebungsluftwaffenmaschinenschlüssel: Blue – "for tactical W/T practices and signals service tests". It split off from Red in October 1939, and was identified regularly until its disappearance from the air in March 1945. Its distribution was widespread but its appearance was generally confined to Luftgau stars, particularly Luftgaue V, XI and XIV. It was used also on the Denmark changers, in Norway, and by the LN Schule at Halle, where the content of the messages was administrative as well as practice. Periodically Luftgau XI issued instructions to reverse the functions of Daffodil and Blue in its area, in which case Blue became tactical. It was used also for tuners, and for a time one message of this nature daily passed in Blue on the Autos from Luftflotte 3. The GAF regulations lay down that special keys are to be issued for large-scale experiments or cover, but during December 1944 Luftflotte 6 passed a considerable quantity of Blue on its Befehlssterne, supposedly for widespread cover and experiments.

Fernschreibluftwaffenmaschinenschlüssel: Indigo – "for secret messages which cannot be sent unencoded between all teleprinter stations of the Luftwaffe." The distribution was naturally widespread, but because the key only appeared on the air in exceptional circumstances, difficult to identify. It was used when Red was compromised, if it was not itself involved, otherwise it appears chiefly on Luftgau networks inside the Reich, Flak stars in North Italy, and the links controlled by Flak Regiment 155, in each case generally with discriminants. It was also used occasionally by fags.

APPENDIX II
LIST OF GERMAN CATEGORIES OF GAF KEYS

	KEY CATEGORY	DISTRIBUTION	ENGLISH NAME	COMMENT
1	Luftwaffenführungs-schlüssel (LF)	OKL and Luftflotten	Pink	
2	Luftwaffenmaschinen-schlüssel	OKL to Flughafe bereiche and Geschwader. Originally to Gruppen and Fliegerhoste	Red	Also known as Luftwaffenmaschinenschlüssel allgemeinbereich or gesamtbereich
3	Luftflottemaschinen-schlüssel	a) Luftflotten and main subscribers	Jaguar, Lion, Gorilla, Beetle, Mosquito, Hyena, Leopard, Chimpanzee	Originally no place for them in key set – first appeared Sept 1943. In Sept 1944 sub-divided to Luftflotten and L.W.Kdo keys
		(b) Fliegerverbindungsschlüssel Luftflotten and liaison officers with Army formations	Ocelot, Puma, Hedgehog, Porcupine	A Luftflotte, not a Fliegerkorps key. First used March 1943
4	Fliegerskorpsmaschinen-schlüssel (FlgM)	Fliegerkorps and subordinate units to level of Gruppen	Wasp, Gnat, Locust, Ermine, Skunk, Hornet, Moth, Mayfly, Firefly	
5	Jagdkorpsmaschinen-schlüssel	Jagdkorps and subordinate units to the level of Gruppen	Cockroach, Cricket	

Appendices

	KEY CATEGORY	DISTRIBUTION	ENGLISH NAME	COMMENT
6	Flakkorpsmaschinen-schlüssel (FlakM)	Flakkorps and subordinate units	Monkey, Weasel, Platypus, Marmoset, Chamois, Goat	First identified 1942. Not used by Lgau Flak units
7	Luftgaumaschinen-schlüssel (LgM)	Luftgaue and subordinate units	Snowdrop, Daffodil, Violet, Narcissus, Gentian, Clover, Primrose, Foxglove, Orchid, Aster, Wallflower, Cowslip, Daisy, Lily, Gorse, Heather, Poppy, Tulip, Speedwell	Also used by Fliegerführer
8	Luftwaffensondermaschinen-schlüssel (LSoM)	Safety Service, Y Service Weather, Geschwader, Special Technical Services, Fliegerführer	Armadillo, RCN, Mustard I and II, Brown I, II, III, Celery, Leek, Garlic, Endive, Otter, Badger, Yak, Civet, Opossum, Gibbon, Leveret, Jerboa, Chipmunk, Llama, Crab, Puce.	
9	Uebungsluftwaffenmaschinen-schlüssel (UebLM)	Luftflotte, Luftgaue and subordinate units	Blue	Practice Key
10	Fernschreibluftwaffenmaschinen-schlüssel (LsLM)	General	Indigo	Teleprinter Key
11	Notluftwaffen-maschinen-schlüssel	General, but not known on Auto	NOT/Guernsey NOT/ATT etc	For emergency use. Not issued by OKL Cipher Office.

APPENDIX III
ALPHABETICAL LIST UNDER ENGLISH NAME OF ALL GAF KEYS

	ENGLISH NAME	GERMAN UNIT	FIRST and LAST IDENTIFIED		COMMENT
1	Armadillo	Flugsicherungs Regiment West	May-44	Aug-44	Special key, with consecutive stecker.
2	Aster	Luftgau VII	May-43	To end	Between 2/44 and 12/44 key replaced by Daffodil.
3	Badger	Kampfgeschwader 3	May-42	May-43	Geschwader Sonderschlüssel.
4	Beaver	Schlachtgeschwader 1	Sep-43	Dec-43	Geschwader Sonderschlüssel.
5	Beetle	Luftflotte 6	Jan-42	To end	
6	Beetroot		Jun-41	Dec-41	A weather key in the West. Probably equivalent to Celery.
7	Blue	General distribution	Oct-39	To end	A practice key.
8	Brown I	IV LN Versuchs Regiment	Beginning	To end	Special key for navigational beam experiments and operations: up to December 1941 known as Brown.
9	Brown II	IV LN Versuchs Regiment	Dec-41	Mar-43	
10	Brown III	IV LN Versuchs Regiment	Sep-43	To end	
11	Celery		Spring 40	Feb-45	A Western weather key: known as Tan to 4/42.
12	Chamois	Flakkorps V	Mar-45	To end	
13	Chimpanzee	Luftflotte 10	Nov-44	To end	

Appendices

	ENGLISH NAME	GERMAN UNIT	FIRST and LAST IDENTIFIED		COMMENT
14	Chipmunk	Versuchsverband ObdL	Jan-44	Mar-45	Geschwader key
15	Civet	Kampfgeschwader 4	Nov-42	Jul-43	Geschwader key
16	Clover	Luftgau I	Mar-43	Apr-45	
17	Cockroach	Jagdkorps I	Jan-42	Feb-45	
18	Cowslip	(?)Luftgau XI	Aug-41	Aug-41	Possible continuity with Daffodil
19	Crab	Fliegerführer Luftflotte 1	Aug-42	Oct-42	Special key
20	Cress	Y Service in Western Europe	May-44	Aug-44	Broadcast key. Known as Aufklärungsmaschinenschlüssel Luftflotte 3
21	Cricket	Jagdkorps II	Dec-43	Nov-44	
22	Daffodil	Luftgau XI	May-42	To end	From 2/44 to 12/44 Daffodil was the only Luftgau key for the area of Luftflotte Reich
23	Daisy	Luftgau Moskau	Mar-43	May-44	Luftgau Moskau was an extension of Luftgau II. Daisy was also used as key name for Luftgau XI in 1941
24	Dingo	Kampfgeschwader 76	Nov-42	Oct-43	Geschwader key
25	Dragonfly	Fliegerkorps Tunis	Feb-43	May-43	
26	Endive		Nov-43	To end	Central German weather key Luftwaffenmaschinenwettersonderschlüssel DZ
27	Ermine	Fliegerkorps I	Sep-42	To end	
28	Ferret	Kampfgeschwader 53	Dec-42	Dec-42	Geschwader key

	ENGLISH NAME	**GERMAN UNIT**	**FIRST and LAST IDENTIFIED**		**COMMENT**
29	Firefly	Fliegerkorps XI Fallschirm AOK 1	Jan-42	Dec-44	Referred to as Armee Maschinen-schlüssel, but had GAF key numbers and discriminants.
30	Foxglove	Luftgau XVII	Mar-43	To end	Foxglove was also known as the key of Luftgau VIII 11/41 and of Luftgau Ost 1/42
31	Gadfly	Luftwaffen Kdo. Süd Ost	Jan-42	To end	Originally Fliegerkorps X but when staff moved to the West and reformed Fliegerkorps X out of Fliegerführer Atlantik, new key was called Gnat, the name Gadfly remaining for Balkan area.
32	Garlic		Apr-42	To end	A weather key for S. Europe. Called Luftwaffen-maschinenwet-tersonderschlüssel Süd
33	Gentian	Luftgau III	Sep-43	To end	
34	Gibbon	Zerstörerge-schwader 1	Jul-44	Aug-44	Geschwader key
35	Glowworm	Fallschirm AOK 1	Jun-44	Sep-44	Used by Italian units only. Confused with Firefly B
36	Gnat	Fliegerkorps X	May-44	Aug-44	Before 5/44 Fliegerkorps X used Snowdrop. Original key of Fliegerführer Atlantik. See Gadfly.
37	Goat	Flakkorps VI	Apr-45	To end	
38	Gorilla	Luftflotte 4	Sep-44	To end	

Appendices

	ENGLISH NAME	GERMAN UNIT	FIRST and LAST IDENTIFIED		COMMENT
39	Gorse	Luftgau XXVI	Mar-43	Nov-44	Before 4/43 known as Foxglove IV
40	Heather	Luftgau Norwegen	Summer 41	Dec-41	Became Narcissus
41	Hedgehog	(Units in area of) Fliegerkorps I, IV, VIII.	Feb-43	Jul-43	Flivo key of Luftflotte 4 known as Luftwaffen-maschinenschlüssel Hammel
42	Hornet	Fliegerkorps IV	Jan-42	Dec-43	
43	Hyena	Luftflotte Reich	Feb-44	To end	
44	Indigo	General Distribution	Oct-43	To end	Teleprinter key of high authority
45	Jaguar	Luftflotte 3 (later) Luftwaffen Kdo. West)	Dec-43	To end	
46	Jerboa	Flak Regiment 155	Jul-44	Feb-45	Special key used by flying bomb sites
47	Leek		Jun-41	To end (?)	A weather key (Eastern)
48	Lemming	Jafue Süd (Norway)	Jan-43	Mar-43	
49	Leopard	Luftflotte 2 (later Komm. Gen. Italien)	Feb-44	To end	
50	Leveret	L N Regiment 200	Nov-43	Jan-45	
51	Light Blue		Jan-41	Dec-41	Operational key in Mediterranean area, allocated for North African campaign and known as Brigitte.
52	Lily	Luftgau Belgien-Nordfrankreich (later Luftgau XIV)	Jun-41	Apr-45	
53	Lion	Luftflotte 5 (later Luftwaffen Kdo Norwegen)	Jun-42	To end	Originally Fliegerführer Nord West

Solving Enigma - The Official History of Bletchley Park's Hut 6

	ENGLISH NAME	**GERMAN UNIT**	**FIRST and LAST IDENTIFIED**		**COMMENT**
54	Llama	Fliegerführer Albanien	Dec-43	Sep-44	Special key, consecutive stecker
55	Locust	Fliegerkorps II	Jan-42	To end	Key remained in S E Europe when Fliegerkorps II moved North. See also Moth
56	Marmoset	Flakkorps IV	Sep-44	Apr-45	
57	Mauve		Feb-41	Mar-41	Probably a GAF key
58	Mayfly	Fliegerkorps XIV	Jun-43	Jan-45	
59	Mole		May-43	Jun-43	A Geschwader key, South Russian area
60	Monkey	Flakkorps II	Feb-45	Apr-45	
61	Mosquito	Luftflotte I	Jan-42	To end	Formerly the key of Fliegerkorps I
62	Moth	Units of Fliegerkorps II (later called Luftwaffen Kdo. Nord Ost)	Mar-45	May-45	New key name for Fliegerkorps II. See also Locust
63	Mouse		Mar-43	Apr-43	A Geschwader key
64	Mustard	German Y Service	Jun-41	To end	After June 1944 there were two Mustards: Mustard II (Balkans) and Mustard I (Western Front)
65	Narcissus	Luftgau Norwegen	Jul-42	Nov-44	
66	Ocelot	Luftflotte 3 (Flivo key)	May-44	To end	The GAF Western Front liaison key
67	Onion		Mar-41	Jul-41	Key connected with navigational beams (cf Brown)
68	Opossum	Kampfgeschwader 100	Jun-44	Aug-44	A Geschwader key

Appendices

	ENGLISH NAME	GERMAN UNIT	FIRST IDENTIFIED	LAST IDENTIFIED	COMMENT
69	Orchid	Luftgau XXV	Mar-43	Nov-44	
70	Otter	Kampfgeschwader 200	Apr-45	Apr-45	A special Geschwader key for Operation Eisenhammer
71	Pink	Führungsnetz subscribers	Feb-41	To end	Highest priority GAF key
72	Platypus	Flakkorps III	May-44	Jan-45	
73	Polecat	Fernaufklärungsgruppe 122	May-42	May-42	A Geschwader key. Some question as to whether it was a genuine key
74	Poppy	Luftgau XII/XIII	Sep-43	Apr-44	
75	Porcupine		Jan-43	Mar-43	A Flivo key on South Russian Front known as Luftwaffenersatzmaschinenschlüssel Spaten
76	Primrose	Luftgau XXVIII	Jan-42	Sep-44	Originally key of Luftgau West
77	Puce		Feb-44	Oct-44	A special key used for reports between Robinson Ost and Luftflotte 4 known as Maxschlüsse
78	Puma	Luftflotte 2 (Flivo key)	Aug 43	To end	GAF Mediterranean liaison key
79	Purple		May-40	Feb-41	
80	Rabbit	Kampfgeschwader 55	Nov-42	Apr-43	A Geschwader key
81	Raccoon	I Kampfgeschwader 66	Jun-44	Jun-44	A Geschwader key.
82	Rat	O.B.de L., O.B.S and Fliegerkorps Tunis	May-43	May-43	Almost certainly merely reserve Red for May 1943

	ENGLISH NAME	**GERMAN UNIT**		**FIRST and LAST IDENTIFIED**	**COMMENT**
84	Scorpion I	Fliegerführer Afrika	Apr-42	Jul-42	
	Scorpion II	Fliegerführer Afrika	Jun-42	Feb-43	
85	Shamrock		Mar-43	Mar-43	Almost certainly merely reserve Red for March 1943
86	Sheep	Jagdgeschwader 53	Aug-43	Aug-43	Really Primrose B
87	Skunk	Fliegerkorps VIII	May-42	To end	
88	Snowdrop	Luftgau Westfrankreich (later Luftgau V)	Apr-42	To end	
89	Speedwell	Luftgau Süd Ost	Jun-41	Jan-42	
90	Squirrel	Fernkampfführer Luftflotte 2	Jul-43	Nov-43	A Sonderschlüssel.
91	Stoat		Jan-43	Feb-43	A key connected with GAF night fighter groups
92	Termite	Fliegerdivision 9	Mar-45	Apr-45	
93	Tulip	Luftgau Holland	Jun-41	Feb-44	
94	Violet	Luftgau VIII	Mar-45	Apr-45	Violet was also the name given to a general Luftgau key used from 11/40 to 1/41.
95	Wallflower	Luftgau VI	Dec-44	Mar-45	
96	Wasp	Fliegerkorps IX	Jan-42	To end	Carried on function of Cockroach from 3/45.
97	Weasel	Flakkorps I	Jul-42	Apr-45	
98	Yak	Fliegerführer Kroatien (later Fliegerführer Nord Balkans)	Nov-43		A special key, with consecutive stecker.

APPENDIX IV
LIST OF COUNTY KEYS

NAME	GERMAN UNIT	IDENTI-FIED	COMMENTS
Buckingham	Flakkorps II	Feb-45	Became Monkey
Cambridge	Luftgau VIII	Feb-45	Became Violet II
Devon		Feb-45	S W Germany
Dorset		Feb-45	S W Germany
Durham	Luftgau 3	Feb-45	Became Gentian B
Florida	LW Kdo. Ost Preussen, Versorgungsstab Nord Ost	Apr-45	Became Clover II
Galway	Flakdivision 9	May-45	N W Germany
Kansas	Lfl. Reich & Luftgau VIII	Apr-45	Became Violet
Kerry	Lfl. Reich & Robinson I Nord	May-45	
Lanark	LW Kdo 4	Mar-45	Became Gadfly
Maryland	All Luftflotten: Kurfürst 2 and 3	Apr-45	Sonderschlüssel: three shuffled versions known as Maryland I, II & III.
Mayo		May-45	Greater Germany
Montana		Apr-45	Became Red B
Nevada		Apr-45	Became Jaguar B
Norfolk	LW Kdo. Ost Preussen: Luftflotte 1	Feb-45	Became Mosquito
Ohio	Kurfürst 1	Apr-45	Used for Auto traffic only known as Sonderschlüssel Kurfürst 1
Oxford	Flakkorps II	Feb-45	Became Monkey A
Salop	Luftgau V	Feb-45	Became Snowdrop
Shetland		Mar-Apr 45	W and S W Germany
Skye	Fliegerdivision 9	Mar-45	Became Termite
Suffolk	Fliegerdivision 4	Feb-45	Eastern Front
Tipperary	Kurfürst Nord	May-45	
Utah		Apr-45	Used for Auto traffic only
Wyoming	LW Kdo. Ost Preussen	Apr-45	
Yorkshire		Feb-Mar 45	W Germany

NOTES TO APPENDICES V & VI
GENERAL USE AND DISTRIBUTION OF ARMY KEYS

The machinery whereby Army traffic was, during the war, identified to keys will not be considered in this section. Here we shall be concerned with the further problem – of equal if not greater difficulty – that arose once the traffic had been identified to keys. These problems fell broadly into two categories:

a. What was the nature and function of any given key, how was it related to the German Army Order of Battle, could it be equated to any specific key in the various (known) categories of keys created by the enemy?

b. Conversely, could any of the keys in the various enemy categories be equated to any particular key that was being identified?

It will be clear that if these two questions were always to be answered at all completely, we should have had to have known at the time any particular Army key was identified exactly what units were passing it and their precise subordination with local Order of Battle, and have had a complete and up-to-date knowledge of the then categories of Army keys in force. If this information had always been available we should, in most cases, have been in the ideal situation of always being able to equate an Army key identified by Hut 6 with the name by which it was known to the Germans. The ideal situation only partly materialised towards the end of the war in the autumn of 1944 and the spring of 1945. It may be useful to state some of the reasons why, for the greater period of the war, classification of Army keys to the German equivalent was tentative, and in some cases, as it subsequently appeared, inaccurate.

a. For various cryptographic reasons Army keys were always more difficult to break than Air keys, at least until the introduction of certain technical security devices in the GAF tended to equalise the position. For this reason, the information from source on the nature and function of any particular key, why it was being used, who held it etc., was correspondingly less.

Appendices

This was especially true of the early years. In fact, it was not until January 1941, apart from Greenshank and Yellow, and exclusive of the SS keys, that the first Army key – Gannet I – was identified.

b. Changes in the different categories, or in the principles on which specific keys were issued, were made occasionally by the Germans. To a certain extent this could be observed from the distribution of any given key, but if the key were only identified only occasionally, or, if identified, broken only occasionally, it might be some time before it was realised such a change had in fact been made. For example, at least as early as November 1943 all Armee Staff keys started to use the same discriminant block, but this was only determined by observing that traffic in the Staff key of X did not decode when the Staff key of Y was broken.

c. After discriminants were generally dropped in September 1943 it became much more difficult to determine the exact distribution of a key when it was not being broken at all frequently, as it would not be known how much and what nondiscriminating traffic would decode, and if the distribution were in doubt it was much more difficult to identify traffic to a specific key, let alone giving this its German name equivalent.

d. The distribution difficulty was accentuated in September and November 1944 when random and encoded callsigns were introduced in place of serials and rows. Hitherto, W/T groups using the same serials, at least in the same area, were occasionally an indication that they might be using the same key or keys.

For these reasons, the following difficulties arose in the identification and naming of Army keys:

a. Identifying an Army key to its German equivalent was sometimes impossible, occasionally tentative, often impracticable.

b. A key might appear in a certain area, at that time seem to be a new key and would be correspondingly named. Later it would prove to be, in fact, a key that was already known but which had not been used, or identified, at the time the "new" key appeared. For example, an apparently new supply key named Goshawk was used by units in Italy in September 1943. In October this key turned out, from discriminant evidence, to be the same key as Kite, the supply key used on the Eastern Front, which had not been identified in September. This incomplete knowledge of the distribution given by the enemy to the various types of keys accounts for a certain number of what were later proved to be wrong key names.

c. Conversely, a key might be identified during a period of time – say, two years – and it might subsequently be shown that at certain times during this period the traffic identified as being encoded in this key was either probably or certainly actually encoded in some other known or unknown (and unnamed) key. That is, the continuity of key name does not always imply that the German name remained the same during the period the particular key was identified. For example, a key called "Falcon I" was identified in the autumn of 1941 and in the autumn of 1944, but continuity between these years is somewhat doubtful. In 1941 the German name was probably Heeresmaschinenschlüssel, in 1944 it was Wehrmachtmaschinenschlüssel Heimatkriegsgebiet.

To sum up, one can say that the identification and naming of a key was made on the lines of as much information as was available on the precise nature and function of the key, the local Order of Battle set-up, and the general category of keys then in force. If it was subsequently proved to be wrong, the key name would either be abolished or changed. The two appendices that follow need some slight explanation.

Appendix V

This sets out the various categories of German Army keys, so far as was known, as in March 1945. Where identified, the English name equivalent is given as well. Numbers for the various keys issued each month were introduced in 1944, but not at the same time for each category of key. It is based on observation and on our knowledge of German key names from source and captured documents. An asterisk by a key name signifies an associated Staff key, denoted in our technology by the suffix II. It is worth pointing out here two differences in the distribution of

Appendices

keys that distinguishes the Army from the Luftwaffe – one, there was never any general Army key corresponding to the Air key Red; two, the different Heeresgruppen did not usually have their own keys, as at the corresponding level in the Luftwaffe did the Luftflotten.

Appendix VI

This is an alphabetical list, by English names, of all Army keys identified during the war. The dates given for the period during which the key was identified are approximate only and do not imply that the key was identified every day during the period. They are only a rough indication of the first and last times the key was identified by Hut 6 – since the fact that a key was not identified does not necessarily mean that the Germans had stopped issuing or using it. It will be observed that many English key names given in Appendix VI do not appear in Appendix V. This is because Appendix V is based on the German division into categories, whilst Appendix VI is merely a list of keys that have been identified, irrespective of in what German category – if any – they should be included.

APPENDIX V

THE VARIOUS CATEGORIES OF GERMAN ARMY KEYS OPERATIVE IN MARCH 1945

GERMAN CATEGORY	FUNCTION	ENGLISH NAME	COMMENT
OKH M/S	OKH - H.Gruppen and Armies		OKH keys have Offizier key signified by III.
* OKH M/S A		Avocet	Used on Eastern Front, Norway.
* OKH M/S B		Puffin	Used on Western Front, Italy and S E Europe.
HEERESTABS M/S	**Inter-Army**		**From 1 Sept 1944 only Staff key for Heeres was issued.**
Heeresstabs M/S Heimatkriegsgebiet		Mallard?	Area of Chef H Ruest and Bde as well as all traffic between the theatres of war, from Army upwards and Dienstellen in area of Chef H Ruest and Bde.
Heeresstabs M/S Ost,			Eastern Front
Heeresstabs M/S Süd		Emu II	Italy and S E Europe and S Russian Front.
WEHRMACHT M/S	**Inter-Service, distribution as for Heeres keys**		
* Wehrmacht M/S Heimatkriegsgebiet		Falcon	
* Wehrmacht M/S Ost			
* Wehrmacht M/S Süd,			
* Wehrmacht M/S West		Bantam	Area of Ob. West.
* Wehrmacht M/S Nord			Area of AOKs in Norway.

Appendices

GERMAN CATEGORY	FUNCTION	ENGLISH NAME	COMMENT
OBERQUARTI-ERMEISTER M/S	**Supply keys**		
Oberquartiermeister M/S A		Kite	Eastern Front, Italy.
Oberquartiermeister M/S B		Peewit	Western Front.
RUND-SPRÜCHE M/S	**Broadcast keys**		
Rundspruch M/S West		Pullet	Used by OBW
Rundspruch M/S H. Gr. B.		Hummingbird	Used by H. Gr. B.
Rundspruch M/S H. Gr. G.		Whinchat	Used by H. Gr. G.
RAILWAY KEYS	**Railway Personnel**		
Eisenbahn Truppen M/S		Blunderbuss	W Europe and N Italy.
Reichsbahn M/S		Rocket	W Europe.
ARMEE M/S	**Army and downwards**	**For English names see Appendix VI**	
SONDER M/S	**Special temporary keys**	See Appendix VI for Probable Sonder M/S	Usually given a trigram "indicator", e.g."Sonder M/SDDY" In the series AAA-ZZZ were originally intended for surrounded "Fortress" units, but were, in fact, used also as replacements for compromised keys and other special purposes.
WEHRKREIS M/S	**Administration and Supply**		
Wehrkreis Fe Fu M/S B.d.E.		Grouse	Key of XVII? Fe Fu = Festefunkstelle
Wehrkreis Fe Fu M/S Sam			Sam = Sammelspruch

GERMAN CATEGORY	FUNCTION	ENGLISH NAME	COMMENT
SS AND POLICE KEYS			
SS Feldnachschub M/S }		Quince I	General SS key. Name changed to SS M/S Sondersatz C probably in March 1945
SS Chef Sonder M/S		Quince II	Staff key to Quince I?
SS Stabs M/S		Orange	General Purpose SS key
SS Querverkehr M/S		Medlar	Key used for W/T cross-working
SS M/S Sondersatz C?		Plum	
Polchi M/S		Roulette I	Senior police commanders.
Bedhörden M/S			Civil Service key?

APPENDIX VI
LIST OF ALL GERMAN ARMY KEYS IDENTIFIED DURING THE WAR

1	Albatross *	Armee M/S	May-43	Apr-45	Key of AOK 10,
2	Apple		Nov-41	Aug-42	Probably used by police formations in Norway and N.Germany,
3	Avocet *	OKH M/S	Jun-44	May-45	OKH Armies, H. Gr. On Eastern Front and Norway. Prior to 7/44 was OKH M/S Nr. II, in probable continuity with Vulture I, II
4	Azure		Aug-40	Jan-41	N W Europe
5	Bantam *	Wehrmacht M/S West	Apr-43	May-45	Western Front Inter-Service key
6	Bittern		Nov-42	Apr-43	Used by Rumanian Army (cf. Stork)
7	Blackbird		May-42	Aug-44	Western Front
8	Blunderbuss	Eisenbahn Truppen M/S	Sep-42	May-45	Used by Reichsbahn personnel (W Europe)
9	Bullfinch		Nov-42	May-43	Rome-Tunis (Special key)
10	Bullfinch		Dec-43	Feb-44	OKH-AOK 10 (Special key)
11	Bunting		Dec-44	Jan-45	Supply key of H. Gr. E and F ?
12	Buzzard		Apr-43	Jun-43	Used in S E Europe
13	Cassowary		Jan-45	Apr-45	Key of Bev. Gen. Ungarn ?
14	Chaffinch I	OKH Stabs M/S I	Feb-41	May-43	Puffin I and II
	Chaffinch II }	Sonder M/S Rom-Panzer Armee	Feb-41	May-43	Puffin I and II
	Chaffinch III	OKH M/S I	Feb-41	May-43	Puffin I and II

15	Chicken	Armee M/S	Apr-43	Apr-45	Key of AOK 15
16	Coot		Jan-44	May-44	Supply key on E Front and S E Europe. May be same as Kite
17	Cormorant		Apr-43	Jun-43	Mediterranean Sonder M/S for traffic Rome-Sardinia
18	Corncrake	Sonder M/S P.W.Kdo. II	Feb-44	Apr-45	Used by units connected with V2 experiments
19	Crow		Sep-41	Oct-41	Used in Yugoslavia
20	Cuckoo		Apr-41	May-41	Used in Balkan campaign
21	Culverin		Oct-44	Nov-44	Used by Army personnel in connection with railway movements in Western Europe.,
22	Curlew		Oct-43	Jun-44	Key of Wehrkreis II ?
23	Diver	Sonder M/S?	Jun-44	Apr-45	Used by 319 Inf. Div. in Channel Islands
24	Dodo *	Armee M/S	Nov-42	Apr-45	Key of Panzer AOK 5.
25	Drake	Armee M/S?	Apr-43	May-43	Used in counter-invasion exercises in Holland
26	Duck *	Armee M/S	Apr-43	May-45	Key of AOK 7
27	Egret	Sonder M/S In the series AAA-ZZZ	Aug-44	Oct-44	Special Western Front key of OKH ?
28	Emu I	Heeres M/S Süd			
29	Emu II	Heeresstabs M/S Süd	Aug-44	May-45	Inter-Army key: Italy and S E urope

Appendices

30	Falcon*	Wehrmacht M/S Heimat-kriegsgebiet	Jun-41	Apr-45	This German name equivalent since autumn 1944: Falcon I, II of 1941-1942 probably not in continuity when German name of Falcon I was probably "Heeres M/S" (see also Merlin)
31	Flamingo	Armee M/S	Jun-44	Aug-44	Key of Panzer AOK 3
32	Flycatcher	Sonder M/S?	Oct-44	Apr-45	OKH Crete
33	Fowl		Aug-43	Dec-43	Used in France
34	Fulmar	Armee M/S	Jan-44	May-44	Key of AOK 8
35	Gannet I	Armee M/S	Jan-41		Key of AOK Norwegen
36	Gannet II	Armee M/S	Apr-42	Apr-45	Key of Gebs AOK 20. Not Staff key of Gannet I
37	Goldfinch		Dec-42	Dec-42	Appeared only in 12/42 when it equalled Bullfinch 11/42. Probably not a genuine key but Bullfinch A, i.e. Bullfinch of 11/42
38	Goose	Armee M/S	Apr-42	May-43	Used in anti-invasion exercises in Holland
39	Goshawk		Sep-43	Sep-43	Wrongly named - was really Kite
40	Gosling *	Armee M/S	May-43	Apr-45	Key of AOK 19
41	Grapefruit		May-44	Apr-45	SS key used in connection with concentration camps
42	Grebe *	Armee M/S	Apr-45	Apr-45	Key of AOK 25
43	Greenshank A and B				Active throughout the war. Used by Wehrkreise
44	Grouse	Wehkreise Fe Fu M/S B.d.E	Jun-44	May-45	Key of Wehrkreis XVII?

45	Guillemot	Sonder M/S	Oct-44	Nov-44	Key of Kommander der Festungsbereich West
46	Hawfinch		Jan-43	Feb-43	Wrongly named - really Chaffinch I
47	Hawk		6/12/41	6/12/41	D/F Lithuanian border
48	Hen		Jun-43	Jul-43	Used in N W France
49	Heron		Oct-42	Dec-42	Used in Norway
50	Hobby	Uebungs M/S von Wehrkreis VI	Aug-43	Oct-43	Practice key of Wehrkreis VI
51	Hummingbird	Rundspruch M/S H. Gr. B	Jan-45	Apr-45	Broadcast key of H. Gr. B
52	Ibis		Oct-44	Apr-45	Used by units in Holland in connection with launching of V2.,
53	Jackdaw		22/9/41	22/9/41	D/F Russian Front
54	Jay		Apr-41	Jun-44	Jay as a key identified 4/41-6/41 and 8/43-6/44 when it was renamed Puffin I. Doubtful if any continuity between Jay of 1941 and Jay of 1943-1944,
55	Kestrel	Rundspruch M/S	Jun-41	Sep-42	During this period four Kestrel keys were identified, corresponding to the different Heeresgruppen on the Eastern Front -Nord, Mitte, Süd etc.
56	Kingfisher *	Armee M/S	May-44	Apr-45	Key of AOK 14
57	Kite	O.Qu.M/S A	Jul-41	Apr-45	Supply key, Eastern Front and Italy. Prior to 8/44 was O.Qu.M/S Nr. II
58	Lemon		Dec-40	Mar-41	Vienna

Appendices

59	Linnet		Mar-41	Aug-41	Forward operational key in Libya
60	Lorient	Sonder M/S	Sep-44	Apr-45	XXV AOK (Lorient) to OBW and H. Gr. B.
61	Magenta		Jan-41	Apr-41	Berlin-Rumania
62	Magpie		Oct-43	Jan-44	Used in Dodecanese.
63	Mallard	Heeres M/S Heimat- kriegsgebiet after 9/44	Aug-42	Apr-45	Continuity of key name is doubtful during these years
64	Medlar, SS	Querverkehr M/S	May-44	May-45	SS key used for W/T cross-working
65	Merlin	Heeresstabs M/S?	Jul-42	Nov-43	See also Falcon
66	Moorhen		Apr-44	May-44	Supply key used in Italy
67	Nightjar	Militär Befel- shaber M/S	Feb-44	Aug-44	Used by military occupation authorities in France
68	Nuthatch		Mid 43	Feb-45	Berlin-Vienna-Belgrade
69	Orange	SS Stabs M/S,	1939	May-45	General purpose SS key
70	Oricle		Oct-44	Apr-45	Y key used between OKH and H. Gr. G
71	Osprey	M/S Organi- sation Todt	Jun-42	Apr-45	Used by Todt organisation: in 1943 there were four separate keys which became indistinguishable when discriminants dropped 9/43
72	Owl *	Armee M/S	Nov-43	Mar-44	Key of AOK 17
73	Peewit	C.Qu.M/S B,	Jun-44	May-45	Prior to 8/44 was O.Qu.M/S Nr. I
74	Pelican	Armee M/S	Mar-44	Jun-44	Key of Panzer AOK 1
75	Penguin		Jun-44,	Jul-44	Used by 12 SS Panzer Division (Western Front)

76	Peregrine		Jun-43	Sep-43	Used between V SS Geb. Korps and Prinz Eugen Division
77	Phoenix	Panzer Armee M/S	Nov-41	May-43	Key of Panzerarmee Afrika (North African campaign)
78	Pigeon		Jul-43 Aug-44	Mar-45,	Pigeon of 7/43 not in continuity with Pigeon of 1944-1945, which was a Western Front Y key
79	Plum	SS M/S Sondersatz C,	Mar-45	Apr-45	SS key - see also Quince
80	Puffin *	OKH M/S B	Aug-43	May-45	Prior to 7/44 was OKH M/S Nr. I. In probable continuity with Chaffinch - see also Jay
81	Pullet	Rundspruch M/S West	Aug-42	Mar-45	Y key of OBW
82	Pumpkin		Apr-44	Apr-45	SS propaganda key
83	Quail *	Armee M/S	Oct-44	May-45	Key used by H.Gr.E. and subordinate Korps
84	Quince I	SS Feldnachschub M/S SS M/S Sondersatz C	Aug-42	May-45	Name changed to SS M/S Sondersatz C in 3/45 General SS key
85	Qince II	SS Chef Sonder M/S	end of 1943	May-45	Staff key to Quince I ?
86	Raven *	M/S Aegaeis Süd (originally Armee M/S of AOK 12)	Sep-41	Apr-45	Key of H.Gr.E. Continuity doubtful
87	Robin		Jul-42	Oct-44	Used in connection with railway system when run by Army personnel - cf. Rocket and Turkey.

Appendices

88	Rocket	Reichsbahn M/S	Jun-40	May-45	Used by Reichsbahn personnel (cf. Robin). Machine on which, Rocket was encoded was different from ordinary machine
89	Rook I		Sep-41	Oct-42	Eastern Front (Connected fwith Panzer units?).,
90	Rook II		Sep-41	Mar 44	(Rook II not Staff key to Rook I). Probably Y key - used between Mikkeli (in Finland) and OKH (Goldap)
91	Roulette I	Polchi M/S	Feb-44	May-45	Used by senior police officials.
92	Seagull		Nov-41	Dec-41	Used in Crete.,
93	Shrike *	Armee M/S	Aug-43	Apr-44	Latterly equated as key of Armee Ligurian, formerly of AOK 14
94	Skylark		Apr-42	May-42	Used for communication between Channel Islands and France
95	Sparrow		Mar-43	Mar-45	Mediterranean Y key
96	Starling		Nov-42	Dec-42	Bucharest to Rostov-on-Don
97	Stork		Oct-43	Nov-43	Used by Hungarian Army. Traffic decoded into Hungarian language
98	Swan *	Armee M/S	May-43	Apr-45	Key of AOK 1
99	TGD				Active throughout war Key of Reichessicherungdienst. Name derived from callsign of, Berlin in 1940.
100	Thrush	Sonder M/S Rom-Malemes	Jul-42	Nov-42	Special Rome-Crete key

Solving Enigma - The Official History of Bletchley Park's Hut 6

101	Tomtit		Nov-44	Feb-45	Used in S E Germany
102	Toucan		Nov-43	Mar-44	Supply key used in Italy
103	Turkey		Apr-43	May-43	Western Front key connected with railway system (cf. Robin)
104	Wagtail		Feb-44	Oct-44	Practice key of Wehrkreis VIII
105	Wheatear	Sonder M/S?	Oct-44	Dec-44	Special key of OBW
106	Whimbrel *	Armee M/S	Jan-45	Feb-45	Key of SS Panzer AOK 6
107	Whinchat	Rundspruch M/S H.Gr.G.	Oct-44	May-45	Y key of H.Gr.G
108	Wood-pecker		Oct-43	Mar-44	Army teleprinter key used in S E Europe
109	Wryneck *	Armee M/S	Aug-43	Mar-45	Key of Panzer AOK 2
110	Vulture I	OKH M/SII	Apr-41	Spring 1944	In probable continuity with Avocet
111	Yellow		Apr-40	Jul-40	Special key used during Norwegian campaign

GLOSSARY

"When I use a word", Humpty Dumpty said, in rather a scornful tone, "it means what I choose it to mean – neither more nor less."
"The question is", said Alice, "whether you can make words mean so many different things."
"The question is", said Humpty Dumpty, "which is to be master – that's all."

Abstimmspruch: A German W/T tuning message.
Abwehr: Security organisation specialising in counter-espionage.
Activity Report: Daily intercept station reports recording, by frequency, the number of messages, type of traffic and all callsigns heard on that frequency.
Adopted Frequency: An agreed measurement of a recognised frequency used by all the intercept stations to assist in identification of traffic, although their frequency readings might vary.
AF5: Army Formation 5.
A-Guide: An order list of all frequencies passing Watch keys (q.v.).
Air Discriminant Foss: A chart recording all identified air discriminants under their initial bigrams designed to throw up alphabetical runs.
Air Key: A key used by the German Air Force.
Air Research: A sub-section of the Research section of Hut 6 which dealt with Research Air keys.
A-Key: The Gebrauch (q.v.) key of the previous month used in the correct order during the current month, e.g., Jaguar A.
Alex: Alexandria.
Alphabetical Discriminant: A discriminant of which the letters are in alphabetical order, e.g., ADM, BLZ.
Alphabetical Run: A relationship between two or more discriminants where the initial bigrams are the same and the last letters of the trigrams alphabetically adjacent, e.g., AFM, AFL, AFK.
Alternative Frequency: One of several frequencies allocated to a particular W/T group other than the one which it is using at any particular time.
Alternative Indicator: A variant version of one or both of the two trigrams forming the indicators of an Enigma message.
AN-Sheet: A Foss sheet (q.v.) recording the first two letters of all messages on any one key.
AOK: Armee Oberkommando, a German Army Command.
A-Order: Result of a hatting (q.v.) of the GAF (q.v.) F Book (q.v.) columns on which the A-Shift (q.v.) was imposed to arrive at the A-Serial (q.v.).
Appease: To identify two or more W/T groups intercepted by different sets on nearby frequencies as the same groups by a comparison of callsigns and traffic.

Appeasement Chart: A chart so arranged as to throw up the common identity of two or more frequencies taken by different sets. It recorded frequency, intercept station and callsign of a given transmission.
Arlington Hall: HQ of the US Signals Security Service.
Army Notation: A number, prefixed by a sorting symbol, allotted to each Army W/T Group.
Army Research: A sub-section of the Research Section of Hut 6 which dealt with Research Army keys.
Army Ringstellung Rule: A rule laid down by the German Army Cipher Office under which, in a period of nine days, the 26 letters of the alphabet were used once each in the ringstellung.
A-Serial: A serial number, fixed for each GAF (q.v.) W/T group, arrived at by imposing the A-Shift on the A-Order (q.v.).
A-Shift: The daily differential factor converting the A-Order (q.v.) into the A-Serial (q.v.).Auto: (1) An automatic transmitting set. (2) The Führungsnetz, the GAF (q.v.) network centred on OKL (q.v.), which employed high-speed transmitting and receiving apparatus.
Autoscritcher: A US machine for recovering unknown reflector wirings.
B: Reflector B, the standard Reflector with fixed wiring used by the Germans 1939-1945.
Banburismus: A mechanical method of counting messages together with the object of discovering fits (q.v.).
Banbury: Two or more messages on the same key at the same machine setting.
Befehlstern: The network linking the superior authority to all important subordinates and adjacent commands.
Beaumanor: The name often given to the main intercept station for German Army traffic, the War Office Y Group, from the place in which it was situated from 1940 onwards.
Beginner: 1. A crib used at the beginning of a message. 2. A hopeful future crib, noted but not established.
Berlinismus: Practice, observed in a series of messages originating from Berlin, of assigning successive outside indicators such that each letter of any one of them was two places further down the alphabet than the corresponding letter in the previous outside indicator (e.g., CRM, ETO, GVQ etc), thereby suggesting that they had as message settings
the letters next to each other (i.e., in the above example, the letters DSN, FUP, HWR etc) – as proved to be the case.
B-Guide: A book of instructions for sorting traffic on frequencies passing identified keys not covered by the A-Guide (q.v.) – in practice, Research keys.
Bible: 1. A complete record, under units, of all evidence relevant to the identification of traffic passed by those units. 2. By transference, any complete record of information relevant to a particular subject.
Bird Book: Rufzeichentafel B, the GAF callsign book used for the first four years of the war.

Glossary

B-Key: The Ersatz (q.v.) key used as Gebrauch (q.v.) in the current month, and liable to be used for the following month, e.g., Jaguar B.

Blean: To clean or purge a blist (q.v.).

Bletchley Park: Location of GC&CS (Government Code and Cypher School).

Blist (Originally Banister List): A register giving details of all messages on any single key; to register on a blist.

Blist Number: Reference number given to each message when registered on the Blist (q.v.).

Block: 1. A set of five adjacent callsigns in the F Book (q.v.). 2. A collection, in order, of 31 or less consecutive sets of discriminants (q.v.).

Block Rule: The Army Ringstellung Rule (q.v.).

Bobbery (from its inventor, Robert Roseveare): A method of recovering D (q.v.) wirings when the wheel order, ringstellung and stecker of the key are known but no crib is available on a message encoded with D.

Boil: A comparison of texts of a routine Enigma message of unknown content, with the object of discovering the clear text, the letters of which will never appear in the Enigma, provided that the clear text is precisely the same on every occasion.

Bombe: A machine for breaking Enigma keys, i.e., ascertaining wheel order, ringstellung and stecker, by testing a crib and its implications in all positions.

Bombe Hour: Unit used in calculating bombe time – one bombe running for one hour.

Bombshell: A weekly publication by Hut 6 Watches readjusting cryptographic cover and giving cover requirements for the immediate future.

Bounce: A Naval key handled in Hut 8.

Callsign: A group, usually of three or more letters and/or figures, sent either in clear or in cipher in the preamble of the message, and serving to identify the sender and/or recipient.

Cataloguer: A technical term in the work of the Duddery (q.v.) used to describe the person who checked in on special tick-offs (q.v.) all duds (q.v.) as they came through from Registration Room 1 (q.v.).

Changes Book: A book in which all alterations to existing sorting instructions were entered for the attention of the Records Party.

Chart: To compare the times of origin (q.v.) of messages on a chart.

Chasing the last Red: Hut 6 jargon for the task of discovering the 4th discriminant to decode on the current Red key, a necessary preliminary to the identification of other discriminants.

Cheap (of a key or job): Requiring little bombe (q.v.) time.

Cilli: Message setting of a message when the finishing position of the wheels has been used as the outside indicator of the succeeding message or teil (q.v.); to use the end position of one message as the outside indicator of the next.

Cilli Menu: A menu (q.v.) using only constatations (q.v.) provided by cillies (q.v.).

Cilli Story: A number of consistent cillies (q.v.) on the same key.

CIP: Short for Current Identification Party (see Identification Party).

C-Key: 1. The key, intended for the Ersatz (q.v.) of the following month, used as the Gebrauch (q.v.) of the current month, e.g., Wasp C. 2. A key, comprised before its period of validity, used currently by a specific unit. This use of 'C' is strictly incorrect, 'C' in this case standing for 'Compromised'.

Clash: To disobey a rule, especially of a wheel order which disobeys the rule forbidding the use of one wheel in the same position on successive days, or of a discriminant which disobeys the rule forbidding the use of one trigram as the discriminant for two different keys on the same day. An example of such disobedience; the identification of a single frequency group to two or more keys.

Clip: The metal lug on the side of an Enigma wheel whereby the ringstellung can be set to any of the 26 possible positions.

Closure: A series of constatations of a menu (q.v.) forming a closed chain.

Codfish: A Fish key.

Colour: A synonym for key.

Column: One quarter (in some books, one half) of one of the pages of a German callsign book.

Compilation and Records Room: see CRR.

Composite Blist: A record of traffic identified to area or W/T (q.v.) system, but not immediately to particular keys used in that area or on that system.

Common Starting Point: The first point in the discriminant strip to which discriminants forming a repeat, bear a common relation.

Compromise: Destruction of security of a cipher. To be compromised (of key), to become insecure.

Composer Keys: GAF (q.v.) three-figure codes.

Consecutive Stecker: A stecker pairing of the type A/B, C/D etc., in which adjacent letters of the alphabet are used.

Consecutive Stecker Knock-Out (CSKO): A device by which a bombe (q.v.) could be made to reject solutions involving consecutive stecker.

Constatation: The association of a cipher letter and its assumed plain equivalent for a particular position.

Control: 1. The central station with which a group of stations is associated. 2. Used loosely for the Control Room (q.v.).

Control Room: That section responsible for the direction of interception and liaison with the intercept stations.

Corrections Party: Sixta (q.v.) department responsible for checking dud (q.v.) messages against the respective logs, and providing, where possible, corrections to the preamble necessary for dedudding the message.

Count: A comparison of two or more Enigma messages to establish, by the number of letters common to both, identical or related settings. To have a large or small number of letters identical with another message.

Cover: To watch any frequency for radio activity. Observation of a frequency by one or more sets.

CQ Message: A message sent, broadcast by Control, to all subscribers using a single so-called CQ callsign.

CR: Crib Room (q.v.).

Glossary

Crash (of a crib or suggested crib): To have one or more letters identical with the equivalent cipher letter or letters.

Crash Analysis: A tally of the number of crashes (q.v.) given by an assumed crib (q.v.) on a number of messages believed to have identical clear texts.

Crib: 1. Plain language equivalent of a stretch of cipher text. 2. A routine message which is so standard in form that it is possible to write out part of the clear text, as opposed to a cilli (q.v.), which was an indicator (q.v.), or an address, which was not a regular message or a re-encodement (q.v.).

Cribbable: So standardised in form that cribs (q.v.) may be used.

Cribbery: Theory and practice of cribbing.

Crib Interception: Special priority interception of certain messages on cryptographic grounds because they contained the crib (q.v.) necessary to break a particular key.

Crib Room (CR): The Hut 6 section engaged in finding cribs (q.v.) for breaking purposes.

CRR (Compilation and Records Room): A department at an intercept station designed to assist interception by providing information about the different W/T (q.v.) groups, especially callsign (q.v.) predictions.

CSKO: Consecutive Stecker Knock-Out (q.v.). Pronounced "Cisko".

Cupboard: To apply the 'five cupboards' (q.v.) substitution cipher to.

Current (of a break): During the 24-hour period the key was valid.

CY: A security device by which the position of the left-hand wheel was altered during the encoding of a message, the new position being indicated to the decoder by the letters CY followed by the new setting.

Cycle: The number indicating the line of the key table used by a particular station for determining the page of the Bird Book (q.v.) on which its callsign (q.v.) is to be found on each of the days of a particular month.

Cyclometer: Two Enigma machines wired together, designed to facilitate the exploitation of females (q.v.).

D: The pluggable reflector introduced by the Germans on Red in January 1944 and later on the GAF (q.v.) keys. Also used on a few Army keys.

D Book: See Dog Book.

'DE' Call: The originator's callsign, particularly where the message is passed on another network.

Decode Evidence: 1. Information contained in a decoded message. 2. Information from the fact that a message decodes on a particular key.

De-Dud: To get out, i.e., to decode a message previously dud (q.v.).

Delayed Hoppity: 1. A type of bombe (q.v.) used to run menus (q.v.) which assume the turnover (q.v.) position of the right-hand wheel after each constatation (q.v.) in turn. 2. A menu prepared for a delayed hoppity (q.v.) bombe.

Depth: The incidence of two or more messages, or portions of messages, on the same key at the same machine setting.

D/F: Direction finding by goniometric measurement. To locate the locality of a W/T (q.v.) station by radio goniometric measurement.

Dingy (of a crib (q.v.): Through variability of form likely to be consistently unsuccessful.

Directed Boil: A synonym for Crash Analysis (q.v.).

Disc: Short for discriminant (q.v.).

Disc-Clash: The appearance of a common discriminant (q.v.) on two or more W/T (q.v.) groups passing different keys, thereby suggesting either the use of another key of wider distribution or incorrect identification.

Disc-Click: Coincidence of a discriminant (q.v.) on two or more hitherto unrelated groups, suggesting a common key.

Discriminant: A three-letter group, normally placed in the preamble (q.v.) indicating the key used for the enciphering of the message.

Discriminant Card: A card recording, in an order as similar to the German order as possible, any discriminants belonging to a particular key-sheet over a period of up to 31 days.

Discriminant Catalogue: A catalogue designed to show on which discriminant card, and on which line of that card, each discriminant appears.

Discriminant Repeat: Repetition of any block of discriminants, whereby it is possible to predict all or some of the discriminants which are available for use with that key until the end of the current month.

Discriminant Strip: The order of discriminant blocks reconstructed in the manner of the master order of the German Cipher Office.

Discriminate: To use discriminants.

Distributor: A member of the Duddery (q.v.) supervising the testing, reblisting (q.v.) and examination of current duds (q.v.).

Dog Book: Rufzeichentafel D, the callsign book used by the German Army until Spring 1942.

Dottery: A hand method of breaking, requiring a knowledge or assumption of wheel order (q.v.), ringstellung (q.v.) and message setting, in which different stecker (q.v.) assumptions are tested by the language distribution of the decode which they give.

Double Bank: To have at least two intercepted operators cover a single W/T (q.v.) group at the same time.

Double Indicator System: The indicating system comprising two trigrams in the preamble of a message, of which the second was the message setting enciphered at the position indicated by the first.

D Position: Situation regarding the distribution and possession of Reflector D (q.v.) on any given network and with reference to any given key.

DR: 1. Decoding Room. 2. Despatch Rider.

Dud: A message which has not decoded on its assumed key. Fail to decode.

Dud Analysis Sheet: A record of all dud messages on one key showing Blist (q.v.)number, TOO (q.v.), TOI (q.v.), outside indicator, frequency, routeing and comments.

Dud-Buster: A machine for getting a message out when the key is known but the message setting unknown.

Glossary

Duddery: The section of TIS (q.v.) responsible for current testing and investigation of duds (q.v.) other than part-duds (q.v.).
Duds Research: The section currently testing and examining part-duds and discriminating duds.
Duds Watch: The Duddery (q.v.).
Duenna: A machine designed to recover unknown reflector wirings.
Dupe: A duplicate (q.v.).
Duplicate: A second copy of a message, intercepted by a second set or in a different transmission, similar in all respects to the first.
E: Short for Enigma (q.v.).
E-Book: See Elephant Book.
E/F: Short for Eastern Front.
Eintrittswalze: A plate of 26 terminals through which current enters the right-hand wheel of the Enigma machine.
Elephant Book: Rufzeichentafel E, the callsign book introduced by the German Army to replace the Dog Book (q.v.).
E-Message: Cipher message enciphered on the Enigma machine.
Encyclopaedia: A record of callsign (c.v.) cycles or serials and their users.
Enigma: 1. Cover name for the high grade machine cipher used by the principal units of the GAF and the German Army for administration and operational traffic. 2. Any cipher machine using normally three-wheels (q.v.), each wheel having an alphabet-bearing tyre capable of being set (according to the ringstellung (q.v.)) in any of 26 positions in relation to the wiring; an Umkehrwalze (q.v.) or reflector (q.v.) wheel connecting the 26 circuits in fixed or variable pairs, and in some models a set normally of ten stecker (q.v.) pairings. The right-hand wheel moves forward one position for each letter enciphered and each of the other two wheels move forward one or more positions for each revolution of the wheel next to it on the right.
Enigma Uhr: An attachment to the Enigma machine whereby the stecker of individual messages on the same key could be varied.
EP (short for 'En Passant'): 1. To note cribs or potential cribs among messages on their way from the DR (q.v.) to Hut 3 (q.v.). 2. To enter details of decodes on EP sheets (q.v.).
EPer: One engaged in EPing (q.v.).
EP Sheet: A form of recording blist (q.v.) number, frequency, TOO (q.v.), TOI (q.v.), outside indicator (q.v.), length, routeing, Reflector B (q.v.) or D (q.v.), Enigma Uhr (q.v.) of decoded messages on their way to Hut 3 (q.v.).
Equidistance: Recurrence of a pair of constatations which are less than 26 letters apart at the same interval at a distance which is a multiple of 26.
Ersatz Key: The key held in reserve for a given month in case the Gebrauch (q.v.) key was compromised. It automatically became the Gebrauch key of the following month.
Expensive (of keys or shots): Requiring much bombe (q.v.) time.
F: 1. (of Enigma messages): The Hut 6 name for messages in which CY (q.v.) was used. 2. Double Playfair traffic.

FAG: 1. Frequency Allocation Group. 2. By transference = W/T (q.v.) system using a FAG. 3. Fernaufklärungsgruppe – long-range reconnaissance unit.
F-Book: A callsign book based on blocks of five calls taken at random from the E Book (q.v.).
FC: Short for Fixed Callsign.
Female: 1. The same constatation (q.v.) occurring at two different positions. 2. Especially at a distance of three as under the old indicating system, when females were used in the breaking process.
FHB: Short for Flughafenbereich, a GAF administrative district controlled by an air base.
Five Cupboards: A British substitution cipher.
Fish: Cover name for a German high-grade cipher system and the traffic enciphered in that system.
Fit: Two or more messages on the same key and at the same machine setting.
Fixed Callsign: An arbitrary call, not based on any callsign system, assigned to a particular unit and always associated with it.
Flakkorps: One of the six GAF anti-aircraft Commands.
Fliegerführer: An operational GAF Command rather smaller than a Fliegerkorps (q.v.).
Fliegerhorst: A German airbase controlling satellite aerodromes.
Fliegerkorps: One of 10 or 11 GAF operational divisions, each of which normally included all types of aircraft.
Flivo (short for Fliegerverbindungsoffizier): A GAF liaison officer attached to Army formations; for Army co-operation.
Flugmelde: The aircraft observation service.
Flugsicherung: The organisation controlling such devices as radio beacons, of which the object was aircraft protection.
Form Sheet: Record of beginnings or endings of Enigma messages, written out to facilitate comparison in making boils (q.v.) or crash analyses (q.v.).
Foss: To record on a Foss sheet (q.v.).
Fosser: One who fosses (q.v.).
Foss Sheet (From its inventor, H R Foss): A squared sheet of 26 lettered columns and rows used (among other purposes) for recording the outside indicators (q.v.) of messages. The third letter of the indicator was entered in the box on the row of the first letter and the column of the second letter.
Fracture: A break.
Fracture Book: A record of all broken keys kept by RR2 (q.v.).
Frequency Band: A name given to the body of currently unidentified traffic after 1 February 1945, arranged in frequency order and laid out on long tables for ready reference in RR Air (q.v.).
Frequency Guide: An index of frequencies designed to show the key most commonly passed on any frequency, thus providing a ready method of sorting traffic.
Frequency Sheet: An ICI (q.v.) sheet.
Führungsnetz: See A-Shift.

Glossary

'Fuer' Call: Callsign of the unit for which a message is intended, especially of a transmission prior to that direct to the final recipient.

Fun and Games: Appearance of two or more messages with texts largely identical, but differing at the end, where the different cipher texts are in depth.

Funkhorchkompanie: A Y unit intended to intercept and read low-grade Allied traffic.

Funkplan: The W/T (q.v.) set-up in a particular area, inclusive of callsign, frequency allocation and times and methods of working.

Funkstelle: A wireless station.

Fusion Room: The Sixta (q.v.) department responsible for collation and distribution of information relevant to cryptographic, intelligence and W/T (q.v.) sections.

GAF: Short for German Air Force

GC&CS: Government Code and Cypher School

Gebrauch Key: The key valid for the current month.

Genuine Dud: A message, sorted to the correct key, but failing to decode by reason of mistakes in encoding, transmission or interception.

Geschwader: GAF Command of normally about 120 aircraft of any type.

Get Out: To decode a message formerly dud (q.v.).

GHQ Netz: German Army W/T (q.v.) system connecting the Armies and Heeresgruppen (q.v.) with OKH (q.v.) and with one another.

Giant: A machine consisting basically of four bombes (q.v.) designed to recover unknown reflector (q.v.) wirings.

GKDOS: Geheimekommandosache – the German 'Top Secret'.

Group: 1. A control and its subscribers working on a given frequency at a given time. 2. Traffic sent by such a group.

Grundstellung: 1. A basic Outside Indicator (q.v.) which formed part of the key and at which position all inside indicators were enciphered.   2. German term for any Outside Indicator.

Gruppe: A small GAF unit roughly corresponding to a RAF squadron.

G-Tail (Geheim or Secret-Tail): A type of crib, widely used on Army messages, assuming that the message ended with its serial number and the classification of the message – Secret or Top Secret.

GTO: Short for German Time of Origin.

Half-Enigma: A type of hand machine in which the terminals of the reflector may be connected direct to the lampboard.

Hand Attempt: An attempt to break an Enigma key by non-mechanical methods, especially by assuming the ringstellung and following out stecker implications from the constatations of a cilli.

Hand Duenna: A method of hand stecker knock-out by using the same principles as those on which the D-breaking machine Duenna was designed to work.

Handwritten Originals: The actual message as written down by the operator as opposed to the teleprinted copies.

Hanky-Panky (named after its inventor, J H Hancock): A chart for recording all incoming discriminants and the frequencies on which they occurred.

Harmonic: A technical freak in interception whereby the frequency is doubled or halved.

Hatted: Random.

Hatting (of keys or discriminants): Re-arrangement of a key-sheet or discriminant block in a random, or even a patterned order.

Heeresgruppe: An Army Group, one of the major operational German Army commands, each of which normally controlled one, two or more Armies (Armeen).

Helio: Short for Heliopolis.

Herivelismus (from its inventor, J W J Herivel): The method of discovering a ringstellung from ringstellung tips (q.v.).

H/F: Short for High Frequency.

High-Speed Bombe: A Delayed Hoppity Bombe (q.v.).

Hoppity: A type of bombe or menu designed to allow for successive turnover assumptions, made possible by knowledge of the position of the right-hand ringstellung clip.

Horrors: Those messages identified too late to blist by day x + 2 in RR1 and x + 3 in RR2.

H/S: Short for Head of Shift.

Hut 3: The section which dealt with the intelligence produced by Hut 6.

Hut 6: The section engaged in registering, breaking and decoding the Enigma traffic of the German Army and Air Force.

Hut 8: The section engaged in breaking Enigma traffic of the German navy.

H/W: Short for Handwritten Original.

IA: The operational department of a German Air or Army unit.

IC: The intelligence department of a German Air or Army unit.

IC Discs: The person in charge of discriminants at the Initial Sorting stage.

ICI (In Charge of Identification): Name given to the person in charge of the current sorting of traffic in RR Air after 1 February 1945.

ICI Sheet: Cover sheet fastened to unidentified traffic in the Frequency Bands (q.v.) on which was recorded all incoming information relative to the traffic on that frequency.

I/C Ops (In Charge of Operations): A member of the Machine Room who determined the order in which jobs should be run on the bombes.

Identification Party: The person concerned with current traffic identification until 1 February 1945 (called latterly CIP).

Illegal: Not legal (q.v.).

Indicating System: A system by which message settings are enciphered or concealed.

Indicator: One or two three-letter groups which help to indicate the Message Setting. (See Single Indicator System and Double Indicator System).

Indicator Correction: A correct sending of an indicator after an original mistake in transmission – thence, loosely, any alternative indicator (q.v.).

Glossary

Initial Sorting: An automatic system of traffic sorting to key blists (q.v.) through guides, based on some form of notation (i.e., frequency, serial, group notation, fixed call) placed on the message by the intercept station.
Instrument Keys: GAF three-figure codes.
Intelligence Group: Groups intercepted for intelligence value.
IP: Identification Party (q.v.).
Italuft: Covername for the commander of the German Air Force in Italy.
Jaeger Code: A five-letter code used principally in the Jägerleitkreis.
Jafue: Short for Jägdführer – O C Fighters.
Jagddivision: One of the divisions of the GAF fighter force.
Jagdkorps: One of the three main commands of the GAF fighter force.
JD: Jagddivison (q.v.).
Jeffreys Sheets: Sheets which record, by means of punched holes, the electrical connections through the reflector and the two left-hand wheels.
JG: Jagdgeschwader (see Geschwader).
Job: A menu or programme of menus prepared for running on the bombe.
Jot: 1. A list of discriminants identified during a particular day. 2. A list of identifications of frequencies compiled and distributed currently by the Control Room.
Jumbo: A type of bombe which distinguished stops having no contradiction and recorded through a typewriter the stecker pairings arrived at.
Kenngruppe: See Discriminant.
Kennwort: The word from which the discriminant of a Notschlüssel was formed by taking the 1st, 3rd and 5th letters to make a trigram.
Key: 1. The wheelorder, ringstellung, stecker, D-plugging (if any) and discriminants (if any) used by a particular group of stations on a particular day or other fixed period. 2. Keysheet (q.v.). 3. An indefinite series of keys as defined in (1) above, with continuity in distribution and use, e.g., Red, the general GAF key.
Keyboard Cilli: A type of Cilli recognisable because it was obtained from, or suggested by, the order of the letters on the keyboard of an Enigma cipher machine, e.g., OKL, QWE, QAP.
Key Message: Schlüssel messages, or key messages, were those decodes which contained information relating to keys. They were one of the types of messages contained in the daily publication known as LFs.
Key-Sheet: A sheet of paper containing 31 keys, normally used for the period of one month.
KG: Kampfgeschwader – a bomber Geschwader (q.v.).
Kiss: A slip of paper on which were marked the time of origin, length, key and number of a message, in order that it could be compared with other similar slips to reveal reencodements by coincidences in time of origin.
Kiss-Lage: A sheet of time of origin clicks thrown up by Kisses.
Kitten: A girl in the Registration Room who carried out the first stage of the sorting process on traffic as it came off the conveyor belt.
Komm.Gen: Short for Kommandierender General – General O/C.

KR (German abbreviation for Kriegsmeldung): An indication of the priority of a message inserted in the preamble. British equivalent of "Immediate".
Kreis: W/T system in which any subscriber can communicate directly with any other.
Lage: A list of jobs waiting to be run on the bombes.
Lage Conference: A daily meeting to discuss priorities on the Lage (q.v.).
Lampboard: A panel on the Enigma hand machine on which the enciphered letter was lit up when the clear text letter was pressed down on the keyboard, or, conversely, on which the clear text letter appeared when the enciphered letter was pressed down.
Legal: Obeying the rules, especially of a wheelorder obeying the "non-clashing" rule (Cf. 'clash').
L/F: Short for Low Frequency.
LFs: A daily publication, translating into English all decoded messages considered to contain information of cryptographic or W/T significance. A single message of this type was frequently referred to as an LF.
LG: Lehrgeschwader, a training or experimental Geschwader (q.v.).
LGau: Short for Luftgau (q.v.).
Library: The room where unbroken traffic was filed under key and date. The dupes of broken traffic were also filed here for a certain period and then thrown away.
Line: A simple wireless set-up consisting of two stations in contact with each other on the same frequency.
Link: 1. A line of communication by teleprinter or W/T between any number of units. 2. A common factor between two or more messages or frequency groups, whether key, discriminant, callsign or dupe. 3. A constatation on a menu.
LN Regiment: Luftnachrichtenregiment, or GAF signals regiment.
Log Book: A record kept by any section of information relevant to the working of that section, entries being made from day to day as occasion demands.
Log Chat: All radio activity recorded on the logs, whether keying, plain language or Q or Z code, exclusive of message.
Logs: Log sheets, the record of radio activity noted by an intercept operator.
LSSAH: Short for Leibstandarte Adolf Hitler, the SS Division which provided Hitler's bodyguard.
Luftflotte: An Air Fleet, one of the highest operational GAF commands, each of which normally controlled at least one Fliegerkorps.
Luftgau: One of the 20 or so areas into which Greater Germany was divided for the purpose of GAF administration. Hence, the authority in such a district (strictly Luftgaukommando).
LW Kdo: Luftwaffenkommando, an operational division of the GAF smaller than a Luftflotte.
Machine Room: The name given at different times to two different sections of Hut 6: 1. The section engaged in work on breaking theory and practice. 2. The section formerly known as the Netz Room (q.v.).

Glossary

Menu: 1. A series of more or less interconnected constatations of which the relative positions are known, and which has been prepared for key-breaking on the bombe. 2. A series of instructions to the Decoding Room to type alphabets at certain machine settings and in a given order, the results being used in a hand attempt at breaking a key.

Message Setting: The initial position of the wheels of the Enigma machine for enciphering a particular message.

M/F: Short for Medium Frequency.

MG Serial: A fixed callsign number allotted to an Army W/T group inside Germany and arrived at by imposing the MG shift (a daily differential factor) on the MG order (a converted E book order).

Middle-Wheel Turnover: A turnover of the left-hand wheel of the Enigma machine caused by the middle wheel reaching the position where it causes the turnover of the lefthand wheel.

Missorts: Those messages incorrectly sorted and identified.

Morrison's Diagrams: Diagrams of W/T communications systems, generally divided into geographical sectors, showing the units and their respective serials and rows, frequencies, cover names, locations and similar information, collated from source and logs. So-called after Major Morrison, whose section was responsible for their compilation and distribution.

Mosse Code: A book of code groups, based on a commercial code compiled by Rudolf Mosse of Hamburg before the war, but developed and expanded during the war. It substitutes semi-pronounceable five-letter groups for common words or phrases – thus Luftgau becomes GELIP.

MR: Machine Room (q.v.).

M/S: Maschinenschlüssel.

M Serial: A fixed callsign number allotted to an Army W/T group whether inside Germany or not, and arrived at by imposing the daily differential factor (the M-shift) on the converted E-book order (the M-order).

Nafue: Short for Nachrichtenführer – signals chief.

Nearness: A type of indicator, especially of a cilli, in which the message setting chosen is near to the outside indicator, e.g., (ABC) BCF, which was known as a (1, 1, 3) or (ABC) ABF, a (0, 0, 3).

Netz: A type of wireless working in which each subscriber had his own receiving frequency.

Netz Method: A way of breaking the Enigma which exploited the weakness of the old indicating system of doubly-enciphered indicators. It was essentially a comparison of females at a distance of three, all occurrences of which were recorded on the Netz sheets (q.v.).

Netz Sheet: Any of 60 sheets, each of 26 differently lettered quadruple Foss sheets having holes punched in them corresponding to females at distances of three, i.e., one set for each possible wheelorder, and one sheet for each position of the right-hand wheel – the positions of the other wheels being represented by the co-ordinates of the holes.

NI: Non-Indicator (q.v.).

Nigelian (From Nigel S Forward, the discoverer of a wheelorder): One of 30 wheelorders which were used in many months on most GAF keys, to the exclusion of the other 30 "non-Nigelian" wheelorders.

No Colour: All traffic which could not be sorted by the Identification Party to key blists or frequency groups. So-called because originally because all keys had colour names, e.g., Red, Blue, Violet.

Non-Clashing Rule: A rule forbidding the use of the same wheel in the same position on two consecutive days in the same month.

Non-Discriminating: Not having a discriminant.

Non-Indicator: A transposition cipher. Traffic enciphered in such a transposition.

Non-Nigelian: See Nigelian.

Non-Turnover Stretch: A stretch of cipher text of a maximum of 26 letters which does not, or is assumed not to, have a turnover of the middle wheel within it.

Notation Number: A number prefixed by the initial letter of the area concerned (e.g., W for West) allotted arbitrarily to all GAF W/T groups after the encoding of callsigns was introduced.

Not-Key: An emergency key specially constructed from a given Schlüsselwort.

Notschlüssel: Not-Key (q.v.).

Number(ed) Group: Traffic on a group or groups, called by one of the principal frequencies used, when there was insufficient evidence to allot a key name, e.g., E 8532, the key used principally on frequency 8532.

OB: Order of Battle (q.v.).

OBdL: Oberbefehlshaber der Luftwaffe – GAF C-in-C.

OBW: Oberbefehlshaber West.

OCB: OC Bombenlage (q.v.).

OC Bombenlage: Members of the Machine Room who assigned bombes to jobs as they came from I/C Ops (q.v.).

OKH: Oberkommando des Heeres – German Army GHQ.

OKL: Oberkommando der Luftwaffe – GAF GHQ.

On Priority (of a W/T group): On the list of those groups to be covered for cryptographic or intelligence reasons.

Op-20-G: The authority in charge of American naval bombes.

Out: Of a key – broken. Of a message – decoded.

Outside Indicator: The setting (i.e., window reading) of the wheels at which the message setting (Inside Indicator) is enciphered.

Overseas Party: A department responsible for the Initial Sorting of traffic intercepted overseas, and the direction of overseas interception.

Parent: A cryptographer to whom the immediate responsibility for the study of a key or group of keys was assigned.

Part-Dud: That part of a multi-teile message which failed to decode when other parts decoded.

Phantom (short for Phantom Link): A link on a menu not used in the bombe run, but designed to allow of the immediate rejection of many incorrect stops.

Glossary

Plist: A blist of messages marked with the letter P, i.e., those encoded with Enigma Uhr.

Pluggable (of the reflector): Capable of having its wiring altered.

PO (part only): A multi-teile message of which one or more parts were missed in interception.

Position: Any one of the 26^3 x 60 possible combinations of wheelorder and ringstellung.

Preamble: The heading of an Enigma message which was transmitted before the beginning of the cipher text and consisted of callsigns, time of origin, priority symbol, length of message and indicators.

Priority Guide: A list of frequencies given special intelligence or cryptographic value. Priority Group: A group "on priority" (q.v.).

Proforma: 1. A type of report set out under fixed, pre-determined headings. 2. Any précis of information set out in a manner designed to facilitate quick reference, especially a log proforma, a précis of the log sheets (q.v.).

Pronounceable (of cillies): A trigram used as a message setting which, if it is a cilli, may be recognised because it is a pronounceable syllable or word, e.g., LOQ, DOF, MUT.

Psilli (psychological cilli): A message setting so related to the outside indicator that it can be inferred from the latter.

QMI: Q code for "cipher machine out of order". Hence used with a key-name or wheelorder to indicate the setting in cases of doubt.

QMO: Q code for notification of key compromise.

QTA: Q code for cancellation of a message on the part of the originator.

Quadrilateral: An interrelation between four keys, whereby two keys of one month were split up, the wheelorder and ringstellung of one key being placed with the stecker and discriminants of the other to form two new keys.

Quatsch (German for "nonsense"): Strings of words, passages from books, poems, etc. encoded in Enigma for practice purposes.

Quiet Room: Originally a sub-section of Control, concerned with traffic research and analysis. Name later changed to TIS2.

Qwatch (Quiet Watch): The part of the Watch intended to deal with rarely broken or nonoperational keys.

QWD: Q code for notification of receipt after decoding.

QZE: Q code for procedure signal meaning "raise your frequency – kcs".

QZF: Q code for the procedure meaning "lower your frequency – kcs".

QZL: Q code for expression of inability to decode a message on the part of the recipient.

Radio Fingerprinting: A method of photographing, with the aid of a cathode ray tube, the individual characteristics of the transmitter in use.

Raster: A hand cipher which replaced Double Playfair as the type of non-machine cipher most closely associated in use and content with Enigma.

RE: Re-encodement (q.v.).

Reblist: To delete messages from one blist and add to another.

Recce: 1. Reconnaissance. 2. The network for communications between units engaged on air reconnaissance.

Re-encodement: A second encoding of a message in a different key.

Reflector (German: Umkehrwalze): The wheel on the left side of an Enigma machine, fixed in a position in some models and designed to turn over in others, serving to connect the 26 circuits constituted by the wiring of the other wheels in pairs.

Registration Room: The section of Hut 6 engaged in registering the traffic.

Reject (of a stretch of cipher text): To produce crashes against a crib or suggested crib. To "reject well" is to reject most of the possible forms of a crib, thereby limiting the forms that need to be run on the bombe.

Repeat(ed) (of a wheelorder): One which has been previously used during the month.

Repeater (Star): A star used for passing on messages originated by a station not one of the subscribers on the star.

Re-Run: A repeat of a message intercepted overseas, obtained in order to check the decoding by the telex operator.

Research Keys: Keys dealt with by the Research Section.

Research Section: The section of Hut 6 engaged in breaking, or trying to break, unbroken, rarely broken, or non-operational keys.

RFP: Radio Fingerprint (q.v.).

Ringstellung: The part of an Enigma key which indicated the tyre-setting of the wheel.

Ringstellung Tip: An indication of the ringstellung or approximate ringstellung obtained from an inspection of the outside indicators of the first message encoded in the key by different cipher clerks.

RO (Receipt Only): A message of which only the preamble, sent as a receipt by the recipient of the message, was intercepted.

Rocket: German railway (Reichsbahn) key, called Rocket from September 1943. Identified by GC&CS in June 1940 and first broken February 1941.

Rod: One of a series of pasteboard strips, of which there are 26 for each wheel, giving the contacts through the wheel at the 26 wheel positions of each letter of the alphabet.

Rod Pairing: An association of two direct rods as of two letters at the same position on a pair of inverse rods, determined or suggested by an unsteckered constatation.

Rod Square: A square of 26 letters by 26 formed by the direct or inverse rods of a particular Enigma wheel arranged in order.

Routine Message: A message appearing at more or less regular intervals, such as a daily report.

Row: 1. Series of callsigns in a callsign book constituting a single row when the book is regarded as a single table having a given number of rows and columns. 2 (by transference): A unit using any particular row.

RR: Registration Room (q.v.).

Glossary

RR1: Registration Room for Watch keys.
RR2: Registration Room for Research keys.
RR Air: Registration Room for Air keys.
RR Army: Registration Room for Army keys.
Run: To try (a crib) on a bombe. A trial of a crib or menu by a bombe.
Sandwich (of an unbroken day): An unbroken day between two broken days (of a wheelorder). The legal wheelorders for such a day.
Schlüsselwort: A word from which the Germans derived a Not-key.
Search Guide: A list of groups, put out by Lovett's section, not important enough to warrant full cover or only occasionally active. Graded as (a) groups requiring cover if active; (b) groups requiring only sufficient cover to keep continuity; (c) groups not requiring cover.
Secondary Sorting System: A specialised method of sorting traffic by rows (q.v.) on certain A-serials which passed more than one key on any given frequency.
Second Channel: A technical error in interception whereby the frequency measurement is 900kcs above or below the actual frequency on which the message is being transmitted.
Sector Investigator: Traffic analyst specialising in a particular geographical sector.
Self-stecker(ed): The term applied to the unsteckered letters (normally six) of any particular key.
Serial: A serial number, fixed for each W/T group, arrived at by imposing the respective shift on the converted M, MG, F or A order.
Set: A radio sending or receiving unit, specially an intercept unit at an intercepting station.
Sheets: Any of the sets of punched paper squares used in breaking, e.g., the Netz sheets or Jeffreys sheets.
Shift: The daily differential factor introduced by the Germans for security reasons in their use of the E and F Books.
Shot: A job (q.v.) for the bombes.
SI: Sector Investigator (q.v.).
Single Indicator System: The early indicating system in which the outside indicator only appeared in the preamble of a message, the doubly enciphered message setting being buried in the cipher groups.
Sixta: Also VI IS. The section concerned primarily with the pure W/T approach to signals intelligence, but embodying also the Fusion Room (q.v.).
Sixta Daily: A summary published daily by Sixta of fresh information affecting the complete W/T picture. It was issued in two parts (a) by Lovett's Section, containing information derived from pure W/T; (b) by Morrison's Section, a collation of information derived from pure W/T
and source.
Sixta Listings: Proformas listing the frequency, callsigns, identification (if any), D/Fs and other relevant information, of all logs not immediately recognised as priority groups.
SKO: Stecker knock-out (q.v.).

Sonderschlüssel: A special key.

Source: General name given to the body of information gained from decoded messages.

Spoof: Dummy traffic, made to look like Enigma, for practice or camouflage purposes.

Staff Key: A key reserved for Top Secret (Geheimkommandosache) matters. (German: Stabsmachinenschlüssel).

Stagger: To try a crib at a number of consecutive positions of the message. A job for the bombes produced by staggering a crib at two or more positions of the message.

Stagger Stretch: Part of a crib considered invariable enough to stagger (q.v.).

Star: A W/T network arranged on the principle of a common control for all subscribers, through which control of all intercommunication between subscribers was theoretically supposed to be passed.

Star-Net: See Star.

Star Number: 1. An arbitrary number assigned to each GAF Star network after the introduction of encoded calls and changing frequencies. 2. A number allocated by the GAF to indicate a particular star, when a unit controlled more than one star.

Station: 1. A wireless intercept station. 2. A wireless transmitting station.

Station Register: Teleprinted list of all messages intercepted by a station, giving message number, TOI, TOO, discriminant (if any), message indicator, first group.

Stecker: Scheme or system of cross-connecting circuits (capable of variation as required, and normally changed by plugging daily), having the effect of a simple reciprocal substitution at the entry points on the right side of the right-hand wheel, affecting usually 20 of the 26 letters. 2. That part of an Enigma key indicating the pluggings to be used.

Stecker Board: Part of the Enigma machine consisting of 26 pairs of plug sockets, one pair for each letter.

Stecker Implication: That characteristic of the Enigma cipher system whereby the assumption of the stecker of one letter of a constatation implies the stecker of the other.

Stecker Knock-Out: A method of determining the stecker of an Enigma key, especially when the pairings of the reflector are unknown, by following out the consequences of a series of stecker assumptions in terms of rod pairings and further stecker deductions until contradictions are produced or a consistent solution reached.

Stecker Pairing: An association of two letters in a daily Enigma key. There were normally ten such pairings in each key, giving the day's stecker (q.v.).

Stecker Plug: A pair of plugs connected by wire, by means of which any letter can be connected with any other on the stecker board (q.v.).

Stop: A point in a run at which a bombe stops. Hence, a possible solution produced by the bombe. (A stop can have stecker contradictions. A stop with no stecker contradictions is known as a story).

Glossary

Story: A possible partial solution of a key produced by hand or mechanical methods, subject to confirmation or rejection by further tests.

Stutterer: A trigram having a repeated letter, such as JJM, JJJ or JMJ. Used of a discriminant or ringstellung.

Subscriber: A station in a W/T group.

Superimposition: The confusion in interception of two W/T groups on close frequencies so that the callsigns of one group become associated with message text of the other group.

SYG: Special Y Group – the earlier name for the intercept station WOYG at Beaumanor (q.v.).

TA: Traffic Analysis or Traffic Analyst.

Tabs: Tagesabschlüsselmeldung.

Tagesabschlüsselmeldung: An "end of day" report, one of a type commonly sent by GAF units, giving the number of messages sent and receive during the day.

Teil (e): Part(s) of a long message. Enigma messages of more than 250 letters were normally divided into parts of approximately 250 letters each, each part having a different message setting.

Teil-Break: A break in a message between parts enciphered with different message settings. See "teil".

Test: To examine a stop or story produced by the bombe to discover if it is a correct solution.

Tester: 1. A person "testing" messages on different keys and settings on the suggestion of the Distributor or Sector Investigator. 2. A member of the Machine Room engaged in testing bombe stops.

Thrice-Daily Stecker: Zusatz stecker (q.v.).

Tick-Off: 1. A sheet numbered serially, on which, according to their blist numbers, messages decoded are ticked, and messages that are dud are marked "dud". 2. A sheet numbered serially, kept by the Duddery, recording the whereabouts of all messages "ticked off" as having been received in that section.

Time Click: Coincidence in time of origin of two or more messages suggesting the possibility of re-encodement.

Time Of Origin: The time at which a message was composed or encoded, which was placed in the preamble of an Enigma message.

TIS 1: Traffic Identification Section 1 (Air).

TIS 2: Traffic Identification Section 2 (Army).

Tl(e): Teil(e) (q.v.).

TOI: Time of Interception (GMT).

TOO: Time of Origin (German).

Top and Tail Menu: A menu using crib constatations from the beginning and the end of a message.

T/P: Teleprinter.

Traffic: Messages sent by wireless.

Try: The testing of a message on a machine on any particular key or setting. To carry out such testing, or cause it to be carried out.

Try-Slip: A form affixed to a message indicating to the tester on what key or keys and wheelorders the message is to be "tried".

Tuner: Message sent by Control of a star, usually CQ (q.v.), to test reception conditions.

Turnover: The periodic forward movement of one position at a time of the middle or left-hand wheel of the Enigma cipher machine.

Typex: The English cipher system used to transmit intercepted traffic from overseas to GC&CS.

Tyre: The moveable alphabet-bearing rim of an Enigma wheel.

Ultra: Intelligence derived from high-grade German cipher.

Uncle: An Umkehrwalze or reflector.

Unduped: Having no duplicate.

Up: Used of a key, when wheelorder and stecker were known, but ringstellung had yet to be worked out.

Upright: The first column of a rod square.

Viennismus: A practice, observed in a series of Enigma messages originating from Vienna, of assigning successive outside indication which formed a sequence (e.g., KCV, LDW, MEX).

V-Key: An Enigma key used by authorities concerned with secret weapons including V1 and V2.

Wahlwort: Any non-textual word or phrase used at the beginning or end of a cipher used to avoid stereotyped beginnings or endings.

Watch: The section of Hut 6 concerned with the current breaking of keys of immediate operational importance.

Watch Keys: Keys dealt with by the Watch (q.v.).

Wehrkreis: 1. One of about 20 administrative military districts of Greater Germany: the authority in such a district (strictly Wehrkreiskommando). 2. The W/T system linking the capitals of these districts. 3. The Enigma key used on this system, otherwise known as Green or Greenshank.

Wehrmacht Key: An Army key for cross-traffic between stations or units of the Army (home forces and field army) and other parts of the Wehrmacht.

W/F: Western Front.

Wheel: One of the three or more components of the Enigma machine, each of which imposes 26 different substitutions at its 26 different positions.

Wheelorder: Order in which the interchangeable wheels of the Enigma machine are arranged. A part of the machine setting for any particular key period.

W/K: Wehrkreis (q.v.).

WOYG: War Office Y Group, the intercept station at Beaumanor (q.v.).

W/T: Wireless Telegraphy.

WTI: Wireless Telegraphy Intelligence.

(Day) X + 1: The day following the day of any particular operation, i.e., interception, breaking.

X-Key: The key of the previous month re-used in a shuffled order, e.g., Jaguar X.

Glossary

"X" Traffic: Intercepts not on adopted frequencies (q.v.) and hence not sorted by the automatic sorting system. Frequencies on traffic of this type were marked with an "X".

"Y" Service: The service concerned with the interception, breaking, analysis and intelligence of enemy wireless traffic.

Zusatz Stecker: A security device whereby two of the stecker pairings were altered during the course of the day.

3L: That section of Hut 3 responsible for liaison with other agencies, including Hut 6.

VI IS: No. VI Intelligence School, later known as Sixta (q.v.).

INDEX

A

Abdulla FAG 187
Abwehr 423
Admiralty 26
Adriatic 281, 309
Adstock 250
Aegaeis Süd 307, 447
Aegean 277, 308, 309
Afrika Korps. *See* Panzerarmee Afrika
Agnus 104
Aitken, James 220, 231
Alamein 24, 277, 284, 291
Albania 111, 374
Alexander, Hugh 26, 35, 168, 174
Algiers 285
American. *See* United States
Angers 316
Anzio Bay 280
AOK Armee Oberkommando (Army High Command)
  AOK 1 319, 417, 429, 448
  AOK 2 306, 308, 348, 449
  AOK 5 295, 319, 443
  AOK 6 319
  AOK 7 321
  AOK 10 298, 299, 300, 348
  AOK 12 303, 447
  AOK 14 298, 299, 300, 448
  AOK 15 321, 443
  AOK 17 348, 446
  AOK 19 319, 444
  AOK 25 444
Ardennes 32, 40
Arlington (Virginia) 117, 239
Asché 72
Athens 276, 284, 295, 378, 382
Auchinleck, General Sir Claude 140
Auschwitz 363
Austria 336, 343, 359
Autoscritcher 35, 179, 180, 184, 356
Avranches 281, 315, 319, 323

B

Babbage, Major Dennis 28, 30, 45, 147, 149, 164, 180, 184, 220, 356
Baker, Robert C. 38
Balkans 119, 253, 255, 275, 276, 282
Banburismus 114, 123
Banbury 87, 102, 123
Banbury sheets 87, 246
Banbury 'stagger' 321
Banister List. *See* Blist
Banister, Michael 20, 31
Beaumanor 15, 34, 40
Belgium 330, 392
Belgrade (see also Balkans, Yugoslavia) 284, 306, 355, 357, 358, 382, 446
Benghazi 277
Bertrand, General Gustav 72
Beta (wheel) 58
Bielefeld 357
Bird Book 282
Bismarck 23, 258
Blist 112, 148, 151, 332, 341, 345, 387
Block A (BP) 26
Block D (BP) 27, 147, 149, 247
Block F (BP) 388
'Bobbery' 178, 343
Bombes 19, 22, 24, 26, 27, 29, 41, 51, 104-107, 108, 115, 117, 121, 140, 147, 153, 157, 158, 162, 168, 170, 189, 211, 215, 221, 225, 239, 240, 241, 247-253, 256, 262, 277, 286, 288, 290, 303, 328, 339, 345, 355, 360
Bombes (Washington) 298, 368, 391
BO Pairing 170, 173, 355
Boulogne 262
BOVO 225, 229, 230, 231, 244, 245
Bovril (see also BOVO) 244
BP (Bletchley Park) 9, 10, 12, 82, 83, 133, 194, 240, 247, 257, 279, 373
Braithwaite, Fran 44
Bream (Fish link) 296, 297

Bruno (reflector) 58
Brussels 320
Bulgaria 282
Bundy, Major William 45

C

Caesar (reflector) 58
Cairo 285, 290
Canadian 327
Canney, June 20
Cape Bon 116
Channel Islands (see also Guernsey,
 Flak Jersey) 312, 322, 443, 448
Cherbourg 262, 322
Cillies 18-22, 24, 26, 28, 84, 87, 90,
 93-95, 101, 102, 104-106, 109,
 110, 112, 113, 131, 148, 151, 154,
 155, 157-159, 169, 206, 210, 211,
 255, 256, 262, 265, 267, 269, 272,
 276, 279, 285-287, 290, 291, 295,
 297, 301-304, 306, 316, 320, 321,
 323, 329, 339, 346, 347, 348, 349,
 351, 356, 357, 362-364, 366-372,
 374, 379, 380, 381, 385-387, 397,
 398, 401
Clarke, Joan (later Murray) 10, 82
Clarke, Lionel E. 125, 173, 180, 184,
 355, 356
Clarkian Wheel Order 125, 126, 127, 129
Clonk method 138, 264, 265, 269
Coblenz 316
Colman, John Stanley 18, 378
Consecutive Stecker Knock-Out
 (CSKO)(see Stecker Knock-Out)
Control Room 15, 38, 43, 44, 271, 378
Crete 23, 294, 304, 309, 381, 444, 448
Crib (including Cribbery) 18, 19, 21-23, 25,
 27, 28, 29, 38, 42, 51, 60-65, 69, 71,
 73, 76-81, 86, 92, 93, 105-109, 113,
 114, 118, 127, 135, 141, 142, 146-155,
 158-160, 168, 170, 173, 175, 178,
 180, 182, 186, 187, 189, 190, 206,
 211-218, 222, 225, 227, 230, 243,
 244, 248, 253-259, 262-265, 267,
 270, 272, 274, 276-295, 297-301,
 303-308, 311, 312, 314-316, 318,
 319, 321, 322, 325-335, 337-339,
 341-343, 345-351, 356-358, 360-
 372, 374-276, 379-383, 386-391,
 396-398, 401, 402
Crib Room (also CR)(BP) 17, 18, 22,
 24-26, 28-29, 31, 51, 104, 107-
 109, 112, 113, 118, 120, 146, 155,
 223, 246, 278, 286, 292, 303
Crimea 336, 338, 348
CSKO (see Stecker Knock-Out)
CY Device 204-206, 209, 369
Czechoslovakia 336, 352, 359

D

Dachau 363
Davies, Sqn. Ldr. Geeorge 33, 42
D-Day 32-38, 115, 163-165, 169, 258,
 275, 300, 310
Decoding Room 24, 37, 38, 43, 46, 48,
 49, 89, 147, 156, 170, 185, 186, 221,
 222, 227, 246, 247, 250, 259, 323
Delayed Hoppity (see Hoppity)
Denmark 272, 330, 421, 424
Denniston, Alistair 83
Depth 76, 85, 86, 87, 101, 106, 112,
 122, 147, 159, 190, 257, 267,
 268, 273, 274, 279, 287, 307,
 322, 329, 381, 396, 402
Derna 279
Dönitz, Grand Admiral Karl 44, 344
Dottery 102, 122, 148, 153, 159, 206
Double encoding 166, 204, 217, 219
Double Playfair 194, 373, 375, 388
Duddery 15, 33, 38, 39, 45
Duds 187, 218, 247, 248, 352
Duenna (also Hand Duenna) 34, 35,
 161, 162, 174, 175, 179-181, 184,
 283, 318, 355, 356
Dunlop, Sheila 45
Durazzo 381, 382
Dutch (see Holland)

E

Eastcote 250
Eastern Front 254, 259, 283, 308,
 317, 334-344, 346-349, 357,
 362, 365, 366, 378-381, 403,
 407, 422, 434, 437, 439, 442,
 445, 448
Edgar, Mr S.C. 20

El Alamein (see Alamein)
Enigma Uhr 34, 36, 122, 154, 163, 166, 178, 182, 185-188, 206, 252, 275, 283, 311, 315-317, 333, 334, 344, 399
EP (En Passant) 109, 222
Eperson, Miss Doreen 248
Erfurt 270
Essen 324
Evans, Lt-Col Geoffrey 376

F

FAG (Frequency Allocation Group) 158, 176, 187, 313, 315
Falaise Gap 40
F Book 34, 35, 36
Fehlanzeige (crib) 113, 216, 217
Feldluftgau XXVIII 280
Finland 357, 448
Fish 30, 119, 285, 294, 296, 346, 358
Flak Jersey (see also Channel Islands, Guernsey)
Flak Korps I 339
Flak Korps 3 314
Flak Korps MVM 337
Fletcher, Harold 45
Flieger Division 318, 419, 434
Fliegerführer Afrika 139, 277, 286, 404, 433
Fliegerführer Kroatien 139, 282, 423, 433
Fliegerkorps Tunis 428
Fliegerkorps I (later Luftflotte I) 338, 339, 344, 405, 419, 428, 430, 431
Fliegerkorps II 278, 280, 283, 310, 313, 344, 345, 431
Fliegerkorps III 329
Fliegerkorps IV 338, 430
Fliegerkorps VIII 336, 338, 339, 344, 405, 418, 430, 433
Fliegerkorps IX 176, 313, 317, 335, 419, 422, 433
Fliegerkorps X 257, 276, 277, 282, 419, 429
Flivo (Fliegerverbindungsoffizier) 279, 281, 310, 313, 342, 347, 419, 430, 431, 432
Forward, Nigel 127
Fossing (Foss Sheet) 85, 101, 133, 134

France 20, 21, 30, 34, 39, 40, 88, 103, 104, 254, 256, 264, 265, 275, 310, 311, 313, 315, 319, 321, 323, 324, 330, 392, 417
Freeborn, Frederick 233
Fricke, Dr Walther 400, 402
Fusion Room 18, 120, 185

G

Gafsa 293
Gamma (wheel) 58
Gaunt, David 20, 30, 33 45, 146, 231
Gayhurst 250
Gazala 286
GHQ Auto 169, 259
Giant 35, 179, 180, 181, 184, 283, 355,
Göring, Reichsmarschall Hermann 372
Graz 359
Greece 276, 294, 302, 306, 309
Guernsey (see also Channel Islands, Flak Jersey) 194, 195, 196, 198, 316, 408, 426

H

Hamburg 330, 422
Hand Duenna (see Duenna)
Hanover 330, 353
Hatted 56, 139, 233, 406
Heeresgruppe B 298, 321, 327
Heeresgruppe C 300, 323, 324
Heeresgruppe E 303, 306, 308, 328
Heeresgruppe F 300, 306
Heeresgruppe G 323, 327
Heeresgruppe HGA 348
Heeresgruppe Kurland 349
Heeresgruppe Mitte 348, 349
Heeresgruppe Nord 349
Heeresgruppe Süd 308
Heidelager 386, 387
Herivel, John 94
Hermann Göring Division 418
Himmler, Reichsführer SS Heinrich 372
Hinsley, Harry 10
Holland (including Dutch, Netherlands) 268, 316, 325, 330, 376, 388, 389, 421, 433
Hollerith punch cards 233

473

Hollington, Miss Eileen 41
Hoppity menus (also delayed hoppity menus) 119, 189, 239, 244, 250, 252, 270, 290
HOR-HUG Reports 119, 120, 122, 131, 135, 363-367, 372
Hungary 309, 343
Hürnum (Danish Station) 335
Husum (Danish Station) 335
Hut 3 (BP) (also 3L, Liaison) 11, 17, 18, 20, 22, 25, 26, 28, 29, 32, 36, 38, 44, 48, 51, 91, 109, 115, 116, 121, 148, 151, 164, 216, 222, 227, 241, 242, 244, 248, 255, 259, 262, 263, 268, 270, 271, 272, 285, 296, 300, 315, 322, 323, 334, 370, 372, 376, 384, 385, 390, 392, 405
Hut 8 (BP) 14, 26, 35, 114, 117, 119, 168, 239, 240, 241, 242, 244, 245
Hut 11A (BP) 250, 251
Hut 23 (BP) 242, 247, 249, 250

I

Indicator (Indicating System) 19, 20, 35, 60, 64, 65, 70-73, 75, 76, 78, 82, 90, 91, 92, 157, 210, 246, 256, 356, 397, 400, 401
118th Infantry Division (German) 306
Innsbruck 359
Italy (also Italian) 353, 366, 370, 371, 372, 378, 381, 382, 418, 420, 424, 429, 439, 440, 443, 445, 446, 449

J

Jagdkorps I 317, 329, 419, 428
Jagdkorps II 313, 317, 419, 428
114th Jaeger Division 306
Jägerleitkreis 257, 417
Jeffreys, John 83
Jeffreys Sheets 83, 84, 169

K

Kampfgruppe Schlieben 322
Kemi (Finland) 357
Kesselring, Field Marshall Albert 259
Keys (also see Appendices)
    AF5 (later Chaffinch) 23, 105, 113, 285
Albatross 31, 116, 119, 122, 135, 212, 280, 296, 297, 299, 300, 301, 305, 306, 348
Armadillo 314
Aster 312, 316, 331, 334
Aviary 253
Avocet 44, 212, 214, 215, 345, 349
Badger 337
Bantam 165, 299, 319, 321-324, 326, 327, 392
Barnyard 164, 204, 253, 301, 323, 325-328
Beetle 129, 145, 177, 183, 186, 188, 233, 335-339, 341-345
Blue 20, 88, 89, 91, 98, 99, 104, 111, 139-141, 254, 255, 258, 313, 330, 331, 335, 390
Blunderbuss (formerly Rocket II) 324, 407
Bounce 239, 241
Brigette (see Light Blue)
Brown 254, 255, 260-274, 384-386, 390
Bullfinch 28, 31, 117, 122, 131, 212, 292-294, 298, 299, 348
Buzzard 212, 304, 305
Celery 142, 233, 339
Chaffinch (also Finches) 23, 25, 105, 109, 111, 113, 118, 122, 130, 131, 134, 140, 211, 277, 285-295, 299
Chicken (see Peewit) 320, 321
Chimpanzee 335
Clover 333, 339
Cockroach 129, 141 150, 177, 183, 233, 235, 258, 272, 311, 316, 317, 329-335, 339, 343
Codfish 304
Cormorant 31, 116, 119, 212, 296
Corncrake 384, 386-388, 391, 393
County 345, 409, 434
Cricket 176, 177, 183, 186, 188, 233, 311, 313-315, 317
Culverin (formerly Stephenson) 235, 325
Daffodil 176, 177, 183, 188, 233,

234, 258, 316, 329-335, 339
Daisy 330
Dingo 255
Diver 322
Dodo 295, 319, 327
Dolphin 322
Dragonfly 278
Duck 165, 319, 322, 323
E/Lorient 324
E/Maryland 344
E/Ohio 344
E/Suffolk 344
E/320 237, 373
E/3730A (Raven) 307
E/6245 (Corncrake) 385
E/6315A (Raven) 307
E/8532 348
Emu 308
Erika 278
Ermine 233, 283, 335, 336, 339, 340, 342, 343, 344
Falcon 295, 305, 324, 325, 326, 328, 351, 353-359, 384
Finches (see Chafinch)
Firefly 314, 316
Flamingo 349
Flycatcher 328
Foxglove 142, 331, 333, 335, 337-341, 379
Gadfly 25, 140, 145, 176, 177, 183, 214, 217, 218-219, 276, 277, 281-283, 286, 336, 341-344
Gannet 119, 357-358
Gentian 177, 183, 188, 215, 331, 333, 334
Gnat 314, 316
Gorilla 145, 177, 178, 183, 283, 284, 316, 336, 337, 342, 343, 344
Gorse 342
Gosling 319
Grapefruit 371, 372
Green (also Greenshank or Wehrkreis) 84, 87, 89, 98, 99, 104, 111-115, 122, 123, 170, 172-173, 179-184, 206, 213, 246, 325, 326, 350-360
Grouse 181, 183, 359-360
Hedgehog 132, 279, 336, 340
Hornet 129, 140, 336, 338-342

Hyena 144, 145, 177, 179, 183, 234, 316, 329, 331-334, 336
Ibis 235, 384, 385, 387-391
Indigo 145, 177, 181, 183, 392
Jaguar 37, 145, 177, 180, 181, 183-188, 192, 204, 233, 257, 281, 310, 312-318, 322, 334, 378, 383, 391, 392
Jay 300
Jerboa 384, 385, 391-392
Kestrel 94, 116, 346, 347
Kingfisher 298, 299, 300
Kite 119, 346
Leek 129, 140, 141, 169, 233
Leopard 177, 183, 188, 280, 281, 284
Leveret 280
Light Blue 21-23, 104, 105, 109, 111, 113, 116, 125, 126, 140, 276, 277
Llama 111, 129, 234
Locust 25, 26, 119, 132, 142, 213, 277-280, 283, 297, 310, 313, 344
Mallard 295, 303, 353, 357-358
Marmoset 177, 181, 183
Mayfly 133, 279
Medlar 371-373
Merlin (later Falcon II) 295, 305
Mosquito 140, 141, 177, 180, 183, 184, 335-339, 341, 342, 343, 345
Moth 177, 183, 188, 345
Mustard 116, 119, 122, 123, 140, 150, 177, 183, 213, 214, 254, 352, 378-383
Narcissus 177, 183, 188, 254, 330, 339
Nightjar 235, 236, 321, 322
Nile 297
Nuthatch 123, 355, 357, 358-359
Ocelet 176
Onion 105, 111
Orchid 283, 337, 339-342
Osprey 119, 255
Orange 111, 113, 114, 119, 120,

475

123, 131, 133, 134, 150, 206, 210, 236, 237, 352, 361-372, 380, 384
Owl 348
Pantellaria 279
Pantrika (see Erika and Pantellaria) 278
Peewit 319, 320, 322
Pelican 349
Penguin 237, 322, 323, 373
Peregrine 370, 371
Phoenix 116, 119, 122, 130, 131, 211, 212, 286, 290-295
Pigeon 327
Pink 177, 183, 254, 258, 259, 260, 280, 300, 344
Platypus 314
Plum 372, 373
Porcupine 340
Primrose 25, 119, 129, 132, 133, 139, 140, 141, 233, 276-280, 296, 339, 379
Puce 337, 342
Puffin 44, 165, 212, 222, 299, 300-301, 307, 319, 323, 324, 327, 328, 392
Pullet 321, 322
Puma 119, 129, 164, 176, 177, 179, 180, 182, 184, 186, 188, 233, 275, 279, 280, 281, 283, 284, 300, 310
Pumpkin 371, 372
Quail 308, 376
Quince 94, 120, 123, 150, 222, 236, 237, 320, 366-369, 377
Rabbit 337
Raccoon 129
Raster (also Rasterschlüssel) 194, 318, 375, 376
Raven 116, 131, 212, 217-218, 303-309, 370
Red 20-23, 34, 39, 87-89, 92, 97-102, 104, 105, 108-111, 113, 114, 116, 119, 123, 125, 126, 132, 139, 140, 142, 144, 145, 167-170, 173-174, 176, 178, 182, 183, 188, 213, 233, 254-258, 259, 260, 275-280, 283, 288, 300, 310-313, 330, 332, 335, 337, 340-343, 353, 376, 378, 379, 381

Rocket 247, 324, 335
Roulette 204, 210, 216, 373, 374, 375, 376, 391
Scorpion 25, 119, 139, 277, 288, 289
Shark 240, 241
Sheep 280
Shrike 31, 119, 131, 212, 298, 299
Skunk 177, 179, 180, 183, 184, 256, 340, 341, 342, 344, 345
Snowdrop 37, 141, 144, 150, 176, 177, 183, 186, 188, 192, 277, 278, 310-316, 330, 333, 334, 339
Sparrow 131, 212, 300, 301-302
Squirrel 129, 280
Stork 255
Swan 319
TGD 362, 373, 377
Thrush 294-295
Tricycle 129, 235
Tulip 312
Violet 105, 111, 139, 331, 333
Vulture 116, 119, 122, 131, 212, 295, 346, 348, 349, 357
Wagtail 235
Wallflower 177, 183, 331, 333
Wasp 176, 177, 179, 183, 188, 311, 313-318, 334, 335
Weasel 337, 339, 340, 342
Whimbrel 319
Woodpecker 358
Wryneck 122, 131, 135, 136, 212, 282, 306-308
Yak 129, 133, 139, 176, 177, 183, 234, 282, 283, 344
Yellow 20, 84, 90-92, 98, 99, 131
KG (Kampfgruppe) 260, 261, 262, 417, 418, 420, 423
Kharkov 266, 268, 366
'Kissing' 119, 227, 312
Klavier 391
Knight, Arthur (Hut 3) 250, 253
Knox, Dilwyn (Dilly) 10, 60, 71, 90
Kommandant General Italien 280, 418, 430
Kooslin 386
Köthen 260, 267, 268, 269, 270, 271
Krakau 365, 366

L

Lage Conference (daily meeting) 121, 224
Lawn, Oliver 21, 162, 169
Legation Fag (also see FAG) 313
Leningrad 341
Letchworth (Hertfordshire) 104
Liaison (see Hut 3)
Libya 130, 275
Limburg 316
L N Versuchs Regiment 260, 261, 266, 419, 423, 427
Lucas, F.L. 20
Luftflotte Reich 316, 329, 331, 332, 418, 419, 422, 428, 430
Luftflotte 1 139, 337, 338, 342, 343, 405, 419, 423, 428, 434
Luftflotte 2 280, 418, 430, 432, 433
Luftflotte 3 257, 310, 312, 313, 316, 322, 418, 419, 422, 424, 428, 430, 431,
Luftflotte 4 256, 283, 337, 340, 342, 343, 344, 429, 430, 432
Luftflotte 6 336, 337, 341, 342, 344, 424, 427
Luftflotte X 335
Luftgau Belgien-Nord Frankreich 316
Luftgau Ost (later Luftgau XVII) 338, 420, 429
Luftgau Reich 332
Luftgau West 311, 315, 316, 420, 432
Luftgau I 333, 339, 420, 421, 428
Luftgau II 330, 420
Luftgau III 331, 421, 429
Luftgau V 311, 316, 421, 433, 434
Luftgau VI 331, 334, 421, 433
Luftgau VII 316, 331, 332, 421, 427
Luftgau VIII 331, 420, 421, 429, 433, 434
Luftgau XI 331, 420, 421, 428, 432,
Luftgau XIV 421
Luftgau XVII 330, 331, 332, 338, 421, 429
Luftgau XVIII 341
Luftgau XXV 339, 421
Luftgau XXVI 342, 430
Luftwaffenkommando Don 339, 405
Luftwaffenkommando Ost (later Luftlotte 6) 336
Luftwaffenkommando Südost 282, 429
Luftwaffenkommando West 430

M

Machine Room (see also Netz Room, Watch) 13, 21, 22, 24, 26, 28, 29, 43, 44, 45, 48, 89, 101-102, 107, 112, 113, 117, 118, 120, 125, 146-149, 155, 169, 190, 221, 223, 225, 227, 228, 242, 243, 246-253, 364, 366
Malta 26, 142
Manisty, Major John 19, 32, 220, 230, 231, 241, 242, 245
Mareth 293
McLaren, Anne 45
Meyer-Bethling, Mr 281
Milner-Barry, Philip Stuart 13, 17, 51-53, 108, 147, 149, 220, 224, 225, 239, 241, 242, 244
Monroe, Major John 45, 129, 220, 225, 230, 231
Monrovian Wheel Order 129
Montgomery, General Bernard 277
Morlaix 262
Mosse Code 166, 204, 216, 217
Mosse, Rudolf 216, 217
20th Mountain Army 357
Münster 326, 327, 356, 357

N

Netz Room (see Machine Room)
Nicoll, Douglas 30, 37, 220, 225, 231
Nigelian Wheel Order 97, 125, 127-130, 232, 234, 249, 282
Normandy (see also D-Day) 37, 275, 310, 312, 318
North Africa 140, 142, 277, 302, 403, 417, 430, 447
Norway 20, 59, 88, 90, 255, 330, 367, 368, 418, 421, 430, 439, 442, 445
Nosegay FAG (see also FAG) 176, 315
Notschlüssel (also NOT-keys) 133, 183, 191-203, 407-409, 423

O

OB (Oberbefehlshaber) Südost 303
OB (Oberbefehlshaber) Südwest 259, 300
Ogre 179

Op-20-G (US) 239, 240, 244-245,
Oranienburg 363
Ordnungspolizei 373
Organisation Todt 255, 446
Owen, Major 388, 389, 391
OXO (see also BOVO) 244

P

Panzer AOK 1 349
Panzer AOK 2 306, 308, 348, 449
Panzer AOK 3 349, 444
Panzer AOK 5 295, 319, 443
Panzerarmee Afrika 286, 447
26th Panzer Division 299
Paris 87, 266, 310, 316, 378
Parker, Reginald 24
Parkerian records 27, 233
Parkerismus 143
Playfair (see Double Playfair)
PLUTO 165
Pola 281
Poland 60, 71-75, 357

Q

QEP (Qwatch Entering Party) 228-230
Queening, Mrs Margaret 45
Qwatch (Quiet Watch) 152, 157, 160, 175, 185, 186, 189, 192, 195, 221-228, 278, 279, 281, 311, 314, 331, 332, 334, 340, 384

R

Radar 268, 270, 329
Raffs 312
Random Indicators 166, 204, 206-211, 369
Read, Arthur 231
Rees, David 21
Reflector B 56, 105, 169, 184, 250, 325, 332, 353, 355, 357, 359, 395
Reflector C 105, 169, 353
Reflector D (Uncle D) 21, 34-36, 39, 42, 56, 57, 143, 154, 162, 166, 167, 169, 170, 173, 174, 175, 176, 188, 200, 201, 237, 252, 257, 275, 281, 283, 311, 315, 325, 331, 332, 334, 335, 336, 343, 344, 345, 353, 355, 356, 359, 360, 382, 398, 399
Registration Room (BP) 20, 22, 24, 26, 30, 36-39, 41, 43, 44, 48, 49, 50, 89, 147, 155, 156, 185, 220, 225, 227, 250, 379
Research Section (BP) 24, 28, 29, 30, 32, 33, 105, 113, 118, 121, 149, 150, 296, 297, 298, 303, 347
Rheims 316
Rhodes 304-307, 309
Rocket Bradshaws 388, 389, 390
Rod (also rodding) 60-65, 73, 76-78, 84, 105, 110, 119, 158, 169, 170, 234, 248, 264, 267, 364, 380
Rome (see also Italy) 275, 276, 281, 284, 286, 292-296, 372, 378, 442, 443, 448
Rommel, Field Marshall Erwin 23, 24, 31, 285, 291-293, 303
Room 64 (BP) 228, 229
Room 76 (BP) 222
Room 78 (BP) 228, 229, 231
Roseveare, Robert 30, 32, 40, 178, 220, 225, 229, 231
Rumania (now Romania) 282, 442, 446
Rundstedt, Field Marshall Gert von 40, 319

S

Salonika 286, 295
Sarafand 279
Sardinia 276, 296, 297, 443,
Schmidt, Hans Thilo (Asché) 72
Seys-Inquart, Reichskommissar Arthur 375
Shitomir 379
Sicily 29, 30, 31, 116, 278, 279, 284, 296, 297,
Sixta 11, 17, 18, 36, 40, 41, 48, 115, 120, 156, 161, 228, 286, 300, 310, 333, 337, 338, 358, 386, 387, 406
SKO (see CSKO)
Smith, Dudley 24, 25, 31
Smith, Howard F.T. 45, 231
Sofia 259
Sonderschlüssel (also Sonder) 111, 139, 268, 269, 294, 371, 387, 404, 408, 417, 419, 420, 440-449

Soviet Union (see Eastern Front)
Spanish Civil War 60
Spider (bombe) 106
Spooner, Malcolm 360
SS Units
    V SS Geb. Korps 371, 447
    6th SS Panzer Army 328
    1st SS Panzer Korps 322
    12th SS Panzer Division 237, 322
    SS Prinz Eugen Division 370, 371, 447
Stalingrad 339, 347
Stecker Knock-Out 77, 133
Stanmore 162, 250
Stolpmünde 271
Stuttgart 311, 312
Stutthof 365
Superlibia (Italian High Command) 291, 293

T

Tarpon (Fish link) 358
Taunt, Derek 30, 32, 40, 228, 229, 231
Tirana 306
TIS (Traffic Identification Section) 15, 33, 36, 39, 41, 48, 161, 164, 174, 220, 385
Tito, Marshal Josip Broz 300, 307
Traffic Indentification Section (see TIS)
Tripoli 275, 278, 284, 289
Tunisia (also Tunis) 24, 27, 29, 275, 278, 285, 292, 294, 295, 296
Turing, Alan 10, 82
Twinn, Peter 9, 64, 409
Typex 290

U

Uncle C (Charlie) 21
United States (also American, Washington - see also Op-20-G, Arlington) 21, 45, 103, 117, 156, 160, 174, 211, 240, 253, 254, 269, 270, 317, 323, 336, 344, 368, 391, 406

V

Vannes 262, 263
Venice 281
VERA 388
'Verenas' 258
Vienna 358, 359, 423, 445, 446
Vosges 312
V-Weapons 254, 384-394

W

Wahlworts 166, 204, 211-216, 281, 289, 292, 293, 297, 298, 304, 333, 335, 349, 361, 374, 380, 382, 399, 401
Walton, Charles 292
War Office Y Group (see WOYG)
Warsaw 378, 379
Washington (see United States)
Watch (BP)(see also Machine Room)
Wehrkreis 89, 235, 350-357, 359, 360
'Weisung' 259
Welchman, Gordon 18-22, 29, 32, 51, 82, 90, 350
Wheel Breaking 60-65
Wiking Division 362
Wilson, Mary 44
Winton, John 33
WOYG 15, 290, 292, 360

Y

Yugoslavia (see also Belgrade, Balkans) 306, 359, 443

Z

Zoo group 312, 315
Zusatzgerät 166
Zusatz Stecker 122, 166, 185, 188-191, 281

FIND OUT MORE

Thank you for taking the time to read *Solving Enigma: The Official History of Bletchley Park's Hut 6* edited by John Jackson. If you enjoyed it please consider posting a short review on Amazon, GoodReads or your preferred book seller's website. You can also help to spread the word by sharing details of the book on social media.

About the Author

John Jackson is a former Fleet Street journalist, magazine editor and publisher. He is a volunteer Bombe demonstrator at Bletchley Park.

Read more about the author, get links his other books & articles at:
www.bletchleyparkresearch.co.uk/authors-researchers/john-jackson

Sign up for the newsletter at Bletchley Park Research to be the first to hear of publication dates and free extracts from some of John Jackson's books as well as other Bletchley Park related news.
www.bletchleyparkresearch.co.uk

You can find out more about their other Bletchley Park and World War 2 codebreaking books by visiting:
www.booktowerpublishing.co.uk.

You can find out more about the work of the Bletchley Park Trust - the official 'Home of the Codebreakers' at:
www.bletchleypark.org.uk